Freedom and the Rule of Law

Freedom and the Rule of Law

Edited by
Anthony A. Peacock

LEXINGTON BOOKS
A division of
ROWMAN & LITTLEFIELD PUBLISHERS, INC.
Lanham • Boulder • New York • Toronto • Plymouth, UK

Published by Lexington Books
A division of Rowman & Littlefield Publishers, Inc.
A wholly owned subsidiary of The Rowman & Littlefield Publishing Group, Inc.
4501 Forbes Boulevard, Suite 200, Lanham, Maryland 20706
http://www.lexingtonbooks.com

Estover Road, Plymouth PL6 7PY, United Kingdom

British Library Cataloguing in Publication Information Available

Library of Congress Cataloging-in-Publication Data

Freedom and the rule of law / Edited by Anthony A. Peacock.
p. cm.
ISBN 978-0-7391-3618-8 (cloth : alk. paper) — ISBN 978-0-7391-3620-1 (electronic)
1. Rule of law—United States—History. 2. Judicial process—United States. I. Peacock, Anthony A. (Anthony Arthur), 1959–
KF382.F74 2010
340.11—dc22 2009038524

∞™ The paper used in this publication meets the minimum requirements of American National Standard for Information Sciences—Permanence of Paper for Printed Library Materials, ANSI/NISO Z39.48-1992.

Printed in the United States of America

Contents

Acknowledgments

This book is the result of a conference on the theme of "Freedom and the Rule of Law" that was held at Utah State University September 15–16, 2008. It was sponsored by the Milton R. Merrill Chair Endowment in the Department of Political Science at Utah State and was the kickoff event for the department's new Project on Liberty and American Constitutionalism. The keynote speaker for the conference was United States Supreme Court Justice Antonin Scalia. Following Justice Scalia's keynote address, all but two of the chapters that appear in this book were presented as papers over the course of the remaining two days.

In addition to Justice Scalia and the contributors to this book, I would like to thank the sponsors of the Milton R. Merrill Chair Endowment for their generosity, without which the "Freedom and the Rule of Law" conference would have never taken place. I would also like to thank Brandee Halverson, Shelly Schiess, Jessica Harrison, Sydney Peterson, Kent Clark, and Ryan Marsh for their extensive help organizing the conference. Thanks are also owed to my departmental colleagues Peter and Carol McNamara and Bobbi Herzberg, as well as to USU president Stan Albrecht and Joyce Albrecht, for their generous assistance with the conference.

At Lexington Books, Joseph Parry showed faith in this collection from the outset and I would like to thank him, Tawnya Zengierski, Jana Wilson, and Julia Loy for their sage advice and never-ending efforts getting this book into print.

My thanks as well to Justin Lee for his extensive assistance putting together the index.

Finally, I would like to thank my wife, Gretchen, and our children Hamilton, Holley, and Spencer for once again tolerating the old man's lengthy absence in the "dungeon" working on yet another writing project.

1

Introduction

American Constitutionalism, Freedom, and the Rule of Law

Anthony A. Peacock

The chapters in this book examine the relationship between freedom and the rule of law in America. Although this is a theme that has been a perennial one since America's founding, it is also one of particular importance today. The rule of law is fundamental to all liberal constitutional regimes whose political orders recognize the equal natural rights of all and whose purpose is to protect those natural rights in addition to the general welfare. The Constitution's limited government objectives, secured through a large federal republic and institutional mechanisms like the separation of powers, checks and balances, and different terms of elections for federal officials, were intended to secure what James Madison in *The Federalist* indicated were the two overarching objects of American constitutionalism: protection of private or individual rights and promotion of the public good.[1]

The rule of law was essential to achieving both of these ends and to reconciling them where necessary. As the preamble to the Constitution makes clear, the Constitution is a popular document ordained by "the People of the United States." American government is popular government and more specifically republican government, government where the people's representatives make the law and where the people, including their representatives, are intended to abide by that law. America is in many respects a law-loving nation not only because the people expect to be governed equally by the law and the law alone—not by the arbitrary dictates of rulers—but because (as the preamble again indicates) Americans seek to establish justice, provide for their safety, and secure the blessings of liberty through the instrument of the law, specifically the Constitution. The Constitution is the supreme law of the land but in many respects it also forms the spirit of America since, along with the Declaration of Independence, Americans see in the Constitution their highest political achievement as well as the keys to their freedom—individual freedom, political freedom, economic freedom, religious freedom, intellectual freedom, the freedom to perfect themselves as they see fit.

But just how free is America today? It was certainly within the contemplation of the Founders that the federal judiciary would have a significant role in interpreting the Constitution, federal laws, and treaties, but it would be difficult to argue that those who framed and ratified the Constitution contemplated a role for the courts, particularly for the United States Supreme Court, of the magnitude they have today. To say nothing of other things, the fact that the article that provides for the federal courts comes third in the Constitution and is the shortest of those defining the branches of the federal government—the first two providing for Congress and the executive—implies that for the Founders the courts were of least importance in the federal government, last in significance in the American constitutional order.

Yet today the Supreme Court would seem to be first in that order, deciding the most important issues of American constitutional life. Political issues like what constitutes "fair" representation, the proper division between federal and state governmental powers, the relationship between the branches of the federal government themselves, campaign finance, the conduct of war, and a host of other matters of fundamental importance are all decided not by Congress or the president but ultimately by the Court. So too hot-button moral and cultural issues like abortion, the relationship between church and state, homosexual marriage, race classifications in educational admissions, federal contracts, and electoral redistricting are all decided by federal courts. It is hard to think of any political or moral issue of the first rank that is not decided today by the courts.

The chapters in this volume focus on three issues that have occupied the U.S. Supreme Court and legal commentators over the last decade: constitutional interpretation, national security, and voting rights and representation. All three of these issues have been critical to defining the relationship between freedom and the rule of law in America and the chapters below review in detail recent developments involving these issues.

However, before turning to these important matters, the first three chapters in part I of the book look at early America, specifically the origins of the rule of law in the United States, administration and the rule of law during the antebellum period, and the prophetic writings of the Anti-Federalist Brutus, who anticipated as well as anyone during the Founding era both the growth of the modern federal state and the increased importance the Supreme Court would assume in American political life.

Joyce Lee Malcolm's chapter introduces the theme of this book, freedom and the rule of law, by examining the English common law roots that provided the foundation for the rule of law in America. Malcolm begins by stressing that although freedom seems to be opposed to the rule of law because the latter restricts individual liberty, the English recognized that without law, freedom was impossible. The protection of the most basic rights—personal security, personal freedom, property rights—required the rule of law. Beginning with Magna Carta (1215), where protection of fundamental rights was first secured from the "vicious king" John, various subsequent developments refined and clarified the English commitment to individual liberty. These included making those individuals acting on behalf of the executive (king) responsible for violation of individual liberties, judges and Parliament reviewing royal actions for their legality, Parliament jealously protecting its right to approve any measures of taxation and penalizing executive attempts to tax without parliamentary authority, and the use of juries to protect individual liberties. This last requirement, not judicial review, Malcolm contends, was what the American Founders insisted was required to protect freedom.

The English clergy were also critical to ensuring respect for the protection of those fundamental common law rights originating in Magna Carta. Even when it was most vociferous in its insistence on obedience to the monarchy, the Church of England distinguished between those commands of the monarch that were lawful and those that were not.

American government was also patterned largely on the structure of English government, with its separate branches and checks and balances. Following the Glorious Revolution of 1688, the ultimate sovereignty of English government would devolve to Parliament and more specifically the House of Commons. Malcolm emphasizes that although over the centuries protecting freedom within the rule of law had focused on restraining the executive rather than the representatives of the kingdom, by the time of the American Revolution it was Parliament that had become all powerful, with only periodic elections and juries restraining its power. Moreover, after having absorbed executive power, in the course of the twentieth century whatever party ruled in the House of Commons had virtually plenary power to alter traditional constitutional provisions and rights through simple majority vote. Malcolm illustrates how from 1920 to the present the right of self-defense has been increasingly undermined in Great Britain to the point where today it is virtually nonexistent. Although there are glimmers of hope—such as the 1998 Human Rights Act and Prime Minister Tony Blair's 2003 proposal to create an American-style supreme court, which may shortly hear cases—Malcolm concludes that only government officials and a vigilant public can protect freedom within the rule of law.

Joseph Postell also reviews the role of the common law in the United States in his chapter, which examines administration and the rule of law in antebellum America. Postell claims that the view prevalent in American history, that prior to the Civil War unregulated economic life predominated, is a myth. The United States never had a laissez-faire or essentially libertarian economy. Rather, from the outset American economic and social life was regulated. However, both the *scope* and, most importantly, the *manner* of such regulation was radically different from the Progressive vision of regulation that came to dominate the United States in the twentieth century.

Typical of antebellum American society was a form of common law regulation that respected the Revolution's natural right principles of self-government. Documenting a host of government interventions such as subsidies for agriculture and manufacturing, investment in internal improvements such as canals, regulatory standards for manufactured goods, occupations, and in support of public morals, Postell points out that many of these governmental activities were seen in early America to fortify property rights and the exercise of liberty, not to undermine them.

However, critical to these regulations were four salient features of antebellum administrative law: (1) legislative supremacy, where legislatures managed the particulars of administrative procedures rather than allowing administrators broad discretion; (2) powerful courts and juries that acted as common law enforcers ensuring citizen control of regulators; (3) decentralization of administration, which recognized the limits of human knowledge and permitted more vigilant supervision of administrators; and (4) robust political parties, which worked to connect public opinion to administration while providing that hierarchical institutional organization that was necessary to make the administrative system manageable.

A second myth Postell dispels is the progressivist assertion that early regulatory activities were impeded because they were irrational and ineffective. Although there were certainly many inefficiencies in early administrative practices, these were largely due to the aforementioned features of administrative law that ensured political accountability or popular control of administrators, what observers such as James Wilson and Alexis de Tocqueville saw as crucial to the preservation of American republicanism. As Postell puts it, American government was based on the natural right principle of self-government, which allowed all individuals to be governed by their own deliberation, however imperfect that deliberation might be. Accordingly, the principal qualification for selecting executive officers was character and prudence, not science and expertise, as twentieth-century progressives would demand.

Seminal progressives like Frank Goodnow decisively rejected the Founders' natural right principles of self-government that moored antebellum administration to consent and the rule of law. Architects of the modern administrative state, like Goodnow, sought to immunize administration from popular accountability and to commit it to rule by experts, bureaucrats separated from politics who would abandon protection of individual rights in favor of promoting broadly defined social interests. The consequence of this sacrificing of the common law economic and civil liberties that defined early America to the corporate regulation characteristic of the modern administrative state is what would so alienate Americans from their government and cause them to view any government activity as a threat to freedom.

Postell concludes by suggesting that the warnings of Tocqueville of succumbing to a blind faith in an omnipotent, centralized "social power" charged with imposing uniform rules in the modern tutelary state has largely come to pass in the United States. Postell does not counsel an unthinking return to the principles of antebellum administration since among other things this would require an enlightened public capable of the sort of self-government of early America. However, looking back might at least remind us what elements of self-government and the rule of law have been sacrificed by our embrace of the modern administrative state and what alternatives exist should we want to take any preliminary steps in an alternative direction.

As one problem confronting freedom and the rule of law today is the problem of the modern administrative state, this is just one aspect of the broader issue of the growth of the federal government per se. In the final chapter of part I, James Strickler examines the writings of the anonymous Anti-Federalist critic Brutus. Strickler claims that Brutus's writings were prophetic, anticipating better than virtually any other writer of the Founding era precisely that growth of the federal government that has become the defining feature of today's national government. Yet the prescience of Brutus has been almost matched by the disregard of his writings by scholars who study the American Founding and those who teach the origins of American government in universities; Brutus is almost never read, explained, or defended by American academics. Strickler's chapter attempts to correct this deficiency.

The most prophetic of Brutus's writings were arguably letters XI through XV on the federal judiciary. Written during the debate over ratification of the Constitution, Brutus demonstrated that the purported constitutional constraints on the national government, such as *Federalist* 51's famous argument that the separation of powers would be maintained by departmental ambition counteracting departmental ambition, were simply ineffectual. Not only would the departments of the federal government not compete with one another for power, they would collude to expand the power of the federal government at the expense of the states and the rule of law. The federal judiciary would be especially prone to expand congressional and executive power since any expansion in the power of these branches of the federal government would enhance the power and prestige of the federal courts. Moreover, unlike Congress and the federal executive, which had some nominal constitutional constraints placed on them, there were virtually no such constraints placed on federal judges once they were appointed. Save for impeachment, they could not be removed from office, could not have their salaries lowered, and could not be punished for erroneous judgments.

Brutus highlighted that the very language of the Constitution would enable the federal judiciary in its task of centralized expansion. Article III extended the judicial power not merely to all cases in law but to all cases in equity as well. It was this latter power, with its opaque meaning unmoored to legal text, that would provide the federal courts unbridled discretion to expand federal law as they saw fit. Strickler provides examples of precisely how the Supreme Court has used its equitable jurisdiction, particularly in the use of remedies, to expand its own power and the power of the federal government. Generous constructions by the Court of other provisions like the Necessary and Proper Clause and the Commerce Clause of Article I, Section 8 have further aided and abetted federal expansion.

Yet other cases demonstrate how federal courts have expanded the power of the federal government by justifying congressional overreach through legal precedents, which precedents are then used by Congress both to justify its expansion and to avoid responsibility for this expansion (since it is explained away by the courts). As Brutus anticipated, the process of judicially sanctioned federal expansion does not have to involve bold usurpations but can take place incrementally and thus can be almost undetectable to the public. This is precisely what occurred during the twentieth century, once again illustrating the depths of Brutus's understanding of the symbiotic relationship between the federal judiciary and Congress, the former's rulings encouraging the latter to push the constitutional envelope of expansion further and further, till virtually every aspect of state and private activity has been enveloped in a web of national control.

Ironically then, the rule of law under the Constitution would be sacrificed to the institutional ambitions of those very guardians entrusted to protect that law. To those judicial originalists, formalists, and textualists so critical of loose interpretations of constitutional and federal law by liberal federal judges, Strickler suggests that they will find an ideological forefather in Brutus.

The four essays in part II again turn to the issue of constitutional interpretation, only this time with a focus on more recent developments in law. Ralph Rossum reviews the textualist jurisprudence of Supreme Court Justice Antonin Scalia, beginning with a 1989 lecture by Justice Scalia titled "The Rule of Law as the Law of Rules." Scalia believes that the rule of law mandates the law of rules. The judiciary is crucial to preserving the rule of law, and the rule of law is best fortified when judges apply rules derived from legal texts and traditions as law.

Rossum explains that Scalia's textualism promotes the law of rules by according primacy to the text, structure, and history of legal documents. On Scalia's reading, judges must begin by looking either at the text of the Constitution or statute or some critical structural principle implicit in that text. If the text of a law is ambiguous, then resort should be made to the specific legal tradition underwriting the text; what specifically did the text mean to the society that embraced it? This distinctive approach to judicial interpretation is why one constantly sees references to "text and tradition" throughout Justice Scalia's opinions.

For the federal judiciary the quintessential dilemma in the American constitutional system involves the question of how to resolve the conflict between majority rule and those individual rights that must be protected against infractions by the majority. Scalia resolves this problem by applying his text-and-tradition approach to judicial review: laws would be found constitutionally infirm only where there is a violation of clear language in the Constitution protecting rights or where a specific legal tradition derivative of the text is infringed. According to Scalia, the Court is to "reflect" and not to "supersede" those national traditions mirroring popular understandings of ambiguous constitutional language. Where no constitutional text or traditions are implicated in constitutional challenges to state and federal laws, there is no rule, and thus no law, for judges to apply, and such challenges must therefore fail. Only in this way, Scalia maintains, can judicial activism or judges slipping their personal preferences into legal decisions be avoided.

Rossum provides numerous examples of cases illustrating the application of Justice Scalia's textualist approach to the law. Perhaps the consummate example in this regard was Justice Scalia's opinion for the Court in its landmark Second Amendment ruling, *District of Columbia v. Heller* (2008).[2] As Rossum suggests, Scalia's interpretive technique is at its finest in *Heller*, where Scalia once again prevented constitutional "backsliding" by vigorously defending an individual right—here the right to keep and bear arms—that is clearly set out in the Constitution.

Rossum analyzes Scalia's *Heller* opinion in detail, documenting why in his opinion it was more comprehensive and incisive than Justice Stevens's own attempt at textual analysis in his dissenting opinion. Scalia's textualist approach was also superior, as constitutional law, to Justice Breyer's "interest-balancing inquiry," which he too proposed in dissent. As Rossum points out, the interpretive methodology adopted by Justice Breyer in *Heller*—essentially the same approach he takes in his book *Active Liberty*[3]—would effectively eviscerate all idea of fixed constitutional rights. If rights can be given or taken away by judges depending on their assessments of policy preferences, as Justice Breyer proposed in *Heller*, Americans do not have constitutional rights. In fact, as Rossum concludes, Justice Breyer's method of constitutional interpretation not only does not require a written constitution but is impossible with one. Only Justice Scalia offered a coherent and defensible approach to constitutional interpretation in *Heller*. Justices Stevens's and Breyer's dissenting opinions, by contrast, exemplified what has become so problematic in recent Supreme Court jurisprudence.

A further review of the *Heller* decision is taken up by Edward Whelan, only this time to exemplify what Whelan refers to as "original-meaning jurisprudence." Since there has been so much misunderstanding of what judicial originalism means, Whelan devotes his chapter to clarifying the meaning of the most popular species of this term, original-meaning originalism, and those common fallacies associated with it.

The term "originalism" itself is new, originating in the 1980s. Until then originalism was so widely accepted as the only legitimate method of constitutional interpretation that there was no need to create a term for it. That is no longer the case. Now there are a litany of competitors to originalism as well as many species of the doctrine itself.

Whelan defines originalism as identifying "the principle that the meaning of various provisions of the Constitution—and of other laws—is to be determined in accordance with the sense they bore at the time they were promulgated." In other words, the Constitution's provisions are to be understood as they were publicly understood at the time they were adopted. It may well be that trying to discern the "original intent" or "original understanding" of the Framers or ratifiers of the Constitution is too subjective or impracticable an enterprise, as critics contend, but this is not so with original meaning. Most provisions in the Constitution have a signification readily discernible in ordinary language. There certainly are phrases in the Constitution that have specialized meaning but even those can be resolved by looking at what those who understood the specialized term publicly meant by it when it was adopted.

Whelan argues that original-meaning jurisprudence is the only theory of constitutional interpretation that can account for how human beings actually communicate in oral and written speech. Only it approaches the common sense and generally accepted meaning of the law and its nature. Other approaches to constitutional interpretation are far removed from such common sense.

Expanding on what the original-meaning approach to constitutional interpretation is by examining what it is not, Whelan reviews a host of fallacies associated with the concept. He points out that contrary to advertisements by its advocates, "living constitutionalism," the approach that seeks to constantly "update" the Constitution to meet ever-evolving social changes, actually "entrenches the current elite's policy preferences in Supreme Court decisionmaking in a manner that deprives future generations of the very adaptability that living constitutionalists say they favor. In short, original-meaning jurisprudence provides the flexibility that the 'living Constitution' falsely promises." The very vice of results-oriented theories like living constitutionalism or pragmatism, another new theory of judicial interpretation, that they can generate desired answers almost at will, is often portrayed by their advocates as a virtue.

It is precisely because theories of constitutional interpretation, like original meaning, cannot answer every question that judicial self-restraint is so crucial, particularly in a democratic republic like the United States. Judges should not "overenforce" the Constitution by construing judicial doctrines so broadly as to invalidate legislative enactments that are in fact constitutional. Second, when originalist methodology fails to yield an adequately clear answer to a constitutional question, a challenged democratic enactment must be left standing. The fact that there is an insufficiently clear response to a constitutional question here is not an indictment of original-meaning jurisprudence but rather an affirmation of its consistency with republican principles.

Whelan concludes that there is no inconsistency in the advocacy of judicial restraint and the overruling of longstanding precedents that themselves wrongfully overruled the democratic process. And the label "liberal judicial activism" is a justifiable one because virtually all of the judicial activism—defined as "the wrongful overriding of democratic enactments"—since the 1960s has involved the judicial entrenchment of the policy preferences of America's Left. When the original-meaning approach to constitutional interpretation is fortified by judicial restraint, the consequence will be the promotion of democratic freedom.

Jeremy Rabkin addresses yet another recent problem in Supreme Court jurisprudence: the reliance by members of the Court on foreign law to interpret the Constitution. Rabkin opens by recounting three recent cases that have done this: *Atkins v. Virginia* (2002),[4] where the Court ruled that capital punishment for the mentally handicapped contravened the Eighth Amendment's proscription against "cruel and unusual punishments"; *Lawrence v. Texas* (2003),[5] where the Court held that laws criminalizing homosexual sodomy violated the Fourteenth Amendment's protection of a general right to liberty; and *Roper v. Simmons* (2005),[6] where the Court in yet another capital case determined that executing defendants younger than eighteen was unconstitutional.

Although in most of these cases foreign authority references were not decisive to the Court's holding, Rabkin points out that the decisions nevertheless revealed novel and disconcerting approaches to judicial review. The Court in the past has certainly appealed to foreign legal commentaries dealing with such things as Western legal traditions or foreign courts' interpretations of treaties, which courts have cited in an attempt to forge a common understanding between the United States and other signatories to treaties. However, as Rabkin points out, in no case prior to *Atkins* had the Court ever invoked a foreign authority to strike down an American law. Beginning with *Atkins*, it did so three times in three years.

Rabkin argues that there are numerous reasons why reliance on foreign authorities as the basis for American constitutional decisions is a bad idea. First, there is the information deficit. It is almost impossible to discern international trends in law. Foreign court decisions are generally not available in English, do not follow the procedures or terminology of the common law, and are not readily accessible in reports to American lawyers. American courts typically have to rely on summaries or surveys of foreign law provided by anonymous intermediaries who too often have a vested interest in partisan legal outcomes. The generalized claims of foreign legal practices that American judges make are thus usually based on only a scintilla of evidence. Rabkin reveals, for instance, that in *Atkins* and *Lawrence* the Court relied on briefs that when examined provided virtually no evidence of the foreign legal trends claimed. The Court simply cherry-picked bits and pieces from briefs that supported its own preferred conclusions.

Second, even if information deficits could be overcome, the ultimate difficulty of how to interpret information from such widely different countries and legal systems remains. Rabkin queries: How are foreign practices to be assessed? Are all foreign legal practices to be adopted or only some? If only some, what are the criteria to be used in selecting those to be emulated and those to be rejected? Do we only want to adopt legal practices from democracies or are we open to other legal practices too? If we are going to rely only on practices from democracies, how do we define a democracy? Do only those countries whose practices resemble American democracy count? What about those countries that claim to be "democracies" but obviously do not respect the freedoms that the American Constitution respects? Rabkin provides examples of a host of practical problems here. Dissenting in a 1999 decision, for instance, Justice Stephen Breyer cited as an authority the Supreme Court of Zimbabwe, a country he later conceded was not a world leader of human rights. Why should Zimbabwe count as an authority for foreign law? If it does not count, are the criteria of disqualification here not applicable to many other countries the Court might rely on for constitutional decisions?

Third, there is the problem of consistency. It seems that those on the Court who wish to rely on foreign authorities wish to adopt only certain foreign practices and not others. The Court frequently relies on practices adopted in Europe, for instance, by the European Union, the European Court of Human Rights, or the Council of Europe. Yet when it comes to access to abortion and free speech rights, the United States is much more permissive than Europe, avoiding for instance the draconian restrictions imposed by hate-speech laws on the European continent. Why should Supreme Court jurisprudence adopt only European practices regarding capital punishment and not abortion or free speech? Again the problem seems to be one of political preference. American judges "want to be able to use foreign or international materials opportunistically: to invoke them when they bolster the outcome they prefer and ignore them when they cut the other way."

Use of foreign authorities also raises the problem of American courts attempting to engage in foreign policy, a role reserved under the Constitution to the executive and Congress. Citing treaties or provisions of treaties that the U.S. Senate has failed to ratify and in some cases has specifically rejected means that in the name of constitutional interpretation courts must disregard "what the Constitution actually says about treaties." Institutionally too, courts are not very well equipped to conduct American foreign policy, and trying to force the Constitution to comport with foreign policy demands of the international community can make American foreign policy excessively legalistic. *Boumediene v. Bush* (2008),[7] where the Court provided constitutional habeas corpus rights to detainees held at Guantánamo Bay, Cuba, provides a good example of this. A decision apparently driven in part by pressure from the international community, *Boumediene* placed new, historically unprecedented restrictions on the conduct of American military policy.

Finally, there is the issue of natural law. Rabkin emphasizes that one of the most common arguments in support of incorporating foreign legal practices into American constitutional law is that it recognizes an emerging consensus on international law much the way the Founders recognized the universal principles of natural law. But Rabkin points out that this argument is misconceived. First, rather than drawing on teachings going back to ancient Greece and Rome the way natural law jurists like Hugo Grotius did, the foreign practices adopted by the Supreme Court today are all recent. The presumption seems to be that "change implies improvement, because history is a story of progress toward higher and better standards." But as Rabkin observes, modern history, especially modern European history, provides us few reassurances in this regard. Nations, like those in twentieth-century Europe, "which allowed themselves to sink into murderous frenzies may not be the best models for nations which managed to hold themselves within reasonable limits." Moreover, it is hard to see such celebrated natural law theorists as Aristotle, Cicero, Grotius, or John Locke expressing qualms about capital punishment or embracing a natural right to sexual liberty—which none of them ever did.

And why is agreement a good thing in and of itself? The Declaration of Independence certainly recognized "the Laws of Nature and of Nature's God" but equally (and obviously) recognized the right to self-determination of nations, the right of a people to establish new governments in whatever form "as to them shall seem most likely to effect their Safety and Happiness." The push for global consensus, Rabkin concludes, could eventuate in a global tyranny where individual nations are stripped of the freedom to follow their own preferred courses of action by global opinion-leaders. The more likely outcome, however, will be political instability engendered by forced adoption of transitory international fashions imposed by judges and diplomats who are not recognized as the people's representatives, a development that could ultimately undermine the rule of law and specifically the law of the Constitution on which American government is based.

Bradley Watson, in his chapter on how progressivism has precipitated a decline in the rule of law in America, examines the progressivist ethos that Rabkin suggests animates, in part, the push for adoption of global standards in American law. Legal historians have focused on the transformations in American law brought about by changes in legal education and legal theory narrowly construed. Watson seeks, by contrast, to look at the philosophical roots of this transformation, roots he maintains have been inadequately examined.

Liberal democracies, like America's, are based on consensual government. The rule of law in such regimes, accordingly, depends on public, consensually adopted norms that bind both government officials and private citizens. The purpose of these public norms is to protect the people's natural rights. As Watson observes, "The rule of law thus cannot be the rule of men, cannot stem from the posting of norms in a manner such that they cannot be known, and cannot involve the alteration of norms in a contingent or nonconsensual manner." But the currently fashionable idea of the Constitution as a "living document" that has to change and grow as the least republican branch of the government, the judiciary, sees fit is incompatible with this idea of the rule of law.

The problem with the "living" Constitution approach to judicial review is that it is fundamentally *historicist* in nature, meaning that the Constitution is not immutable over time but requires updating by judicial elites according to what they perceive to be the progress of history—that is, a history that has a definitive meaning and that evolves in an evermore democratic, egalitarian direction. As Watson points out, this is the antithesis of what the rule of law requires and what America's Founders understood to be the form of constitutionalism mandated by the Declaration of Independence's "Laws of Nature and of Nature's God," a constitutionalism that would create a government of limited and dispersed powers. How did the American judiciary come to adopt such a living, organic view of the Constitution—a progressive historicist rather than legalistic understanding of jurisprudence?

After surveying recent opinions in cases involving abortion, homosexual conduct, equal protection, and the "right to die" that demonstrate the sort of progressivist reasoning that assumes the Constitution has no fixed meaning and must evolve over time, Watson then proceeds to examine the origins of this transformation in American political thought. The most distinctive origins are in social Darwinism and pragmatism, two early movements that coalesced into intellectual progressivism. It was this latter ideology that would infiltrate institutional attitudes and behaviors and that would have such a decisive effect in the early twentieth century on the federal judiciary.

Watson stresses that it was the thinking of such social Darwinists as John Dewey and later pragmatists like William James that would set the foundation for the judicial philosophy of the living Constitution. Dewey was critical to popularizing the idea that Charles Darwin's *On the Origin of Species* was essential to revolutionizing not only the natural sciences but the human sciences too. Change was good, even essential, to the organic world as well as the inorganic world. So Dewey taught. Watson, however, has his doubts. On Darwinian terms, change may be the essence of the good and "identified with organic adaptation, survival, and growth," but as Watson stresses, in "the absence of fixity, morals, politics, and religion are subject to radical renegotiation and transformation." And this is not always a good thing. In fact, it usually is not.

Although the connections between pragmatism and the movement of twentieth-century discussions away from the Constitution may at times seem remote, James's doing away with the categories of nature and natural law, which Watson documents, helped the process along. So too did Dewey, who like so many of the intellectuals of his day was deeply opposed to classical economics, liberal individualism, and the natural rights philosophy on which these were based. It was "in Dewey that we can see how social Darwinism and pragmatism together become an intellectual and political force to be reckoned with; a modern liberalism whose goal is to help history along its democratic path, relying on the intellectual inputs of an elite vanguard that need not directly consult the people or ask for their consent." In Dewey, liberal individualism becomes collective liberalism where social action through elites in government becomes the preferred modus operandi.

This vision will serve as the animating ethos of progressivism, an ideology impatient with any inherent limits or constitutional restraints on state power. Modern liberalism, Watson concludes, is dedicated to liberation through social policy. The judiciary is a critical element of this liberation. What will count in progressive jurisprudence is neither text, nor tradition, nor logic, nor constitutional structure. Rather, what will count is what a judge feels is most critical to facilitating social and personal growth. Art will trump economics; expression, the common good; subjectivity, morality; freedom, natural law; and will, deliberation. The success of progressive jurisprudence "is marked by the fact that it no longer seeks victory, only legitimation in a constitutional order formally dedicated to the rule of law."

Since the events of 9/11 there have been a number of Supreme Court decisions and numerous editorial and academic publications that have suggested that greater judicial supervision of executive war powers is necessary, that both the Constitution and the rule of law require greater "legalization" of war. On the other hand, there has been alternative commentary, such as books by John Yoo and Jack Goldsmith, both former members of President Bush's Office of Legal Counsel, that have suggested that the executive is already engulfed in a labyrinth of legal regulations that threaten to strangle the presidency in times of war.[8]

This dispute is nothing new. The extent to which the executive should be restrained by formal legal regulations and whether the judiciary should get engaged in questions involving war powers rather than having these issues decided solely by the political branches of government—the president and Congress—have been subjects of contention in American constitutionalism since before the Constitution was ratified. The chapters in part III by Louis Fisher and me address these issues.

In his chapter on the judiciary's role in national security law, Fisher suggests that members of the federal judiciary should be less concerned about whether they have the jurisdiction or institutional competence to deal with questions of war and national security since there is an extensive basis in American law and practice for judicial intervention in such questions. It was not until the Vietnam War that judges began to have qualms about intervening in matters of war and national security. Fisher's chapter is an attempt to try to disabuse the judiciary and others of this misgiving since its constitutional and political consequences have been severe. As Fisher puts it, "Without a judiciary comfortable and knowledgeable about its duties and authority, broad assertions by executive officials of emergency power will undermine constitutional rights and individual liberties."

Fisher begins by examining the fundamental principles of constitutional law. He contends that the Framers recognized an implied authority of the president to respond to military actions taken against the United States but that this grant was narrowly defined. He cites a number of prominent Founders in support of the proposition that Congress, not the executive, has the constitutional power to initiate military hostilities. The Supreme Court also weighed in early on questions of war and national security in two cases emanating from the United States' conflict with France in the Quasi-War (1798–1800).

One of the great fallacies that has contributed to misunderstanding about the role of the president in American politics has been the "sole organ" doctrine, which holds that the president is the sole representative of the country in foreign affairs—and by implication in matters of war and national security. The principal culprit for this line of thinking was *United States v. Curtiss-Wright Corp.* (1936),[9] where a seven-man majority in an opinion by Justice George Sutherland claimed *in dicta* that the president had inherent constitutional powers to act as the sole organ in international affairs. As Fisher writes, "Of all the misconceived and poorly reasoned judicial decisions that have inflated presidential power in the field of national security, confused the judiciary, weakened the rule of law, and endangered individual rights, *Curtiss-Wright* stands in a class by itself."

Cases from 1789 to the Vietnam War make clear that Justice Sutherland's opinion in *Curtiss-Wright* cannot be squared with constitutional law or practice. For instance, as a result of the War of 1812, the Court ruled that seizing enemy property required a legislative, not executive or judicial, act; the Mexican War saw the Court restrictively interpreting the Commander-in-Chief Clause of Article II to that of carrying out congressional statutes; in another case of that era the Court held that constitutional authority to create courts inferior to the Supreme Court in conquered countries, the responsibility for administering the law of nations, and the authority to make rules regarding capture, were all powers Congress had under Article I. In *The Prize Cases* (1863),[10] the Court gave its imprimatur to President Lincoln's blockade of the rebellious states but admonished that the president as commander in chief "has no power to initiate or declare a war either against a foreign nation or a domestic State."

Fisher acknowledges that there have been cases following the Civil War where the Court ruled it lacked jurisdiction on the basis of what came to be known as the "political questions" doctrine, a doctrine where the Court distinguished between judicial and political powers, taking the position that matters of war and foreign policy were issues best dealt with by the political branches of government rather than the judiciary. Fisher suggests that these cases were anomalies since the Court through most of the twentieth century was prepared to hear war powers disputes. Even in the World War II cases involving the upholding of a curfew order and then the internment of Japanese Americans, the Court, although deferential to the executive and the military, nevertheless decided the cases. In some federal district court cases judges were even willing to challenge military leaders.

It was not until the Vietnam War that courts began to use the political questions doctrine, or some variant of it, to consistently avoid deciding constitutional challenges to executive exercises of war powers. This went on from 1966 to 1970, at which point federal courts again began to consider the merits of claims. However, even through the early 1970s courts still relied on denying plaintiffs standing and asserting the political questions doctrine to dismiss a host of cases.

Since 1973 many cases challenging the exercise of war powers have been deemed unsuitable for judicial resolution because Congress and the president failed to reach a constitutional impasse, what courts had begun to demand as the precondition for making a legal challenge to executive action "ripe" for adjudication. This was the case in *Dellums v. Bush*,[11] where members of Congress brought suit against President George H. W. Bush in 1990 when, in preparation for war, he amassed American troops on the Saudi Arabian border with Kuwait following Saddam Hussein's invasion of the latter country. Instead of declaring that the case had not ripened for judicial resolution because Congress as a body had not voted for or against war with Iraq, Fisher asks why relief could not have been provided by Judge Harold Greene, who heard the case. Green "could have decided on the merits that if the President proceeded to mount an offensive war, it could begin only after Congress either declared or authorized the war. He could have issued an injunction, as requested by the plaintiffs, subject to the condition that the injunction would be lifted if Congress passed a declaration or authorization."

Although critical of federal court decisions like these reluctant to decide war powers cases on the merits, Fisher is reassured by the four major detainee cases the Supreme Court has decided since 2004 involving national security post-9/11: *Hamdi v. Rumsfeld* (2004),[12] *Rasul v. Bush* (2004),[13] *Hamdan v. Rumsfeld* (2006),[14] and *Boumediene v. Bush* (2008).[15] All four decisions saw the Court actively involved in national security questions, agreeing to resolve a host of legal issues and prepared to deny powers asserted by President Bush where warranted. As Fisher concludes, "Throughout the past two centuries, judges have reviewed a broad range of issues involving foreign and domestic conflicts: the Executive's right to seize property in wartime, annex territory, establish duty rates, suspend the writ of habeas corpus, and define when war begins and ends. Recent cases on detainees and military tribunals fit well within the jurisdiction and duties of federal courts."

In my contribution to this book I contest this role for the courts in intervening in war powers disputes. Specifically, I defend Justice Thomas's dissenting opinion in *Hamdi v. Rumsfeld* (2004),[16] where Justice Thomas held that the judiciary could decide whether the executive's detention of Yaser Hamdi was lawful but *not* whether his designation as an enemy combatant was correct. That was a decision for the political branches, specifically the executive, to make, not the judiciary.

My defense of Justice Thomas's position centers on his use of *The Federalist* to buttress his opinion. *Hamdi* was unique among Supreme Court cases in the number of references made to *The Federalist*, an obvious authority on the issues in dispute. *The Federalist* was cited eleven times by three justices in the case—Justices Souter, Scalia, and Thomas. Obviously, however, each justice's use of *The Federalist* could not be consistent with the teaching of that seminal work since each adopted a different interpretation of what that work had to say about executive war powers. Accordingly, I review the opinions of Justices Souter, Scalia, and Thomas, as well as the plurality opinion in *Hamdi*, with a view to resolving which of them is most consistent with the teaching of *The Federalist*. I argue that Justice Thomas's opinion in support of the unitary executive most closely comports with *The Federalist*'s teaching on the issue of war and necessity.

I also emphasize that the dispute over the meaning of *The Federalist* is not merely some ethereal academic quibble but a dispute with real practical consequences since *The Federalist*, perhaps better than any other work in American political thought, sheds light on the theory underlying the Constitution's war powers. *The Federalist* may also go a long way to explaining the substance of the numerous criticisms lodged against the Court since *Hamdi*.

What *The Federalist* reveals on the issue of war powers is that as much as America is a nation of laws, the idea that the rule of law can apply to all political decisions is a fallacy—and a dangerous fallacy. This is especially true in the case of war, where unforeseen contingencies that may threaten national security can arise and where these have to be left to executive discretion. To try to "legalize" discretionary executive war powers by encumbering them with a raft of legal rules and regulations, as *Hamdi* and subsequent Court decisions have done, may not only threaten national security but undermine the rule of law since it will require that the law be broken to save American lives.

Decisions like *Hamdi* are dangerous not only because they handcuff the political branches of government when making war powers decisions but because they presume that the federal judiciary has both the constitutional authority and institutional capacity to resolve national security dilemmas. Both *The Federalist* and earlier Supreme Court decisions suggest otherwise. So too do dissenters in *Hamdi, Rasul, Hamdan,* and *Boumediene,* in addition to lawyers who have been involved in the war on terror post-9/11. The last part of my chapter reviews recent literature critical of the post-1960s legalization or lawyerization of warfare in addition to the consequences of judicializing war powers for the rule of law that *Hamdi* and the other detainee cases the Court has recently decided have had. I conclude that trying to reconcile individual rights with the demands of national security during a time of war is the most difficult issue tasked to the Constitution. It is an issue that cannot be resolved in any fixed, legalistic way readily addressed through judicial decision making.

Throughout the 1990s and early 2000s some of the most important equal protection cases the Supreme Court heard involved questions of race and representation under the Voting Rights Act (VRA). In her contribution to part IV, Katharine Inglis Butler addresses how the VRA and other developments in American law have led to the demise of that most fundamental building block of American politics, geographically based representation. Butler surveys how this element of American republicanism that has been in place since America's Founding is now being undermined by the imposition of a novel form of interest-group representation. The interests typically sought to be represented under this new model of representation are either racial, ethnic, or political in character. Either way they detract from the promotion of the public interest in American politics.

America's geographic form of representation was not designed to accommodate group representation. It does so very poorly. Although most other democracies in the world have adopted systems of proportional representation specifically designed to accommodate a diversity of political interests and parties, such a system of representation is alien to Americans. Our representatives represent geographic districts, and whether Republican or Democrat, those elected from geographic districts are expected to represent all their constituents, not just their party. Butler contends that "if we expect our geographic system to function effectively, we must continue to follow, or in many cases return to, the standards that produce districts for that purpose. If on the other hand, interest group representation is now thought to be essential for minorities, it should be provided directly and not by manipulation of district boundaries."

The challenges to geographic districting over the last half century have come primarily from the Supreme Court. They began with the reapportionment—"one person, one vote"—decisions of the 1960s. These decisions required states to reconfigure congressional and state electoral districts so that they were all more or less equally populated. The reapportionment cases precipitated the demise in the importance of counties and other traditional political subdivisions used for purposes of representation. This was especially so after the Supreme Court began to restrict the amount of deviation from equipopulous districts it would tolerate. As the Court's jurisprudence evolved, making more and more demands, states found it increasingly difficult to maintain a connection between counties and election districts. Once counties could no longer serve well for such districts, the use of alternative principles such as mandating compact districts and respect for "communities of interest" helped inoculate against undue gerrymandering. But this did not help for very long.

Further fueling the Court's assault on geographic representation was its jurisprudence under the VRA, which would turn out to be the principal culprit causing the decline of traditional geographic representation. Cases decided under the act beginning in 1969 increasingly mandated proportional representation of minorities as the measure of "fair" minority representation. States charged with complying with the VRA would increasingly have to abandon traditional districting principles to do so. The demands of the act got so extreme that in the 1990s a number of majority-minority districts drawn to comply with it were so bizarrely configured that they were successfully challenged before the Court as unconstitutional racial gerrymanders. Butler points out that by the 1990s, census data and redistricting technology had become so sophisticated that racial gerrymandering down to the tiniest segment of geography could be achieved, thus allowing for the creation of the bizarre districts in question.

Ironically, the cases that the Court decided in the 1990s holding that the VRA did not require jurisdictions to create racially gerrymandered districts inconsistent with traditional districting principles would have the effect of encouraging, rather than discouraging, gerrymandering, although this time for nonracial reasons. This was because the Court's focus in the cases was on the use of race as the predominant factor in drawing the districts in dispute. The Court was interested in geographic distortions of the districts only insofar as these were indicia of racial classifications. Moreover, in post-2000 cases the Court has explicitly endorsed the use of political data, specifically the political affiliations of racial groups, as a cover for racial redistricting, thus encouraging further such redistricting.

Butler points out that political interests of the nonracial variety have also benefited from racial gerrymandering because of the precedent-setting disregard for traditional districting criteria racial gerrymandering has set. Distorted districts, once created, tend to become permanent fixtures in American politics because whatever unsavory features these distortions present to American politics, politicians elected from the districts find their irregular boundaries just fine. As Butler puts it, "Once hooked on the personal and partisan advantages of districts drawn without regard to traditional districting standards, it was easy to draw more districts with even less regard for standards." Yet such districts increasingly undermine the ability of citizens to participate in politics as voters and candidates.

Butler concludes that there is little likelihood of electoral districts returning to their traditional association with independently significant geographic units absent legislators, who benefit from the status quo, taking the initiative. The 2006 VRA, now extending a key provision of the act (Section 5) for an additional twenty-five years, almost ensures yet more pressure for racial maximization policies that have to date so undermined geographic districting. Bizarre districts, whether conceived for racial or other partisan reasons, Butler declares, "disrupt basic political participation from voting to running for office, and serve the interests only of the 'group' for which they were designed. Those of us who are not strongly supportive of incumbents, highly partisan, or minorities, are effectively limited in our ability to impact electoral outcomes. We have become 'filler' for districts specifically designed to further interests not our own." As unwanted as this development in American politics has been, there is little prospect it will be resolved anytime soon

NOTES

1. Alexander Hamilton, John Jay, and James Madison, *The Federalist: A Commentary on the Constitution of the United States*, ed. and intro. Robert Scigliano (New York: Modern Library, 2001); *Federalist* 10, 57.
2. 128 S. Ct. 2783.
3. Stephen Breyer, *Active Liberty: Interpreting Our Democratic Constitution* (New York: Alfred A. Knopf, 2005).
4. 536 U.S. 304.
5. 549 U.S. 577.
6. 543 U.S. 551.
7. 128 S. Ct. 2229.
8. See, for instance, John Yoo, *The Powers of War and Peace: The Constitution and Foreign Affairs after 9/11* (Chicago: University of Chicago Press, 2005), and Jack Goldsmith, *The Terror Presidency: Law and Judgment inside the Bush Administration* (New York: W. W. Norton, 2007).
9. 299 U.S. 304 (1936).
10. 67 U.S. 635.
11. 752 F. Supp. 1141 (D.D.C. 1990)
12. 542 U.S. 507.
13. 542 U.S. 466.
14. 126 S. Ct. 2749.
15. 128 S. Ct. 2229.
16. 542 U.S. 507.

I

THE ORIGINS OF THE RULE OF LAW, ADMINISTRATION, AND THE ANTICIPATED GROWTH OF THE AMERICAN STATE

2

Freedom and the Rule of Law

The Ingenious English Legacy

Joyce Lee Malcolm

At first blush, freedom and the rule of law seem opposites, since freedom is the lack of fetters while law, like the fictional barrister Horace Rumpole's wife Hilda, must be obeyed. As the English, our constitutional forebears, appreciated, everything depends on what is in that rule of law. They knew firsthand that freedom without law was no freedom, but law that did not protect basic human rights was to their minds slavery and, as the song insists, "Britons never, never, never shall be slaves."[1] One of medieval England's most draconian punishments was being thrust out of the protection of law, to be made an "outlaw." While the outlaw was free from restraint, in *The History of English Law* Pollock and Maitland point out he was branded a public enemy, his outlawry "the sentence of death." "To pursue the outlaw and knock him on the head as though he were a wild beast" was, they added, "the right and duty of every law-abiding man."[2] He was said to bear the head of the wolf. Just how grim was life outside the rule of law? Pollock and Maitland elaborate:

> The outlaw's life is insecure. In Bracton's day he ought not to be slain unless he is resisting capture or fleeing from it; but it is every one's duty to capture him. And out in Gloucestershire and Herefordshire on the Welsh march custom allows that he may be killed at any time. If knowing his condition we harbour him, this is a capital crime. He is a "lawless man" and a "friendless man." Of every proprietary possessory, contractual right he is deprived; the king is entitled to lay waste his land and it then escheats to his lord; he forfeits his chattels to the king; every contract, every bond of homage or fealty in which he is engaged is dissolved. If the king inlaws him, he comes back into the world like a new-born babe . . . capable indeed of acquiring new rights, but unable to assert any of those that he had before his outlawry.[3]

The specter of the entire realm being plunged into a lawless state by rebellion or civil war was always in the background and convinced many people that however unfair the law might be, however vicious those who enforced it, it was preferable to life without the rule of law. On those grounds and the biblical admonition to render unto Caesar the things that are Caesar's, English clergy in the sixteenth and seventeenth centuries argued for the necessity of obedience, even to cruel, oppressive kings. "Without king, rule and judges," they taught, "no man shall ride or go by the highway unrobed, no man shall sleep in his own house or bed unkilled, no man shall keep his wife, children, and possessions in quietness, all things shall be common."[4] By "common" they did not mean that all things would be shared but that all would be vulnerable, a return to Hobbes's state of nature, the war of all against all. The picture of modern Iraq immediately after the fall of Saddam Hussein's brutal government is an instance of the bedlam let loose by the collapse of law.

The customary definition of the rule of law, however, ignores the extent of freedom within that law. Dr. Johnson's *Dictionary*, for example, defines the rule of law merely as a "particular form or mode of trying and judging," and—skipping from the eighteenth to the twentieth century—*Black's Law Dictionary*, only slightly more particular, dubs it a system in which "decisions are made by the application of known principles or laws without the intervention of discretion in their application." Of course the Third Reich had a rule of law as did France during the Terror.

The American Bar Association has turned its attention to the rule of law. In the August 2008 issue of the *ABA Journal* William Neukom, the outgoing president, described the organization's World Justice Project, which "brings rule of law to the fore as the highest priority for all." This ABA project, however, is far from neutral about the content of that law. It has devised a Rule of Law Index by which countries can measure their own rule of law.[5] The index's criteria, we are told, includes "dozens of indices" such as "competitiveness or human rights" and "whether a nation's laws are fairly and efficiently enforced, whether they protect the security of people and property, and whether they provide an effective remedy for violations of fundamental rights."[6] This effort to ensure key protections for freedom within the law is what the English had been laboring to achieve since Magna Carta. Over the centuries, periods of backsliding and acquiescence were ultimately trumped by those of effort, ingenuity, and courage to provide their nation a legacy of freedom within the rule of law. Unfortunately, recent shifts in the traditional British constitutional balance have eroded customary protections, consequently giving the majority party in Parliament and particularly its leader almost unchecked power. America's Founders, however, benefited from the original protections and it is that earlier range of constitutional strategies this chapter will briefly outline.

The primary English effort to embed rights within law was Magna Carta, which forced a vicious king, John, to agree at sword-point to abide by a host of rules meant to preserve what William Blackstone later summarized as the three great and primary rights: "personal security, personal liberty, and private property," at least for all free men.[7] John pledged to honor ancient custom; refrain from seizing persons or property without lawful judgment in the first case, and consent in the second; not to interfere with the processes of law; to respect the freedom of the church; to levy no tax without the approval of his Great Council; to permit trial by jury; and to abide by an assortment of other rights, some of great import at that time, others timeless. Notwithstanding John's vow that he and his heirs were granting all "the underwritten liberties" forever, his opponents had no illusions that a document signed by a notoriously faithless king on the battlefield would stand.[8] Indeed, barely a month after signing it John complained to the pope, who dutifully annulled Magna Carta and vowed to excommunicate anyone who abided by it. Happily, John died soon thereafter, leaving an infant heir; subsequent kings prudently reaffirmed his promises.

What I find most intriguing about Magna Carta was the attempt to ensure it would be no parchment barrier. In one of its final articles, the drafters created a watchdog group of twenty-five barons to monitor the king's performance, hear complaints of violations, then petition the king for redress. Should he refuse to mend his ways, John had agreed that the barons could gather the community and, in the words of the charter:

> Distrain and distress us in all possible ways, namely, by seizing our castles, Lands, possessions, and in any other way they can, until redress has been obtained as they deem fit, saving harmless our own person, and the persons of our queen and children; and when redress has been obtained, they shall resume their old relations toward us. [9]

Although this watchdog committee with its license to revolt proved unworkable, the same article included a more lasting tactic. The king promised to "procure nothing from anyone, either personally or through another, by which any of these concessions and liberties shall be revoked or diminished; and if any such thing is procured, it shall be void and null, and we will never use it either ourselves or through another."

Over the years a variety of other techniques were devised to ensure that freedom, or at least freedoms, remained within the rule of law. It was no easy task to bind a king who could not be held accountable in any court to respect his subjects' rights. But each monarch at his coronation was expected to take an oath to preserve "the Statutes Laws and Customs" of the realm and the inhabitants in "their Spirituall and civill rights and Properties."[10] And if the king was not punishable, each of his subjects was. In 1253, during the reign of John's son, Henry III, a statute was passed to threaten with punishment anyone who assisted in a violation of Magna Carta. As Pollock and Maitland point out, "[T]he anathema was launched, not merely against all who should break the charter, but also against all who should take any part whatever, even the humble part of mere transcribers, in making or promulgating or enforcing any statutes contrary to the sacred text."[11] To ensure that someone would be liable for any illegal act, other checks were added. As government bureaucracy grew, offices were taken out of the king's household and his seals were transferred to the hands of royal servants who "were bound to consider the rules of their office as well as the king's wishes."[12] The use of their countersignatures and seals meant the king could not act alone. The fact that the irresponsible king was joined in every action by a responsible individual or council had the beneficial effect, as one scholar put it, of "crippling his independent action."[13]

Other practices evolved, some focusing on the king, some on the judges, servants of the Crown but also the chief guardians of the law. A statute of Edward I's reign made it illegal for the king to refuse to redress wrongs when a subject submitted a petition of right.[14] A key legal tenet claimed, "The King could do no wrong." While this is often interpreted to mean the king was above the law, it also meant that any wrongful command was void in the act.[15] It was to be ignored. As an anonymous author pointed out in 1643, "[T]he King can doe no wrong, because his juridical power and authority is allwayes to controle his personal miscarriages."[16] On the other hand, if judges neglected their obligation to uphold the rights enshrined in Magna Carta, such a judgment was "to be undone and holden for naught."[17] Any judgment contrary to law was never to be drawn on as a precedent. And while the king pledged not to interfere with the processes of the law, from the time of Edward III a judge's oath of office required him to ignore even direct orders from the king. He was sworn to "deny no man common Right by the King's Letters."[18]

Religion played a role in protecting freedom within the rule of law as well, for although the clergy of the Church of England insisted that the faithful render unto Caesar the things that are Caesar's, that famous biblical text cautioned believers to "render unto God the things that are God's." As Howard Nenner reminds us, even when the Church of England seemed most insistent on obedience to the monarch, its teaching distinguished between lawful and unlawful commands.[19] "[O]bedience was not due to the ungodly command, but [only] to the duty to suffer the tyrannical prince's wrath."[20]

The responsibility of ensuring that the rule of law included freedom for individuals was not left to kings, royal officials, and judges. Parliament, the highest court of the realm and representative of its people, was not to tolerate illegal royal actions. Not surprisingly, its members were especially anxious to protect the institution's own rights, as will be discussed below. Much was asked of ordinary subjects as well. A tract of 1689 justifying the Glorious Revolution contended:

> Although . . . a King may require things not inconsistent with the Law of God, yet if they are beyond that Authority which the Constitutions of England have assigned to him, his Subjects are not bound in conscience to obey those Commands, and tho in some case they may comply by a voluntary concession, yet they are obliged to condemn and withstand such proceedings if they increase so far as to threaten a fatal subversion of the Government.[21]

Any officials appointed by the king "to oppress his Subjects contrary to Law their commissions being illegal, must be without authority: and therefore the subject is not bound in conscience to submit to them."[22] The ironic result of imposing on the subject the necessity of testing the legality of doubtful commands while freeing the king from the need to ascertain the legality of his orders meant, as David Ogg sees it, that "everyone except the king, is supposed to know the whole law of England."[23]

All of this asked a great deal of the entire community, from royal officials and judges down to the ordinary man. Few people are up to civic martyrdom. But there are striking examples of individuals and institutions standing fast for freedom under the rule of law. There are instances when judges nullified royal actions that they considered beyond the king's legitimate prerogative. In 1602, judges circumscribed the royal power to create monopolies when they declared that Queen Elizabeth's grant of a monopoly on the production of playing cards was void because "every grant made in grievance or prejudice of the subject is void."[24] Three years earlier they had found that a royal charter to the Merchant Tailors of London authorizing them to make ordinances was too broad. The tailors had restricted cloth dressing to their members, creating, in the judges' opinions, a monopoly that was "against the common law because it was against the liberty of the subject."[25] More often though, rather than confront the Crown, judges silently amended a law they found improper or tiptoed around doubtful royal commands. This could be risky. When James I and his successors tried to use the judges to push an agenda that clipped freedoms, and the judges failed to defend the rights of the people, there was popular outrage. A glaring instance was the Ship Money Case. Ship money was a tax levied on counties bordering the sea to provide for ships to protect the coast. Charles I unilaterally extended ship money to inland counties claiming there was an emergency. Many individuals refused to pay on the plea that since Parliament had not approved the levy and there was no emergency, it was illegal. John Hampden, one of the refusers, was taken to court, where his attorneys pleaded that the levy was null and void since there was no emergency. Seven of the twelve justices hearing the case held that the king was the sole judge of when a threat existed, thereby giving him a means to raise taxes without consulting Parliament. Indignant at this reasoning, Edward Hyde, future royalist, affirmed it a civic responsibility to resist illegal acts, even acts royal justices had pronounced legal, fuming: "[W]hen they [the public] heard this demanded in a court of law as a right, and found it by sworn judges of the law adjudged so, upon such grounds and reasons as every stander-by was able to swear was not law . . . and by a logic that left no man anything which he might call his own . . . they thought themselves bound in conscience to the public justice not to submit."[26] When the Long Parliament met in 1640, among the first to feel its wrath were those judges who had failed to protect Magna Carta. There was also anger that Charles I had changed the judges' customary tenure from serving during good behavior to serving during pleasure, the better to control their actions. This change became one of Parliament's grievances against that ambitious monarch.[27]

Many protests involved taxation. Individual justices of the peace scattered throughout the realm refused to carry out orders they felt were against law. When James I tried to raise money through a benevolence, a form of taxation abandoned nearly a century earlier, there was widespread opposition from justices of the peace because he hadn't gotten parliamentary approval. One justice explained, "[W]e are constrained to refuse to render unto His majesty such satisfaction as in our harts wee desyer."[28] Charles I requested the same tax in 1626, only to be told that local constables "made some question whether this course now holden were not against law."[29] A year later, attorneys for men who refused to pay Charles I's "forced loan" argued that since the loan was illegal, those who failed to advance the money requested had committed no offense.[30]

The requirement that Parliament approve taxation was the key to its survival, and members were necessarily jealous of the right. The most dramatic instance of Parliament's exercise of this responsibility came in 1628. Charles I had been collecting the customary taxes of tonnage and poundage without parliamentary approval and in direct violation of the recently passed Petition of Right. Customs officers confiscated the goods of those who refused to pay, including John Rolle, a member of the House of Commons. Rolle's colleagues pronounced the king's collections illegal and announced that anyone who paid would be punishable at law. This led to the infamous scene in which the speaker of the House of Commons was forcibly held in his seat when he tried to adjourn the house, while there was read a declaration that condemned as enemies of the commonwealth anyone who "shall counsel or advise the taking and levying of the subsidies of tonnage and poundage, not being granted by parliament or shall be an actor or instrument therein" shall be "reputed an innovator in the government, and a capital enemy to the kingdom and Commonwealth," while any merchant or person who voluntarily paid the subsidies of tonnage and poundage, "not being granted by parliament, he shall likewise be reputed a betrayer of the liberties of England, and an enemy to the same."[31]

Two incidents in which individuals refused to tolerate royal infringement on Magna Carta deserve mention. When Sir William Coryton, a Cornish knight, refused to pay the forced loan, he told county commissioners he would gladly serve the king but he could not disobey the law citing medieval statutes that no aids or taxes should be levied without consent of Parliament. Summoned before the Privy Council, Coryton explained that the loan was illegal, whereupon in his words, the council "gave me leave to depart with fair respect."[32] Even more indicative of the strength of feeling for the rule of law and individual rights among ordinary Englishmen is the example of Charles II's professional soldiers camped at Blackheath in 1673, when they were asked to take a vague new oath of obedience to the king. The secretary of the Privy Council was notified that the soldiers were nearly ready to mutiny because the articles of war included an exceptionally broad oath. "They scruple the oath in it," he was informed, "and say that to swear at large to obey the King's commands is strange: for then he may command things for which the persons that do them shall afterwards be hanged."[33] "That English paid soldiers should have objected to this 'horrid' oath," David Ogg finds "one of the most striking tributes to the preeminence of common-law traditions; for in some general way, these men on Blackheath believed that, unlike foreigners, they had over them the protection of Magna Carta and the Petition of Right."[34]

Individuals were also in a position to protect liberty through their role on juries. Jurors' keen sense of right and justice led them to refuse to find guilt if they believed the punishment too severe or unfair. In his fine study of medieval juries, Thomas Green found that jurors tended to refuse to convict indigents for theft and law-abiding individuals for an unpremeditated act of violence. "Juries frequently manipulated the fact-finding process," Green writes, "to prevent the imposition of capital punishment."[35] A striking example of this power occurred during the eighteenth century when the notorious Waltham Black Act created more than 250 new capital crimes, many for minor thefts.[36] The act was meant to deter, but instead victims were reluctant to bring charges; few of those who were charged were indicted, and juries and even judges committed what Blackstone termed "a kind of pious perjury" distorting the facts in order to avoid extreme penalties.[37] Larceny, for example, had been set at twelve pence over eight hundred years earlier. In light of the considerable inflation over the centuries, Sir Henry Spelman had complained in the seventeenth century that "while everything else has risen in its nominal value, and become dearer, the life of man had continually grown cheaper." Sympathetic juries simply claimed the stolen item was worth less than twelve pence. Lord Holland told of a case in which the charge was stealing a ten-pound note. In this instance the jury, "in the warmth of their humane feelings," committed perjury and reduced it in their verdict to the nominal value below forty shillings.[38]

America's Founders had resorted to sympathetic juries during tense disputes with the English government and insisted that freedom depended not on judicial review, but on the right to trial by jury. During the Massachusetts ratification convention, for example, Theophilus Parsons, future chief justice of the Massachusetts Supreme Court, replied to concerns about the new federal government usurping the people's rights with this testament to the jury's importance:

> But, sir, the people themselves have it in their power effectually to resist usurpation, without being driven to an appeal to arms. An act of usurpation is not obligatory; it is not law; and *any man* may be justified in his resistance. Let him be considered as a criminal by the general government, yet only his fellow-citizens can convict him; they are his jury, and if they pronounce him innocent, not all the powers of Congress can hurt him.[39]

The English clergy, when it served their purposes, defended Magna Carta's common law rights. The bishop of London, Henry Compton, was arraigned in 1688 for refusing to suspend a rector who had delivered two antipopery sermons in defiance of the warning by the Catholic King James II against polemical preaching.[40] Compton's lawyers pleaded that he could not have suspended the erring cleric without a citation and trial, for a citation "is *jure gentium* and can never be taken away by any positive command or law whatsoever," adding that "no man can be obliged to do an unlawful act . . . this rule obliges all men in the world, in all places, and at all times."[41]

The most famous case of clergy taking their stand on English rights was the Seven Bishops case of 1688. James II had ordered the bishops to have his Declaration of Indulgence dispensing with penal laws against Roman Catholics and Protestant dissenters read from every pulpit in the land on three successive Sundays. Rather than obeying, six bishops and the archbishop of Canterbury petitioned the king, pleading that they were obliged to preserve the Act of Uniformity and challenging his power to suspend the penal acts.[42] The seven were arrested and clapped in the Tower for "preferring, composing, making, and publishing, and causing to be published, a seditious libel." They responded that what was asked of them was against the law. At their trial the solicitor general insisted they had no right to petition the king outside of Parliament but should have acquiesced. The judges debated whether the king had the power to dispense with laws for ecclesiastical affairs, Justice Powell arguing that "if there be no such dispensing power in the king, then that can be no libel . . . which says that the declaration, being founded upon such a pretended power is illegal."[43] Other judges, however, felt that any contradiction of a royal order was itself a libel. The case was decided by a jury, though, and the jury found the bishops not guilty. When the Convention Parliament met after James II had fled the realm, it commended the bishops "for the great Services they had done their Religion and Country, by the Opposition they had made . . . and their refusing to read the King's Declaration for a Toleration, which was then founded upon the Dispensing Power."[44]

In addition to these common law strategies, the very structure of English government, from which our own was patterned, was crucial to the preservation of freedom. The arrangement was designed to ensure a division of power. While the English constitution didn't, and doesn't, have the strict separation of branches that Montesquieu insisted on, it did have a series of balances and checks. The English balance of king, lords, and commons was a combination of government by the one, the few, and the many. As for checks, William Blackstone boasted that "all parts" of the English constitution "form a mutual check upon each other":

> In the legislature, the people are a check upon the nobility, and the nobility a check upon the people . . . while the king is a check upon both, which preserves the executive power from encroachments. And this very executive power is again checked, and kept within due bounds by the two houses. . . . Like three distinct powers in mechanics, they jointly impel the machine of government in a direction different from what either, acting by themselves, would have done, but at the same time in a direction partaking of each, and formed out of all; a direction which constitutes the true line of the liberty and happiness of the community.[45]

England's political theorists explained that the king and lords had a genuine and permanent interest in the preservation of the kingdom. The king's power depended on the prosperity of the realm and as an heir and father he would feel duty bound to preserve the prerogatives of his office. The lords were large landowners with a permanent stake in the general welfare and subject to taxation and common law. They saw themselves as holding the balance between the king and the people. Both king and lords had an interest beyond a short-lived political career. During the Virginia ratification convention, Patrick Henry argued that in contrast to Britain's "real balances and checks," the proposed American constitution had "only ideal balances."[46] The new American president and senators would have nothing to lose, while the divisions between branches relied on technical checks that stemmed from shared or distinct functions.[47] More than is, or was, generally acknowledged, the American government structure was patterned on the British model with an executive and a two-house legislature; their roles, although not their source of personnel, often mirrored those of the Mother Country. But the American government boasts stricter separation of powers and a more independent judiciary, which has taken final responsibility for protection of freedom within the rule of law. Just as important, both the new American state constitutions and the federal constitution incorporated common law thinking, procedures, and rights. James Stoner in *Common-Law Liberty* attributes the restraint with which this country was able to change from a monarchy to a republic as "testimony, in part, to the continuous power of a common law that focused its attention not on the question of regime but on the rights of individuals in particular cases and thus on the whole array of institutions in civil society in the midst of which the people went about their lives."[48]

Even as the American Constitution was being drafted borrowing from English models for protecting rights, the English constitution was changing. During the seventeenth century the growing pretensions of contenders for sovereignty in England shattered the nice balance and clever means devised to preserve freedom. A brutal civil war between Crown and Parliament swept the British Isles. The king lost and was tried for treason by members of Parliament and executed. When all other means failed, the traditional constitution simply had no way to hold an untrustworthy king to account. The monarchy and House of Lords were abolished and with this the traditional checks on Parliament and the executive disappeared. The impromptu republican regime that followed proved so unpopular it had to rely on military force to maintain power. The monarchy was restored in 1660 but once again traditional rights were threatened by ambitious kings. Finally, in 1688 during the Glorious—because bloodless—Revolution, James II fled. A Convention Parliament elevated William and Mary to the throne on condition they consent to a bill of rights. While the Crown still had considerable power, the issue of ultimate sovereignty was settled in favor of Parliament and gradually, within Parliament, devolved on the House of Commons. The old balance with its built-in checks was vanishing. There was still freedom within the rule of law, even increased democracy, but it was secure only as long as Parliament agreed to preserve individual rights.

English efforts to protect freedom within the rule of law had always focused on controlling the executive, not the representatives of the kingdom. It was assumed that members of Parliament would never trample on ancient rights, being protected by these themselves. Judges had quietly modified the operation of parliamentary statutes for centuries, but modern scholars are skeptical about their treating acts as null and void. One study claims the high-water mark of judicial review was Dr. Bonham's case of 1610, the very case that explicitly proclaimed "that in many cases, the common law will controul Acts of Parliament, and sometimes adjudge them to be utterly void: for when an Act of Parliament is against common right and reason, or repugnant, or impossible to be performed, the common law will controul it, and adjudge such Act to be void."[49] This is probably setting the "high-water mark" of judicial review in England too early, but that is of less significance than its later collapse.

By the late eighteenth century, the only check remaining on Parliament, apart from petitions, periodic elections, and juries, was the stipulation that an act be rational, not whether it infringed on a longstanding right.[50] Yet on the eve of the American Revolution, even this meager protection seemed no longer to hold. Writing in 1765, Blackstone affirmed that "acts of parliament that are impossible to be performed are of no validity; and if there arise out of them collaterally any absurd consequences, manifestly contradictory to common reason, they are, with regard to those collateral consequences void."[51] Well and good. However, Blackstone added that Parliament could "change and create afresh even the constitution of the kingdom, and of parliaments themselves," and in short "do every thing that is not naturally impossible."[52] As long as Parliament was clear about its intent, however unreasonable, "no court has power to defeat the legislature." Champion as he was for individual rights, Blackstone was clearly troubled by the unfettered power of Parliament over the British constitution and the rights of individuals. He cited Sir Matthew Hale's foreboding a century earlier, that as Parliament was the kingdom's highest court, "if by any means a misgovernment should any way fall upon it, the subjects of this kingdom are left without all manner of remedy." In the final edition of his *Commentaries of the Laws of England*, Blackstone modified the statement of its power to read: "But if parliament will positively enact a thing to be done that is unreasonable, I know of no power *in the ordinary forms of the* constitution that is vested with authority to control it."[53]

As the sovereignty of Parliament solidified, other traditional checks were eclipsed or removed. English judges were poorly situated to protect freedom within the old rule of law. Parliament was the highest court. Judges were never as independent as the public wished or as the judicial branch of the United States would be. They were appointed by the Crown and later by the Lord Chancellor, a member of the cabinet; they sat in the House of Lords and felt it their duty to defer to the "democratic branch," rather than proclaim any statute against law. Maybe that reticence was proper. But it spelled doom for ancient rights. As for the people's power, petitions and elections are little security when major parties share the desire to expand government powers at the expense of individual rights.

Within Parliament, power has continued to shift. The House of Commons first absorbed the power of the executive—the Crown—then in the course of the twentieth century the ruling party in the Commons began to exercise near-dictatorial control over the legislature. Its leader now has virtual carte blanche over his party in Parliament and with it the country. Matthew Hales's fears have been realized. Time and again by an ordinary act the majority party in the British Parliament has altered the traditional constitution and infringed ancient rights through a simple majority vote. In 1911 the House of Commons curbed the ancient powers of the hereditary House of Lords. While it was probably long past due to change the hereditary nature of the Lords, the use of a simple vote was a perilous omen. In 1999 after a defiant House of Lords, one packed with life appointees, repeatedly thwarted the Commons' desire that voters elect EU representatives by slate, not as individuals, Parliament voted to abolish the hereditary lords entirely. Apart from ninety-two hereditary lords who were "grandfathered in," all future peers will be appointed for life by the party in power. Tony Blair's government promised that the reconfiguration of the House of Lords would be settled in a formal, constitutional manner, but that issue has never been revisited. It suits the leaders of the Commons to leave the upper house weak, its constitutional role unclear.

Ancient rights have also fallen victim to government policies. Both Labour and Conservative governments have insisted on a monopoly on the use of force, claiming this is a matter of public safety. The repercussions for both traditional rights and public safety have been dire. The right to self-defense, long regarded by political philosophers as the first law of nature, could not, Blackstone insisted, be taken away by the law of society.[54] Yet during the twentieth century the right of the people to have arms for their defense, a right specifically guaranteed in the 1689 Bill of Rights, was increasingly pruned, then completely removed. From 1920, firearms were required to be registered and applicants had to have a suitable reason to own a gun. Secret directives from the Home Office gradually tightened restrictions on what constituted a suitable reason until in 1969 police were instructed that "[i]t should never be necessary for anyone to possess a firearm for the protection of his house or person."[55] There could no longer be arms for personal defense.

In the meantime, the 1953 Prevention of Crime Act made it illegal to carry an offensive weapon.[56] Any item carried with the idea that it might be used for self-defense was automatically defined as an offensive weapon and therefore illegal. The same act gave police broad power to stop and search whomever they liked, and anyone found with such a device was guilty until proven innocent. The public was required to depend on the police for personal protection, and even advised to walk on by if they witnessed an attack on a fellow citizen. Desperate situations were to be left to the professionals to handle.

The Criminal Law Act of 1967 then changed the rules of what was permissible self-defense, leaving everything to be based on what seemed reasonable later.[57] In his textbook on English criminal law, Glanville Williams found the requirement that an individual's efforts to defend himself be "reasonable" was "now stated in such mitigated terms as to cast doubt on whether it still forms part of the law."[58] The authors of the popular Smith and Hogan criminal law textbook warn that the prohibition against carrying any item that could be used for protection together with the narrow definition of reasonableness "may qualify the important principle that a man cannot be driven off the streets and compelled not to go to a public place where he might lawfully be because he will be confronted by people intending to attack him. If he decides that he cannot go to that place unless armed with an offensive weapon, it seems that he must stay away. He commits an offence if he goes armed."[59]

When crime continued to escalate, the government set about stripping other rights with a view to getting more convictions. At the end of its 2003 session, Parliament repealed the eight-hundred-year old guarantee against double jeopardy. Anyone acquitted of a serious crime now can be retried if "new and compelling evidence" is brought forward. Parliament tinkered with the definition of "new" to make that burden easier to meet. The test for "new" in these criminal cases, Lord Neill pointed out, is lower than "is used habitually in civil cases. In a civil case, one would have to show that the new evidence was not reasonably available on the previous occasion. There is no such requirement here." The benefits to be reaped by chucking the ancient prohibition against double jeopardy seemed so promising that Parliament extended the repeal beyond murder cases to cases of rape, manslaughter, kidnapping, drug trafficking, and some twenty other serious crimes. For good measure it also made the new act retroactive. Henceforth, no one who has been, or will be, tried and acquitted of a serious crime can feel confident he will not be tried again. The attorney general conceded the new law would uproot an ancient right but pointed out: "[T]hat does not necessarily mean that it is right for all time. I recognize that the provision carries a price, but it is a price worth paying, because of the justice that it will bring about."

During the same session the government announced it was overturning other time-honored protections. Prosecutors are now permitted to introduce hearsay evidence as well as a defendant's prior record into Court, and since juries are unreliable, able to be intimidated, and inefficient, the number of jury trials is being reduced.

Blackstone, ever the optimist, was aware that rights, even great and primary rights, were at times trampled on, but was convinced that the English constitution was sufficiently resilient to restore them:

> The absolute rights of every Englishman . . . as they are founded on nature and reason, so they are coeval with our form of government; though subject at times to fluctuate and change: their establishment (excellent as it is) being still human. At some times we have seen them depressed by over-bearing and tyrannical princes; at others so luxuriant as even to tend to anarchy. . . . But the vigour of our free constitution has always delivered the nation from these embarrassments, and, as soon as the convulsions consequent on the struggle have been over, the balance of our rights and liberties has settled to it's [*sic*] proper level, and their fundamental articles have been from time to time asserted in parliament, as often as they were thought to be in danger.[60]

Indeed, there are two hopeful signs that protections for rights may be restored. The first is the Human Rights Act passed in 1998.[61] To avoid the embarrassment of British citizens appealing for protection to the European Court of Human Rights in Strasbourg, the new act enables individuals to appeal in British courts for a remedy to a breach of a convention right. This act injects some measure of judicial review into the British courts but not on the American model. British judges are to take account of decisions of the Strasbourg court and to interpret parliamentary legislation for its compatibility with the European Convention on Human Rights. While they can declare legislation incompatible with the convention, the legislation will still be valid. The idea is to find a remedy for the individual plaintiff, not to nullify a law passed by Parliament. Nor does the European Convention on Human Rights include the full range of common law rights. There is no right to self-defense, for example.

Secondly, the Blair government announced in 2003—the same year it moved to eliminate ancient rights of defendants—the intention to establish a supreme court on the American style, independent of Parliament and able to review its acts. In fact, no other constitutional democracy has its highest court as part of its legislature. The manner in which this change was announced, though, demonstrates what has become of the British constitution. At a press conference the prime minister simply informed the public that he was abolishing the post of Lord Chancellor, the chief minister for 1,400 years, and creating an independent supreme court. The two were tied. The Lord Chancellor's duties had kept the judiciary entangled in politics since he served as the Lords' speaker, cabinet minister responsible for civil law, and head of the judiciary in England and Wales who appointed judges. There was surprise and dismay at the announcement. Neither members of the parliamentary opposition parties nor the public had been consulted or given advance notice.[62] The Conservative shadow home secretary, Oliver Letwin, complained, "To remake constitutions on the hoof, on the basis of personnel changes within the cabinet [the former chancellor, an old friend of Blair's, had stepped down] is the height of irresponsibility. To announce it in a press release at 5:45 pm on a Thursday evening is nothing short of a disgrace." The shadow leader of the Lords, Lord Strathclyde, described the proposals as "trendy reforms cobbled together on the back of an envelope." Still the idea is sound. Twelve justices, no longer members of Parliament, will serve as the final court of appeal. It isn't clear whether the court will be able to declare a law unconstitutional, however. The current law lords will be the first justices, then vacancies will be filled by an independent commission. It is now five years since that announcement but the Supreme Court only heard its first case in October 2009, much time having been spent in selecting an appropriate building to house the court.

In addition to these measures, and in extremis, one can fall back on that old guarantee from Magna Carta restated in the 1918 case of *Bowles v. Bank of England*: "[T]he Bill of Rights still remains unrepealed, no practice or custom, however prolonged, or however acquiesced in on the part of the subject, can be relied on by the Crown as justifying any infringement of its provisions."

To conclude, it seems freedom can exist within the rule of law only if clever strategies, embedded in a government's constitution and law, are protected by government officials and a public concerned with preserving the rights of the people. As the great American justice Benjamin Cardozo summed it up:

> The great ideals of liberty and equality are preserved against the assaults of opportunism, the expediency of the passing hour, the erosion of small encroachments, the scorn and derision of those who have no patience with general principles, by enshrining them in constitutions, and consecrating to the task of their protection a body of defenders.[63]

That body of defenders is the crucial ingredient.

NOTES

1. See "Rule, Britannia!" first published in the eighteenth century.
2. Sir Frederick Pollock and Frederic William Maitland, *The History of English Law before the Time of Edward I*, 2nd ed., 2 vols. (London: Cambridge University Press, 1968), 1:476.
3. Pollock and Maitland, *History of English Law*, 1:477. According to Pollock and Maitland, this punishment was very common with ten men outlawed for one who is hanged (478). Bracton lived in the thirteenth century.
4. Joyce Lee Malcolm, ed., *The Struggle for Sovereignty: Seventeenth-Century English Political Tracts*, 2 vols. (Indianapolis: Liberty Fund, 1999), 1:xxx.
5. Samuel Johnson, *A Dictionary of the English Language*, abridged from the Rev. H. J. Todd, corrected and enlarged edit. by Alexander Chalmers, repr. (USA, 1994); Henry Campbell Black, *Black's Law Dictionary*, 5th ed. (St. Paul, Minn.: West Publishing 1979); *ABA Journal* (August 2008): 9.
6. *ABA Journal* (August 2008): 9.
7. William Blackstone, *Commentaries on the Laws of England*, 4 vols. (1765–1769; repr. Chicago, 1979), 1:136.
8. Magna Carta, 1215, art. 1.
9. Magna Carta, art. 61.
10. See discussion on the coronation oath devised for William and Mary, Joyce Lee Malcolm, "Doing No Wrong: Law, Liberty, and the Constraint of Kings," *Journal of British Studies* 38 (April 1999): 184.
11. T. E. Tomlins et al., eds., *Statutes of the Realm* [to 1713], 11 vols. (London, 1810–1828), 1:6; Pollock and Maitland, *History of English Law*, 1:179.
12. J. E. A. Jolliffe, *The Constitutional History of Medieval England: From the English Settlement to 1485*, 4th ed. (London: A. and C. Black, 1961), 393. Henry III was an infant when his father died; this left power in the hands of others until he came of age. Also see William Anson, *The Law and Custom of the Constitution*, 2 vols. (Oxford: Clarendon Press, 1892), 1:15.
13. Anson, *Law and Custom*, 2:41. The Thirty Articles of 1410 required the king to govern by advice of a permanent council.
14. Sir William Holdsworth, *A History of English Law*, 2nd ed., 12 vols. (London, 1938), 9:8. Holdsworth points out that while ordinary writs did not lie against the king in his court, he was "morally bound to do the same justice to his subjects as they could be compelled to do to one another" (9:10).
15. For an analysis of this tenet and its meaning and history, see Malcolm, "Doing No Wrong," 161–86.
16. Anon., *Touching the Fundamental Laws* (London, 1643), 11.

17. 25 Edw. I, cap. 2.

18. 18 Edw. III, cap. 7. And see David Jenkins, *The Kings Prerogative and the Subjects Privileges Asserted according to Law and Reason* (London, 1645; repr., 1680), 8. Medieval judges were still the king's servants according to Ralph V. Turner, *Judges, Administrators and the Common Law in Angevin England* (London: Hambledon Press, 1994), 113.

19. Howard Nenner, "The Later Stuart Age," in *The Varieties of British Political Thought, 1500–1800*, ed. J. G. A. Pocock, Gordon J. Schochet, and Lois Schwoerer (Cambridge: Cambridge University Press, 1993), 205.

20. Nenner, "The Later Stuart Age," 205. Nenner concludes: "As the divinely appointed guarantor of the faith, the church was effectively denying that God's truth was alterable by the king alone or even by the king-in-parliament."

21. Samuel Masters, *The Case of Allegiance in Our Present Circumstances Considered: In a Letter from a Minister in the City, to a Minister in the Country* (London, 1689), 12.

22. Masters, *Case of Allegiance*, 14.

23. David Ogg, *England in the Reign of Charles II*, 2nd ed. (Oxford: Oxford University Press, 1967), 453.

24. *Darcy v. Allein*, Trin. 44 Eliz. in Sir Edward Coke, *The Reports of Sir Edward Coke* (London, 1826), 6 vols., pt. 11, 87e.

25. *Davenant and Hurdies*, Trin. 41 Eliz.rot.92, in Coke, *Reports*, pt. 11, 86b.

26. Edward, Earl of Clarendon, *The History of the Rebellion and Civil Wars in England*, ed. W. Dunn Macray, 6 vols. (Oxford, 1888), 1:150.

27. This change of tenure was complained of in clause 38 of the Grand Remonstrance as meant "the better to hold a rode over them." See Gardiner, *Constitutional Documents*, 213.

28. Richard Cust, *The Forced Loan, 1626–1628* (Oxford: Clarendon Press, 1987), 154.

29. Cust, *Forced Loan*, 161–62.

30. J. P. Sommerville, *Politics and Ideology in England, 1603–1640* (London: Longman, 1986), 42.

31. Protestation of 2 March 1628 in John P. Kenyon, ed., *The Stuart Constitution, 1603–1688: Documents and Commentary*, 2nd ed. (Cambridge: Cambridge University Press, 1986), 71.

32. Kevin Sharpe, *The Personal Rule of Charles I* (New Haven, Conn.: Yale University Press, 1992), 19–20. And see Cust, *Forced Loan*, 165–70. Coryton's comment is cited by Sharpe, *Personal Rule*, 20.

33. Henry Ball to Williamson, 18 July 1673, quoted in Ogg, *Charles II*, 505. Ogg included the text of the oath.

34. Ogg, *Charles II*, 505.

35. Thomas A. Green, *Verdict according to Conscience: Perspectives on the English Criminal Trial Jury, 1200–1800* (Chicago: University of Chicago Press, 1985), xv.

36. The most thorough study of this act is E. P. Thompson, *Whigs and Hunters: The Origin of the Black Act* (London: Allen Lane, 1975). Also see Joyce Lee Malcolm, *Guns and Violence: The English Experience* (Cambridge, Mass.: Harvard University Press, 2002), 67–77.

37. Blackstone, *Commentaries*, 4:238–39.

38. T. C. Hansard, ed., *The Parliamentary Debates from the Year 1803 to the Present Time*, 1st ser., 20:297. See William S. Holdsworth, *A History of English Law*, 2nd ed.,

12 vols. (London: Methuen & Co., 1924–1938), 11:559; Blackstone, *Commentaries*, 3:336.

39. Jonathan Elliot, ed., *The Debates in the Several State Conventions on the Adoption of the Federal Constitution*, 5 vols. (Philadelphia, 1863), 2:94 (emphasis added).

40. J. R. Jones, *The Revolution of 1688 in England* (London: Weidenfeld and Nicolson, 1972), 67–73.

41. Mark Goldie, "The Political Thought of the Anglican Revolution," in *The Revolutions of 1688: The Andrew Browning Lectures, 1988*, ed. Robert Beddard (Oxford: Clarendon Press, 1991), 120.

42. W. C. Costin and J. Steven Watson, *The Law and Working of the Constitution: Documents 1660–1914*, 2 vols. (London: A. and C. Black, 1952), 1:258–71.

43. Costin and Watson, *Constitution*, 268.

44. The resolution was passed on February 1, 1688/1689. See *The Tryal of Dr. Henry Sacheverell, before the House of Peers for High Crimes and Misdemeanors: Upon an Impeachment* (London, 1710), 28.

45. Blackstone, *Commentaries*, 1:150–51.

46. See Elliot, *Debates*, 3:165–66. And see John Murrin, "The British and Colonial Background of American Constitutionalism," in *The Framing and Ratification of the Constitution*, ed. Leonard Levy and Dennis J. Mahoney (New York: Macmillan, 1987), 34–35.

47. Eliot, *Debates*, 3:165–66.

48. James R. Stoner Jr., *Common-Law Liberty: Rethinking American Constitutionalism* (Lawrence: University Press of Kansas 2003), 16.

49. See T. F. T. Plucknett, "Dr. Bonham's Case and Judicial Review," *Studies in English Legal History* 14 (1983): 34, 53.

50. Plucknett, "Judicial Review," 53–54.

51. Blackstone, *Commentaries*, 1:91.

52. Blackstone, *Commentaries*, 1:156.

53. Plucknett, "Judicial Review," 60 (emphasis added). The only limit to Parliament's authority is that one parliament cannot control the next.

54. Blackstone, *Commentaries*, 3:4.

55. 10 & 11 Geo. V. c. 43 (1920), Firearms Act; "Memorandum for the Guidance of the Police," Home Office, September 1969, 22.

56. 1 & 2 Eliz. II. cap. 14 (1953), and see Malcolm, *Guns and Violence*, 171–89.

57. Criminal Law Act, c. 58 (1967).

58. Glanville Williams, *Textbook of Criminal Law*, 2nd ed. (London: Stevens, 1983), 504, 507.

59. J. C. Smith, *Smith and Hogan Criminal Law*, 9th ed. (London: Butterworths, 1999), 450–51 and nn. 20, 1.

60. Blackstone, *Commentaries*, 1:120, 125, 123.

61. Human Rights Act, 1998, c. 42.

62. Patrick Wintour and Clare Dyer, "Blair's Reforming Reshuffle," *Guardian*, June 13, 2003.

63. Benjamin Cardozo, *The Nature of the Judicial Process* (New Haven, Conn.: Yale University Press, 1921).

3

Regulation, Administration, and the Rule of Law in the Early Republic

Joseph Postell

> As a matter of fact the American democracy both in its central and in its local governments has always practiced both [natural and artificial] selection. The state governments have sedulously indulged in a kind of interference conspicuous both for its activity and its inefficiency.[1]
>
> —Herbert Croly, *The Promise of American Life*

According to a prevalent myth in American history, economic life in America was almost entirely unregulated in the antebellum period due to the predominant natural right doctrines of the American Revolution. This conception of unregulated economic life in America has influenced a vast array of legal, economic, and political historians. The historian Harry Scheiber wrote as recently as 1987 that "the reader of recent literature on industrial policy would gain scarcely any sense of whether state law and administration historically have mattered in the ordering of economic affairs."[2]

This typical narrative claims that America was essentially libertarian in economic matters up to the period following the Civil War, when there emerged industrialization and a new theory of government, which rejected the natural right doctrines of the Founding upon which a supposedly "laissez-faire" society was established. This chapter opens by examining some examples to demonstrate the prevalence of regulation in the first seventy years of the republic. Once this is established, it will be useful to examine the particular administrative arrangements of nineteenth-century regulation, to provide some background against which to compare administrative arrangements and theories of the twentieth-century administrative state. Thus, the chapter will proceed to discuss in particular four salient features of nineteenth-century regulation and administration, and the principles upon which these arrangements rested, including self-government and the rule of law, before examining the Progressives' rejection of the arrangements that preserved these ends, for the sake of promoting centralized, executive justice by experts.

The regime established by the American Founders, in short, did not lead to a laissez-faire approach to economic activity in the nineteenth century. However, the *locus* of regulatory authority in the Founders' regime was far different from that of the administrative society the Progressives envisioned, and the manner in which administration was conducted was opposed to basic principles of Progressive thought. As Jack Rakove frankly puts the issue, the statesmen of the Founding "understood how much the multifarious duties of courts defined the essence of government in a society completely devoid of anything resembling a bureaucracy or the apparatus of a modern state."[3] While there are important philosophical differences between the Founders' and Progressives' views regarding the *scope* of government authority (and the corresponding relationship between the public and private spheres), perhaps the crucial difference between the Founders and the Progressives lies in the *manner* in which government authority is exercised. This chapter will discuss the institutional arrangements governing regulation that were born from the ideas that prevailed during the Founding.

I. ACTIVE SOCIETY AND REGULATION IN THE EARLY REPUBLIC

In recent decades, a wide group of economic and legal historians have explored the extent to which the governments of the several states, and the federal government, intervened in economic matters for the sake of ensuring a well-regulated society. By the mid-1990s, it could be confidently proclaimed by one historian that "it has become impossible to speak of laissez-faire in the antebellum American context."[4] The work of these scholars has revealed that, as the natural right principles of the Founding were being worked out in practice in the nineteenth century, citizens and statesmen saw no inconsistency between the principles of the revolution and the existence of a prevalent system of government regulation that touched on and even dictated the economic and social actions of citizens. A few examples and a brief overview will suffice to show the prevalence of regulation during the early republic.

Governments during this period assumed authority to grant subsidies and otherwise promote useful enterprises in agriculture and manufacturing. This was famously debated at the federal level, but it was prevalent and widely accepted at the state level. New York State, according to L. Ray Gunn, "resorted to bounties, premiums, and grants to individuals or companies engaged in agriculture, manufacturing, or transportation."[5] "Between 1785 and 1826," he also notes, "New York expended some $6.5 million in aid of agriculture, banking, manufacturing, and transportation."[6] Sidney Fine also notes that various states "subsidized agricultural and industrial fairs, provided bounties for the growing of certain crops," and generally became involved in actively promoting economic development by funding private enterprise.[7]

Connected to this, the various states (and to a limited extent, the federal government) engaged in robust schemes of internal improvements, particularly in the form of canals. Typically, the state purchased stock in these enterprises, or simply granted subsidies outright for the sake of supporting these endeavors. In Illinois, over $10 million was invested in internal improvements in 1837, much of which was dedicated to constructing railroads in the state. Indiana similarly spent approximately $10 million in 1836 subsidizing internal improvements.[8] New York, Ohio, Pennsylvania, and many other states invested even greater resources in these quasi-public improvements projects.

Furthermore, government was understood to have legitimate authority to inspect manufactured goods to ensure their conformity to regulatory standards. In Massachusetts, according to Oscar and Mary Handlin, rules were developed to ensure the quality of manufactured goods, including systems of inspection. These inspection procedures were applied to a wide variety of goods such as lumber, beef and pork, tobacco, and stone lime. Inspectors were either chosen by municipalities, or appointed by the governor.[9] In Pennsylvania, the inspection system also applied to a wide array of products, including flour, fish, beef, tobacco, and gunpowder. Inspections included regulations governing "packing, dimensions of containers, brand marks of dealers, and inspection methods and markings."[10] Contrary to the widely accepted popular myth that inspection of products is a relatively new phenomenon, a robust system of government inspection was in place throughout the states in the early republic. These systems were not confined to a few isolated states; William Novak notes that "[s]urveys of the statute books of Maryland, South Carolina, Michigan, and Ohio reveal similar stories" of closely regulated manufacturing. In Maryland, for example, a law "regulating the sale, inspection, and export of pickled or salted fish was typical" of the kinds of regulations that prevailed during this period. These regulations governed packaging, branding, quality, and other aspects of manufacturing.[11]

Also, contrary to popular view, in early America the regulation of occupations by licensing was a common practice in the various states and municipalities. In Pennsylvania, a system of licensing governed innkeepers, liquor merchants, tavern owners, and other occupations.[12] Similarly, in Massachusetts licenses were required to keep a ferry, operate a tavern, or become a lawyer or auctioneer.[13] Also in Massachusetts, the convictions of "an unlicensed bonesetter and healer of sprains"[14] and a citizen "selling intoxicating liquors without a license" were upheld by the Supreme Court on similar grounds.[15]

Finally, states and municipalities commonly promulgated regulations designed to support public morals. These regulations were particularly prominent in the area of prohibition. In Massachusetts, rather than opt for outright prohibition of liquor, temperance reformers opted for the more practicable approach of using licensing regulations to restrict the injurious abuse of liquor. As Oscar and Mary Handlin explain, "It was easier to take advantage of certain prudential regulations always attached to licensing, regulations that forbade sales to minors, servants, idlers, and excessive drinkers. The temperance forces put these precedents to a new use."[16] But, in general, regulations governing and even prohibiting the sale of liquor were upheld in the face of objections that they were contrary to basic natural rights possessed by all citizens. In addition to regulations on liquor sales, early nineteenth-century criminal law enforced a host of penalties for violating moral standards, and the common law of nuisance was employed to abate morally repugnant nuisances to the community.[17]

The upshot of this is that the Founders did not see any inconsistency between a theory of government that required the protection of natural rights of liberty and property, and the practice of ensuring the noninjurious exercise of these rights through regulation. As Justice Lemuel Shaw explained in *Commonwealth v. Blackington*:

> The preamble of the [Massachusetts] constitution announces one of its objects to be, to secure to individuals the power of enjoying in safety and tranquility their natural rights, one of the most important of which is, that of acquiring, possessing and protecting property . . . such laws are necessary to define, secure and give practical efficacy to the right itself. . . . All the inspection laws, providing for the inspecting and marking of the principal products of our agriculture and manufacturers, with a view to benefit our commerce in those articles, at home and abroad; all laws made with a view to revenue, to health, to peace and good morals, are of this description.[18]

Shaw grounds the legitimacy of regulations such as inspections not on the principle that consumers must be protected from the potential (but not yet actual) injury that comes from poorly manufactured goods, but rather on the principle that they are necessary to "give practical efficacy to the right itself." In particular, these regulations were understood to *promote* the right to property by supporting the competition of the market. Free markets depend on individuals who can trust those with whom they enter into contracts, and liberty and property are more secure when government establishes rules of fair dealing that prevent fraudulent transactions between consenting individuals.

Or, as James Wilson put it, "[W]ise and good government . . . instead of contracting, enlarges as well as secures the natural liberty of man." Wilson describes "the very close and interesting connexion, which subsists between the law of nature and municipal law."[19] For Wilson, regulation was viewed as entirely consistent with natural liberty and the law of nature. Therefore, Wilson says that

> [t]rue it is, that, by the municipal law, some things may be prohibited, which are not prohibited by the law of nature: but equally true it is, that, under a government which is wise and good, every citizen will gain more liberty than he can lose by these prohibitions. He will gain more by the limitation of other men's freedom, than he can lose by the diminution of his own. He will gain more by the enlarged and undisturbed exercise of his natural liberty in innumerable instances, than he can lose by the restriction of it in a few.[20]

In short, the view of jurists and political figures of this era was that these activities *supported* the right to acquire property and exercise liberty, by fostering a competitive system where the rewards of honest labor were available to all.

II. REGULATION, ADMINISTRATION, AND THE RULE OF LAW IN THE EARLY REPUBLIC

In the economic histories that acknowledge regulation during this period, a common refrain emerges. This refrain asserts that while there was a robust and active regulatory policy in the various states, the administrative mechanisms by which this policy was carried out led to disastrous consequences. The rise of a more laissez-faire orientation in public policy after 1850 is often attributed to the fact that the states during the early republic simply could not figure out how to administer their schemes of regulation effectively. Thus, the myth of the stateless society in the early republic is replaced with a second myth: that the regulatory activities of government in this period were crippled by irrational and ineffective systems of administration. One might call this myth the "myth of failed administration." Richard L. McCormick's view of antebellum administration is typical: "Forever giving things away, governments were laggard in regulating the economic activities they subsidized. . . . 'Policy' was little more than the accumulation of isolated, individual choices."[21]

Let us recall Croly's statement (cited at the opening of this chapter) that "[t]he state governments have sedulously indulged in a kind of interference conspicuous both for its activity and its inefficiency."[22] Croly acknowledges that regulation existed in early America but claims that this "interference" was "conspicuous" for "its inefficiency." In a common assumption of Progressive intellectuals and historians, Croly identifies the active role government played in the economic sphere in the early American republic but assumes that it is primitive, irrational, and inefficient compared to the advances made by modern administrative techniques. Woodrow Wilson concurs with Croly's explanation in his famous essay "The Study of

Administration," asserting as if uncontroversial that "in spite of our vast advantages in point of political liberty, and above all in point of practical political skill and sagacity, so many nations are ahead of us in administrative organization and administrative skill."[23]

Croly's argument is echoed by the economic historians who have written about regulation at the state level. Donald Pisani, for instance, writes that "[t]he federal and state governments were too weak to regulate the economy effectively until the 1930s."[24] In the area of insurance companies, he continues, "close cooperation between regulator and regulated" was not considered problematic.[25] In sum, Pisani echoes Croly's assessment of early regulatory efforts as devoid of expertise, effective enforcement power, and ethics.

In his study of regulation in antebellum Pennsylvania, Louis Hartz similarly argues that because "[p]olitical thought . . . was gradually overwhelmed by an exaggerated belief in rotation and the joyous acceptance of inexperience," administration suffered and became irrational: "[E]ven specialized administrative personnel were not quite exempted from the impact of these attitudes."[26] This led to extraordinary difficulties: "However excellent the principles of rotation or election may have been as applied to legislative, gubernatorial, or even judicial offices, they clearly had serious shortcomings in the administrative field. . . . It was in the realm of administration, more clearly than anywhere else, that the age was misled by the glamour of its democratic dreams."[27] According to Hartz, regulatory and administrative efficiency was undermined by the political principles of the day, which did not favor independent expertise and efficiency. In his view, "other contributions of the democratic theory" led to the failure of administration in Pennsylvania. These contributions "were not traceable *entirely* to its inexperience." The failures

> were partially traceable also to the prevalent belief in an amateur intelligence in government, a fundamental aspect of the democratic faith and one bound to be disastrous in a setting where administrative competence was imperative. In the broadest sense it was this belief that rationalized the reluctance of the legislature to delegate technical responsibilities, the enforcement of political rotation in administrative services, and the extension of the elective process which, in the case of the canal board, ended all hope for the redemption of the most important administrative body of the era.[28]

L. Ray Gunn concurs with the assessments of these scholars in his survey of regulation in antebellum New York. He writes, "[T]he attributes of a political system which make it representative are not necessarily those most conducive to effective government." The "very representativeness" of New York in this period "produced a bargaining style of politics and political outcomes so disaggregated as to virtually defy, except in a few instances, the rational consideration of policy alternatives."[29] It was the adherence to principles of representative government that prevented "rational" government from taking place, according to Gunn. In his account, "there was little in the way of formal administrative integration . . . there was no institutionalized central direction; effectiveness almost certainly suffered, therefore, as a result of a fusion of functions and overlapping of roles." Moreover, "[t]he role of the legislature in the appointing process . . . virtually assured that the administration would be highly politicized."[30] In short, according to Gunn, the effectiveness of administration was fatally undermined by notions like representative government, legislative supremacy, the rule of law, and so forth. The final picture of administration we get is that of a feeble administration, because it was unsophisticated and politically accountable. In his own words, "For all the accumulation of power by state officers . . . administration, as Tocqueville correctly observed, was hardly imposing . . . the specific structures created exhibited characteristics directly contrary to modern notions of effective administration."[31]

That intellectuals and historians influenced by progressivism should come away with this diagnosis of the ills of antebellum regulation should hardly be surprising. For these historical accounts measure the quality of administration in early America by standards that are by definition contrary to the principles of natural right that animated the Founders. It may be true that administration was less rational, in the sense of being based on empirically and statistically verifiable data reviewed and implemented by experts. It may also be true that administration was more political because of principles of representation. And it may finally be true that administration was less efficient because expert executives were bound by judicial review and the rule of law. The argument of the Progressive intellectuals and historians is that while these principles *explain* why administration possessed these characteristics in antebellum America, they hardly *justify* the practical effects that followed from these arrangements. And, again, this makes perfect sense once one recalls that embedded in the Progressive orientation is the view that we have progressed beyond the primitive and antiquated administrative techniques of earlier periods. These writers insufficiently considered the principled justification for these administrative arrangements because they assumed that there is nothing to be learned from such obviously inferior institutions.

In what follows, I consider how principles such as the rule of law and representative government informed the methods of antebellum administration, and potentially can teach us something about good government and administration in our current state. As legal scholar Jerry Mashaw has argued in a recent article, it is not the case that administrative law failed to exist in the early republic; in his words, "The constitutional politics of the whole of the ante-bellum period tends to obscure the relatively continuous growth and organizational development of national administrative capacity in the first century of the American Republic."[32] And this is to say nothing of the more thorough growth and development of state and local administrative capacity during the same period.

Several salient features of administration in the early republic can be identified. These features can all be explained by recourse to a few central principles at the center of the Founders' political theory. These features have been sometimes noted in passing by various observers. Ellis W. Hawley writes that "in the nineteenth century we developed our own peculiar form of the modern state. It lodged power not in a bureaucratic elite, but in patronage-based political parties, local governmental units, and a strong judicial system."[33] In a famous speech to the American Bar Association in 1916 called "Public Service by the Bar," Elihu Root noted that "we are entering upon the creation of a body of administrative law quite different in its machinery, its remedies, and its necessary safeguards from the old methods of regulation by specific statutes enforced by courts."[34] In Hawley's and Root's statements we identify several characteristics of what one might call "antebellum administrative law": legislative supremacy, a strong judicial system based on common law as enforcer, decentralized administration, and a robust party system. After laying out these features, I will juxtapose Tocqueville and the Progressives' treatments of this subject to reveal their fundamental disagreement about the principles that gave rise to these characteristics, namely, self-government, the rule of law, and democratic participation.

III. FOUR CHARACTERISTICS OF ADMINISTRATION IN THE EARLY REPUBLIC

The proclivity of legislatures to enter into the particulars of administration is the first salient characteristic of regulation in the early republic. This can be demonstrated by examining the wide array of statutes that descended into the details of administration, responded to constituents through the petition process, and generally constrained the discretion of executive agents.

In general, at all levels of government, the trend was to grant as little discretion to such officials as possible. At the federal level, Leonard White notes that "[a]mong a people as devoted to liberty as were eighteenth century Americans, we would expect official discretion to be looked upon with concern and to be strictly limited. So far as subordinate officials were concerned, there is much evidence to show that they were intended to possess not more than a minimum" of discretion.[35] And as Jerry Mashaw notes,

> By the time that Andrew Jackson took office as President, Congress had already institutionalized itself in ways that promoted oversight of administration. It had begun to exercise its investigatory powers to publicize and correct administrative malfeasance, and it has put in place a number of reporting requirements that kept Congress systematically informed about administrative operations, particularly the use of public revenue.[36]

In the early years of the republic, the Congress at times placed very specific directions in statutes. For instance, Congress designated the ports of entry pertaining to the collection of taxes on imports, and also specified in a statute the precise route of post roads.[37] Alexis de Tocqueville also observed that "[i]n the New England states, the legislative power extends to more objects, than among us. The legislator penetrates in a way into the very heart of administration; the law descends to minute details . . . it thus encloses secondary bodies and their administrators in a multitude of strict and rigorously defined obligations."[38] In a more critical explanation of this fact, Tocqueville writes that "[e]very day legislative assemblies swallow up the dregs of governmental powers; they tend to gather them all to themselves, just as the [National] Convention had done" during the French Revolution.[39] Even in cases where the statute seemed to grant discretion to the executive agents charged with carrying it out, "superior officers tended to circumscribe that discretion by the formulation of administrative rules."[40] Commentators have dubbed this the "internal law of administration," or the use of internal hierarchical authority to ensure fidelity to the statutory mandate. This hierarchy was present at the federal level, but it was often missing (as Tocqueville observes) at the state and local levels.[41]

State legislatures and Congress also utilized the petition as a means of making particular decisions. These petitions involved citizens asking for government aid for debt relief, assistance for military veterans, and reduction of taxes on particular commodities.[42] For example, the Jacksonian period marked "the establishment of America's first, continuous Article I court, the Court of Claims." Though Congress had established a Committee on Claims in 1794, this committee "had, by 1831, metastasized into five specialized claims committees to handle differing species of claims."[43] Congress had set up a scheme to manage the deluge of petitions, but by the 1830s the tide had nearly overwhelmed it. This system has been called "legislative adjudication."

In the second feature of antebellum administration, regulations were typically enforced by a combination of courts and juries, frequently in lieu of statutes through the common law. Donald Pisani writes that "[r]egulation in the nineteenth century was largely the application of well-worn principles of the common law at the state level."[44] Various commentators have described the importance of courts to regulation in the early republic. Richard Ellis observes that in the 1760s, "the courts, particularly on the county level—even in New England . . . had extensive administrative powers. They assessed local taxes and administered their spending on the building and repairing of roads, bridges, jails, workhouses, and courthouses."[45] Leonard White also describes the importance of courts in enforcing federal law during the early republic. As he explains, the Sedition Act was entirely enforced by courts and juries, and "[t]he act for the government and regulation of seamen in the merchant service depended entirely upon courts for implementation."[46] Also, the laws requiring the registration and licensing of vessels utilized judicial enforcement; when the terms of a license were violated, only the courts (not the collectors of customs) could revoke the license.[47]

This reliance on courts required the initiative of private citizens in order to be effective. Thus private enforcers were commonly employed to ensure that violations of the law would reach the courts for adjudication.[48] At the state level, the use of private informers was also prevalent. The Massachusetts Prohibition regulations were enforced through the use of informers,[49] and as noted earlier, enforcement by private citizens bringing suit in court was widespread in both Massachusetts and Pennsylvania.[50] This fact is critically described by Tocqueville: "Americans are obliged to interest denouncers by calling on them in certain cases to share in fines. This is a dangerous means that assures the execution of the laws while degrading mores."[51]

This approach to common law rested on two primary factors, namely, a strong judicial role in carrying the law into effect, and decentralization to allow common law to rest on the social consensus established in self-governing communities. As Ernst Freund, a Progressive jurist who opposed the common law approach to regulation that prevailed in the early republic, put it, "It is not inconceivable that a highly centralized and powerful court should set the considerations of easy administration of justice above the highest type of substantive justice."[52] The virtues of centralization entailed easy administration of justice, but at the potential cost of the "highest type of substantive justice." For, as Freund noted, "a centralized system of justice is naturally unfavorable to differentiation of legal rules," to "its close adjustment to varying conditions."[53]

This leads us into the third prominent feature of antebellum regulation and administration, namely, the decentralization of administrative activity. This was also most famously observed by Alexis de Tocqueville.[54] Interestingly, in this period authority was actually delegated by the state governments to municipalities; as Delba Winthrop has noted, "[d]ecentralization is equated with local government and opposed to state or even county government"[55]—it is not intended to serve as a defense of federalism or the importance of policymaking at the state level. In New Jersey, New York, Illinois, Georgia, and many other states, the state government granted authority to local governments to deal with matters that were properly under their superintendence.[56]

One of the primary effects of decentralization of administration was to render administration subject to the close supervision of popular opinion and control. This effect was increased by the practice of electing executive officials. In the township of New England, Tocqueville explains, "the greatest part of administrative powers is concentrated in the hands of a small number of individuals elected each year whom they name selectmen."[57] In Massachusetts during the Prohibition years, selectmen and county commissioners were elected by the people for the sole reason that they promised to refuse to grant any further licenses to sell liquor.[58] Annual elections of executive officials, combined with a great degree of discretion in jury enforcement of the law, led to a great degree of popular control over administration.

With regard to the decentralization of administration, Tocqueville and the Founders are in complete agreement. Both Tocqueville and the Founders agree that it is inadvisable to have administrative centralization because it is *impossible* for a centralized administrative state to function efficiently. Madison remarks in *Federalist* 46 that "it is only within a certain sphere, that the federal power can, in the nature of things, be advantageously administered."[59] This almost mirrors Tocqueville's famous observation that "[a] central power, however enlightened, however learned one imagines it, cannot gather to itself alone all the details of the life of a great people. It cannot do it because such a work exceeds human strength."[60] The premise underlying both of these comments is that human understanding and knowledge are limited, and cannot be applied to circumstances that are not intimately known. What follows from this premise is that administration must take place at a local level where those who are governed by regulation have the knowledge of practical circumstances that alone can guide government policy. Technical and abstract knowledge cannot be imposed from above, because such an approach cannot adjust to account for particular circumstances. The importance of this should not be overlooked; Tocqueville at one point calls "township independence . . . the principle and the life of American freedom."[61]

A final salient feature of antebellum regulation and administration was the dominance of the political party, which provided the institutional organization necessary to render the entire system workable. Under a theory of government that supported legislative supremacy, decentralization of administration, popular election of executive officials, and enforcement through courts and juries, the absence of hierarchy would render administration chaotic unless some sort of organization is devised for bringing order to the system. In New York, for example, L. Ray Gunn explains that Martin Van Buren and the Albany Regency "brought to the disparate elements of state government a level of efficiency, continuity, integration and centralization which tends to obscure the contradictions built into formal governmental structures." By articulating competing visions of a well-ordered and regulated society, the competing political parties could channel public opinion's influence on the administrative system to ensure cohesion in administration. In Gunn's words, "The extraconstitutional agency of party and political influence served as the glue that prevented the centrifugal forces inherent in the structure of the system from producing complete confusion and disintegration" in administration.[62] In other words, to ensure the connection between public opinion and administration, a strong system of political parties became necessary. Conversely, as Sidney Milkis has shown, with the rise of administrative government out of the New Deal came the decline of political parties in America.[63] As independent administration rises, parties decline. Once again, this brings us back to the subject of popular control over the administration of the law. In the view of early Americans, administration is not removed from politics but is the essence of day-to-day politics.

One might summarize the system of regulation and administration in the early republic as local, political, and popular. It was also buttressed by a judicial system based on the common law as the foundation for preserving the rule of law and individual liberty from the arbitrary enforcement of the law by an external or foreign authority.

IV. COMPETING ASSESSMENTS OF NINETEENTH-CENTURY ADMINISTRATIVE LAW

This account of antebellum administration and administrative law provokes two further questions. First, did these institutional arrangements rest on a coherent political theory, and if so, what are the contours of that theory? Second, why were these arrangements attacked by later theorists and what were the central points of contention? I will now address these questions in turn.

These disparate elements of antebellum regulation and administration are often explained as merely the outgrowth of traditional legal institutions and the product of the physical characteristics of early America. As we have seen, for many later historians these elements were the result of an ignorance of the true principles of good administration. Yet in Tocqueville's qualified defense of administration in early America one discerns the contours of a theoretical justification of these arrangements, which may suggest to the reader that the abandonment of the Founders' approach to regulation and administration could produce some problematic effects.

Decentralization and Self-Government

According to Tocqueville, administrative decentralization and the spirit of township government are derived from a simple maxim: "[T]hat the individual is the best as well as the only judge of his particular interest, and that society has the right to direct his actions only when it feels itself injured by his deed or when it needs to demand his cooperation. This doctrine is universally accepted in the United States."[64] In other words, administration in antebellum America was structured around a simple principle derived by the Founders from their views on natural right; although there may be differences in the talents and characteristics of individuals, no human being is so naturally superior to another that he has the rightful authority to direct that person's actions without their consent. In the antebellum paradigm of administration, individuals are not governed by an extrinsic force, a distant sovereign, but rather by their own deliberation. This is the definition of self-government, the idea that Tocqueville points to as the foundation of antebellum administration.

This principle of self-government is connected to the various arrangements of antebellum administrative law. In accordance with the idea that the practical judgments at the heart of self-government can only be fully considered by those individuals who are immersed in the community being governed, the primary qualification for appointment to executive office was based on character and prudence rather than science and expertise. In Tocqueville's words, "The justice of the peace," an important administrative official in township government, "is an enlightened citizen, but who is not necessarily versed in knowledge of the law. So they charge him with keeping the order of society, a thing that demands more good sense and rectitude than science."[65]

Tocqueville notes that from the basic maxim governing administration—that each individual is the most proper judge of his interests and conduct—several institutional arrangements follow. We have had the opportunity to review these arrangements in the previous section, but it is useful now to recur to them to note the connection to the principle of self-government. Tocqueville identifies three primary consequences of the principle of popular sovereignty for administration. He writes, "The first consequence of this doctrine has been to have all the administrators of the township and the county chosen by the inhabitants themselves, or at least to have those magistrates chosen exclusively from among them."[66] While Publius recognized the consistency between republican principles and the indirect appointment (but not election) of certain officials,[67] Tocqueville notes that at the township level popular sovereignty is understood to produce direct election of administrators. The "cult of expertise" was absent in the administrative theory of the early republic. This was evident not only in the area of executive officials but also in the area of courts, for juries were given wide discretion to decide questions of both law and fact.[68] Furthermore, technical expertise in a particular area was not viewed as the predominant qualification for selection to hold office. At the local level, character was, rather, an overriding consideration, and followed this principle during George Washington's administration.[69]

One result of the direct election of administrators, resulting from the principle of self-government, according to Tocqueville, is "that no one has been able to introduce rules of hierarchy anywhere. . . . Administrative power is found diffused in a multitude of hands."[70] Tocqueville explains that a final consequence of the principle of self-government for administration is "the obligation to introduce courts, more or less, into administration" in order to impose some order on the nonhierarchical administration.[71] So that the administration of the laws could be held accountable to some higher authority, courts and juries were authorized to review and carry out administrative acts. The higher authority to which administration should be subordinated, according to citizens in the early republic, is the people through their immediate superintendence.

The Rule of Law, Common Law, and Judicial versus Executive Justice

The centrality of the common law in the Founders' approach to regulation, the second feature of antebellum administration discussed above, cannot be overstated. Common law, with its reliance on custom and community norms, was the way to preserve self-government and popular rule with regulation of individual activity, since individuals participated in their own self-rule through common law regulation. This was central also to preserving the rule of law. As William Novak has pointed out, the Founders thought that common law and consent were perfectly compatible and intimately bound together.[72] James Wilson explained the rationale behind this proposition:

> How was a custom introduced? By voluntary adoption. How did it become general? By the instance of voluntary adoption being increased. How did it become lasting? By voluntary and satisfactory experience, which ratified and confirmed what voluntary adoption had introduced. In the introduction, in the extension, in the continuance of customary law, we find the operations of consent universally predominant.[73]

It should be noted in this context that the common law to which courts and juries both appealed was not synonymous with judge-made law. For jurists of this period, the common law was not crafted by judges but grounded in principles of natural right that were merely discovered and applied by judges and juries. In fact, juries were, according to Tocqueville, "the part of the nation charged with assuring the execution of the laws, as the houses [of the legislature] are the part of the nation charged with making the laws."[74] Thus, what appears to us today to be "judicial activism" was nothing more than a judicial branch protecting citizens from arbitrary administrative action by applying principles of natural right. In 1929 W. F. Willoughby of the Brookings Institution noted and criticized the extensive reliance on courts for administration and enforcement. He advocated

> removing whole categories of cases from the courts and vesting their handling in administrative authorities or in administrative tribunals of a quasi-judicial character. The extent to which our courts in the past have been burdened with the task of acting as auxiliary agencies for securing the administration of public law is not generally appreciated. This has arisen from the emphasis that the English speaking people have placed upon rights and the deep-rooted belief that adequate protection of such rights can be secured only through the judi-

> cial branch of the government. As a necessary consequence of this position, the American people, in common with other English speaking people, have been loath to grant to administrative officers other than the most limited powers to enforce, through their own action, compliance with provisions of law.[75]

The crucial proposition in this context is that enforcement by courts and juries rather than centralized executive officials promotes the rule of law and protects against arbitrary administrative decision making. This seems counterintuitive, since in contemporary thought courts and juries are equated with nonexperts, as opposed to the scientific and technical expertise found in the bureaucracy. When one accepts this framework, it is easy to draw the conclusion that regularity and consistency of execution is promoted by granting more authority and deference to executive officials.

Yet the Founders would have rejected this conclusion. In their view, the solution to the potential problem of arbitrary administration was not to delegate this authority to experts, but to ensure that administration is carried out in the branch where the greatest protections to individual liberty are placed. In their view, this was the judicial branch. To understand this, we must recall the distinction between the rule of law and the rule of men. Under the rule of law, citizens are self-governed, though the orbit of self-government is widened to include the norms of the community. Under the rule of men, law is imposed on individuals by an extrinsic force, and the community has no active role in the enforcement and administration of the law.

The distinction between the rule of law, intimately tied to the common law and decentralized method of administration, and the arbitrary rule of men is neatly explained by Roscoe Pound, a Progressive legal scholar who nevertheless was critical of the New Deal's implementation of centralized administration:

> It seemed that judicial justice, administered in courts, was to be superseded by executive justice administered in administrative tribunals or by administrative officers. In other words there was a reaction from justice according to law to justice without law, in this respect entirely parallel to the present movement away from the common-law courts in the United States. In place of the magistrate limited by law and held to walk strictly in the paths fixed by the custom of the realm, men sought to set up a benevolent guardian of social interests who should have power to do freely whatever in his judgment protection of those interests might involve.[76]

In Pound's view, the traditional common law method of regulation limited the magistrate by requiring him "to walk strictly in the paths fixed by the custom of the realm." Though common law was not written, it was "fixed" in the sense that it was based on custom and tradition, as opposed to the arbitrary and ad hoc decisions of "a benevolent guardian of social interests" who could make the law according to his judgment about what social interests may require. The rule of law, he implied, is incompatible with the rise of

> offhand administrative tribunals in which the relations of individuals with each other and with the state were adjusted summarily according to the notions for the time being of an administrative officer as to what the general interest or good conscience demanded, unencumbered by many rules.[77]

In this second feature of antebellum regulation, a reliance on courts, juries, and the common law, we therefore see the principle of the rule of law as a justification for this arrangement. Tocqueville appeals to this principle, and the Progressives who rejected the antebellum mode of regulation specifically rejected it, as we shall subsequently observe.

Relatedly, courts do not seem to have been inclined to defer to executive branch agencies in the early years of the republic. Preserving judicial review was seen as a crucial component of the rule of law, rather than meddling in business that was outside the province of the courts. There were, to be sure, limits to the proper scope of judicial review, but this was not understood to cut against the practice of judicial review itself. To cite only one example, in the famous case of *Kendall v. United States*, the Supreme Court argued that the courts could issue a writ of mandamus when executive officials failed to act in accordance with the express terms of a statute. This is not to say, however, that advocates of judicial deference to executive agencies were nonexistent during the antebellum period. In fact, in an 1853 case, *Bartlett v. Cain*, Chief Justice Taney strenuously advocated judicial deference and executive predominance, arguing that "[t]he interference of the courts with the performance of the ordinary duties of the executive department of the government would be productive of nothing but mischief; and we are satisfied that such a power was never intended to be given to them."[78]

Moreover, the idea of self-government and the rule of law suggested to people with whom Tocqueville interacted that executive officials must be subject to the independent review of courts and citizens as a matter of right. As opposed to the current view of many conservatives, which holds that courts should remain out of the business of executive officials and defer to agencies when reviewing agency actions, in the early republic citizens and courts regularly oversaw administrative activity. The relevant passages from *Democracy in America* merit citing at length:

> [A]mong a free people like the Americans, all citizens have the right to accuse public officials before ordinary judges and all judges have the right to sentence public officials, so natural is the thing.
>
> It is not to grant a particular privilege to the courts to permit them to punish agents of the executive when they violate the law. To forbid them to do so would be to deny them a natural right. . . .

> In year VIII of the French Republic, a constitution appeared in which article 75 was conceived thus: "Agents of the government, other than ministers, can only be prosecuted for deeds relative to their offices by virtue of a decision of the Council of State. . . ."
>
> I have often tried to make the sense of this article 75 understood by Americans or English, and it has always been very difficult for me to succeed. . . .
>
> [W]hen I sought to make them understand that the Council of State was not a judicial body in the ordinary sense of the word, but an administrative body whose members depended on the king, in such a way that the king, after having sovereignly commanded one of his servants, called a prefect, to commit an iniquity, could sovereignly command another of his servants, called a counselor of state, to prevent the first from being punished; when I showed them the citizen, injured by the order of the prince, reduced to demanding from the prince himself authorization to obtain justice, they refused to believe in enormities like this and accused me of lying or ignorance.[79]

In this regard, what Tocqueville and Pound find so pernicious about modern administrative theory is not that it allows government to do more than it previously had done, but rather that it grants wide discretion to administrators who are insulated from political accountability and the rule of law, including judicial review. As Richard Epstein has remarked, "[T]he independent agencies . . . do not today constitute the main threat to the rule of law. That place of honor must be assigned to the substantive expansion of administrative discretion, particularly on questions of law."[80]

I have posited that the difference between antebellum administration and the modern administrative state does not lie exclusively (or perhaps even primarily) in the *scope* of regulation, but rather in the *manner* in which regulation takes place. Tocqueville concurs in this assessment. He argues that authority in America is not weak; "on the contrary, they imposed on [citizens] more varied social obligations than elsewhere." For Americans, according to Tocqueville, freedom is not preserved by simply exempting or "removing from society the right or ability to defend itself in certain cases," that is, carving out particular areas of individual freedom where government cannot interfere with individual liberty. It is preserved primarily by "dividing the use of [authority] among several hands; of multiplying officials while allocating to each of them all the power he needs to do what he is destined to execute."[81] In other words, authority and regulation in antebellum America are not limited by explicit limitations on the scope of authority; they are limited in their application by certain institutional and legal arrangements that allow society to govern itself rather than be governed by an extrinsic authority.

To summarize, then, the character of antebellum regulation and administrative law is informed by core principles of natural right that are central to the Founding, but rarely connected to administrative practices. These principles—popular self-government, prudence as opposed to science as the basis for policymaking, and the protection of liberty through procedural checks on authority, including the rule of law and common law—serve as the basis for understanding antebellum administration.

Efficiency as a Principle of Administration

One final point is in order. Tocqueville admits that these arrangements are not productive of administrative efficiency, but he defends them nevertheless. Whereas the Progressives (as we will see) criticized the inefficiency of antebellum administration, and viewed this inefficiency as sufficient justification for abandoning the antebellum model, Tocqueville admits that these arrangements are attended with inconveniences but argues that the benefits outweigh the costs.

Tocqueville agrees that "[c]ertain undertakings interest the entire state and nevertheless cannot be executed because there is no national administration to direct them. Abandoned to the care of townships and counties, left to elected and temporary agents, they lead to no result or produce nothing lasting."[82] He also admits that

> in the United States one often regrets not finding those uniform rules that seem constantly to be watching over each of us [in France]. From time to time one encounters great examples there of insouciance and social negligence. . . . Some useful undertakings that demand a continual care and a rigorous exactitude are often abandoned in the end; for, in America as elsewhere, the people proceed by momentary efforts and sudden impulses.[83]

Because of this, Tocqueville continues, "I shall admit, if one wishes, that the villages and counties of the United States would be more usefully administered by a central authority located far away from them, and that would remain foreign to them, than by officials taken from within them." Nevertheless, "[t]he *political* advantages that Americans derive from the system of decentralization would still make me prefer it to the contrary system."[84] The most obvious political advantages of the system of decentralization are the liberty and self-determination that are intrinsically tied to the theory of self-government that predominates in the system. The "development of provincial freedoms," to use Tocqueville's term, is necessary as a bulwark against despotism.[85]

However, Tocqueville also describes a subtler advantage that is derived from decentralization. In a regime where individuals are governed by a force that is extrinsic to them, there is no support for the government of that regime. Conversely, in a regime where a system of decentralization predominates, the authority of the self-governing community "excites neither jealousy nor hatred . . . each person guides, supports, and sustains it."[86] Because of the rise of the ubiquitous modern administrative state, we are accustomed to think of government activity as the antithesis of freedom. Tocqueville draws the connection between the two: insofar as citizens are subject to an external authority that is foreign to them, they will be jealous of the power of government and view it as a necessary evil. On the other hand, as Tocqueville observes in the self-governing township, citizens identify the regulations of the community as the regulations of self-government, the limits that they have imposed on their own activity by their own volition.

Because of the benefits derived from administrative decentralization, Tocqueville accepts it as a positive good, even while admitting that it comes with some inconveniences.

V. THE PROGRESSIVES' REJECTION OF THE EARLIER APPROACH TO REGULATION

The natural right principles of self-government that grounded the antebellum system of administration were specifically and decisively rejected by the Progressive architects of the modern administrative state. To expound on this, for the sake of brevity I will focus primarily (but not exclusively) on Frank Goodnow, one of the central Progressive theorists on administrative law.

In his most famous work, *Politics and Administration*, Goodnow lays out the famous distinction between the function of politics and the function of administration. To summarize, the former is concerned with expressing the will of the state and the latter is tasked with carrying that will into effect.[87] Because the task of carrying will into effect is instrumental, some superintendence over administration by politics is necessary. However, a distinction must be drawn between different types of administration. According to Goodnow, there is "the administration of justice" that is entrusted to "the judicial authority," and that is distinct from the administration of government.

Yet, "[t]he administration of government is also susceptible of differentiation."[88] One part of "the administration of government is to be found in the mere execution of the expressed will of the state—the law."[89] And another part is derived from the fact that "a very complex governmental organization must be established, preserved, and developed" to execute the will of the state.[90]

Having differentiated the functions of administration, "we are in a position to answer the question put at the beginning of this chapter: What parts of this function of administration should be subjected to the control of the function of politics to the end that the expressed will of the state may be executed?"[91] Goodnow answers this question by affirming that the purely executive function must be subjected "to the control of the body intrusted [*sic*] ultimately with the expression of the state will," that is, politics. However, he asserts that no political control should be exercised over "the other branches of the administration of government."[92] This is a crucial point. Whereas Tocqueville and the Founders asserted that administration is rightfully subject to the control of popular opinion—that realm Goodnow calls "politics"—the Progressives argue that a certain kind of administration must be removed from political control.

According to Goodnow, the earlier paradigm of administration confused the various kinds of administration, and therefore subjected all of administration to political control. This had disastrous consequences: "The distinctly administrative functions naturally were confused with the executive function" in the early republic. "It was regarded as proper to attempt to exercise the same control over administrative matters as was exercised, and properly exercised, over the executive function."[93] Goodnow concurs with the assessments of the historians we examined earlier: "[w]hen so undertaken by governmental organs," administration in the early republic was "inefficiently done, and inefficiently done because of our failure to recognize the existence of an administrative function which should be discharged by authorities not subject to the influence of politics."[94] The difficulty with self-government as applied to administration is that it leads to inefficiency.

The fundamental difference between Tocqueville's qualified defense of antebellum administration and Goodnow's thoroughgoing critique of it, therefore, boils down to foundational principles of self-government and the rule of law. For Tocqueville, as for Goodnow, the peculiar features of regulation and administration in the early republic are derived from the natural right foundation of self-government. Therefore, when Goodnow critiques the basis for applying this principle to administration, it comes as no surprise when he criticizes all the salient characteristics of "the system which was either adopted by the states of the American Union at the time of their formation or was soon after developed."[95]

First, Goodnow attacks the idea of frequent elections and short tenure for administrators, arguing that without "permanence of tenure . . . the maximum of administrative efficiency is impossible of attainment."[96] In general, the administrative system where officials "are vested with no discretion at all, being merely the instruments of other state organs which determine, not only what shall be done, but also how the thing determined upon shall be done," describes precisely the evils of the Founders' arrangement that must be overcome.[97] The control of administrative officials and limitation of their discretion by political organs of the state is the central problem of the earlier paradigm of administration, according to Goodnow. When the idea of popular government predominates in a regime, "[t]he people, the ultimate sovereign in a popular government, must . . . have a control over the officers who execute their will," which leads to short terms in office for executive officials and "a popular control which may be frequently exercised because of frequent elections."[98]

Goodnow critiques the other features of regulation and administration in the early republic, which this essay has already touched on. Second, he notes critically that the legislature sought to control executive officers through specific statutes. He states, "All the legislature could do, if it were dissatisfied with the way in which officers acted who were intrusted [*sic*] with the execution of the law, was to regulate their duties more in detail, trusting to the courts to enforce its mandates."[99] For example, with regard to Prohibition, Goodnow writes, "The laws passed by the legislatures . . . descended successively into greater and greater detail, in the hope that in this way the execution of the will of the state might be secured."[100]

Finally, Goodnow criticizes the influence of political parties on administration in this period. He states, "[I]f the government was to go on harmoniously, some means of coordinating the expression and execution of the will of the state had to be found. Such means could not be found in the governmental system, as has been shown. It had therefore to be found . . . in the political party."[101] At this point, it should hardly require explanation of Goodnow's criticism of using the political party to coordinate the disparate elements of this system, namely, that it prevented the removal of administrative discretion from political control: "The spoils system had, however, two great faults," which are essentially identical. "In the first place, when applied to ministerial appointive officers, it seriously impaired administrative efficiency. In the second place . . . it tended to aid in the formation of political party machines, organized not so much for facilitating the expression of the will of the state as for keeping the party in power."[102]

In general, Goodnow understands that the Founders' mode of regulation relied on administrative decentralization:

> This system of administration is usually accompanied by extreme decentralization from the point of view of the relations of the state to the local communities. It has been termed "a government of laws, and not of men." It has unquestioned advantages, particularly in retarding the development of despotism and in preventing arbitrary administrative action; but it makes the development of the administrative function free from the influences of politics almost impossible, since it tends to promote interference by the legislature, a distinctly political body, in all matters of government. The judicial control by which it is accompanied is not suited to secure anything except obedience to the law.[103]

Remarkably, Goodnow admits that decentralization and the extension of political control through legislatures, courts, and juries (as well as the limits on executive discretion) serve important principles like the rule of law and prevention of despotism through arbitrary administrative action. Yet, in his view, it renders the separation of politics and administration impossible, and therefore can no longer be accepted.

What is interesting about this juxtaposition between Tocqueville and Goodnow's account of administration in the early republic is that they agree largely on the facts. They agree that administration was not always efficient, and that it was not separated from political control. They agree that it was accomplished through institutional features such as the election of public officials, curtailment of discretion by detailed legislation, political parties, and enforcement by courts and juries. They also agree that these arrangements, despite their relative inefficiency, served important political principles by preventing despotism and preserving liberty and popular government. The crucial disagreement, then, is over which principles of administration should take precedence.

The Progressives argued that the form of regulation in early America, with its reliance on common law, the rule of law, decentralization, and a general distrust of wide-ranging executive authority unchecked by the legislative and judicial branches, was outmoded and tailored too closely to protecting individual rights rather than social interests. As Ernst Freund states, "If policy means the conscious favoring of social above particular interests, the common law must be charged with having too much justice and too little policy. It has fallen to the task of modern legislation to redress the balance."[104] The problem, simply put, was that this mode of regulation was still too individualistic; although it sought to prevent the use of individual freedom from being injurious to the community, it still preserved an individualistic attitude: according to Freund, this approach understood the law "with a primary view to abstract and equal justice between private and presumably equivalent interests. While this individualistic attitude has been criticized, it represents a perfectly intelligible method and principle."[105] According to Freund, this was a perfectly intelligible principle on which to base the law; it was simply the wrong principle.

The common law method of regulation could not simply be loosened by legal reforms; it had to be scrapped altogether in favor of a new theory of regulation. Freund continued, "[T]he common law has carried the right of ownership to extremes from which in part at least it has been found necessary to recede, but the modifications are slight as compared with the power that remains."[106] "Put in other words," Freund continued, "the common law treated a certain quantum of liberty as protected from corporate regulation. Here, then, we have realized the idea of economic liberty secured against governmental action, a common-law right of civil liberty as against unreasonable regulation."[107] And this idea, from the Progressives' point of view, was the problem.

Tocqueville himself had warned against the emergence of the Progressives' view of administration, which was on the ascendance in Europe in his day. He writes that during his time, in Europe, "[t]he unity, ubiquity, and omnipotence of the social power, the uniformity of its rules, form the salient feature characterizing all newly born political systems of our day." There are two claims in this passage—the absence of limits on the social power, and the uniformity of its operation and its rules. Tocqueville emphasizes this latter point as it pertains to the new view of administration that is emerging in Europe: "[F]or the first time they comprehend that the central power they represent can and ought to administer all affairs and all men by itself, and on a uniform plan."[108] Tocqueville repeats that the uniformity and centralization of the new administrative powers of Europe are a striking break from the administrative system of the early American republic, and from the earlier political principles of European kings: "This opinion . . . had never been conceived before our time by the kings of Europe," but it now "penetrates the intelligence of these princes most profoundly."[109] Whereas in America such an enterprise is understood to "exceed human strength," in Europe the movement is toward greater centralization and uniformity, due to a faith in the power of the central government to understand and coordinate the affairs of a large nation.

It must be admitted that even Tocqueville thought some of the unstable elements of antebellum administration could imperil freedom. He writes,

> I think that in changing their administrative processes as often as they do, the inhabitants of the United States compromise the future of republican government. Constantly hindered in their projects by the continuous volatility of legislation, it is to be feared that men will in the end consider the republic as an inconvenient way of living in society; the evil resulting from the instability of secondary laws would then put the existence of fundamental laws in question, and would indirectly bring a revolution; but that period is still very far from us.[110]

Yet in his critique of the "volatility" and mutability of administration in antebellum America, Tocqueville implies that the solution is not to abandon republican government, but to temporize with these inconveniences so that people do not become disillusioned with republicanism. If they do, the consequences will be worse than the disease the people seek to remedy. Tocqueville's solution is far different from Goodnow's, in the end.

CONCLUSION

As a historical matter, it is important to trace the contours of the institutional arrangements that characterized antebellum regulation and administrative law. It provides us with a theoretical and historical perspective from which to view the salient features of modern administrative law and consider possible disadvantages that attend the current system of centralized administration we have adopted from the Progressives.

The key basic insight is that the alternative is not between the modern administrative state and the laissez-faire state; rather, the premodern regulatory state contained a coherent theory of regulation and administration that permitted an active government, but that was oriented around preserving key concepts of natural right such as self-government, the rule of law, and democratic participation rather than modern ends such as efficiency and scientific expertise.

The foregoing does not necessarily mean that an unthinking return to the antebellum administrative paradigm is warranted. As Tocqueville suggests, such an arrangement can work only "when the people are enlightened, awakened to their interests, and habituated to thinking about them as they are in America" during his time.[111] Otherwise, perhaps the inconveniences of decentralized administration would outweigh the salutary benefits Tocqueville describes as following from the arrangement. Yet there are important sacrifices that we have made in the adoption of the modern administrative state involving harm to concepts like self-government and the rule of law, and it is at least worth considering whether these sacrifices are justified by any benefits we have gained from the advance of modern, centralized, bureaucratic government. Though it would be a laborious task to restore the earlier understanding of regulation and administration, a view of the fundamental alternatives will at least inform our judgment as to whether and how to take the first steps in that direction.

NOTES

1. Herbert Croly, *The Promise of American Life* (Boston: Northeastern University, 1989; orig. pub. 1909), 191.
2. Harry N. Scheiber, "State Law and 'Industrial Policy' in American Development, 1790–1987," *California Law Review* 75, no. 1 (1987): 415, 417.
3. Jack Rakove, *Original Meanings: Politics and Ideas in the Making of the Constitution* (New York: Random House, 1996), 322.
4. Colleen A. Dunlavy, *Politics and Industrialization: Early Railroads in the United States and Prussia* (Princeton, N.J.: Princeton University Press, 1994), 19; cited in Clifford F. Thies, "The American Railroad Network during the Early 19th Century: Private versus Public Enterprise," *Cato Journal* 22, no. 2 (Fall 2002): 229.
5. L. Ray Gunn, *The Decline of Authority: Public Economic Policy and Political Development in New York State, 1800–1860* (Ithaca, N.Y., and London: Cornell University Press, 1988), 101.
6. Gunn, *Decline of Authority*, 114.
7. Sidney Fine, *Laissez Faire and the General Welfare State; a Study of Conflict in American Thought, 1865–1901* (Ann Arbor: University of Michigan Press, 1956), 22.
8. See Thies, "American Railroad," 242.
9. See Oscar Handlin and Mary Handlin, *Commonwealth; a Study of the Role of Government in the American Economy: Massachusetts, 1774–1861* (New York: New York University Press, 1947), 64–66. It is worth noting, for later purposes, that the practice of authorizing local officials (as opposed to officials appointed by and answerable to state officials) was objected to; this led to the centralization of administrative

authority over inspections in Massachusetts by 1816. After 1816, "the governor appointed inspectors of pot and pearl ash, of pork and beef, nails, butter and lard and pickled fish" (Handlin and Handlin, *Commonwealth,* 66). It is also worth noting that the law often employed informers by paying them from the fines collected, and also paid appointed officers with a "reward from prosecutions" (Handlin and Handlin, *Commonwealth,* 67). These regulations appear to have been justified on the grounds that inspection of goods contributed to the prestige of produced goods and therefore supported competition and the right to acquire property through honest labor. See Handlin and Handlin, *Commonwealth,* 68 ("there was a general belief that inspection added prestige to Massachusetts goods in foreign ports").

10. Louis Hartz, *Economic Policy and Democratic Thought: Pennsylvania, 1776–1860* (Cambridge, Mass.: Harvard University Press, 1948), 205. As in Massachusetts, enforcement took place primarily at the local level, and informers were employed as an enforcement tool. See Hartz, *Economic Policy,* n. 129. The primary justification of these regulations was not the protection of consumers, but the support of commerce and the right to acquire property through honest labor. See Hartz, *Economic Policy,* 204: "Inspection policy was most heavily emphasized in connection with articles produced for export, since the reputation of Pennsylvania merchants in interstate commerce depended on it."

11. William J. Novak, *The People's Welfare: Law and Regulation in Nineteenth-Century America* (Chapel Hill: University of North Carolina Press, 1996), 88–89. Novak points out that "[n]o fish could be exported from Maryland without certification of inspection and an oath by the ship's master that all fish on board had been properly inspected" (Novak, *People's Welfare,* 89).

12. See Hartz, *Economic Policy,* 206–7.

13. Handlin and Handlin, *Commonwealth,* 69–74.

14. Howard Gillman, *The Constitution Besieged: The Rise and Demise of Lochner Era Police Powers Jurisprudence* (Durham, N.C., and London: Duke University Press, 1993), 52.

15. Handlin and Handlin, *Commonwealth,* 52–53.

16. Handlin and Handlin, *Commonwealth,* 252.

17. See Novak, *People's Welfare,* 155–56.

18. *Commonwealth v. Blackington,* 24 Pick, 352, 357.

19. James Wilson, "Lectures on Law: Chapter II: 'Of the Natural Rights of Individuals,'" in *Collected Works of James Wilson,* ed. Kermit L. Hall and Mark David Hall (Indianapolis: Liberty Fund, 2007), 1055.

20. Wilson, "Lectures on Law," 1056. It is worth noting in this context that Wilson seems to draw a distinction between liberty and freedom. Freedom, he admits, is subject to "limitation" and "diminution." Liberty, he argues earlier, is never alienated or diminished by government and regulation.

21. Richard L. McCormick, "The Party Period and Public Policy: An Exploratory Hypothesis," *Journal of American History* 66 (1979): 279, 284–85; cited in Novak, *People's Welfare,* 286n17.

22. Croly, *Promise of American Life,* 191.

23. Woodrow Wilson, "The Study of Administration," in *Woodrow Wilson: The Essential Political Writings,* ed. Ronald. J. Pestritto (Lanham, Md.: Lexington Books, 2005), 237.

24. Donald Pisani, "Promotion and Regulation: Constitutionalism and the American Economy," *The Journal of American History* 74, no. 3 (December 1987): 740.

25. Pisani, "Promotion and Regulation," 740.

26. Hartz, *Economic Policy*, 31.

27. Hartz, *Economic Policy*, 33.

28. Hartz, *Economic Policy*, 310. (emphasis added).

29. Gunn, *Decline of Authority*, 83.

30. Gunn, *Decline of Authority*, 89.

31. Gunn, *Decline of Authority*, 90. See also p. 93: "[I]n this period at least, the distrust of authority and the desire to implement the principles of representation overshadowed any desire for the rationalization and centralization of authority." For further statements along these lines see p. 116 ("the inability to conceive of a public interest beyond that of the locality prevented the rational allocation of the state's resources" in internal improvements), 128 (the New York Bank Commission "could not develop the independence, continuity, and expertise generally regarded as essential in effective, modern regulatory agencies"), and 141 ("the failure to base public economic policies on the firm foundation of a systematic and rational tax structure had profound implications for the distribution of wealth in the state").

32. Jerry M. Mashaw, "Administration and 'The Democracy': Administrative Law from Jackson to Lincoln, 1829–1861," *Yale Law Journal* 117 (2008), 1583.

33. Ellis W. Hawley, "The New Deal State and Anti-Bureaucratic Tradition," in *The New Deal and Its Legacy: Critique and Reappraisal*, ed. Robert Eden (Westport, Conn.: Greenwood Press, 1989), 78.

34. Elihu Root, "Public Service by the Bar," in *Addresses on Government and Citizenship*, ed. Robert Bacon and James Brown Scott (Cambridge, Mass.: Harvard University Press, 1916), 534–35.

35. Leonard Dupree White, *The Federalists: A Study in Administrative History* (Westport, Conn.: Greenwood Press, 1978), 448.

36. Mashaw, "Administration," 1667.

37. See Gary Lawson, "Delegation and Original Meaning," *Virginia Law Review* 88, no. 2 (April 2002): 402–3.

38. Alexis de Tocqueville, *Democracy in America*, trans. Harvey C. Mansfield and Delba Winthrop (Chicago: University of Chicago Press, 2000), 69. Subsequent references to Tocqueville will cite the page number in the Mansfield translation.

39. Tocqueville, *Democracy in America*, 85.

40. Mashaw, "Administration," 1618. The use of administrative rules to curb the discretion granted to the executive officer, therefore, is not a new phenomenon. This became a substantial issue in the debate over the "new nondelegation doctrine," but its roots seem to be traceable back to the early republic.

41. Mashaw, "Administration," 1619. Moreover, the "internal law of administration" model seemed to develop in the Jacksonian period, some decades into the practice of administration in the United States. Earlier administrations did not rely on this model nearly as extensively, even at the federal level. Although the Congress was more willing to grant discretion to the State and War Departments in the early years of the republic, it was notoriously concerned with strictly delineating the duties of the Treasury Department, entering into the details of its operations. This can possibly be explained in three ways. First, the Treasury was a department that concerned domestic affairs, as opposed to the other departments that dealt with foreign and, hence, executive matters. Second,

because the Treasury was feared by most during this period as the locus of true power in the fledgling republic, Congress was more exacting in laying out the requirements of the office. Third, because Congress was given the explicit power over the purse by the Constitution, it may have been more jealous in the granting of discretion to officers in the Treasury Department.

42. See, for instance, Sara M. Shumer, "New Jersey: Property and the Price of Republican Politics," in *Ratifying the Constitution*, ed. Michael Allen Gillespie and Michael Lienesch (Lawrence: University Press of Kansas, 1989), 79–80. Laura Jensen's recent study of pension benefits for Revolutionary War veterans also describes the widespread use of the petition to address claims of particular individuals seeking pension benefits. According to Jensen, Congress actually established standing committees specifically to deal with these petitions on a case-by-case basis. See Laura Jensen, *Patriots, Settlers, and the Origins of American Social Policy* (New York: Cambridge University Press, 2004), 68–69, 45–47. For an overview see Christine A. Desan, "The Constitutional Commitment to Legislative Adjudication in the Early American Tradition," *Harvard Law Review* 111 (1998): 1381.

43. Mashaw, "Administration," 1538–39.

44. Pisani, "Promotion and Regulation," 755. Pisani argues that "the Constitution . . . suggested that the courts were the best arbiters of legal rights and that regulatory commissions were more like courts than like legislatures."

45. Richard Ellis, *The Jeffersonian Crisis: Courts and Politics in the Young Republic* (New York: W. W. Norton, 1974), 5. See also William E. Nelson, *The Americanization of the Common Law* (Cambridge, Mass.: Harvard University Press, 1975), 15.

46. White, *The Federalists*, 442. White also explains that "[t]here are many examples of the enforcement of statutory rights of persons through the courts alone." He mentions patents and copyrights in this context. See White, *The Federalists*, 443n24.

47. White, *The Federalists*, 438–39.

48. As White notes, "Reliance upon private informers to bring law violations to the attention of prosecutors or courts was a part of English procedure in the eighteenth century and was widely adopted by Congress" (White, *The Federalists*, 415).

49. See Novak, *People's Welfare*, 173, 181.

50. See sup. notes 9, and 10.

51. Tocqueville, *Democracy in America*, 75.

52. Ernst Freund, *Standards of American Legislation:* (Chicago and London: University of Chicago Press, 1965; org. pub. 1917), 43.

53. Freund, *Standards of American Legislation*, 44, 43.

54. Tocqueville, *Democracy in America*, vol. 1, pt. 1, chap. 5, "On the Political Effects of Administrative Decentralization in the United States," 82–93. Perhaps the most explicit statement of this phenomenon is on p. 79: "[G]enerally, one can say that the salient characteristic of public administration in the United States is to be enormously decentralized."

55. Delba Winthrop, "Tocqueville on Federalism," *Publius: The Journal of Federalism* 6, no. 3 (Summer 1976): 95.

56. For New Jersey, see the New Jersey Constitution of 1776, Article XIV, in Francis Thorpe, *Federal and State Constitutions*, 5:2597; for New York, see Gunn, *Decline of Authority*, 202; for Illinois see Novak, *People's Welfare*, 155n38; and for Georgia see Milton Sidney Heath, *Constructive Liberalism: The Role of the State in Economic*

Development in Georgia to 1860 (Cambridge, Mass.: Harvard University Press, 1954), 388–89.

57. Tocqueville, *Democracy in America*, 59.

58. See Novak, *People's Welfare*, 173.

59. *Federalist* 46, 317.

60. Tocqueville, *Democracy in America*, 86.

61. Tocqueville, *Democracy in America*, 40.

62. Gunn, *Decline of Authority*, 95.

63. See Sidney M. Milkis, *The President and the Parties: The Transformation of the American Party System Since the New Deal* (New York: Oxford University Press, 1992).

64. Tocqueville, *Democracy in America*, 62. Tocqueville elsewhere offers the following similar formulation: "[T]he organization of the township and the county in the United States rests on this same idea everywhere: that each is the best judge of whatever relates only to himself, and is in the best position to provide for his particular needs" (*Democracy in America*, 77). See also p. 381: Americans believe that "Providence has given to each individual, whoever he may be, the degree of reason necessary for him to be able to direct himself in things that interest him exclusively. Such is the great maxim on which civil and political society in the United States rests."

65. Tocqueville, *Democracy in America*, 70–71.

66. Tocqueville, *Democracy in America*, 77.

67. See *Federalist* 39: "It is sufficient for [republican] government, that the persons administering it be appointed, either directly or indirectly, by the people." James Madison, Alexander Hamilton, and John Jay, *The Federalist Papers*, ed. Jacob E. Cooke (Hanover, N.H.: Wesleyan University Press, 1961), 251.

68. See, for example, Nelson, *Americanization of the Common Law*, 3, 21.

69. White, *The Federalists*, 257–62, is replete with examples of Washington's policy in selection of officials, which was consistently concerned with "fitness of character."

70. Tocqueville, *Democracy in America*, 77–78. Tocqueville elsewhere remarks that France and America during this period differ on how to control administrative officials, to prevent arbitrariness; "In France, we seek that final guarantee in *administrative hierarchy*; in America, they seek it in *election*" of officials (*Democracy in America*, 73). This stands in stark contrast to Hegel's argument that "[t]he security of the state and its *subjects* against the misuse of power by ministers and their officials lies directly in their hierarchical organization and their answerability." G. W. F. Hegel, *Philosophy of Right*, trans. T. M. Knox (New York: Oxford University Press, 1943), 192 (emphasis added).

71. Tocqueville, *Democracy in America*, 78.

72. Novak, *People's Welfare*, 38–40.

73. Wilson, "Lectures on Law," 1:494–95. See also Wilson, "Lectures on Law," 1:469–70: "The knowledge of [the laws] may be disseminated by long and universal practice. 'Confirmed custom,' says a writer on Roman jurisprudence, 'is deservedly considered as a law. For since written laws bind us for no other reason than because they are received by the judgment of the people; those laws, which the people have approved, without writing, are also justly obligatory on all. . . .' Of all yet suggested, the mode for the promulgation of human laws by custom seems the most signifi-

cant, and the most effectual. It involves in it internal evidence, of the strongest kind, that the law has been introduced by common *consent*; and that this consent rests upon the most solid basis—experience as well as opinion. This mode of promulgation points to the strongest characteristic of liberty, as well as of law."

74. Tocqueville, *Democracy in America*, 261.

75. W. F. Willoughby, *Principles of Judicial Administration* (Littleton, Colo.: F. B. Rothman, 1981; orig. pub. 1929), 18.

76. Roscoe Pound, *The Spirit of the Common Law* (Francestown, N.H.: Marshall Jones, 1921), 72–73. It should be noted that Pound is here describing the conflict between James I and Sir Edward Coke in seventeenth-century Great Britain, but he clearly seeks to draw a comparison between that conflict and the conflict in his day over the implications of New Deal–style centralized administration.

77. Pound, *Spirit of the Common Law*, 73. Pound had made this observation several years earlier in a speech to the law association of Pennsylvania, where he made the precise connection to America in the early twentieth century: "The movement away from the common law was a movement from judicial justice administered in courts to executive justice administered in administrative tribunals or by administrative officers. In other words, it was a reaction from justice according to law to justice without law, and in this respect again the present movement away from the common law courts is parallel." Pound, "The Organization of Courts" (Law Association of Pennsylvania, 1913), 5.

78. 57 US 263 (1853). Moreover, in the very first American administrative law treatise, Bruce Wyman claims that several key precedents in nineteenth-century administrative law point to the proposition that Congress cannot "provide an appeal to the federal courts from an adjudication by any non–Article III tribunal." Mashaw, "Administration," 161.

79. Tocqueville, *Democracy in America*, 98–99. Incidentally, the passage containing the phrase translated as natural right reads thus: *C'est leur enlever un droit naturel que de le leur défendre.*

80. Richard Epstein, "Why the Modern Administrative State Is Inconsistent with the Rule of Law," *N.Y.U. Journal of Law and Liberty* 3 (2008): 491, 504.

81. Tocqueville, *Democracy in America*, 85.

82. Tocqueville, *Democracy in America*, 85.

83. Tocqueville, *Democracy in America*, 87.

84. Tocqueville, *Democracy in America*, 88 (italics in original).

85. Tocqueville, *Democracy in America*, 91.

86. Tocqueville, *Democracy in America*, 90.

87. Frank Goodnow, *Politics and Administration* (New York: Macmillan, 1900), 18: "Enough has been said, it is believed, to show that there are two distinct functions of government, and that their differentiation results in a differentiation, though less complete, of the organs of government provided by the formal governmental system. These two functions of government may for purposes of convenience be designated respectively as Politics and Administration. Politics has to do with policies or expressions of the state will. Administration has to do with the execution of these policies."

88. Goodnow, *Politics and Administration*, 73.

89. Goodnow, *Politics and Administration*, 76.

90. Goodnow, *Politics and Administration*, 77.

91. Goodnow, *Politics and Administration*, 78.
92. Goodnow, *Politics and Administration*, 79.
93. Goodnow, *Politics and Administration*, 83. The foregoing analysis, as a side note, is important because it deepens and in some way qualifies the surface understanding that the Progressives simply separated politics and administration. In Woodrow Wilson as well as Goodnow's writings, there is a constant tension regarding the extent of political control of administration (see "The Study of Administration"—decisive critic, but too meddlesome). To make sense of this paradox, Goodnow's distinction between the various kinds of administration ought to be kept in mind.
94. Goodnow, *Politics and Administration*, 87.
95. Goodnow, *Politics and Administration*, 98.
96. Goodnow, *Politics and Administration*, 88.
97. Goodnow, *Politics and Administration*, 94.
98. Goodnow, *Politics and Administration*, 98.
99. Goodnow, *Politics and Administration*, 102.
100. Goodnow, *Politics and Administration*, 103.
101. Goodnow, *Politics and Administration*, 104–5.
102. Goodnow, *Politics and Administration*, 112–13.
103. Goodnow, *Politics and Administration*, 96–97.
104. Freund, *Standards of American Legislation*, 48.
105. Freund, *Standards of American Legislation*, 69.
106. Freund, *Standards of American Legislation*, 185–86.
107. Freund, *Standards of American Legislation*, 188–89.
108. Tocqueville, *Democracy in America*, 642.
109. Tocqueville, *Democracy in America*, 642.
110. Tocqueville, *Democracy in America*, 382.
111. Tocqueville, *Democracy in America*, 85–86.

4

Constitutional Cassandra

The Prophetic Fears of Brutus, the Anti-Federalist

V. James Strickler

I. WHY READ BRUTUS?

During the public debate over ratification of the United States Constitution, an anonymous Anti-Federalist who called himself "Brutus" wrote a series of open letters to the citizens of New York State urging them to reject the new compact.[1] These letters, published in the *New York Journal*, often anticipated or responded to the proratification arguments advanced by "Publius" in what became known as *The Federalist Papers*.[2] Most notably, in letters XI through XV, Brutus attacked the proposed federal judiciary, prompting Alexander Hamilton's defense of the national courts offered in *Federalist* 78 through 83.[3] In the end, Brutus's efforts failed to control the actions of New York's forty-six Anti-Federalist delegates, or sway the opinions of the nineteen Federalists who attended the state's ratifying convention.[4] Faced with the possibility of their state remaining a sovereign nation surrounded by, yet isolated from, a newly empowered federal union,[5] the New York convention reluctantly approved the federal Constitution by a narrow vote of thirty to twenty-seven.[6]

Though the writings of Brutus did not accomplish the purpose for which they were written, they may well be the finest example of Anti-Federalist rhetoric and reasoning. One scholar of the antiratification cause has judged that the "Antifederalists had no publicist more able than [Brutus,] . . . [whose] letters are outstanding for their logical development of possible implications and ramifications of specific clauses [of the Constitution]."[7] Another historian of the era concluded that "[n]o wiser, more perspicacious, or farsighted Antifederalist analyses of the Constitution were composed than the essays by 'Brutus.'"[8] In particular, the "essays of 'Brutus' are generally viewed as the most comprehensive and penetrating critique of the Constitution's proposed arrangements for the federal judiciary."[9]

But, despite Brutus's skills as a constitutional critic, and the importance of his arguments in representing significant political views from the days when they were written,[10] his voice is not commonly heard by students of the Founding.[11] Because Brutus and his fellow opponents of ratification were the losers in the constitutional debate, his writings are routinely brushed aside by historians of the period.[12] When they are now mentioned, it is generally to provide brief Anti-Federalist contrast to the primary subject—the Federalist cause in general and *The Federalist Papers* in particular.[13]

The common academic opinion of Brutus goes beyond merely seeing him as irrelevant, however. All too often, Brutus's arguments are dismissed as being "fallacious,"[14] and his writings are described with exaggerated—and, thus, delegitimizing—terms, such as "apocalyptic."[15] The modern attitude toward Brutus is well described by William Jeffrey:

> To any historian or any reader even slightly conversant with the present-day doctrines of the Supreme Court[, Brutus's arguments] . . . will, almost certainly, appear to be the most flagrant kind of linguistic prestidigitation, entirely inappropriate—indeed, virtually unheard of—in legal or constitutional interpretation. . . . "Brutus" appears to present-day readers as somehow "false and misleading" in his opposition to the Constitution. His seemingly wild and extravagant mode of reasoning is regarded as the plainest kind of evidence establishing the far-fetched and desperate nature of his objections to the proposed national Constitution.[16]

Even Jack Rakove, renowned historian of the Founding, while praising the plausibility, cogency, and sincerity of Brutus's "dark musings" about the federal judiciary, criticizes him for not resisting "the Anti-Federalist tendency to locate grave threats in seemingly innocuous clauses."[17]

Such criticisms, however, evaluate Brutus's worth against a mistaken standard. Federal undertakings—particularly the exploits of an activist judiciary—that may seem common and innocuous to many modern scholars were by no means settled practices at the time of the Founding.[18] Nor are they even yet settled among theorists of constitutional law.[19] Some of the questions that Brutus asked—Are constitutional restraints on national power effective? How much discretion should judges have? Are there any effective checks on judicial power? Is the Supreme Court of the United States more an enemy than an ally of the rule of law?—are still being asked today.

Though Brutus's answers to these questions had been nearly forgotten, they have ironically grown more accurate and powerful as the intervening centuries have passed. Brutus believed that the proposed Constitution would allow, and even encourage, dramatic expansions of federal power—well beyond the politically acceptable predictions of the Federalists—and that the federal courts would be a major conduit of that expansion.[20]

Clearly, at least some of Brutus's "dark musings" have come to pass, leading some commentators to even call him "prophetic."[21]

Brutus deeply feared the consequences of such developments, and his anxious arguments will undoubtedly resonate with many modern readers.[22] Judicial "formalists," "originalists," and "textualists"—who often blame the lawless interpretations of liberal federal judges for the expansion of national governmental powers beyond what the text and intent of the Constitution appear to allow—will undoubtedly find in Brutus an ideological brother, or even a forefather.[23]

Even those who would dismiss Brutus's concerns about the abuse of federal power should find it enlightening to know that some Americans at the time of the Founding foresaw a dramatic expansion of national power through the enabling interpretations of an activist judiciary, and they publicly debated that possibility during the constitutional ratification process. The modern relevance of Brutus's analysis is laid bare by the Federalist tactic of denying that his predictions were either likely to come to pass or intended by the Framers of the Constitution. If such things as the development of a national police power, the collapse of state sovereignty, and the rise of an imperial judiciary were viewed with dread or denial by *both* camps in the constitutional ratification debate, it is problematic to justify these things as intended features of America's constitutional structure. Thus, Brutus's analysis of constitutional dangers is a seminar in what both sides of the original ratification debate believed that the Constitution was not or should not be!

Whatever a reader's political persuasion or views on the efficacy of national power, the writings of Brutus demand thoughtful consideration. Much like *The Federalist,* the arguments found in Brutus's letters are often more carefully reasoned and effectively presented than what is found in comparable debates today.[24] In many ways, the questions have not changed and the answers have not either. Thus, one should seek out the finest voices in the struggle, even if they are more than two hundred years old.

In short, an uncommon reading of the arguments of Brutus (in addition to the common study of *The Federalist*) should be an essential component of any balanced inquiry into the American Founding in general and into the proper extent of national power and the role of the federal judiciary in particular.[25] As is eloquently argued by Herbert Storing, "If the foundation of the American polity was laid by the Federalists, the Anti-Federalist reservations echo through American history; and it is in the dialogue, not merely in the Federalist victory, that the country's principles are to be discovered."[26]

It is unfortunate that Brutus's letters are largely unknown—for his predictions of ever-growing national power enabled by an unchecked judiciary have, to a great extent, come true. Though he did not always correctly predict the exact mechanisms through which his fears would be realized, Brutus foresaw such developments as the near-ubiquitous reach of federal court jurisdiction, the looseness of constitutional interpretation, the ascent of the federal judiciary to the summit of national power, and, most insightfully, the development of a symbiotic relationship between the branches of the national government, leading to an unbridled expansion of national power at the expense of the states.

II. SAMPLING BRUTUS'S FEARS

In Brutus's public letters he expressed doubts about constitutional provisions and omissions as varied as the apportionment of representation, the potential for a standing army, and the collection of taxes. But, much of his critical effort was directed toward a single perceived threat: the proposed federal courts. A brief sampling of Brutus's worries in this area can illustrate both his foresight and the limits of his vision.

Brutus believed that the federal courts would continually seek to expand their official jurisdiction. He speculated that large numbers of traditionally state-adjudicated cases would be removed to the federal court system, creating difficulties and disadvantages for many citizens—and leading to a significant loss of power for state courts and thus for the states. He envisioned elaborate schemes by which the national courts would assume diversity jurisdiction in purely intrastate cases through the fiction of individuals claiming citizenship in separate states, though they live in the same state.[27] The purpose of the federal courts allowing such thinly veiled deceptions would be to give a pretext for their expansion of power to more and more cases.[28] But it was not merely the potential for an expanding scope for federal jurisdiction or the flimsy pretext on which it would be based that concerned Brutus. He was also troubled by the practical consequences of common citizens having to fight in federal court:

> [T]he operation of the appellate power in the supreme judicial of the United States, would work infinitely more mischief than any such power can do in a single state. . . . The trouble and expense to the parties would be endless and intolerable . . . therefore the poorer and middling class of citizens will be under the necessity of submitting to the demands of the rich and the lordly, in cases that will come under the cognizance of this court.[29]

Though fictions of citizenship have not been as heavily used as Brutus had expected, the federal courts *have* adopted flexible definitions of diversity—particularly to allow suits against corporations to be brought into the federal system (where it is assumed that the individual will receive fairer treatment).[30] But the primary avenue that has developed for individuals to enter the federal court system is through raising a "federal question"—a claim that a privilege under federal law or a right under the Constitution is being infringed. With the great expansion of subjects over which the federal courts claim jurisdiction—via the Bill of Rights being "selectively incorporated" against the states,[31] and the reaching of the Congress into a multitude of private activities via the Commerce Clause[32]—a vast array of federal questions have become available for citizens to use to gain access to the federal courts. These federal questions can touch almost all relationships public and private.

While Brutus did not correctly envision all the specific processes that have brought the tendrils of the federal courts into realms formerly reserved to the state courts, he nonetheless realized that the federal government would have incentives to expand the federal judicial scope—one way or another.[33]

A more significant concern of Brutus's, and one more easily recognized in a modern context, was his observation of the consequences of giving the federal judiciary unbridled opportunities for discretionary interpretation. More specifically, Brutus was troubled that the Constitution specifically granted the judiciary the power to decide constitutional issues according to equitable principles. He wrote:

> This art.icle [art. 3d, sec. 2d] . . . vests the judicial with a power to resolve all questions that may arise on any case on the construction of the constitution, either in law or equity . . . [and] with authority to give the constitution a legal construction, or to explain it according to the rules laid down for construing a law—These rules give a certain degree of latitude of explanation. . . . The judicial are not only to decide questions arising upon the meaning of the constitution in law, but also in equity. . . . By this they are empowered, to explain the constitution according to the reasoning spirit of it, without being confined to the words or letter. . . . [Equity] is thus defined by Grotius, "the correction of that, wherein the law, by reason of its universality, is deficient.[34]

This equitable power is most easily recognized today in the judicial practice of not merely deciding winners and losers, but also fashioning specific remedies through the use of injunctions and constructive orders that may even require the restructuring of governmental operations and procedures. The most famous example of the exercise of such powers can be seen in the Supreme Court's school desegregation cases and their lower-court progeny, wherein the courts redrew attendance zones, rerouted buses, and redirected funds.[35]

Brutus believed that the troubling aspects of the granting of equitable power to the federal judiciary would be further exacerbated by interpretation of the Necessary and Proper Clause:

> The clause which vests the power to pass all laws which are proper and necessary. . . . [I]t implies that the constitution is not to receive an explanation strictly, according to its letter; but more power is implied than is expressed. . . . [D]eclaring, that the construing of the articles conveying power, the spirit, intent and design of the clause, should be attended to, as well as the words in the common acceptation.[36]

As a result of these opportunities for discretionary interpretation, Brutus thought it clear that "in their decisions [the federal courts] will not confine themselves to any fixed or established rules, but will determine, according to what appears to them, the reason and spirit of the constitution."[37] Such freedom creates a natural tendency to not treat the Constitution as a codified law, with explicit, expressed powers, but rather as a common law document—to be molded as the judge sees fit, to bring about his or her view of "justice" in future cases. If any principles do guide such unfettered judicial choices, "it is not difficult to see, that they may, and probably will, be very liberal ones."[38]

Brutus's dark vision of a judiciary run amok, placing their personal preferences and purely subjective values above the vision of the constitutional text has arguably come to pass. Though the federal courts may be loath to call their actions "common law constructions" or "equitable remedies," and will rarely admit that they are divining "the spirit" of the document as a justification for their opinions (though, on occasion, they have even admitted this!),[39] it is clear to many that these are exactly the kinds of things that the modern Supreme Court does.

Another way in which Brutus departed dramatically from the future visions of his Federalist counterparts was in his unwillingness to accept the need for an independent judiciary. Because the United Sates, under the Constitution, would have no absolute authority, such as a monarch—who was not electorally accountable to the people—there would be no need for judicial independence to check absolute power. Brutus argued that the people could be the ultimate check, through the process of elections—that is, unless it was the judiciary itself that assumed ultimate authority.[40]

Yet, despite there being no need to do so (in Brutus's view), the Federalists were intent on guaranteeing judicial independence. The plan of the new Constitution, in Brutus's mind, left the Supreme Court not only independent, but totally unchecked. He wrote: "[T]he adjudications of this court are final and irreversible, for there is no court above them to which appeals can lie, either in error or on the merits. . . . [And t]hey cannot be removed from office or suffer a dimunition of their salaries, for any error in judgement or want of capacity."[41] This was something of an ironic problem, for the Federalists had elsewhere championed the need for checking the powers of the new government by pitting interest against interest.[42]

By granting judges the independent power of judicial review, Brutus feared that the judiciary would then control Congress, "for the supreme court are authorised in the last resort, to determine what is the extent of the powers of the Congress."[43] Given their control of Congress, judges would then reign supreme and untouchable within the federal system, with no checks on them, and thus no accountability for their choices. This possibility led Brutus to lament, "I question whether the world ever saw, in any period of it, a court of justice invested with such immense powers, and yet placed in a situation so little responsible."[44]

Brutus did not believe that the Court could resist such power, but like all humans would be corrupted by it. "In short, they are independent of the people, of the legislature, and of every power under heaven. Men placed in this situation will generally soon feel themselves independent of heaven itself."[45] And they would then take advantage of their absolute power to implement their own political agenda. "This power in the judicial, will enable them to mould the government, into almost any shape they please."[46] Modern critics of "judicial activism" will surely recognize the ring of truth in Brutus's fears.

III. THE FEDERALIST RESPONSE

In addition to making claims about the power of the proposed federal judiciary, Brutus addressed deficiencies in the counterarguments put forth by Federalists. He characterized those arguments as being of two types. The first recognized the potential for judicial abuse, but placed faith in the power of Congress to prevent those abuses. This argument he dismissed as an admission of a problem that the Federalists were simply unwilling to fix:

> To obviate the objections made to the judicial power it has been said, that the Congress . . . will make provision against all the evils which are apprehended from this article. On this I would remark, that this way of answering the objection made to the power, implies an admission that the power is in itself improper without restraint, and if so, why not restrict it in the first instance.[47]

The second counterargument that Brutus described placed similar faith in the people to raise an alarm and check the power of usurping courts. Brutus thought this approach irrational:

> [I]f the habits and sentiments of the people of America are to be relied upon, as the sole security against the encroachment of their rulers, all restrictions in constitutions are unnecessary . . . for the habits and principles of the people will oppose every abuse of power. This I suppose to be the sentiments . . . of the advocates of this new system. An opinion like this, is . . . repugnant to the principles of reason and common sense.[48]

If the people would so clearly stop abuses of power, then there would be no need for any checks to be designed into the government—the entire effort of the Constitutional Convention was an indictment of this counterargument.

Alexander Hamilton dismissed Brutus's worries with the flimsy critique that his concerns should be equally directed at state courts and constitutions as well (never acknowledging the relevant differences between the two levels of government):

> [T]here is not a syllable in the plan under consideration which *directly* empowers the national courts to construe the laws according to the spirit of the Constitution, or which gives them any greater latitude in this respect than may be claimed by the courts of every State. . . . There can be no objection, therefore, on this account to the federal judicature which will not lie against the local judicatures in general, and which will not serve to condemn every constitution that attempts to set bounds to the legislative discretion.[49]

Hamilton also seemed naively (or, perhaps, disingenuously) convinced that judges could be relied on to keep themselves in check, just because they "ought to."[50]

The only convincing argument that Hamilton could offer, to counteract fears of judicial power run wild, is his famous description that the courts, lacking "sword or purse," would exercise "neither FORCE nor WILL but merely judgment; and must ultimately depend upon the aid of the executive arm even for the efficacy of its judgments."[51] This lack of judicial power to self-enforce their decisions seemed to be confirmed when, in 1832, in response to the Supreme Court's decision in the case of *Worcester v. Georgia* (involving the Cherokee tribe),[52] Andrew Jackson ignored the Court's ruling and is reported to have said, "Well, John Marshall has made his decision; now let him enforce it!"[53]

Hamilton, however, did not consider the slow accumulation of power that eventually would allow the Court to assert its authority in ways that were only imagined by Brutus—even in the face of executive opposition. For example, in *U.S. v. Nixon*, the Court forced the president to surrender secret tapes, despite his claim to executive privilege in the matter.[54] But, there is an even more fundamental response to Hamilton's assertions of judicial weakness, which can best be understood by examining Brutus's rebuttal to one of James Madison's most famous arguments.

IV. BRUTUS AND THE MADISONIAN MISTAKE

To understand how Brutus's critique of Madison is also an answer to Hamilton, it is useful to first restate Hamilton's argument. In essence, Hamilton seems to assert, the courts would be unable to expand their reach beyond their constitutionally defined limits because doing so would require executive cooperation which, he assumed, would not be forthcoming. Viewed this way, Hamilton's description of a weak Court in need of executive support is similar to Madison's claim that the Constitution was designed with "auxiliary precautions" to keep the powers of government in check.[55] Madison argued that

> [t]he great security against a gradual concentration of the several powers in the same department, consists in giving to those who administer each department

> the necessary constitutional means and personal motives to resist encroachments of the others. . . . Ambition must be made to counteract ambition. . . . [T]he constant aim is to divide and arrange the several offices in such a manner as that each may be a check on the other.[56]

Essentially, none of the three branches of government would overstep its bounds, because the other two branches, jealously guarding their own power, would push back against the third's attempted expansion.

Brutus provides a devastating critique of this now long-held conventional wisdom—a critique that has unfortunately been all but forgotten. To fully appreciate Brutus's argument, it is helpful to begin with a review of some fundamental principles of the construction of America's federal union. These principles can be illustrated using a series of Venn diagrams. In figure 4.1, a circle is used to encompass all the powers and rights of mankind. In terms of social contract theory, this circle represents all the things that one might do in a world "[w]here there is no common power, [where] there is no law."[57] This state is described by John Locke this way:

> [W]e must consider, what state all men are naturally in, and that is, a state of perfect freedom to order their actions, and dispose of their possessions and persons, as they think fit, within the bounds of the law of nature, without asking leave, or depending upon the will of any other man. A state also of equality, wherein all the power and jurisdiction is reciprocal, no one having more than another.[58]

During America's revolutionary period, the thirteen newly independent states adopted new charters of rights and constitutions. These documents were designed to invest these state governments with sovereign authority derived directly from the people, to replace authority that was lost with sev-

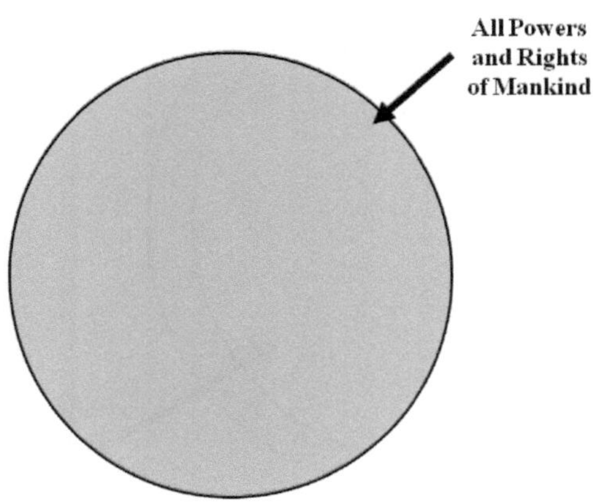

Figure 4.1. All the Powers and Rights of Mankind

erance from the English Crown. These grants of power were generally considered to be comprehensive, except as limited by the "inalienable rights of man," often listed in accompanying bills of rights. This new distribution of legal authority can be overlaid on the circle of power shown in figure 4.1, to give us the diagram presented in figure 4.2.

This expansive view of state power was so commonly assumed at the time of the Founding that during the New York ratifying convention, Alexander Hamilton—no friend of the states—made this simple allusion to the pervasive reach of the state police power,[59] and its relationship to federally delegated powers:

> [There is an] obvious and important principle in confederated governments, that whatever is not expressly given to the federal head is reserved to the members. The truth of this principle must strike every intelligent mind. *In the first formation of government, by the association of individuals, every power of the community is delegated, because the government is to extend to every possible object; nothing is reserved but the unalienable rights of mankind*[. B]ut, when a number of these societies unite for certain purposes, the rule is different, and from the plainest reason—they have already delegated their sovereignty and their powers to their several [state] governments; and these cannot be recalled, and given to another [federal government], without an express act.[60]

James Madison concurred with Hamilton's view of the great reach of state sovereignty. In *Federalist* 45, he wrote that "the powers delegated by the proposed Constitution to the federal government are few and defined. Those which are to remain in the State governments are numerous and *indefinite*."[61]

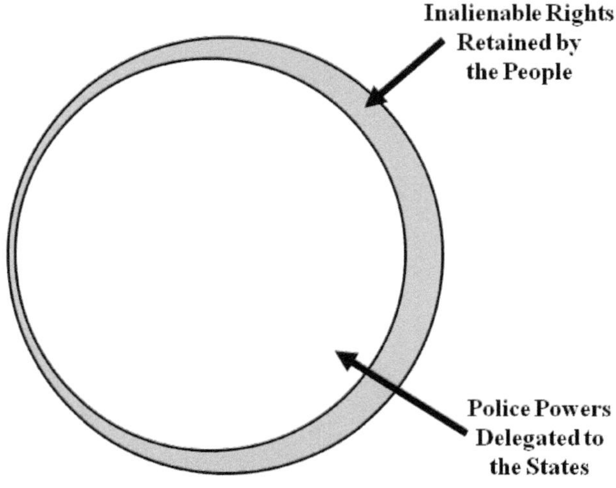

Figure 4.2. Original Delegation of Governmental Power

The virtually unlimited scope of the "police power" allowed the states, at the time of the Founding, to do things that would be thought outrageous today. As examples: The 1776 constitution of North Carolina instituted Protestantism as the state's official religion, stating in part that "no person, who shall deny the being of God, or the truth of the Protestant religion, or the divine authority either of the Old or New Testaments, or who shall hold religious principles incompatible with the freedom and safety of the State, shall be capable of holding any office or place of trust or profit in the civil department within this State."[62] In 1787, New York imposed special entrance and clearance fees on all vessels heading to or from New Jersey or Connecticut.[63] At the same time in Pennsylvania, branding, whipping, and mutilation (such as the cropping of ears) were accepted punishments within the state's criminal justice system.[64] And in South Carolina, a 1789 ordinance regulating the behavior of slaves and free blacks in Charleston included the following provisions: "Not more than seven male slaves were ever to be allowed to assemble together, except for a funeral; no gathering was to last later than ten at night in summer, and nine in winter; no negro could on his own account buy, sell, or barter . . . and no negro was to engage in any mechanic or handicraft trade for himself."[65]

Since the powers of the states to this point in time had been nearly unlimited within their own borders, the granting of a supreme authority to the new central government obviously necessitated the states surrendering some of those powers.[66] In addition, the Constitution specifically eliminates the power of states to (among other things)

> enter into any Treaty, Alliance, or Confederation . . . coin Money . . . pass any . . . ex post facto Law, or Law impairing the Obligation of Contracts. . . . [Or] without the Consent of the Congress, lay any Imposts or Duties on Imports or Exports . . . keep Troops, or Ships of War in Time of Peace, enter into any agreement or Compact with another State, or with a foreign Power, or engage in War, unless actually invaded.[67]

The delegation of some powers—"few and defined"—to the national government, which had formerly been held by the states, is illustrated in figure 4.3.

The concern for Brutus was that this ceding of state power was not limited to the powers expressly delegated to the national government in the text of the Constitution. He feared that the nationalization of governmental power would become an ongoing process, bounded only by the hungry desires of the national Congress and the federal courts.[68] Eventually the federal appetite would entirely consume the sovereignty of the states.

Brutus was not alone in his fear of unbounded federal growth. His sentiments were echoed in the writings of other Anti-Federalists,[69] and in amendment proposals put forward in the state ratifying conventions.[70] It even seems that the desire to expressly limit the powers of the national

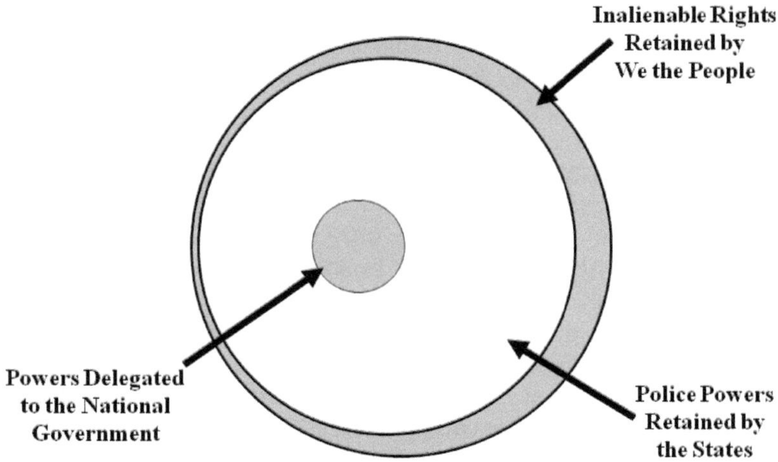

Figure 4.3. The Delegation of Federal Power

government was *the* foremost concern of the various state ratifying conventions.[71] The lists of amendments that the states separately proposed almost always began with a suggestion to limit national power. Of the eight states that formally proposed amendments, all eight included such a proposal. As examples: the Massachusetts ratifying convention asked that "it be explicitly declared, that all powers not expressly delegated by the aforesaid Constitution are reserved to the several states, to be by them exercised";[72] the New Hampshire convention proposed that "it be Explicitly declared that all Powers not expressly & particularly Delegated by the aforesaid Constitution are reserved to the several States to be, by them Exercised";[73] and the Virginia ratifying convention began its list of desired amendments to the body of the Constitution with "1st. That each state in the Union shall respectively retain every power, jurisdiction, and right, which is not by this Constitution delegated to the Congress of the United States, or to the departments of the federal government."[74]

Such fears were common enough that James Madison felt the need to placate them in *The Federalist*. In *Federalist* 45 he wrote (as partially quoted earlier):

> The powers delegated by the proposed Constitution to the federal government are few and defined. Those which are to remain in the State governments are numerous and indefinite. The former will be exercised principally on external objects, as war, peace, negotiation, and foreign commerce; with which last the power of taxation will, for the most part, be connected. The powers reserved to the several States will extend to all the objects which, in the ordinary course of affairs, concern the lives, liberties, and properties of the people, and the internal order, improvement, and prosperity of the State.[75]

But such reassurances were not sufficient, and the issue was again addressed in the First Congress, as the members considered the composition of a bill of rights. On June 8, 1789, James Madison proposed a series of amendments,[76] including one that read in part: "The powers not delegated by the Constitution, nor prohibited by it to the States, are reserved to the States respectively."[77] Eventually this amendment—in slightly modified form—was approved without opposition by both houses of Congress, and by the states, to become the Tenth Amendment to the United States Constitution.[78]

The adoption of the Tenth Amendment could have rendered Brutus's concern about the destruction of state sovereignty moot, if it had not been drafted in a neutered form. During the House debate over Madison's proposed amendment, Thomas Tudor Tucker of South Carolina suggested that the word "expressly" be inserted so that it would deprive the federal government of "powers not *expressly* delegated by this Constitution" (emphasis added).[79] Three days later, Elbridge Gerry of Massachusetts suggested the same change.[80] Both proposals, opposed by Madison, were defeated.[81] The absence of this one word has had serious consequences for the power of the amendment. As historian Kenneth R. Bowling has aptly explained, "The omission of this limiting word gutted the amendment and left interpretation of the Constitution open to the doctrine of implied federal powers, the great enemy of states' rights."[82] Thus Brutus's concerns were left intact—and the fate of states would be decided by interpretations of national power rendered by the federal courts.

Brutus had no confidence in the federal courts policing the boundaries of national power. He claimed that "the judicial power of the United States, will lean strongly in favour of the general government, and will give such an explanation to the constitution, as will favour an extension of its jurisdiction."[83] As the federal courts have interpreted the Tenth Amendment, they seem to have fulfilled some of Brutus's worst fears. In 1819, Chief Justice Marshall claimed that the Tenth Amendment had been created only "for the purpose of quieting the excessive jealousies which had been excited . . . thus leaving the question, whether the particular power . . . has been delegated to the one government, or prohibited to the other, to depend on a fair construction."[84] By 1941, the Supreme Court had come to consider the Tenth Amendment to be nothing but a "truism that all is retained which has not been surrendered," because "[t]here is nothing in the history of its adoption to suggest that it was more than declaratory of the relationship between the national and state governments."[85] It is interesting that these interpretations consider only the purpose for which the Congress may have drafted the amendment, and not the purpose for which the states originally proposed it or later ratified it. By taking such a view, the federal courts have essentially read the Tenth Amendment—and its potential limits on federal power—out of existence.

What then would hold the powers of the national government in check? In *Federalist* 51 (as partially quoted earlier), James Madison explains that the maintenance of constitutional boundaries cannot be entrusted to the political process, but requires structural safeguards:

> [T]he great security against a gradual concentration of the several powers in the same department, consists in giving to those who administer each department the necessary constitutional means and personal motives to resist encroachments of the others. The provision for defense must in this, as in all other cases, be made commensurate to the danger of attack. Ambition must be made to counteract ambition. The interest of the man must be connected with the constitutional rights of the place. It may be a reflection on human nature, that such devices should be necessary to control the abuses of government. But what is government itself, but the greatest of all reflections on human nature? If men were angels, no government would be necessary. If angels were to govern men, neither external nor internal controls on government would be necessary. In framing a government which is to be administered by men over men, the great difficulty lies in this: you must first enable the government to control the governed; and in the next place oblige it to control itself. A dependence on the people is, no doubt, the primary control on the government; but experience has taught mankind the necessity of auxiliary precautions.[86]

Madison's "auxiliary precautions," wherein "ambition" is used to "counteract ambition" within the structural design of the national government, is illustrated in figure 4.4.

Madison, in *Federalist* 51, is arguing (much as Hamilton did in *Federalist* 78), that the internal struggles for power within the central government, between that government's three branches, would result in those branches

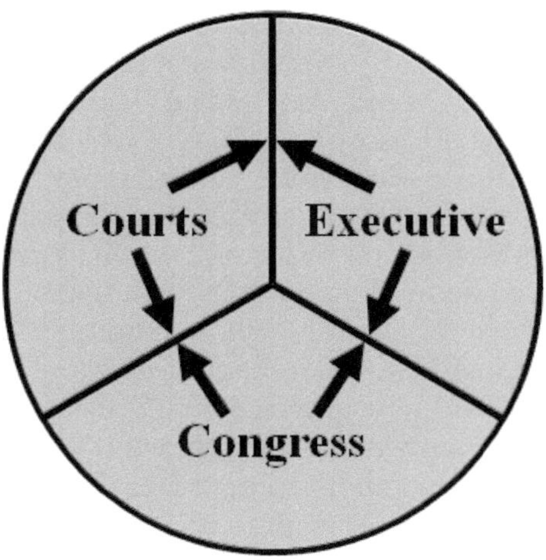

Figure 4.4. Madison's "Auxiliary Precautions"

securing the boundaries of each other's power. To see how much sense this argument makes within the greater federal system, we can insert Madison's design into the Venn diagram we have been building, as seen in figure 4.5. This illustration immediately hints at the critical weakness in Madison's argument. All the forces of Madison's auxiliary precautions point inward, maintaining internal boundaries only. The external boundaries of national power remain unsecured. But, even worse for a proponent of state power, Brutus recognized that not only would the branches of the national government not be arrayed to stop intrusions on state power, but they would actually have reason to conspire together to the detriment of the states. The federal courts, Brutus believed, would play a critical role in this process.

Alexander Hamilton, in *Federalist* 78, claimed that it would be the national courts that would be responsible for maintaining the fixed boundaries of national power:

> No legislative act . . . contrary to the Constitution can be valid. . . . It is . . . rational to suppose that the courts were designed to be an intermediate body between the people and the legislature in order, among other things, to keep the latter within the limits assigned to their authority. The interpretation of the laws is the proper and peculiar province of the courts. A constitution is, in fact, and must be regarded by the judges, as a fundamental law. It therefore belongs to them to ascertain its meaning, as well as the meaning of any particular act proceeding from the legislative body. If there should happen to be an irreconcilable variance between the two, that which has the superior obligation and validity ought, of course, to be preferred; or, in other words, the Constitution ought to be preferred to the statute, the intention of the people to the intention of their agents.[87]

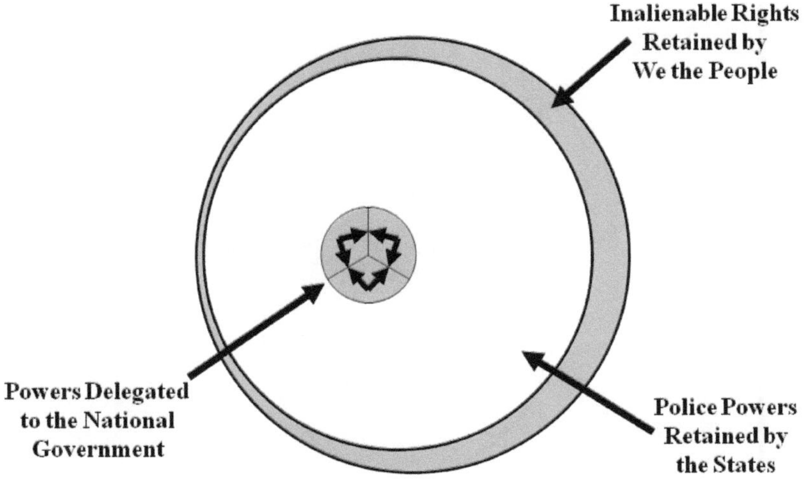

Figure 4.5. Madison's Precautions in the Federal System

In making this argument, Hamilton fails to deal with the fact that the federal courts are part of the very entity—the national government—that they are supposed to police.

In contrast, Brutus argues, judges, like all who are invested with power, would wish to expand their own power.[88] As a result, federal judges will "give such a meaning to the constitution in all cases where it can possibly be done, as will enlarge the sphere of their own authority."[89] But it will not be just their own authority that they will expand. In fact, Brutus recognized, a symbiotic relationship exists between the federal courts and the Congress: "Every extension of the power of the general legislature . . . will increase the powers of the courts; and the dignity and importance of the judges."[90] This is true because the federal courts will then claim jurisdictional authority over each new area of congressional intrusion. Thus, it is in the self-interest of federal judges to expand the power of the entire federal government, to thereby expand their own. Fortunately, from the point of view of the judges and their national coconspirators, there is a direction for their expanding power to go and still avoid the internal conflicts of Madison's "auxiliary precautions." As illustrated in figure 4.6, the branches of the national government can expand their powers outward!

Brutus explains this process in detail. Its foundation is built by judges transforming their questionable parchment decisions into undeniable bedrock principles by burying them under the weight of continually accumulating decisions. The judiciary then will repeatedly cite its own expansive readings as precedents and the legislature will intentionally become dependent on them.

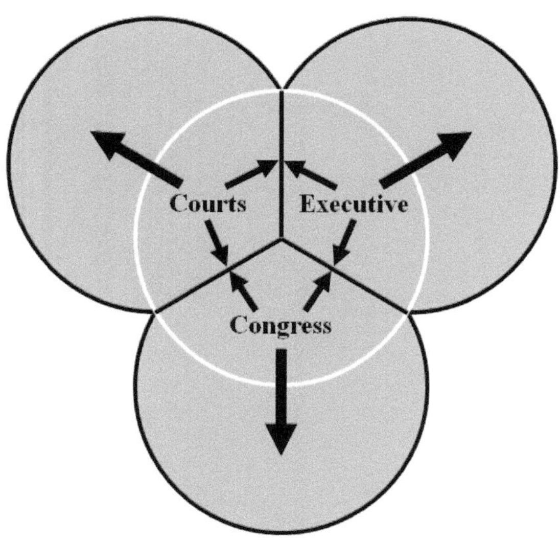

Figure 4.6. Madison's Mistake

> In determining these questions, the court must and will assume certain principles. . . . These principles . . . when they become fixed, by a course of decision, will be adopted by the legislature, and will be the rule by which they will explain their own powers. . . . And there is little room to doubt but that they will come up to those bounds, as often as occasion and opportunity may offer.[91]

Brutus also realized that this process—in addition to expanding judicial power to then supervise all new realms entered into by the legislature—provides the Congress with the dual benefit of increasing their power while having an excuse to avoid responsibility for their usurping expansion. The Congress can simply say that it is the Court that polices the bounds—that decides what is constitutionally permissible—not they.

> [O]ne adjudication will form a precedent to the next, and this to a following one. . . . [A] series of determinations will probably take place before even the people will be informed of them. In the mean time all the art and address of those who wish for the change will be employed to make converts of their opinion. . . . In this situation, the general legislature, might pass one law after another, extending the general and abridging the state jurisdictions, and to sanction their proceedings will have a course of decisions of the judicial to whom the constitution has committed the power of explaining the constitution.[92]

This situation is illustrated in figure 4.7. Brutus posited that such expansions would not necessarily involve dramatic power grabs by any branch, but could be had through slow, mutually beneficial accretion, almost undetectable to the people.

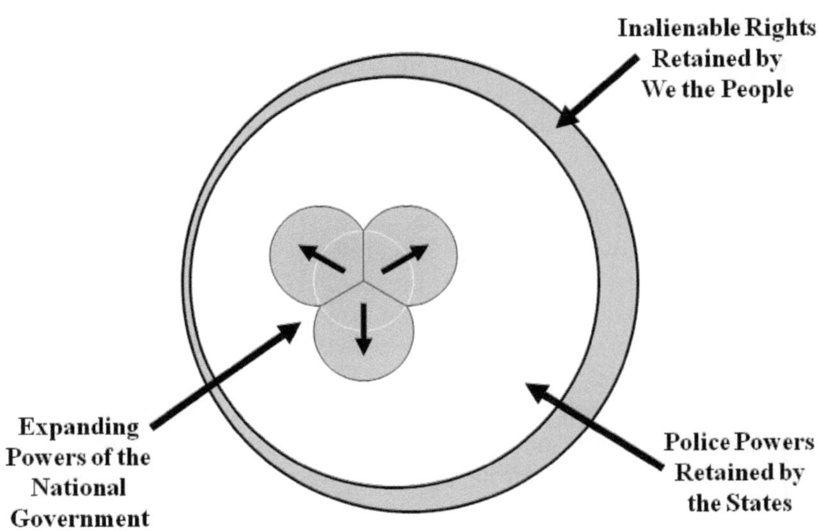

Figure 4.7. Madison's Mistake in the Federal System

We can see such a process—of slowly legitimizing the extension of federal power, as was envisioned by Brutus—manifest in the historical development of the Commerce Clause. For over fifty years in the twentieth century, every act of Congress directed at private behavior, which the Congress claimed was authorized by powers granted by the Commerce Clause, was endorsed by the courts, no matter how much of a stretch it was to classify the activity as "interstate commerce."[93] As the courts approved each incremental power grab by Congress, they simply encouraged legislators to push the envelope farther, until, it would seem, every possible corner of state and private authority had been enveloped by the national government. Eventually, the U.S. Supreme Court endorsed this very reasoning: "We live in a Nation knit together by two centuries of scientific, technological, commercial, and environmental change. Those changes, taken together, mean that virtually every kind of activity, no matter how local, genuinely can affect commerce, or its conditions, outside the State—at least when considered in the aggregate."[94] The Court has then left us to "wonder why anyone would make the mistake of calling it the Commerce Clause instead of the 'Hey, you-can-do-whatever-you-feel-like Clause.'"[95] And, it must not be forgotten, by assisting in the expansion of congressional power, the courts have, as a result, dramatically expanded their own powers. They can then oversee compliance with a multitude of new laws, in new areas, where the Founders may never have dreamed the courts would have authority. It is in such a process that we can see an arguably prophetic fulfillment of Brutus's warning:

> [I]n expounding the constitution, [the federal courts will] give every part of it such an explanation, as will give latitude to every department under it, to take cognizance of every matter, not only that affects the general and national concerns of the union, but also of such as relate to the administration of private justice, and to regulating the internal and local affairs of the different parts.[96]

Alexander Hamilton, in defending the judiciary against Brutus's assaults, observed that "liberty can have nothing to fear from the judiciary alone, but would have every thing to fear from its union with either of the other departments."[97] But, unlike Brutus, he did not seem to realize (or, at least, admit) that incentives would exist for the three branches of the national government to in fact unite in their pursuit of power at the expense of the states. Internal expansion of the relative power of a given branch *might* be checked by Madison's auxiliary precautions, but this would not prevent the three branches of national government from cooperating to expand externally and infringe significantly on the realm of retained state powers.

Brutus thought he saw an obvious outcome for the states, if federal power was continually expanded through self-serving judicial interpretations:

> [Because] the laws of the state legislatures must be repealed, restricted, or so construed, as to give full effect to the laws of the union on the same subject.

> . . . [I]t is easy to see, that in proportion as the general government acquires power and jurisdiction, by the liberal construction which the judges may give the constitution, will those of the states lose its rights.[98]

In another place he summed up the same idea, when he wrote that "[e]very adjudication of the supreme court, on any question that may arise upon the nature and extent of the general government, will affect the limits of the state jurisdiction. In proportion as the former enlarge the exercise of their powers, will that of the latter be restricted."[99] This situation is illustrated in figure 4.8.

History has shown this to be a defensible assertion. In virtually every area where the states and the national government have both claimed power, the national government has prevailed and the realm of state sovereignty has shrunk a bit more. This is, to an extent, an expected outcome, given that the Constitution contains the Supremacy Clause.[100] But it becomes a threat to the states—as sovereign entities—and a partial fulfillment of Brutus's worst fears when one considers the stunning range of activities into which federal power now reaches, thus preempting traditional state powers (and, by extrapolation, imagine where federal power might yet assert its authority).

One example of this reach is exhibited in the case of *Garcia v. San Antonio Metropolitan Transit Authority*.[101] In *Garcia*, the Supreme Court ruled that states "as states" are required, just as are private employers, to obey federally mandated maximum hours and minimum wage laws.[102] In another case, *South Dakota v. Dole*,[103] the Court ruled that Congress could, under its spending power, force states to set their mandatory drinking age at twenty-one, or risk having their federal highway funds withheld.[104] In *Perez v. United*

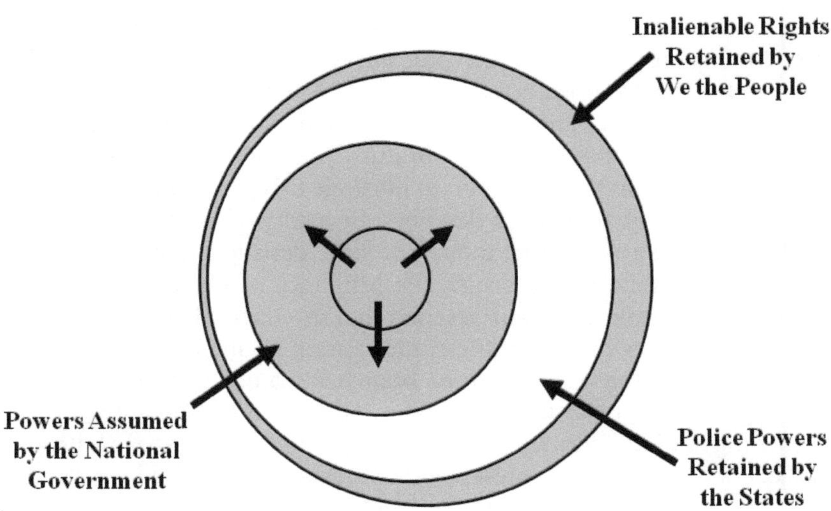

Figure 4.8. The Expansion of National Power

States,[105] the Court upheld a federal statute outlawing local "loan-sharking" as an inappropriate act of interstate commerce.[106] In the case of *City of Philadelphia v. New Jersey*,[107] the Court forced a landfill operated by the State of New Jersey to accept waste from other states, for, it claimed, to do otherwise would impede interstate commerce.[108] And, in a final stunning example, the Court, in *United States v. Ohio*,[109] upheld penalties assessed against the State of Ohio under the Agricultural Adjustment Act of 1938,[110] which Congress had enacted under its expressly delegated power to regulate interstate commerce.[111] Ohio was penalized for growing wheat on state-owned farms, for consumption by prisoners, in excess of federally mandated quotas, despite the fact that none of the wheat entered, or could have entered, interstate or foreign commerce, directly or indirectly, due to an express prohibition in the Ohio State Constitution.[112]

Thus, by flexing its delegated powers in expansive—judicially approved—new ways, the federal government has told the states (among other things) what the states have to pay their own workers, who the states may allow to purchase booze, what local activities entirely within the states will be considered crimes, whom the states have to accept garbage from, and how the states must go about feeding their prisoners. These were areas in which the states had previously regulated their own affairs—but not after Congress and the courts had extended federal dominion. (Additional examples of national-power-expanding decisions rendered by the federal courts could be given ad nauseam, but such an accounting is well beyond the scope of this chapter.)[113]

When all the above evidence is considered, one must ask whether the states—as viable, sovereign governments (and not merely convenient administrative entities)—truly do continue to exist only at the mercy of the national government (and, in particular, at the mercy of the federal judiciary). Yes, there remains great variety in the policies and practices of the states, but, when push comes to shove, can they still tell the national government "No!" in any area? Such a circumstance, if one's imagination is allowed reasonable liberties, is uncomfortably close to Brutus's predictions of doom. We can make final use of our Venn diagram to illustrate this possibility in figure 4.9, and ask ourselves how closely it describes the reality of today.

Perhaps Brutus's worst nightmares of state destruction have not come true,[114] but this should not tarnish the brilliance of his argument. While Hamilton and Madison naively asserted that the internal checks of the national government would be sufficient to restrain its abuse of power, Brutus correctly pointed out that the three branches would have good cause to cooperate to steal power from the states. At least in this area, the canonical teachings of *The Federalist* should be required to share space with their Anti-Federalist critics when presented to students of American government today. For, at least on this point, it is the anonymous Anti-Federalist who was right, and the too-oft-praised "brilliance" of Publius that was wrong.

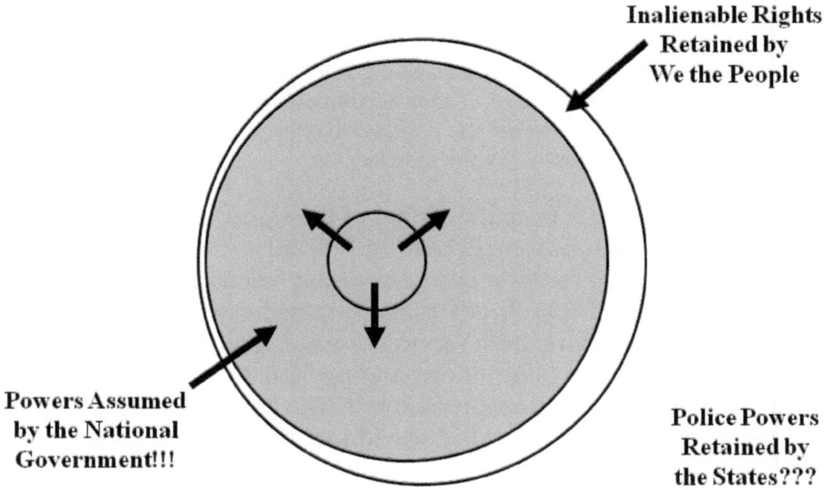

Figure 4.9. The Death of Federalism

V. POSTSCRIPT

Brutus's concerns about the three branches of national government cooperating to abuse power were frighteningly realized just ten years after the Constitution's ratification, with the passage of the Sedition Act of 1798.[115] That congressional act prohibited the publication of materials that were critical of the Federalist president and Congress.[116] Though clearly a violation of both the letter and spirit of the First Amendment,[117] the Federalist-filled federal judiciary was willing to enforce the act and at least ten persons were convicted under it.[118]

In response to this conspiracy of the three branches of the national government to undermine the constitutionally protected rights of free speech and freedom of the press, Thomas Jefferson and James Madison were compelled to face the deficiencies of the Constitution's structural checks on power. They authored resolutions for the legislatures of Kentucky and Virginia, declaring the Sedition Act "altogether void, and of no force."[119] If all three branches of the federal government had been sufficiently captured so as to allow their unanimous support for a clearly unconstitutional measure, then a check must be found elsewhere—in the defiance of the states.[120] Madison specifically argued in the Virginia House of Delegates:

> [I]t is objected, that the judicial authority is to be regarded as the sole expositor of the Constitution in the last resort. . . . On this objection it might be observed . . . if the decision of the judiciary be raised above the authority of the sovereign parties to the Constitution, the decision of the other departments . . . must be

> equally authoritative and final. . . . But the proper answer to the objection is, that . . . [in] those great and extraordinary cases, in which all the forms of the Constitution may prove ineffectual against infractions dangerous to the essential rights of the parties to it . . . that the ultimate right of the parties to the Constitution, to judge whether the compact has been dangerously violated, must extend to violations . . . by the judiciary."[121]

Yet, despite such pleas from the "father of the Constitution," the Virginia and Kentucky resolutions were decried in Federalist strongholds as an unconstitutional attempt to wrest power from the federal judiciary. In 1799, state legislatures in at least Rhode Island, Massachusetts, New York, Connecticut, New Hampshire, and Vermont passed resolutions condemning Jefferson's and Madison's resolutions and praising the virtues of a constitutionally independent national judiciary.[122] The Rhodes Island legislature, while declaring the Sedition Act to "be within the powers delegated to Congress," argued that "the Constitution of the United States . . . vests in the federal courts, exclusively, and in the Supreme Court of the United States, ultimately, the authority of deciding on the constitutionality of any act or law of the Congress of the United States."[123] Similarly, the legislature of Vermont asserted that "[i]t belongs not to state legislatures to decide on the constitutionality of laws made by the general government; this power being exclusively vested in the judiciary courts of the Union."[124] Clearly, the textual barriers found in the Constitution, and the structural barriers created by it, would not restrain the extraconstitutional goals of a determined political party, at least when that party included allies in the federal judiciary who could "interpret" the document as needed to serve their purposes.

When Brutus, whoever he was, viewed the tumultuous political events of 1798 and 1799—maybe from a modest home in Albany, New York, rather than from a seat of great renown or power—perhaps he thought, with disappointed satisfaction, "Mr. Madison, I told you so!"[125] Had he lived to see our day, it would be a refrain he could have repeated many times throughout the country's subsequent history.

NOTES

1. The title of "Brutus" appears to have been taken in response to Alexander Hamilton's use of the pseudonym "Caesar" in letters published in New York's *Daily Advertiser* (which were in reply to the Anti-Federalist writings of New York governor George Clinton, who wrote as "Cato" in the *New York Journal*). The authorship of Brutus's essays, however, remains a mystery, though he has been variously identified by different historians (and, in at least one case, by the same historian) as Abraham Yates Jr., Richard Henry Lee, George Clinton, Melancton Smith, Thomas Treadwell, or others. Most commonly Brutus's writings are attributed to Robert Yates, a former delegate from New York to the Constitutional Convention in Philadelphia and chief

justice of New York's Supreme Court; but this identification is not certain. See the introductory note to Brutus, I, in John P. Kaminski and Gaspare J. Saladino, eds., *The Documentary History of the Ratification of the Constitution*, vol. 13 (Madison: State Historical Society of Wisconsin, 1981), 411–21; also see Paul Leicester Ford, ed., *Pamphlets on the Constitution of the United States* (New York: Da Capo Press, 1968), 117, 424; Herbert J. Storing, ed., *The Complete Anti-Federalist*, vol. 2 (Chicago: University of Chicago Press, 1981), 358; and William Jeffrey Jr., "The Letters of 'Brutus'—a Neglected Element in the Ratification Campaign of 1787–88," *University of Cincinnati Law Review* 40, no. 4 (1971): 643, 644–46.

2. "Publius" was the pseudonym under which Alexander Hamilton, James Madison, and John Jay authored *The Federalist Papers*. *The Federalist Papers* were published variously in three New York newspapers—the *Independent Journal*, the *New-York Packet*, and the *Daily Advertiser*—from October 27, 1787, through August 13, 1788. See Alexander Hamilton, James Madison, and John Jay, *The Federalist Papers*, ed. Clinton Rossiter (New York: New American Library, 1961).

3. Brutus's letters XI through XV were published from January 31, 1788, through March 20, 1788. Alexander Hamilton's *Federalist* 78 through 83 were first publicly released on May 28, 1788, and were serialized in New York's *Independent Journal* from June 14, 1788, through July 12, 1788.

4. John P. Kaminski, "New York: The Reluctant Pillar," in *The Reluctant Pillar: New York and the Adoption of the Federal Constitution*, ed. Stephen L. Schechter (Madison: Madison House Publishers, 1985), 79.

5. The Federal Convention officially sent its proposed Constitution to "the United States in Congress" on September 17, 1787. Congress then unanimously submitted the document to the states for ratification on September 28, 1787. Delaware, by a thirty to zero vote in its ratifying convention, became the first state to approve the Constitution on December 7, 1787. With New Hampshire becoming the ninth state to ratify the document on June 21, 1788, the Constitution, according to the terms found in it (see U.S. Constitution art. VII, cl. 1), went into effect. When word reached the New York ratifying convention on July 2, 1788, that Virginia had become the tenth state to ratify the Constitution, the Federalists in attendance withdrew from debate. Enough Anti-Federalists then broke ranks and the convention accepted membership in the union on July 26, 1788. See Jack Rakove, *Original Meanings: Politics and Ideas in the Making of the Constitution* (New York: Alfred A. Knopf, 1997), 125.

6. The approval of New York was particularly important for the success of the Constitution. After ratification had reached the required threshold of nine states to go into effect, the states of Virginia and New York were still debating approval, with the outcome unsure. If these two large states had refused to ratify, it would have left the new union geographically, economically, and politically fragmented, and its long-term survival would have been questionable. But Virginia did approve the Constitution on June 26, 1788, by a narrow eighty-nine to seventy-nine vote, followed a month later by New York. Once the successful creation of the new constitutional union was assured by the approval of these two pivotal states, the Congress set about organizing elections for the new government. A resolution setting the date for national elections and establishing that the seat of government (temporarily in New York City) was passed by the sitting Congress on September 13, 1788. It was then not until the first Congress constituted under the new Constitution met and

submitted a bill of rights to the states for ratification (on March 4, 1789) that the recalcitrant state of North Carolina reconvened its ratifying convention and joined the union on November 21, 1789. Only under the threat of being treated as a small foreign nation did Rhode Island finally ratify the Constitution by a narrow thirty-four to thirty-two vote on May 29, 1790, thus uniting the thirteen original colonies as one federated republic.

7. Cecelia M. Kenyon, ed., *The Antifederalists* (Indianapolis: Bobbs-Merrill, 1966), 323.

8. Morton Borden, ed., *The Antifederalist Papers* (East Lansing: Michigan State University Press, 1965), 82.

9. Arthur E. Wilmarth Jr., "Elusive Foundation: John Marshall, James Wilson, and the Problem of Reconciling Popular Sovereignty and Natural Law Jurisprudence in the New Federal Republic," *George Washington Law Review* 72 (December 2003): 113, 137.

10. Acknowledgment of the theoretical importance of Brutus's writings should not be confused with a claim about their practical importance at the time they were published. As Larry Kramer concludes, "Federalist 78 had no influence on Ratification. This is because hardly anyone saw either it or Brutus's essays during the campaign. Brutus was well regarded among a small circle of the most intellectual participants in Ratification, but he was not widely circulated or read. Of Brutus's three essays on judicial review, two were not reprinted anywhere—not even in New York—while the third was reprinted only twice. Publius's audience was hardly larger, the canonical status of The Federalist most definitely being a post-ratification phenomenon. This is particularly true of Federalist 78, which was not included in the original newspaper series and first saw the light of day only upon publication of the second volume of The Federalist at the end of May, 1788—too late to influence any ratifying convention except (possibly) that of New York." Larry D. Kramer, "The Supreme Court 2000 Term: Foreword: We the Court," *Harvard Law Review* (November 2001): 4, 67 (footnotes omitted).

11. William Jeffrey Jr. observed that in comparison to the frequent republication of Hamilton's, Madison's, and Jay's *Federalist*, "the history of the republication of the letters of 'Brutus' has been a tale of a quite different kind. These letters were left perfectly undisturbed in the libraries' files of the *New York Journal* until 1856, when *Letters I–IV* were reprinted in an edition of the proceedings of the Massachusetts ratifying convention, stimulating no discoverable response, scholarly or otherwise. There followed a second period of unbroken obscurity, not interrupted until the era of the 'Roosevelt court fight,' when Professor Edward Corwin appended three of the letters to his *Court over Constitution*. . . . After a third period of neglect, however, 'Brutus' began at long last, in the middle 1960s, to achieve the recognition properly owed him. His letters were extensively drawn upon by Professor Borden in the preparation of the *Antifederalist Papers*, published in 1965, and in the next year Professor Kenyon reprinted four of the letters in her valuable anthology entitled *The Antifederalists*." Jeffrey, "The Letters of 'Brutus,'" 644. Though some scholars began to pay attention to Brutus in the 1960s, it was not until 1981, with publication in two multivolume sets—*The Documentary History of the Ratification of the Constitution* and Herbert J. Storing's *The Complete Anti-Federalist*—that all of Brutus's letters could be found in print (though in *The Documentary History of the Ratification of the Constitution*, his letters are scattered chronologically among five large volumes). More than

a decade later they were included in another multivolume work: Bernard Bailyn, ed., *The Debate on the Constitution: Federalist and Antifederalist Speeches, Articles, and Letters during the Struggle over Ratification* (New York: Library of America, 1993). But, these scholarly aids to serious researchers did not make Brutus available to the masses; that had to wait until the twenty-first century. Most recently, the *Cambridge Texts in the History of Political Thought* edition of *The Federalist* includes all sixteen of Brutus's letters. See Alexander Hamilton, James Madison, and John Jay, *The Federalist: with Letters of "Brutus,"* ed. Terence Ball (New York: Cambridge University Press, 2003). Fortunately, despite the relatively limited availability of Brutus's writings in print, his letters can finally be easily accessed together and in their entirety on a variety of Internet sites. A sampling of such sites, as of September 15, 2008, can be found at http://www.constitution.org/afp/brutus00.htm, http://www.infoplease.com/t/hist/antifederalist/brutus.html, and http://www.angelfire.com/pa/sergeman/foundingdocs/antifedpap/main.html. In contrast to the rare examples of Brutus in print, a quick search on www.amazon.com reveals that at least half a dozen different editions of *The Federalist* papers are in popular publication today (and quite likely even more). Often, some edition of *The Federalist* papers is packaged with American government texts, for study in basic college courses. Exposure of American readers and students to the whole collection of *The Federalist* papers is both convenient and common. Exposure to Brutus is sporadic and limited.

12. The short shrift that is given to Brutus can be seen in the limited exposure that his writings receive in some important works of noted historians. In Gordon S. Wood's *The Creation of the American Republic 1776–1787* (Chapel Hill: University of North Carolina Press, 1998), the index does not contain a single entry for Brutus or his writings. The same is true of Julius Goebel's *History of the Supreme Court of the United States*, vol. 1, *Antecedents and Beginnings to 1801* (New York: Macmillan, 1971). Yet both of these books contain dozens of references to the corresponding *Federalist* papers. In Leonard Levy and Dennis J. Mahoney's edited volume, *The Framing and Ratification of the Constitution* (New York: Macmillan, 1987), though a number of references to Brutus are listed in the index, almost without exception the corresponding passages contain only general comments about Anti-Federalist ideas, or the words of Brutus are presented as brief, specific counterpoints to *Federalist* passages. More general-use American history textbooks and reference sources often fail to mention the existence of Brutus, though they lavish praise on *The Federalist* papers. For examples, see James A. Henretta, David Brody, Susan Ware, and Marilynn Johnson, *America's History*, 4th ed. (Boston: St. Martin's, 1999), and Paul S. Boyer, ed. *The Oxford Companion to United States History* (New York: Oxford University Press, 2001). The scholarly dismissal of Brutus is even more extreme in legal volumes, considering the direct relevance that Brutus's arguments may have to the subject matter. As an example, see Robert N. Clinton, Richard A. Matasar, and Michael G. Collins's textbook, *Federal Courts: Theory and Practice* (Boston: Little, Brown and Company, 1996), which deals explicitly with theoretical arguments concerning Article III of the Constitution. While quoting major portions of Alexander Hamilton's six *Federalist* papers dealing with the federal judiciary, it does not even mention Brutus or his arguments.

13. Brutus's second-fiddle status to Publius is true, despite the fact that "Hamilton's attempt . . . in Federalist Nos. 78 and 81, to rebut Brutus' conclusions on the danger of judicial supremacy constituted, in the final analysis, an abject failure."

Shlomo Slonim, "Federalist No. 78 and Brutus' Neglected Thesis on Judicial Supremacy," *Constitutional Commentary* 23 (Spring 2006): 7, 28.

14. Kramer, "The Supreme Court 2000 Term," 66.

15. Norman R. Williams, "The Failings of Originalism: The Federal Courts and the Power of Precedent," *U.C. Davis Law Review* 37 (February 2004): 762, 816.

16. Jeffrey, "The Letters of 'Brutus,'" 648. Interestingly, after pointing out the modern perception that Brutus's arguments must be disingenuous, Jeffrey goes on to justify those arguments as being sincerely rooted in the legal culture of Brutus's day.

17. Rakove, *Original Meanings*, 187. A possible explanation for why Rakove finds "innocuous" what Brutus found threatening may be found in the closing pages of *Original Meanings*, where Rakove reveals his own inclination to allow constitutional content to be altered by judicial will instead of by formal, constitutionally mandated processes. He writes: "It is one thing to rail against the evils of politically unaccountable judges enlarging constitutional rights beyond the ideas and purposes of their original adopters; another to explain why morally sustainable claims of equality should be held captive to the extraordinary obstacles of Article V or subject to the partial and incomplete understandings of 1789 or 1868." Rakove, *Original Meanings*, 367–68.

18. "[T]he substance of the Ratification debate was precisely what the experience of the 1780s would have led one to expect. A handful of participants saw a role for judicial review, though few of these imagined it as a powerful or important device, and none seemed anxious to emphasize it. Others were opposed to the notion of judicial review, citing its possibility as one of the proposed Constitution's liabilities. The vast majority of participants were still thinking in terms of popular constitutionalism and so focused on traditional political means of enforcing the new charter; the notion of judicial review simply never crossed their minds. There is, in fact, only a single exchange on judicial review that can be described as anything other than cursory, that between Brutus and Publius in the New York press." Kramer, "The Supreme Court 2000 Term," 66 (paragraph break omitted).

19. For a few prominent examples of this ongoing debate, see Bruce Ackerman, *We the People: Transformations* (Cambridge, Mass.: Belknap Press of Harvard University Press, 1998); Randy E. Barnett, *Restoring the Lost Constitution: The Presumption of Liberty* (Princeton, N.J.: Princeton University Press, 2005); Raoul Berger, *Government by Judiciary: The Transformation of the Fourteenth Amendment* (Cambridge, Mass.: Harvard University Press, 1977); Alexander Bickel, *The Least Dangerous Branch: The Supreme Court at the Bar of Politics* (Indianapolis: Bobbs-Merrill, 1962); Robert Bork, *The Tempting of America: The Political Seduction of the Law* (New York: The Free Press, 1990); Stephen Breyer, *Active Liberty: Interpreting Our Democratic Constitution* (New York: Alfred A. Knopf, 2005); Ronald Dworkin, *Freedom's Law: The Moral Reading of the American Constitution* (Cambridge, Mass.: Harvard University Press, 1996); Michael J. Perry, *The Constitution in the Courts: Law or Politics?* (New York: Oxford University Press, 1994); Richard A. Posner, *Overcoming Law* (Cambridge, Mass.: Harvard University Press, 1996); Antonin Scalia, *A Matter of Interpretation: Federal Courts and the Law* (Princeton, N.J.: Princeton University Press, 1997); Cass Sunstein, *Radicals in Robes: Why Extreme Right-Wing Courts Are Wrong for America* (New York: Basic Books, 2005); and Mark Tushnet, *Taking the Constitution Away from the Courts* (Princeton, N.J.: Princeton University Press, 1999).

20. "This government is a complete system, not only for making, but for executing laws. And the courts of law, which will be constituted by it, are not only to decide upon the constitution and the laws made in pursuance of it, but by officers subordinate to them to execute all their decisions. The real effect of this system of government, will therefore be brought home to the feelings of the people, through the medium of the judicial power." Brutus, XI, *The Documentary History of the Ratification of the Constitution*, XV, 512.

21. Ann Stuart Diamond, "The Anti-Federalist 'Brutus,'" *Political Science Reviewer* 6 (Fall 1976): 249–81.

22. For discussions of the favorable political attention that the writings of Anti-Federalists, including Brutus, have recently received, see Kevin E. Broyles, "Federalism and Political Life," in *Saving the Revolution: The Federalist Papers and the American Founding*, ed. Charles R. Kessler (New York: The Free Press, 1987); and Saul A. Cornell, "The Changing Historical Fortunes of the Anti-Federalists," *Northwestern University Law Review* 85 (Fall 1990): 39. Also, for a sampling of the scholarly attention, both positive and negative, that has been given to the writings of Brutus, in particular, in recent years, see Anthony V. Baker, "'So Extraordinary, So Unprecedented an Authority': A Conceptual Reconsideration of the Singular Doctrine of Judicial Review," *Duquesne University Law Review* 39 (Summer 2001): 729, 744–48; Henry J. Bourguignon, "The Federal Key to the Judiciary Act of 1789," *South Carolina Law Review* 46 (Summer 1995): 647, 663–66; William N. Eskridge Jr., "All About Words: Early Understandings of the 'Judicial Power' in Statutory Interpretation, 1776–1806," *Columbia Law Review* 101 (June 2001): 990, 1047–57, 1086; The Goldwater Institute and the Federalist Society, "Federalism and Judicial Mandates: Edited Transcripts from the Panel Discussions Held in Phoenix, Arizona on November 3rd and 4th, 1995," *Arizona State Law Journal* 28 (Spring 1996): 17, 18–51; Shawn Gunnarson, "Using History to Reshape the Discussion of Judicial Review," *Brigham Young University Law Review* 1994, no. 1 (1994): 151, 172–83; Larry D. Kramer, "Putting the Politics Back into the Political Safeguards of Federalism," *Columbia Law Review* 100 (January 2000): 215, 246–49; Helen K. Michael, "The Role of Natural Law in Early American Constitutionalism: Did the Founders Contemplate Judicial Enforcement of 'Unwritten' Individual Rights?" *North Carolina Law Review* 69 (January 1991): 421, 483–89; Saikrishna B. Prakash and John C. Yoo, "The Puzzling Persistence of Process-Based Federalism Theories," *Texas Law Review* 79 (May 2001): 1459, 1473, 1518–20; James Etienne Viator, "The Losers Know Best the Meaning of the Game: What the Anti-Federalists Can Teach Us about Race-Based Congressional Districts," *Loyola Journal of Public Interest Law* 1 (Spring 2000): 1, 15–22.

23. For a discussion of the Brutus-like bent of the Rehnquist Court, see John O. McGinnis, "Reviving Tocqueville's America: The Rehnquist Court's Jurisprudence of Social Discovery," *California Law Review* 90 (March 2002): 485; Christopher H. Schroeder, "Causes of the Recent Turn in Constitutional Interpretation," *Duke Law Journal* 51 (October 2001): 307; Mark Tushnet, "Mr. Jones & the Supreme Court," *Green Bag* 4, no. 2 (Winter 2001): 173; and Mark Tushnet, "What Is the Supreme Court's New Federalism?" *Oklahoma City University Law Review* 25 (Fall 2000): 927.

24. There are sound reasons for looking to the political discourse of the Founding in general, and the New York debate in particular, even if one does not think such evidence is binding for modern questions. As was eloquently stated by Jack Rakove (though undoubtedly with Madison in mind more than Brutus):

"[B]ecause the meditations about popular government that we encounter there remain more profound than those that the ordinary politics of our endless democratic present usually sustains." Rakove, *Original Meanings*, 368. Showing a similar sentiment, law professor Norman R. Williams explains that "[t]he Federalist Papers do not have authoritative significance because they are evidence of a collective, shared understanding of the Constitution by those who framed and ratified the document. Rather, their interpretive value lies in the fact that they provide a comprehensive, normatively attractive interpretation of the Constitution espoused by several of the most prominent Framers to have given their attention to the matter. Stated differently, the interpretive value of the Federalist Papers lies not in their value as a historical record of the shared views of the Framers but rather in their attractiveness as a coherent explanation of the Constitution's meaning offered at the time of the Founding." Williams, "The Failings of Originalism," 812n199. Likewise, it is the coherency of Brutus's fears about federal power that make his writings of lasting importance. "[Brutus] is incomparably better than the mass of Anti-Federalist writing and a good deal of Federalist writing. . . . One of the most reassuring qualities of Brutus is the extent to which he views political questions theoretically and takes theory seriously. The essays are full of examples: the small republic theory of government, the social contract, a theory of representation, the principle of limited government, of political economy, the implications of constitutionalism. This outlook testifies also to the fact that the debate over ratification took place in terms of great theoretical questions on both sides, dare one say great philosophical questions? If Brutus had believed that his readers would only be convinced by practical concerns, by bread and butter issues as we now say, he certainly would have used only them. Instead he spoke in the accepted 'language' of his time and was one of the more influential Anti-Federalist publicists." Diamond, "The Anti-Federalist Brutus," 279–80.

25. I am certainly not the first to make this suggestion. For examples, see Lino A. Graglia, "The Goldwater Institute and the Federalist Society, Federalism and Judicial Mandates: Edited Transcripts from the Panel Discussions Held in Phoenix, Arizona on November 3rd and 4th, 1995," *Arizona State Law Journal* 28 (Spring 1996): 17, 27 ("It is now widely recognized that the Antifederalists were right in seeing that the Constitution created a potentially all-powerful national government, leaving no area of policy-making exclusively for the states. . . . The Antifederalists, particularly Brutus and the Federal Farmer, saw the Constitution's potential not only for concentrated legislative power, but also for despotic judicial power. It has been to the detriment of the welfare of the nation that their warning has gone unheeded. It would make for a healthier and more realistic understanding of the role of the Courts in our system of government if students were not subjected to the specious reasoning of Hamilton in Federalist No. 78 and Marshall in *Marbury* [*v. Madison*, 5 U.S. 137 (1803)] without being given the writings of Brutus and the Federal Farmer as an antidote.") and Mark R. Killenbeck, "A Strange Apparent Cruelty?" *Arkansas Law Review* 57, no. 1 (2004): 93, 94 ("The Antifederalist vision played a crucial role in the story of the founding. And any account of those events that hopes to do them justice must be just as aware of and sensitive to the musings of say, The Federal Farmer and Brutus, as it is to the thoughts and impulses of Alexander Hamilton or James Madison.").

26. Storing, *The Complete Anti-Federalist*, 72.

27. The Constitution grants that "[t]he judicial Power shall extend to all cases . . . between Citizens of different states. . . ." U.S. Constitution art. III, sec. 2. When a federal court exercises authority over such a case, it is said to be invoking "diversity jurisdiction."

28. Brutus, XII, *The Documentary History of the Ratification of the Constitution*, XVI, 120–22, 121.

29. Brutus, XIV, *The Documentary History of the Ratification of the Constitution*, XVI, 328–32, 328.

30. For purposes of diversity jurisdiction, corporations are considered to be "citizens" of both the state in which they are incorporated (often Delaware, for tax purposes) and the state where they do their business. See 28 USCS sec. 1332 (c) (1). This characterization of business "citizenship" allows individuals to bring suit against most large corporations, which almost surely are "citizens" of a different state than the individual, either through their place of incorporation or their place of business.

31. The process of making states accountable for honoring select provisions of the Bill of Rights, via the Due Process Clause of the Fourteenth Amendment, began with the case of *Gitlow v. New York*, 268 U.S. 652 (1925), wherein the First Amendment's Freedom of Speech Clause was incorporated. Though Brutus could not foresee the events that led to the Civil War Amendments, nor the eventual impact that they specifically would have, he certainly did recognize the tendencies, put in place through the new Constitution, for the federal government, including the federal judiciary, to expand their control over the states through whatever constitutional passages were available to them. Thus, though the specific means of federal expansion may not have been in Brutus's view, the general process and the ultimate ends surely were.

32. U.S. Constitution art. I, sec. 8, cl. 3. A prime example of the expansive construction of this constitutional clause is seen in the case of *Wickard v. Filburn*, 317 U.S. 111 (1942), wherein the Supreme Court ruled that Congress could prevent a man from growing a small amount of wheat as feed for his own livestock, in excess of his allotment under the Agricultural Adjustment Act of 1938, because to do so was an act of "interstate" commerce that Congress was authorized to regulate in the Commerce Clause.

33. Interestingly, it did not require the vast modern expansion of federal powers to open up the federal courts to heavy use. According to a study of federal courts in Kentucky shortly after the Founding, business in these courts became brisk immediately, with a much heavier volume recorded in the court records than scholars had ever supposed. See Mary K. Bonsteel Tachau, *Federal Courts in the Early Republic 1789–1816* (Princeton, N.J.: Princeton University Press, 1978), 11.

34. Brutus, XI, *The Documentary History of the Ratification of the Constitution*, XV, 512–17, 513–14.

35. See, as examples, *Green v. County School Board of New Kent County*, 391 U.S. 430 (1968) and *Swann v. Charlotte-Mecklenburg Board of Education*, 402 U.S. 1 (1971). "'The image of the heroic Court, stepping in where others dared not, to free an oppressed people and relieve the nation of the crippling legacy of segregation, is cherished in the American memory.' And, one might plausibly extrapolate, if the Court could end the legal oppression of African-Americans, why could it not do the same for women, gays and lesbians, political radicals, and so forth." Michael J. Klarman, "Rethinking the Civil Rights and Civil Liberties Revolutions," *Virginia Law*

Review 82 (February, 1996): 1, 19, quoting John C. Jeffries Jr., *Justice Lewis F. Powell, Jr. and the Era of Judicial Balance* (New York: C. Scribner's Sons, 1994), 330.

36. Brutus, XI, *The Documentary History of the Ratification of the Constitution*, XV, 515.

37. Brutus, XI, *The Documentary History of the Ratification of the Constitution*, XV, 514.

38. Brutus, XII, *The Documentary History of the Ratification of the Constitution*, XVI, 72–75, 73. On this point, at least well after ratification was achieved, Alexander Hamilton clearly agreed with Brutus. As secretary of the Treasury, he wrote the following in defense of the constitutionality of his proposed Bank of the United States: "[T]he powers contained in a constitution of government . . . ought to be construed liberally in advancement of the public good." Alexander Hamilton, "Opinion as to the Constitutionality of the Bank of the United States," in *The Works of Alexander Hamilton*, vol. 3, ed. Henry Cabot Lodge (New York: G. P. Putnam's Sons, 1904), 446.

39. A rare occasion when the Supreme Court admitted that it was relying on the "spirit" of the Constitution to reach its decision was seen in the case of *Hepburn v. Griswold*, 75 U.S. 603 (1870), wherein the Court had to decide if a contract signed before but enforced after the federal issuance of paper money had to still be paid in silver or gold coin. In that case, the Court decided that Griswold had to be paid in coin. Chief Justice Salmon P. Chase wrote for the Court that the statute in question, wherein Congress established paper money as legal tender, would have to be read in a way "consistent with the spirit of the Constitution." *Hepburn v. Griswold*, 75 U.S. 603, 622 (1870). Chase reasoned that it was "clear that those who framed and those who adopted the Constitution, intended that the spirit of [the] prohibition [that 'no State shall pass any law impairing the obligation of contracts' (U.S. Constitution art. I, sec. 10)] should pervade the entire body of legislation, and that *the justice which the Constitution was ordained to establish* was not thought by them to be compatible with legislation of an opposite tendency." *Hepburn v. Griswold*, 75 U.S. 603, 623 (1870) (emphasis added). Not only does Chase rely on a divination of the spirit of the document to render his decision, but he seeks that spirit not in the document's legally binding text, but rather in the rhetoric of the Constitution's preamble, as evidenced by his reference to "the justice which the Constitution was ordained to establish," which is so closely related to the preamble's language, which reads in part: "We the people of the United States, in order to form a more perfect Union, establish justice . . . ordain and establish this Constitution." This is exactly the kind of legal maneuver that Brutus predicted and for which modern critics dismiss him for having thought possible.

40. Brutus, XV, *The Documentary History of the Ratification of the Constitution*, XVI, 431–35, 432.

41. Brutus, XV, *The Documentary History of the Ratification of the Constitution*, XVI, 431–35, 432–33. In fulfillment of Brutus's claim that Supreme Court justices could not be removed from office, in the history of the United States only one justice has been impeached—Samuel Chase in 1805—but he was not convicted and removed. This fact severely discredits Alexander Hamilton's counterargument to Brutus, that impeachment would be a significant check on the judiciary. Hamilton wrote: "It may in the last place be observed that the supposed danger of judiciary encroachments on the legislative authority which has been upon many occasions reiterated is in reality a phantom. . . . This may be inferred with certainty from the general

nature of the judicial power, from the objects to which it relates, from the manner in which it is exercised, from its comparative weakness, and from its total incapacity to support its usurpations by force. And the inference is greatly fortified by the consideration of the important constitutional check which the power of instituting impeachments in one part of the legislative body, and of determining upon them in the other, would give to that body upon the members of the judicial department. This is alone a complete security." See Alexander Hamilton's *Federalist* 81, in Alexander Hamilton, James Madison, and John Jay, *The Federalist Papers* (New York: Mentor, 1961), 481–91 at 484–85. Perhaps the reason that impeachment has not been a check on the judiciary is the judiciary's tendency to uphold expansions of congressional power while encroaching on other areas of government—particularly the states.

42. See James Madison's *Federalist* 10, in Alexander Hamilton, James Madison, and John Jay, *The Federalist Papers* (New York: Mentor, 1961), 77–84.

43. Brutus, XV, *The Documentary History of the Ratification of the Constitution*, XVI, 431–35, 431.

44. Brutus, XV, *The Documentary History of the Ratification of the Constitution*, XVI, 431.

45. Brutus, XV, *The Documentary History of the Ratification of the Constitution*, XVI, 432.

46. Brutus, XI, *The Documentary History of the Ratification of the Constitution*, XV, 512–17, 517.

47. Brutus, XIV, *The Documentary History of the Ratification of the Constitution*, XVI, 328–32, 331.

48. Brutus, IX, *The Documentary History of the Ratification of the Constitution*, XV, 393–98, 395–96.

49. Hamilton, *Federalist* 81, 482–83.

50. Hamilton, *Federalist* 78, 467.

51. Hamilton, *Federalist* 78, 465.

52. *Worcester v. Georgia*, 31 U.S. 515 (1832).

53. John Meachan, *American Lion: Andrew Jackson in the White House* (New York: Random House, 2008), 204.

54. *U.S. v. Nixon*, 418 U.S. 683 (1974).

55. Madison, *Federalist* 51, 322.

56. Madison, *Federalist* 51, 321–22.

57. Thomas Hobbes, *Leviathan* (New York: Penguin Classics, 1982), 188.

58. John Locke, *Second Treatise of Government* (Indianapolis: Hackett, 1980), 8.

59. "The authority of the state to enact this statute is to be referred to what is commonly called the police power,—a power which the state did not surrender when becoming a member of the Union under the Constitution. . . . [T]his court has . . . recognized the authority of a state to enact . . . all laws that relate to matters completely within its territory and which do not by their necessary operation affect the people of other states." *Jacobson v. Massachusetts*, 197 U.S. 11, 24–25 (1905).

60. Jonathan Elliot, ed., *Debates in the Several Conventions, on the Adoption of the Federal Constitution, as Recommended by the General Convention at Philadelphia in 1787*, 2nd ed. (Washington, D.C.: Jonathan Elliot, 1836), 2:362–63 (emphasis added).

61. Madison, *Federalist* 45, 292–93 (emphasis added).

62. North Carolina Constitution of 1776 art. XXXII.

63. Alan Nevins, *The American States: During and After the Revolution: 1775–1789* (New York: Macmillan, 1924), 561.

64. See Harry Elmer Barnes, *The Evolution of Penology in Pennsylvania: A Study in American Social History* (Montclair, N.J.: Patterson Smith Barnes, 1968), 39; and Michael Meranze, *Laboratories of Virtue: Punishment, Revolution, and Authority in Philadelphia, 1760–1835* (Chapel Hill: University of North Carolina Press, 199), 22.

65. Alan Nevins, *The American States*, 450.

66. The Constitution expressly grants Congress supreme authority to (among other things) "lay and collect Taxes, Duties, Imposts and Excises . . . To borrow money . . . To regulate Commerce with foreign Nations, and among the several States, and with the Indian Tribes; To establish a uniform Rule of Naturalization, and uniform Laws . . . of Bankruptcies . . . To coin Money . . . and fix Standards of Weights an Measures; To provide for the Punishment of counterfeiting . . . To establish Post Offices and post Roads; To . . . secur[e patents] . . . To constitute Tribunals inferior to the supreme Court; To declare War . . . To raise and support Armies . . . To provide and maintain a Navy . . . To provide for the calling forth of Militia to . . . suppress Insurrections and repel Invasions; . . . To exercise exclusive Legislation in all cases whatsoever, over [the] District [of Columbia] . . . [and] To make all Laws necessary and proper for carrying into execution the foregoing powers." U.S. Constitution art. I, sec. 8. These are all powers that the states had held individually—and supremely, within their own borders—prior to ratification of the Constitution.

67. U.S. Constitution art. I, sec. 10.

68. Brutus did not think the states would be eliminated in one bold stroke (though he thought this possible), but rather through an inevitable process. In his first letter he wrote: "[A]ll laws made, in pursuance of this constitution, are the supreme law of the land . . . any thing in the constitution or laws of the different states to the contrary notwithstanding. . . . By such a law, the government of a particular state might be overturned at one stroke. . . . It is not meant, by stating this case, to insinuate that the constitution would warrant a law of this kind. . . . But what is meant is, that the legislature of the United States are vested with the great and uncontroulable powers, of laying and collecting taxes, duties, imposts, and excises; of regulating trade, raising and supporting armies, organizing, arming, and disciplining the militia, instituting courts, and other general powers. And are . . . invested with the power of making all laws, proper and necessary, for carrying all these into execution; and they may so exercise this power as entirely to annihilate all the state governments, and reduce this country to one single government. And if they may do it, it is pretty certain they will; for it will be found that the power retained by individual states, small as it is, will be a clog upon the wheels of the government of the United States; the latter therefore will be naturally inclined to remove it out of the way. Besides, it is a truth confirmed by the unerring experience of ages, that every man, and every body of men, invested with power, are ever disposed to increase it, and to acquire a superiority over every thing that stands in their way. This disposition, which is implanted in human nature, will operate in the federal legislature to lessen and ultimately to subvert the state authority. . . . It must be very evident then, that what this constitution wants of being a complete consolidation of the several parts of the union into one complete government, possessed of perfect legislative, judicial, and executive powers, to all intents and purposes, it will necessarily acquire

in its exercise and operation." Brutus, I, *The Documentary History of the Ratification of the Constitution*, XIII, 416–17.

69. Another anonymous Anti-Federalist author, the "Federal Farmer" (often thought to be Richard Henry Lee of Virginia or Melancton Smith of New York), convincingly explained: "To make declaratory articles [such as a bill of rights] unnecessary in an instrument of government, two circumstances must exist; the rights reserved must be indisputably so, and their nature defined; the powers delegated to the government, must be precisely defined by words that convey them, and clearly be of such extent and nature as that, by no reasonable construction, they can be made to invade the rights and prerogatives intended to be left in the people." Federal Farmer, XVI, in *The Founder's Constitution*, ed. Philip B. Kurland and Ralph Lerner (Chicago: University of Chicago Press, 1987), 5:402.

70. As examples: In South Carolina, "[t]his Convention doth declare that no Section or paragraph of the said Constitution warrants a Construction that the states do not retain every power not expressly relinquished by them and vested in the General Government of the Union." William R. Davie, "William R. Davie to James Madison," in *Creating the Bill of Rights: The Documentary Record from the First Federal Congress*, ed. Helen E. Veit, Kenneth R. Bowling, and Charlene Bangs Bickford (Baltimore: Johns Hopkins University Press, 1991), 15. The New York convention also requested "[t]hat the Powers of Government may be reassumed by the People, whensoever it shall become necessary to their Happiness; that every Power, Jurisdiction and Right, which is not by the said Constitution clearly delegated to the Congress of the United States, or the departments of the Government thereof remains to the People of the several States, or to their respective State Governments to whom they may have granted the same; And that those Clauses in the said Constitution, which declare, that Congress shall not have or exercise certain Powers, do not imply that Congress is entitled to any Powers not given by the said Constitution; but such Clauses are to be construed either as exceptions to certain specified Powers, or as inserted merely for greater Caution." Davie et al., *Creating the Bill of Rights*, 22. In the Pennsylvania convention, "[t]he amendments proposed [included]. . . . I. That Congress shall not exercise any powers whatever, but such as are expressly given to that body by the Constitution of the United States; nor shall any authority, power, or jurisdiction, be assumed or exercised by the executive or judiciary departments of the Union, under color or pretence of construction or fiction; but all the rights of sovereignty, which are not by the said Constitution expressly and plainly vested in the Congress, shall be deemed to remain with, and shall be exercised by, the several states in the Union, according to their respective Constitutions; and that every reserve of the rights of individuals, made by the several constitutions of the states in the Union, to the citizens and inhabitants of each state respectively, shall remain inviolate, except só far as they are expressly and manifestly yielded or narrowed by the national Constitution." Elliot, *Debates in the Several Conventions*, 2:545. The Maryland convention declared that "[t]he following amendments to the proposed Constitution were separately agreed to by the committee, most of them by a unanimous vote, and all of them by a great majority. 1. That Congress shall exercise no power but What is expressly delegated by this Constitution. By this amendment, the general powers given to Congress by the first and last paragraphs of the 8th sect. of art. 1, and the 2d paragraph of the 6th article, would be in a great measure restrained; those dan-

gerous expressions, by which the bills of rights, and constitutions, of the several states may be repealed by the laws of Congress, in some degree moderated; and the exercise of constructive powers wholly prevented." Elliot, *Debates in the Several Conventions*, 2:550. And the North Carolina convention proposed that "1. Each state in the Union shall respectively retain every power, jurisdiction, and right, which is not by this Constitution delegated to the Congress of the United States, or to the departments of the general government; nor shall the said Congress, nor any department of the said government, exercise any act of authority over any individual in any of the said states, but such as can be justified under some power particularly given in this Constitution; but the said Constitution shall be considered at all times a solemn Instrument, defining the extent of their authority, and the limits of which they cannot rightfully in any instance exceed." Elliot, *Debates in the Several Conventions*, 4:249.

71. Though not an official resolution or even a part of debate within the proceedings of a ratifying convention, a letter sent from William R. Davie to James Madison provides this illuminating summary of the greatest concern of his fellow ratifying convention delegates in North Carolina: "Instead of a Bill of rights attempting to enumerate the rights of the Indivi[du]al or the State Governments, they seem to prefer some general negative confining Congress to the exercise of the powers particularly granted, with some express negative restriction in some important cases." Elliot, *Debates in the Several Conventions*, 3:659.

72. Elliot, *Debates in the Several Conventions*, 2:177.

73. Davie et al., *Creating the Bill of Rights*, 16.

74. Elliot, *Debates in the Several Conventions*, 4:249.

75. Madison, *Federalist* 45, 288, 292–93.

76. When Madison introduced the proposed Tenth Amendment in the House of Representatives, he explained that "I find, from looking into the amendments proposed by the State conventions, that several are particularly anxious that it should be declared in the Constitution, that the powers not therein delegated should be reserved to the several States. Perhaps words which may define this more precisely than the whole of the instrument now does, may be considered as superfluous. I admit they may be deemed unnecessary: but there can be no harm in making such a declaration, if gentlemen will allow that the fact is as stated. I understand it so, and do therefore propose it." "House of Representatives, Amendments to the Constitution (June 8, 1789)," in *The Founder's Constitution* (Chicago: University of Chicago Press, 1987), 5:28.

77. *Annals of Congress*, 1st Cong., 1st sess., ed. Joseph Gales (Washington, D.C.: Gales and Seaton, 1834), 453.

78. It reads: "The powers not delegated to the United States by the Constitution, nor prohibited by it to the States, are reserved to the States respectively, or to the people." U.S. Constitution amend. 10.

79. *Annals of Congress*, 1st Cong., 1st sess., 790.

80. *Annals of Congress*, 1st Cong., 1st sess., 797.

81. *Annals of Congress*, 1st Cong., 1st sess., 790, 797.

82. Bowling continues his discussion of the drafting of the Bill of Rights with this interesting observation: "When describing Madison's proposals, both Federalists and Antifederalists turned to the popular ship of state metaphor. They called his proposals 'a tub to the whale,' an allusion to Jonathan Swift's *Tale of a Tub* (1704). In

his satire, Swift described how sailors, encountering a whale that threatened to damage their ship, flung it 'an empty tub by way of amusement' to divert it. Madison's contemporaries used the allusion to illuminate the fact that he had proposed mostly rights-related amendments rather than ones designed to alter the structure and balance of the new government. As a result, the Antifederal leviathan would be diverted and the ship of state could sail away intact." Kenneth R. Bowling, "Overshadowed by States' Rights: Ratification of the Federal Bill of Rights," in *The Bill of Rights: Government Proscribed*, ed. Ronald Hoffman and Peter J. Albert (Charlottesville: University Press of Virginia, 1997), 79. See also Kenneth R. Bowling, "'A Tub to the Whale': The Founding Fathers and the Adoption of the Federal Bill of Rights," *Journal of the Early Republic* 8 (Fall 1988): 223.

83. Brutus, XI, *The Documentary History of the Ratification of the Constitution*, XV, 515.

84. *McCulloch v. Maryland*, 17 U.S. 316, 406 (1819).

85. *United States v. Darby*, 312 U.S. 100, 123–24 (1941). Even Justice Sandra Day O'Connor, generally considered a friend of states' rights, in a decision striking down a portion of a federal act as an infringement on state sovereignty, admitted her belief that "[t]he Tenth Amendment . . . restrains the power of Congress, but this limit is not derived from the text of the Tenth Amendment itself, which, as we have discussed, is essentially a tautology." *New York v. United States*, 505 U.S. 144, 157 (1992). See post notes 65–67 and accompanying text.

86. Madison, *Federalist* 51, 322.

87. Hamilton, *Federalist* 78, 467 (some punctuation altered).

88. This pessimistic view of human nature was common among those on both sides of the constitutional debate. As examples, James Madison and Alexander Hamilton seemed to agree with Brutus's basic assessment of the compelling power of self-interest. In *Federalist* 10, Madison argues that "[t]he latent causes of faction are thus sown in the nature of man. . . . A zeal for different opinions concerning religion, concerning government, and many other points . . . have, in turn, divided mankind into parties, inflamed them with mutual animosity, and rendered them much more disposed to vex and oppress each other than to co-operate for their common good. So strong is this propensity of mankind to fall into mutual animosities, that where no substantial occasion presents itself, the most frivolous and fanciful distinctions have been sufficient to kindle their unfriendly passions and excite their most violent conflicts." Madison, *Federalist* 10, 77, 79. In *Federalist* 51 Madison further builds on this perspective: "Ambition must be made to counteract ambition. . . . It may be a reflection on human nature, that such devices should be necessary to control the abuses of government. But what is government itself, but the greatest of all reflections on human nature? If men were angels, no government would be necessary." Madison, *Federalist* 51, 320, 322. Similarly, in *Federalist* 15, Hamilton claims that "there is, in the nature of sovereign power, an impatience of control, that disposes those who are invested with the exercise of it, to look with an evil eye upon all external attempts to restrain or direct its operations. . . . Power controlled or abridged is almost always the rival and enemy of that power by which it is controlled or abridged. This simple proposition will teach us how little reason there is to expect, that the persons intrusted with the administration of the affairs of the particular members of a confederacy will at all times be ready, with perfect good-humor, and an unbiased regard to the public weal, to execute the resolutions

or decrees of the general authority. The reverse of this results from the constitution of man." Hamilton, *Federalist* 15, 105, 111.

89. Brutus, XI, *The Documentary History of the Ratification of the Constitution*, XV, 516.

90. Brutus, XI, *The Documentary History of the Ratification of the Constitution*, XV, 516.

91. Brutus, XII, *The Documentary History of the Ratification of the Constitution*, XVI, 72–75, 73.

92. Brutus, XV, *The Documentary History of the Ratification of the Constitution*, XVI, 431–35, 434.

93. Until the decisions in *U.S. v. Lopez*, 514 U.S. 549 (1995) (involving a law banning the carrying of handguns in school zones) and *U.S. v. Morrison*, 529 U.S. 598 (2000) (involving a law creating a federal cause of action for gender-related violence) struck down two Commerce Clause based laws (for not being sufficiently related to the congressional power to regulate interstate commerce), no act of Congress, regulating private activity, that was founded on the Commerce Clause power, had been struck down in over fifty years—no matter how outlandishly unrelated to interstate commerce it was. But these two cases, so clearly unrelated to interstate commerce, show just how far the legislature had managed to nurse a power-expanding line of judicial precedents prior to these decisions.

94. *Heart of Atlanta Motel v. U.S.*, 379 U.S. 241, 251 (1964).

95. Alex Kozinski, introduction to vol. 19, *Harvard Journal of Law & Public Policy* 19 (Fall 1995): 1, 5.

96. Brutus, XII, *The Documentary History of the Ratification of the Constitution*, XVI, 72-75, 74.

97. Hamilton, *Federalist* 78, 467

98. Brutus, XII, *The Documentary History of the Ratification of the Constitution*, XVI, 122.

99. Brutus, XI, *The Documentary History of the Ratification of the Constitution*, XV, 515.

100. U.S. Constitution art. VI, sec. 2. This reads in part: "This Constitution and the Laws of the United States which shall be made in pursuance thereof . . . shall be the supreme Law of the Land; and Judges in every State shall be bound thereby, any Thing in the Constitution or Laws of any State to the Contrary notwithstanding." Though this passage establishes that a state law will fall if it is "Contrary" to the Constitution or federal law, the Supreme Court long ago adopted a less-exacting standard. In two of the earliest and most significant cases regarding the intersection of state and federal sovereignty, Chief Justice John Marshall wrote opinions that implied that merely "interfering" with a federal law is a sufficient cause to nullify a state law. See *McCulloch v. Maryland*, 17 U.S. 316, 430 (1819) and *Gibbons v. Ogden*, 22 U.S. 1, 262–63 (1824).

101. *Garcia v. San Antonio Metropolitan Transit Authority*, 469 U.S. 528 (1985).

102. *Garcia* overruled a decision in the case of *National League of Cities v. Usery*, 426 U.S. 833 (1976). The *National League of Cities* decision was a rare example of the courts attempting to limit the power of the national government. But in the end, less than a decade later, even the relatively conservative Rehnquist Court of 1985 upheld the federal regulation of state hours and wages.

103. *South Dakota v. Dole*, 483 U.S. 203 (1987).

104. This ruling was made despite the existence of the Twenty-first Amendment, which repealed Prohibition and granted the states authority over the liquor trade. That amendment reads in part: "The transportation or importation into any State, Territory, or possession of the United States for delivery or use therein of intoxicating liquors, in violation of the laws thereof, is hereby prohibited." U.S. Constitution amend. 21, sec. 2. The only direct way for the national government to manage the sale of alcohol is through its delegated power to "regulate Commerce . . . among the several States" (U.S. Constitution art. I, sec. 8), but this area of interstate commerce has been reserved for the states by the Twenty-first Amendment, so it can be persuasively argued that state authority over the alcohol industry is plenary (or at least should be).

105. *Perez v. United States*, 402 U.S. 146 (1971).

106. This case is particularly noteworthy because the Supreme Court was willing to uphold the federal Extortionate Credit Transactions Act (18 U.S.C. secs. 891–96 [1976]) as a valid exercise of Congress's delegated power to "regulate Commerce . . . among the several States" (U.S. Constitution art. I, sec. 8) despite the fact that this criminal statute did not require any proof that the prohibited activity in any way directly affected interstate commerce, nor that any instrument of interstate commerce was used in committing the crime. In dissent, Justice Potter Stewart argued that loan-sharking was just another local crime, and that "the definition and prosecution of local, intrastate crimes are reserved to the States under the . . . Tenth Amendment." *Perez v. United States*, 402 U.S. 146, 158 (1971) (Stewart, J., dissenting). See also *United States v. Perez*, 426 F2d 1073 (2d Cir., 1970), wherein the appeals court admitted that "almost all federal criminal statutes are so drafted that the connection with federal interests . . . must be proved in each case" (at 1075).

107. *City of Philadelphia v. New Jersey*, 437 U.S. 617 (1978).

108. See U.S. Constitution art. I, sec. 8, granting Congress power to "regulate Commerce . . . among the several States." Significantly, the Court made this determination despite the fact that Congress had not chosen to regulate this type of commerce. Justice Stewart, writing for the Court, justified making such a ruling, despite a lack of congressional sanction, by arguing that "[a]lthough the Constitution gives Congress the power to regulate commerce among the States, many subjects of potential federal regulation under that power inevitably escape congressional attention 'because of their local character and their number and diversity.' *South Carolina State Highway Dept.* v. *Barnwell Bros., Inc.*, 303 U.S. 177, 185 [(1938)]. In the absence of federal legislation, these subjects are open to control by the States so long as they act within the restraints imposed by the Commerce Clause itself. See *Raymond Motor Transportation, Inc. v. Rice*, 434 U.S. 429, 440 [(1978)]. The bounds of these restraints appear nowhere in the words of the Commerce Clause, but have emerged gradually in the decisions of this Court giving effect to its basic purpose." *City of Philadelphia v. New Jersey*, 437 U.S. 617, 623 (1978).

109. *United States v. Ohio*, 385 U.S. 9 (1966) (reversing *United States v. Ohio*, 354 F. 2d 549 (6th Cir., 1965).

110. Agricultural Adjustment Act of 1938, 7 U.S.C. sec. 1281 et seq. (2009), Pub. L. No. 75-430, 52 Stat. 31 (1938).

111. U.S. Constitution art. I, sec. 8.

112. Ohio Constitution art. II, sec. 41, which reads in part: "Laws shall be passed providing for the occupation and employment of prisoners sentenced to the several penal institutions and reformatories in the state; and no person in any such penal

institution or reformatory while under sentence thereto, shall be required or allowed to work at any trade, industry or occupation, wherein or whereby his work, or the product or profit of his work, shall be sold, farmed out, contracted or given away. . . . Nothing herein contained shall be construed to prevent the passage of laws providing that convicts may work for, and that the products of their labor may be disposed of to, the state or any political sub-division thereof, or for or to any public institution owned or managed and controlled by the state or any political subdivision thereof." (Adopted September 3, 1912.)

113. A comprehensive list of additional such decisions would certainly include the following Supreme Court cases, among many others: *National Labor Relations Board v. Jones & Laughlin Steel*, 301 U.S. 1 (1937); *United States v. Darby*, 312 U.S. 100 (1941); *Wickard v. Filburn*, 317 U.S. 111 (1942); *Heart of Atlanta Motel v. United States*, 379 U.S. 241 (1964); *Katzenbach v. McClung*, 379 U.S. 294 (1964); *Maryland v. Wirtz*, 392 U.S. 183 (1968); *California Bankers Association v. Shultz*, 416 U.S. 21 (1974); *Hodel v. Virginia Surface Mining & Reclamation Association*, 452 U.S. 264 (1981); and *C & A Carbone, Inc. v. Town of Clarkstown, New York*, 511 U.S. 383 (1994). In addition, a compilation of similar cases from lower federal courts could easily number in the thousands. To thoroughly explain the ongoing negative impact of all these federal cases on state powers would undoubtedly be the masterwork of a lifetime, requiring several volumes.

114. "I will venture to predict, without the spirit of prophecy, that if [the Constitution] is adopted without amendments . . . that the same gentlemen who have employed their talents and abilities with such success to influence the public mind to adopt this plan, will employ the same to persuade the people, that it will be for their good to abolish the state governments as useless and burdensome." Brutus, XV, *Documentary History of the Ratification of the Constitution*, XVI, 434. Brutus's concern that the states would be abolished was certainly not outrageous at the time he voiced it. In an era of profound political flux, the destruction of the states seemed a real possibility. James Madison even admitted that abolition of the states was advocated by some members of the Constitutional Convention: "The . . . due partition of power between the General and local Governments, was perhaps, of all [the objects of the convention], the most nice and difficult. A few contended for an entire abolition of the States." James Madison, letter to Thomas Jefferson, October 24, 1787, in *Letters and Other Writings of James Madison, Published by Order of Congress*, ed. Philip R. Fendall (Philadelphia: Lippincott, 1865), 348.

Alexander Hamilton was among those who appeared to advocate the annihilation of the states. Early in the convention, Hamilton avowed to "being fully convinced, that no amendment of the [Articles of] Confederation, leaving the States in possession of their Sovereignty could possibly answer the purpose [of the convention]." He argued that a "dissolution of the [States] would still leave the purposes of Gov^{t} attainable to a considerable degree." And he lamented that "[a]lmost all the weight of [governmental influence] is on the side of the States; and must continue so as long as the States continue to exist." Therefore, Hamilton continued, the power of the general government "must swallow up the State powers. Otherwise it will be swallowed up by them." He concluded that "[i]f [the States] were extinguished [a] great æconomy might be obtained by substituting a general Gov^{t}. . . . They are not necessary for any of the great purposes of commerce, revenue, or agriculture." The following day, Hamilton defended his previous comments by explaining that "[b]y an abolition of the States, he meant that no boundary could be drawn between the National & State Legislatures; that the former must have indefinite authority. If it were limited at all, the rivalship of the States would gradually subvert it. . . . As *States*, he thought they ought to be abolished." Madison, *Notes of Debates in the Federal Convention*, 129, 131, 133, 134, 152. A decade after the new national government was established, Hamilton seemed still willing to fulfill Brutus's worst expectations. In a letter to Jonathon Dayton, the Speaker of the House of Representatives, Hamilton lobbied for reorganization of the states into convenient administrative subunits, as soon as possible. See John C. Livingston, "Alexander Hamilton and the American Tradition," *Midwest Journal of Political Science* 1 (November, 1957): 209, 217.

James Madison did not merely report the anti-state tendencies of some attendees at the Constitutional Convention, but seemed himself sympathetic to the annihilation of the states. He concluded that "Supposing therefore a tendency in the Gen[l] Government to absorb the State Gov[t]s, no fatal consequences could result." Madison, *Notes of Debates in the Federal Convention*, 166. If one considers that both Hamilton and Madison—two of the most famous and influential of Federalists politicians—had already to some degree publically considered the elimination of the states, it should not surprise us to find that Brutus believed the Federalists would pursue this end once their proposed constitution was established as the supreme law of the land.

115. An Act for the Punishment of Certain Crimes against the United States, 1 Stat. 596 (1798).

116. Among other things, the Sedition Act made it a crime if "any persons shall unlawfully combine or conspire together, with intent to oppose any measure or measures of the government of the United States, which are or shall be directed by proper authority, or to impede the operation of any law of the United States, or to intimidate or prevent any person holding a place or office in or under the government of the United States, from undertaking, performing or executing his trust or duty . . . [or if] any person shall write, print, utter or publish, or shall cause or procure to be written, printed, uttered or published, or shall knowingly and willingly assist or aid in writing, printing, uttering or publishing any false, scandalous and malicious writing or writings against the government of the United States, or either house of the Congress of the United States, or the President of the United States, with intent to defame the said government, or either house of the said Congress, or the said President, or to bring them, or either of them, into contempt or disrepute; or to excite against them, or either or any of them, the hatred of the good people of the United States." Richard Peters, ed., *Public Statutes at Large of the United States of America*, vol. 1 (Boston: Little and Brown, 1850), 74.

117. "Congress shall make *no law* . . . abridging the freedom of speech, or of the press." U.S. Constitution, amend. 1 (emphasis added).

118. Craig R. Ducat and Harold W. Chase, *Constitutional Interpretation*, 5th ed. (St. Paul, Minn.: West, 1992), 903.

119. Elliot, *Debates in the Several Conventions*, 4:538, 540. The second resolution of the Kentucky Resolutions of 1798 reads: "That the Constitution of the United States, having delegated to Congress a power to punish treason, counterfeiting the securities and current coin of the United States, piracies, and felonies committed on the high seas, and offenses against the law of nations, and no other crimes, whatsoever; and it being true as a general principle, and one of the amendments to

the Constitution having also declared, that 'the powers not delegated to the United States by the Constitution, not prohibited by it to the States, are reserved to the States respectively, or to the people,' therefore the act of Congress, passed on the 14th day of July, 1798, and intituled 'An Act for the punishment of certain crimes against the United States,' as also the act passed by them on the day of June, 1798, intituled 'An Act to punish frauds committed on the bank of the United States,' (and all their other acts which assume to create, define, or punish crimes, other than those so enumerated in the Constitution,) are altogether void, and of no force; and that the power to create, define, and punish such other crimes is reserved, and, of right, appertains solely and exclusively to the respective States, each within its own territory." Elliot, *Debates in the Several Conventions*, 4:540.

120. In the Virginia Resolutions, Madison argued that "[t]hat this Assembly doth explicitly and peremptorily declare, that it views the powers of the federal government as resulting from the compact to which the states are parties, as limited by the plain sense and intention of the instrument constituting that compact, as no further valid than they are authorized by the grants enumerated in that compact; and that, in case of a deliberate, palpable, and dangerous exercise of other powers, not granted by the said compact, the states, who are parties thereto, have the right, and are in duty bound, to interpose, for arresting the progress of the evil, and for maintaining, within their respective limits, the authorities, rights and liberties, appertaining to them." Elliot, *Debates in the Several Conventions*, 4:528. In an early draft of the Kentucky Resolutions, Jefferson was more explicit, resolving "that in cases of an abuse of the delegated powers, the members of the General Government, being chosen by the people, a change by the people would be the constitutional remedy; but, where powers are assumed which have not been delegated, a nullification of the act is the rightful remedy: that every State has a natural right in cases not within the compact, (casus non foederis,) to nullify of their own authority all assumptions of power by others within their limits: that without this right, they would be under the dominion, absolute and unlimited, of whosoever might exercise this right of judgment for them." Paul Leicester Ford, ed., *The Writings of Thomas Jefferson, 1795–1801* (New York: G. P. Putnam's and Sons, 1896), 7:301. The Kentucky Resolution of 1799 (not written by Jefferson) publicly asserted what had been edited out of the 1798 final version: "Resolved, . . . That, if those who administer the general government be permitted to transgress the limits fixed by that compact, by a total disregard to the special delegations of power therein contained, an annihilation of the state governments, and the creation, upon their ruins, of a general consolidated government, will be the inevitable consequence: That the principle and construction, contended for by sundry of the state legislatures, that the general government is the exclusive judge of the extent of the powers delegated to it, stop nothing short of despotism—since the discretion of those who administer the government, and not the *Constitution*, would be the measure of their powers: That the several states who formed that instrument, being sovereign and independent, have the unquestionable right to judge of its infraction; and, *That a nullification, by those sovereignties, of all unauthorized acts done under color of that instrument, is the rightful remedy*: That this commonwealth does, under the most deliberate reconsideration, declare, that the said Alien and Sedition Laws are, in their opinion, palpable violations of the said Constitution; and however cheerfully it may be disposed to surrender its opinion to a majority of its sister states, in matters of ordinary or doubtful policy, yet,

in momentous regulations like the present, which so vitally wound the best rights of the citizen, it would consider a silent acquiescence as highly criminal." Elliot, *Debates in the Several Conventions,* 4:545 (emphasis in original).

121. Elliot, *Debates in the Several Conventions,* 4:549.

122. Elliot, *Debates in the Several Conventions,* 4:533–39.

123. Elliot, *Debates in the Several Conventions,* 4:533.

124. Elliot, *Debates in the Several Conventions,* 4:539.

125. If "Brutus" was in fact Robert Yates, he did not retire from the New York Supreme Court until 1798 and did not die until September 9, 1801.

II

CONSTITUTIONAL INTERPRETATION AND THE RULE OF LAW

5

Antonin Scalia and the Rule of Law

The Textualist Foundation of the "Law of Rules"

Ralph A. Rossum

On February 14, 1989, Justice Antonin Scalia delivered the Oliver Wendell Holmes Jr. Lecture at Harvard Law School, which he entitled "The Rule of Law as the Law of Rules."[1] This chapter explores the textualist foundations of Scalia's jurisprudence and how they are in service of the law of rules and therefore the rule of law.

Scalia argues that primacy must be accorded to the text, structure, and history of the document being interpreted and that the job of the judge is to apply the clear textual language of the Constitution or statute, or the critical structural principle necessarily implicit in the text. If the text is ambiguous, yielding several conflicting interpretations, Scalia turns to the specific legal tradition flowing from that text—to "what it meant to the society that adopted it."[2] "Text and tradition" is a phrase that fills Justice Scalia's opinions. Judges are to be governed only by the "text and tradition of the Constitution," that is, by its original meaning, not by their "intellectual, moral, and personal perceptions."[3] As he remarks in his concurring opinion in *Schad v. Arizona*: "[W]hen judges test their individual notions of 'fairness' against an American tradition that is deep and broad and continuing, it is not the tradition that is on trial, but the judges."[4]

For Scalia, reliance on text and tradition is a means of constraining judicial discretion. Scalia believes that "the main danger in judicial interpretation of the Constitution—or, for that matter, in judicial interpretation of any law—is that the judges will mistake their own predilections for the law."[5] Faithful adherence to the text of a constitutional or statutory provision or, if that is ambiguous, to the traditional understanding of those who originally adopted it, reduces the danger that judges will substitute their beliefs for society's.

Scalia fully understands that the Constitution creates two conflicting systems of rights: one is democratic—the right of the majority to rule individuals; the other is antidemocratic—the right of individuals to have certain interests protected from majority rule. He relies on the Constitution's text to define the respective spheres of majority and minority freedom, and when that fails to provide definitive guidance, Scalia turns to tradition. He argues that tradition, and not the personal values of the justices, is to tell the Court when the majoritarian process is to be overruled in favor of individual rights.[6] He believes that by identifying those areas of life traditionally protected from majority rule, the Court can objectively determine which individual freedoms the Constitution protects.[7] As he argued in his combined dissent in the companion cases of *Board of County Commissioners, Wabaunsee County v. Umbehr*[8] and *O'Hare Truck Service v. Northlake*,[9] "I would separate the permissible from the impermissible on the basis of our Nation's traditions, which is what I believe sound constitutional adjudication requires."[10]

Scalia therefore would overrule the majority only when it has infringed on an individual right explicitly protected by the text of the Constitution or by specific legal traditions flowing from that text.[11] In his dissent in *United States v. Virginia*,[12] in which the Court proclaimed that the exclusively male admission policy of the Virginia Military Institute violated the Equal Protection Clause of the Fourteenth Amendment, he declared that the function of the Court is to "preserve our society's values, not to revise them; to prevent backsliding from the degree of restriction the Constitution imposed upon democratic government, not to prescribe, on our own authority, progressively higher degrees." The Court is not to "supersede" but rather is to "reflect" those "constant and unbroken national traditions that embody the people's understanding of ambiguous constitutional texts." [13]

Scalia believes that "the rule of law [i]s the law of rules." He argues that, when the text in question embodies a rule, judges are simply to apply that rule as the law.[14] When the text and traditional understanding of that text fail to supply a rule, there is no rule, no law for judges to apply to contradict the actions of the popular branches, and therefore no warrant for judicial intervention. Thus, in *Troxel* v. *Granville*,[15] he dissented from the Supreme Court's invalidation of a Washington State statute—providing visitation rights for nonparents of a child if a judge found that it would be in the best interests of the child—on the grounds that it unconstitutionally infringed on the fundamental right of parents to rear their children. Scalia found the law offensive, declaring that, "[i]n my view, a right of parents to direct the upbringing of their children is among the 'unalienable Rights' with which the Declaration of Independence proclaims 'all Men . . . are endowed by their Creator.'"[16] But, he continued, offensive laws are not unconstitutional in the absence of clear text making them so.

> Judicial vindication of "parental rights" under a Constitution that does not even mention them requires not only a judicially crafted definition of parents, but also—unless, as no one believes, the parental rights are to be absolute—judicially approved assessments of "harm to the child" and judicially defined gradations of other persons (grandparents, extended family, adoptive family in an adoption later found to be invalid, long-term guardians, etc.) who may have some claim against the wishes of the parents. If we embrace this unenumerated right, I think it obvious . . . that we will be ushering in a new regime of judicially prescribed, and federally prescribed, family law. I have no reason to believe that federal judges will be better at this than state legislatures; and state legislatures have the great advantages of doing harm in a more circumscribed area, of being able to correct their mistakes in a flash, and of being removable by the people.[17]

Likewise, since his first term on the Court, Scalia has consistently opposed what he calls the Court's "'negative' Commerce Clause jurisprudence,"[18] which holds that the Commerce Clause of Article I, Section 8 not only grants power to Congress to regulate commerce among the states but also confers power on the Court to protect the "right to engage in interstate trade free from restrictive state regulation."[19] It holds that "the very purpose of the Commerce Clause was to create an area of free trade among the several States" and that the Clause "by *its own force* created an area of trade free from interference by the States."[20] Therefore, irrespective of whether Congress has itself acted on the basis of its delegated power to prohibit this interference, it holds that the Court is constitutionally authorized to protect this "area of free trade" and to vindicate this right to engage in interstate commerce free from state interference by weighing the burdens that state regulation of commerce imposes against the benefits it provides and invalidating all discriminatory burdens it concludes are unjustified.

Scalia has opposed this "'negative' Commerce Clause jurisprudence," first and foremost, because it has "no foundation in the text of the Constitution."[21] As he declared in *American Trucking Association v. Smith*, "The text from which we take our authority to act in this field provides only that 'Congress shall have Power . . . to regulate Commerce . . . among the several States.' It is nothing more than a grant of power to Congress, not the courts."[22] He has opposed the negative Commerce Clause as well because, as he has said, it takes the Court, "self-consciously and avowedly, beyond the judicial role itself" and casts it in an "essentially legislative role."[23] It requires the justices to weigh "the imponderable" and balance "the importance of the State's interest in this or that (an importance that different citizens would assess differently) against the degree of impairment of commerce."[24] This weighing and balancing by the Court, he argues, is often impossible for the political interests on the opposite sides of the scale are often "incommensurate." As he noted in *Bendix Autolite Corp. v. Midwesco Enterprise*, the Court is often asked to judge "whether a particular line is longer than a particular rock is heavy," a role inconsistent with its "function as the nonpolitical branch." Weighing "the governmental interests of a State against the needs of interstate commerce is," he insists, "a task squarely within the responsibility of Congress."[25]

However, Scalia's insistence that "the rule of law [i]s the law of rules" means more than merely opposing efforts by the judiciary to "prescribe, on . . . [its] own authority new rules that "supersede" the text of the Constitution or the specific legal traditions that flow from it in order to create new rights or new powers for itself; to quote again from his dissent in *United States v. Virginia*, it also means preventing "backsliding" by vigorously and courageously protecting those rights spelled out in the Constitution and ensuring that the "degree of restriction" they "impose upon democratic government" is honored by judges otherwise enamored with the idea of the "Living Constitution." As Scalia puts it in his book, *A Matter of Interpretation*:

> It certainly cannot be said that a constitution naturally suggests changeability; to the contrary, its whole purpose is to prevent change—to embed certain rights in such a manner that future generations cannot readily take them away. A society that adopts a bill of rights is skeptical that "evolving standards of decency" always "mark progress," and that societies always "mature," as opposed to rot.[26]

An excellent example of Scalia's objection to "backsliding" is his opinion for the Court in *Kyllo v. United States*.[27] *Kyllo* involved the warrantless use from a public street of a thermal-imaging device aimed at a private residence occupied by someone suspected of growing marijuana. The device detected relative amounts of heat within the residence and whether high-intensity halide lights were being used to grow marijuana indoors. Scalia found the use of the thermal imager to be "unreasonable" because it violated "that degree of privacy against government that existed when the Fourth Amendment was adopted."[28]

> [I]n the case of the search of the interior of homes—the prototypical and hence most commonly litigated area of protected privacy—there is a ready criterion, with roots deep in the common law, of the minimal expectation of privacy that *exists*, and that is acknowledged to be *reasonable*. To withdraw protection of this minimum expectation would be to permit police technology to erode the privacy guaranteed by the Fourth Amendment. We think that obtaining by sense-enhancing technology any information regarding the interior of the home that could not otherwise have been obtained without physical "intrusion into a constitutionally protected area" constitutes a search—at least where (as here) the technology in question is not in general public use. This assures preservation of that degree of privacy against government that existed when the Fourth Amendment was adopted. On the basis of this criterion, the information obtained by the thermal imager in this case was the product of a search.[29]

The Court's duty is, Scalia insisted, to prevent "advancing technology" capable of "discern[ing] all human activity in the home"[30] from "shrink[ing] the realm of guaranteed privacy."[31]

Other superb examples of Scalia's objection to "backsliding" are his opinions concerning a criminal defendant's right to trial by jury that culminate in *Blakely v. Washington*.[32] The right is clearly mentioned in the text of both Article III, Section 2, and the Sixth Amendment. As Scalia declares in his dissent in *Neder v. United States*, it is the only guarantee "to appear in both the body of the Constitution and the Bill of Rights" and is nothing less than "the spinal column of American democracy."[33] For Scalia, it also reflects "that healthy suspicion of the power of government which possessed the Framers" and which led them "to reserve the function of determining criminal guilt to [the people] themselves, sitting as jurors."[34] As he declares in his opinion for the Court in *Blakely v. Washington*, "Just as suffrage ensures the people's ultimate control in the legislative and executive branches, jury trial is meant to ensure their control in the judiciary."[35]

The right to trial by jury in a criminal case means for Scalia the right of a defendant "to have the jury determine his guilt of the crime charged [and that] necessarily means his commission of *every element* of the crime charged."[36] It also means that "absent a voluntary waiver of the jury right, the Constitution does not trust judges to make determinations of criminal guilt."[37] The judges, after all, are "officers of the Government";[38] as he says in his concurring opinion in *Apprendi v. New Jersey*, they "are part of the state—and an increasingly bureaucratic part of it, at that."[39] When it comes to depriving individuals of their liberty or their lives, the Framers were of the view that "the state should suffer the modest inconvenience of submitting its accusations to 'the unanimous suffrage of twelve of his equals and neighbors' rather than a lone employee of the state."[40]

In *Apprendi v. New Jersey*, Scalia applied these principles and held unconstitutional New Jersey's "hate-crime" statute authorizing a twenty-year sentence instead of the usual ten-year maximum if a judge found the crime to have been committed "with a purpose to intimidate . . . because of race, color, gender, handicap, religion, sexual orientation, or ethnicity." He insisted that the Sixth Amendment requires that "all the facts which must exist in order to subject the defendant to a legally prescribed punishment *must* be found by the jury."[41] In his concurring opinion in *Ring v. Arizona*, he applied his argument in *Apprendi* to an Arizona law that authorized the death penalty if the judge found there was present in the case one of ten possible aggravating factors, and concluded that the defendant's constitutional rights had been violated because the aggravating factor had been neither admitted by the defendant nor found by the jury and because the judge had imposed a sentence greater than the maximum he could have imposed without the challenged factual finding.

Apprendi and *Ring* were merely preliminary rounds to the main event: *Blakely v. Washington*. In his 2004 opinion for a five-member majority, Scalia struck down Washington's sentencing process because it allowed judges, not juries, to decide facts that resulted in enhanced sentences. As he put it, when the judge sentenced the defendant who had been found guilty by a jury of kidnapping his estranged wife to ninety months (thirty-seven months more than the fifty-three-month statutory maximum of the standard range of Washington's sentencing guidelines) because the judge found the defendant to have acted with "deliberate cruelty," the judge ordered a punishment "that the jury's verdict alone does not allow" and "exceed[ed] his proper authority."[42]

In his 1998 dissent in *Monge v. California*, Scalia had explained why it is so important that all facts—all elements of the crime—be found by the jury. He offered a hypothetical: "Suppose that a State repealed all of the violent crimes in its criminal code and replaced them with only one offense, 'knowingly causing injury to another,' bearing a penalty of 30 days in prison, but subject to a series of 'sentencing enhancements' authorizing additional punishment up to life imprisonment or death on the basis of various levels of *mens rea*, severity of injury, and other surrounding circumstances." If the state provided the defendant a jury trial, with the requirement of proof beyond a reasonable doubt, solely on the question whether the defendant "knowingly caused injury to another" but then left it up to the judge to enhance the thirty-day sentence based on the judge's own findings whether the defendant acted intentionally or accidentally and whether the victim ultimately died from the injury the defendant inflicted, would, Scalia asked, the Sixth Amendment be violated? For Scalia the answer was obvious, and he declared: "If the protections extended to criminal defendants by the Bill of Rights can be so easily circumvented, most of them would be . . . 'vain and idle enactments,'" and the Court, by upholding such a procedure, would have mapped the way to "the El Dorado sought by many in vain since the beginning of the Republic: a means of dispensing with inconvenient constitutional 'rights.'"[43]

These examples of Scalia's efforts to prevent backsliding (and many others) have been previously assessed.[44] The remainder of this chapter will focus instead on Scalia's most recent effort to prevent backsliding in his seminal interpretation of the Second Amendment in the landmark case of *District of Columbia v. Heller*.[45] It will contrast, in particular, Scalia's textualist defense of the "rule of law as the law of rules" with Justice Stephen Breyer's dissent, in which Breyer proposed what he called an "interest-balancing inquiry"[46] as his own particular road map to "El Dorado."

The Second Amendment provides: "A well regulated Militia, being necessary to the security of a free State, the right of the people to keep and bear Arms, shall not be infringed." The question before the Court in *Heller* was which of two very different interpretations of the amendment was correct.

The District of Columbia argued that, given its prefatory clause, the Second Amendment protects only a "collective right" to possess and carry a firearm in connection with militia service and that, therefore, its total ban on handguns, as well as its requirement that lawfully owned long guns in the home be kept nonfunctional even when necessary for self-defense, were constitutional. Dick Heller, a D.C. special police officer authorized to carry a handgun while on duty at the Federal Judicial Center, argued that, given its operative clause, the Second Amendment protects an "individual right" to possess a firearm unconnected with service in a militia, and to use that arm for traditionally lawful purposes, such as self-defense within the home. He had won with this argument before the Court of Appeals for the District of Columbia Circuit in *Parker v. District of Columbia*.[47] In a five-to-four decision,[48] Scalia wrote the majority opinion affirming the D.C. Circuit's ruling and declaring that "on the basis of both text and history," the Second Amendment "conferred an individual right to keep and bear arms."[49]

Scalia's majority opinion was a classic expression of his textualist jurisprudence; in it, he systematically explored the original meaning of the words in the text of the Second Amendment. He began by noting: "In interpreting this text, we are guided by the principle that '[t]he Constitution was written to be understood by the voters; its words and phrases were used in their normal and ordinary as distinguished from technical meaning.' Normal meaning may of course include an idiomatic meaning, but it excludes secret or technical meanings that would not have been known to ordinary citizens in the founding generation."[50] He then quoted its text, pointing out that it is divided into a prefatory clause and an operative clause, and remarking that "the former does not limit the latter grammatically, but rather announces a purpose."[51] He continued by stating that "logic demands that there be a link between the stated purpose and the command" and that the requirement of a logical connection can allow the prefatory clause to "resolve an ambiguity in the operative clause." (He supplied an example by offering the following statement: "The separation of church and state being an important objective, the teachings of canons shall have no place in our jurisprudence." As he explained, "The preface makes clear that the operative clause refers not to canons of interpretation but to clergymen.") But, he went on, "apart from that clarifying function, a prefatory clause does not limit or expand the scope of the operative clause."[52] Based on that understanding, he turned to a textual analysis of the operative clause, announcing he would "return to the prefatory clause to ensure that our reading of the operative clause is consistent with the announced purpose."[53]

He began with the words, "the right of the people." For him, "[t]he first salient feature of the operative clause" was that it codified the preexisting "right of the people to keep and bear arms"[54]—a preexisting right that "shall not be infringed."[55] Scalia noted that the same words, "the right of the people," are also found in the First Amendment's Assembly-and-

Petition Clause and in the Fourth Amendment's Search-and-Seizure Clause and that "very similar terminology is found in the Ninth Amendment." And, in all three of these instances, these words "unambiguously refer[red] to individual rights, not 'collective' rights, or rights that may be exercised only through participation in some corporate body."[56] Furthermore, these words "contrast[ed] markedly" with the words "the militia" in the prefatory clause. Previewing his subsequent analysis of the prefatory clause, he observed that the militia in colonial America "consisted of a subset of 'the people'—those who were male, able bodied, and within a certain age range." He was prompted to remark that "reading the Second Amendment as protecting only the right to 'keep and bear Arms' in an organized militia therefore fits poorly with the operative clause's description of the holder of that right as 'the people.'" His textual analysis of the very first words of the operative clause led him to conclude, therefore, that there is "a strong presumption that the Second Amendment right is exercised individually and belongs to all Americans."[57]

He then turned to the words "keep and bear arms." As he analyzed these words, he did in *Heller* what he has done so often throughout his judicial career when seeking insight into the original meaning of constitutional language: he turned to dictionaries of the era.[58] Thus, concerning the meaning of the word, "arms," he found that "[t]he 1773 edition of Samuel Johnson's dictionary defined 'arms' as 'weapons of offence, or armour of defence.' *Dictionary of the English Language* 107 (4th ed.). Timothy Cunningham's important 1771 legal dictionary defined 'arms' as 'anything that a man wears for his defence, or takes into his hands, or useth in wrath to cast at or strike another.' *A New and Complete Law Dictionary* (1771); see also N. Webster, *American Dictionary of the English Language* (1828) (similar)." His conclusion: "The term was applied, then as now, to weapons that were not specifically designed for military use and were not employed in a military capacity."[59]

Concerning the word "keep," he noted that "Johnson defined 'keep' as, most relevantly, '[t]o retain; not to lose,' and '[t]o have in custody.' Johnson 1095. Webster defined it as '[t]o hold; to retain in one's power or possession.' No party has apprised us of an idiomatic meaning of 'keep Arms.' Thus, the most natural reading of 'keep arms' in the Second Amendment is to 'have weapons.'"[60]

And, concerning the word "bear," he reported that "[a]t the time of the founding, as now, to 'bear' meant to 'carry.' See Johnson 161; Webster; T. Sheridan, *A Complete Dictionary of the English Language* (1796); 2 Oxford English Dictionary 20 (2d ed. 1989). When used with 'arms,' however, the term has a meaning that refers to carrying for a particular purpose—confrontation." For Scalia, "the natural meaning" of "bear arms" was the "carrying of the weapon for the purpose of 'offensive or defensive action,'" without any connotation of "participation in a structured military organization."[61]

The issue, however, was complicated by the fact that, unlike the phrase "keep arms," the phrase "bear arms" also had at the time of the Founding "an idiomatic meaning that was significantly different from its natural meaning: 'to serve as a soldier, do military service, fight' or 'to wage war.'" Justice Stevens made much of this idiomatic meaning in his dissent, as he advanced his argument that the Second Amendment protects only the right to possess and carry firearms in connection with militia service.[62] But as Scalia noted, the phrase "bear arms" bore that idiomatic meaning "only when followed by the preposition 'against,' which was in turn followed by the target of the hostilities. See 2 Oxford 21. (That is how, for example, our Declaration of Independence used the phrase: 'He has constrained our fellow Citizens taken Captive on the high Seas to bear Arms against their Country. . . .')" And, he continued, "Every example given by petitioners' amici for the idiomatic meaning of 'bear arms' from the founding period either includes the preposition 'against' or is not clearly idiomatic."[63]

Putting together "all of these textual elements" in the operative clause, Scalia confidently concluded "that they guarantee the individual right to possess and carry weapons in case of confrontation." He then moved from text to tradition and found this meaning "strongly confirmed"[64] by "the historical background" of the amendment, including language found in the English Bill of Rights and Blackstone's *Commentaries* and employed by the pamphleteers of the American Revolution.[65] But, before proceeding, Scalia turned to a textual analysis of the prefatory clause, to determine whether it "comports with our interpretation of the operative clause."[66]

He began with the words "well-regulated militia." He noted that in *United States v. Miller*,[67] the Court had defined the militia as comprising "all males physically capable of acting in concert for the common defense." He found that definition to comport with Founding-era sources, quoting from Webster, *The Federalist*, and Jefferson. He rejected the argument of the District of Columbia and Justice Stevens in dissent that the militia were the state and congressionally organized military forces described in the Militia Clauses, that is, Article I, Section 8, Clauses 15–16. Giving each word its due, he noted that "unlike armies and navies, which Congress is given the power to create ('to raise . . . Armies'; 'to provide . . . a Navy'), the militia is assumed by Article I already to be *in existence*. Congress is given the power to 'provide for calling forth the militia' and the power not to create, but to 'organiz[e]' it—and not to organize 'a' militia, which is what one would expect if the militia were to be a federal creation, but to organize 'the militia, connoting a body already in existence." This, he continued, was "fully consistent with the ordinary definition of the militia as all able-bodied men." That meaning was not altered by the adjective "well-regulated," which dictionaries of the era make clear "implied nothing more than the imposition of proper discipline and training."[68]

He continued with the phrase "security of a free state," which he said meant simply the "security of a free polity," not the security of each of the several states as Judge Karen L. Henderson had argued in her dissent in *Parker*.[69] With regard to why the militia was thought to be "necessary to the security of a free state," Scalia offered three reasons, all connected to the traditional understanding of the relation of the militia to republican government: "First, of course, it is useful in repelling invasions and suppressing insurrections. Second, it renders large standing armies unnecessary. . . . Third, when the able-bodied men of a nation are trained in arms and organized, they are better able to resist tyranny."[70]

With the words of the prefatory clause thus defined, Scalia then asked whether they "fit with an operative clause that creates an individual right to keep and bear arms[.]" His answer: "It fits perfectly, once one knows the history that the founding generation knew." That history, he continued, shows "that the way tyrants had eliminated a militia consisting of all the able-bodied men was not by banning the militia but simply by taking away the people's arms, enabling a select militia or standing army to suppress political opponents." For Scalia, it was "therefore entirely sensible that the Second Amendment's prefatory clause announces the purpose for which the right was codified: to prevent elimination of the militia." But, he continued, "[t]he prefatory clause does not suggest that preserving the militia was the only reason Americans valued the ancient right; most undoubtedly thought it even more important for self-defense and hunting." As he explained, the preexisting "right of the people to keep and bear arms" was codified in the Constitution (including the right to self defense, which he described as "the central component of the right itself") not because of worries that the right to self-defense would be taken away but because of worries that "the new Federal Government would destroy the citizens' militia by taking away their arms."[71]

Scalia then proceeded to show how his interpretation was "confirmed by analogous arms-bearing rights in state constitutions that preceded and immediately followed adoption of the Second Amendment;[72] by postratification commentary from "St. George Tucker's version of Blackstone's *Commentaries*,"[73] William Rawle,[74] and Joseph Story's "famous *Commentaries*, in which the English right in the English Bill of Rights was equated with the Second Amendment";[75] by pre–Civil War case law "that interpreted the Second Amendment universally [in] support [of] an individual right unconnected to militia service";[76] by post–Civil War legislation;[77] and by post–Civil War commentators, "the most famous"[78] of which was Thomas McIntyre Cooley who had declared: "Among the other defences to personal liberty should be mentioned the right of the people to keep and bear arms."[79]

He finished by confirming that his interpretation was also consistent with precedent. The only perceived precedent promoted by the District of Columbia and Justice Stevens in his dissent as contrary to Scalia's "individual rights" interpretation was *United States v. Miller*. According to Justice

Stevens, the Court in *Miller* held that the Second Amendment "protects the right to keep and bear arms for certain military purposes, but that it does not curtail the legislature's power to regulate the nonmilitary use and ownership of weapons."[80] But, as Scalia pointed out:

> Nothing so clearly demonstrates the weakness of Justice Stevens' case. *Miller* did not hold that and cannot possibly be read to have held that. The judgment in the case . . . is not only consistent with, but positively suggests, that the Second Amendment confers an individual right to keep and bear arms (though only arms that "have some reasonable relationship to the preservation or efficiency of a well regulated militia"). Had the Court believed that the Second Amendment protects only those serving in the militia; it would have been odd to examine the character of the weapon [in this case, a sawed-off shotgun] rather than simply note that the two crooks [in this case, the two defendants] were not militiamen.[81]

He concluded, therefore, that "nothing in our precedents forecloses our adoption of the original understanding of the Second Amendment,"[82] that is, that it conferred an individual right to keep and bear arms.

Scalia readily conceded that the right secured by the Second Amendment, "like most rights," is "not unlimited." It is "not a right to keep and carry any weapon whatsoever in any manner whatsoever and for whatever purpose."[83] He gave a list of examples that he was quick to assert was not "exhaustive":[84] "[N]othing in our opinion should be taken to cast doubt on longstanding prohibitions on the possession of firearms by felons and the mentally ill, or laws forbidding the carrying of firearms in sensitive places such as schools and government buildings, or laws imposing conditions and qualifications on the commercial sale of arms."[85] He then acknowledged "another important limitation on the right to keep and carry arms." Scalia found persuasive *Miller*'s explanation "that the sorts of weapons protected were those 'in common use at the time.' We think that limitation is fairly supported by the historical tradition of prohibiting the carrying of 'dangerous and unusual weapons.'" As he noted, "[T]he conception of the militia at the time of the Second Amendment's ratification was the body of all citizens capable of military service, who would bring the sorts of lawful weapons that they possessed at home to militia duty."[86]

Scalia finally turned to the District of Columbia's total ban on handgun possession in the home and its requirement that any lawful long gun in the home be disassembled or bound by a trigger lock at all times and considered them in light of the Second Amendment's "inherent right of self-defense." The handgun ban amounted to "a prohibition of an entire class of 'arms' that is overwhelmingly chosen by American society for that lawful purpose." Moreover, the prohibition extended "to the home, where the need for defense of self, family, and property is most acute." Scalia refused to apply either intermediate or strict scrutiny but declared that under "any of the standards of scrutiny that we have applied to enumerated constitutional rights, banning from the home 'the most preferred firearm in the nation to keep and use for protection of one's home and family' would fail constitutional muster."[87]

Scalia also rejected the District's argument that the possession of handguns could be banned so long as the possession of long guns was allowed. The handgun, he noted, is "the quintessential self-defense weapon," and there are reasons for that: "It is easier to store in a location that is readily accessible in an emergency; it cannot easily be redirected or wrestled away by an attacker; it is easier to use for those without the upper-body strength to lift and aim a long gun; it can be pointed at a burglar with one hand while the other hand dials the police." But, he continued, whatever the reasons, handguns "are the most popular weapon chosen by Americans for self-defense in the home, and a complete prohibition of their use is invalid."[88] And he rejected the District of Columbia's requirement that long guns in the home be rendered and kept inoperable at all times. "This makes it impossible for citizens to use them for the core lawful purpose of self-defense and is hence unconstitutional."[89] He concluded with a classic Scalia finale: "[T]he enshrinement of constitutional rights necessarily takes certain policy choices off the table. These include the absolute prohibition of handguns held and used for self-defense in the home. Undoubtedly some think that the Second Amendment is outmoded in a society where our standing army is the pride of our Nation, where well-trained police forces provide personal security, and where gun violence is a serious problem. That is perhaps debatable, but what is not debatable is that it is not the role of this Court to pronounce the Second Amendment extinct."[90] Scalia had delivered a towering "text and tradition" opinion.

There were two dissents: Justice Stevens wrote the first, in which he gave his own textualist reading of the amendment or, more precisely, its prefatory clause. It is an opinion that highlights the perils of those who attempt to employ that approach disingenuously; it concludes that

> [t]he Second Amendment was adopted to protect the right of the people of each of the several States to maintain a well-regulated militia. It was a response to concerns raised during the ratification of the Constitution that the power of Congress to disarm the state militias and create a national standing army posed an intolerable threat to the sovereignty of the several States. Neither the text of the Amendment nor the arguments advanced by its proponents evidenced the slightest interest in limiting any legislature's authority to regulate private civilian uses of firearms. Specifically, there is no indication that the Framers of the Amendment intended to enshrine the common-law right of self-defense in the Constitution.[91]

Stevens, however, failed to address—much less answer—a trenchant question posed by Chief Justice Roberts during oral argument: "If the

Second Amendment . . . is limited to State militias, why would they [the members of the First Congress] say 'the right of the people' [in the operative clause]? In other words, why wouldn't they say 'state militias have the right to keep arms'?"[92]

He also failed to explain why "the right of the people to keep and bear arms" in the Second Amendment is a collective right, while "the right of the people to . . . petition the government for a redress of grievances" in the First Amendment and "the right of the people to be secure in their persons, houses, papers, and effects" in the Fourth Amendment are individual rights.

Additionally, he failed to explain why James Madison, when he submitted a series of amendments in the First Congress that ultimately became the Bill of Rights, proposed placing the Second Amendment in Article I, Section 9 of the Constitution. To understand his failure, some background is essential here.

Madison intended for his set of amendments to be incorporated into the text of the original Constitution—not appended at the end. He explained why: "[T]here is a neatness and propriety in incorporating the amendments into the Constitution itself; in that case the system will remain uniform and entire; it will certainly be more simple, when the amendments are interwoven into those parts to which they naturally belong, than it will if they consist of separate and distinct parts. We shall then be able to determine its meaning without references or comparison."[93] Madison failed, however, to persuade his colleagues to do so. Roger Sherman successfully argued that the amendments should be added at the end of the Constitution, as any attempt to "interweave" these amendments into the Constitution itself would "be destructive of the whole fabric. We might as well endeavor to mix brass, iron, and clay."[94]

Had Madison prevailed in his efforts to incorporate the amendments into the text of the Constitution itself, "the right of the people to keep and bear arms" would have been included in Article I, Section 9 alongside other provisions securing individual rights including the habeas corpus privilege and the proscriptions against bills of attainder and ex post facto laws and would have been there together with his proposed protections for speech, press, and assembly. Yet Stevens argued that what became the Second Amendment was intended by Madison merely to amend the Militia Clauses of Article I, Section 8, Clauses 15 and 16. If that had in fact been Madison's intention, he would have proposed placing the Second Amendment there and not in Article I, Section 9.

And, it is not that Stevens was unaware of what happened in the First Congress. The Respondent's Brief expressly made this argument.[95] So did Solicitor General Paul D. Clement during oral argument in response to a question from Stevens: "[I]f the Second Amendment had the meaning that the District of Columbia ascribes to it, one would certainly think that James Madison, when he proposed the Second Amendment would have proposed it as an amendment to Article I, Section 8, Clause 16. He didn't. He proposed it as an amendment to Article I, Section 9, which encapsulates the individual rights to be free from bills of attainder and ex post facto clauses."[96]

This "placement" argument is powerful, but Scalia never uses it in his majority opinion to refute Stevens's claim. Scalia's textualism keeps him from consulting any form of "legislative history" (including the debates in the Constitutional Convention or the work of the First Congress),[97] even when doing so would have allowed him to expose Stevens's false textualism.

One final word on Stevens's dissent: His preoccupation with the prefatory clause and his disregard for the operative clause's language of the "right of the people to keep and bear arms" should also give pause to anyone who holds a copyright or patent. After all, Article I, Section 8, Clause 8 grants Congress power "[t]o promote the Progress of Science and useful Arts, by securing for limited Times to Authors and Inventors the exclusive Right to their respective Writings and Discoveries." Until Stevens's opinion, writers and inventors did not have to fear that their copyrights and patents protected by the clause's operative language might be unenforceable because they fail to "promote the Progress of Science and useful Arts" as spelled out in the clause's prefatory language. For example, Justice Stevens might well find unworthy of protection, because not promoting anything he would find useful, this very chapter.

Justice Breyer wrote the second dissent. While he joined completely in Stevens's dissent, he wrote separately to "show that the District's law is consistent with the Second Amendment even if that Amendment is interpreted as protecting a wholly separate interest in individual self-defense." That is so, he argued, "because the District's regulation, which focuses upon the presence of handguns in high-crime urban areas, represents a permissible legislative response to a serious, indeed life-threatening, problem."[98] He engaged in what he called "an interest-balancing inquiry" because "important interests [lay] on both sides of the constitutional equation." For him, the D.C. handgun ban "significantly implicate[d] competing constitutionally protected interests in complex ways," and, therefore, the Court majority should have asked "whether the statute burdens a protected interest [i.e., the right of personal self-defense] in a way or to an extent that is out of proportion to the statute's salutary effects upon other important governmental interests."[99]

Just as Scalia's majority opinion tracked the approach to constitutional interpretation he advanced in *A Matter of Interpretation*, so, too, Breyer's dissent reflected his approach to constitutional interpretation as laid out in his book, *Active Liberty*.[100] In it, Breyer argued that liberty is more than "freedom from governmental coercion"; it is also the more important "freedom to participate in government itself"—what he called "active liberty."[101] And, while he acknowledged that active liberty can place in jeopardy "the individual's right to freedom from the majority," he nonetheless urged his fellow judges to "take greater account of the Constitution's democratic nature" when interpreting the Constitution."[102] Breyer asserted that the "primary objective" of the Constitution was to create "a form of government in which all citizens share the governmental authority, participating in the creation of public policy."[103]

In *Active Liberty*, Breyer interpreted the First Amendment against that "primary objective." The First Amendment "seek[s] primarily to encourage exchange of information and ideas necessary for citizens themselves to shape that 'public opinion which is the final source of government in a democratic society.'" Campaign finance laws, he noted, "seek to further a similar objective," by "broadening the base of a candidate's meaningful financial support, and encouraging greater public participation." Breyer therefore argued that "insofar as they achieve these objectives, those laws, despite the limits they impose [on free speech], will help to further the kind of open public discussion that the First Amendment seeks to sustain, both as an end and as a mean of achieving a workable democracy."[104]

For Breyer, at the end of the day, everything depends on "consequences."[105] Directly responding to Scalia's textualist argument in *A Matter of Interpretation*, Breyer asserted that "[w]hatever 'subjectivity-limiting' benefits a more literal, textual, or originalist approach may bring, and I believe those benefits are small, it will also bring with it serious accompanying consequentialist harm."[106] So, with regard to the First Amendment, its protection of free political speech that begins with the words, "Congress shall make no Law," must yield to Congress's interest in broadening the base of a candidate's meaningful financial support and encouraging greater public participation when it passed the Bipartisan Campaign Reform Act. In *Active Liberty*, Breyer laid out for all to see his "consequentalist" map to "El Dorado."

In his *Heller* dissent, he follows the map to "El Dorado" that he laid out in *Active Liberty* regarding the First Amendment. What were the "consequences" of interpreting the Second Amendment to protect the inherent right of individuals "to keep and bear arms"? For Breyer, they were intolerable: they would make "saving lives, preventing injury, and reducing crime" more difficult.[107] So, despite its express words, Breyer argued that the Second Amendment had to yield to the public-safety judgment of the City Council of the District of Columbia when in 1976 it banned the possession of handguns and required that all lawfully owned long guns in the home be kept nonfunctional even when necessary for self-defense. There was, he insisted, "no less restrictive way to achieve the problem-related benefits that it seeks."[108]

If the Second Amendment protects an individual right to gun ownership, as Breyer was willing to accept *arguendo*, but if that right can be trumped by the consequences of a "public-safety" exception as determined by local politicians and justices affirming them, then what is the value of the Second Amendment? How does Breyer's "interest-balancing inquiry" prevent "backsliding" and protect the principle of the law of rules? At the end of the day, what value does a written constitution have for Breyer if it can be revised by Supreme Court justices doing their own balancing of interests? Active liberty requires no written constitution and is, in fact, rendered impossible by one. Protection from majority tyranny does, however, require a written constitution, as Madison, the Framers, and Scalia all well knew. Scalia's "rule of law as the law of rules" rebuttal to Breyer's argument was devastating: "A constitutional guarantee subject to future judges' assessments of its usefulness is no constitutional guarantee at all. Constitutional rights are enshrined with the scope they were understood to have when the people adopted them, whether or not future legislatures or (yes) even future judges think that scope too broad." The First Amendment, Scalia insisted, protects against backsliding when it comes to "the expression of extremely unpopular and wrong-headed views," and "the Second Amendment is no different."[109] Scalia shredded Breyer's map to El Dorado, reducing it to confetti.

A. V. Dicey, in his *Introduction to the Study of the Law of the Constitution*, describes the "rule of law" as containing three key principles: (1) "It means, to begin with, the absolute supremacy or predominance of regular law as opposed to the influence of arbitrary power, and excludes the existence of arbitrariness, of prerogative, or even of wide discretionary authority on the part of the government"; (2) "It means, again, equality before the law, or the equal subjection of all classes to the ordinary law of the land administered by the ordinary Law Courts"; and (3) "The rule of law, lastly, may be used as a formula for expressing the fact that with us . . . the constitution . . . [is] not the source but the consequence of the rights of individuals."[110] Scalia's textualist opinion in *Heller* perfectly captured all three of these key principles of the rule of law as Dicey defined them.

First, Scalia gave primacy to the text of the Second Amendment and rejected out of hand Breyer's claim that judges should exercise their discretionary authority and employ their worries about the consequences for public safety of invalidating D.C.'s handgun ban as a justification for "dispensing with inconvenient constitutional 'rights.'"[111] Second, he ensured that "all Americans" were equally protected in their "inherent right of self-defense" by having access to the "quintessential self-defense weapon," the handgun; he denied that it was limited simply to those with "the upper-body strength to lift and aim a long gun." And third, he observed that the Second Amendment speaks of a preexisting right of the people to keep and bear arms that shall not be infringed, noting that this right was neither granted by the Constitution nor was it in any manner dependent on that instrument for its existence. For Scalia, the Second Amendment was a law of rules to be enforced, and by faithfully adhering to its text, Scalia contributed, as he has so often, to the rule of law.

NOTES

1. Antonin Scalia, "The Rule of Law as the Law of Rules," *University of Chicago Law Review* 56 (1989): 1175.

2. "What I do when I interpret the American Constitution is, I try to understand what it meant, what was understood by the society to mean when it was adopted. And I don't think it changes since then." "Transcript of Discussion between U.S. Supreme Court Justices Antonin Scalia and Stephen Breyer," American University, Washington College of Law, January 13, 2005, 12.

3. *Callins v. Collins*, 510 U .S. 1141 (1994).

4. 501 U.S. 624, 650 (1991).

5. Antonin Scalia, "Originalism: The Lesser Evil," 57 *University of Cincinnati Law Review* (1989): 857.

6. "[U]nder either the procedural component or the so-called 'substantive' component of the Due Process Clause[, i]t is precisely the historical practices that *define* what is 'due.'" *Schad v. Arizona*, 501 U.S. at 650 (emphasis in original).

7. The meanings of those constitutional provisions that are ambiguous are not fixed in time; tradition can evolve, and, for Scalia, the appropriate way for such evolution to take place is through the people via their elected state legislatures and Congress. As he says in *Burnham v. Superior Court*, 495 U.S. 604, 627 (1990): "The difference between [me] and Justice Brennan has nothing to do with whether 'further progress [is] to be made' in the 'evolution of our legal system.' It has to do with whether changes are to be adopted as progressive by the American people or decreed as progressive by the Justices of this Court."

8. 518 U.S. 668 (1996).

9. 518 U.S. 712 (1996).

10. 518 U.S. 695.

11. Timothy Raschke Shattuck, "Justice Scalia's Due Process Methodology: Examining Specific Traditions," *Southern California Law Review* 65 (1992): 2743, 2776–78.

12. 518 U.S. 515 (1996).

13. 518 U.S. 568. See Scalia/Breyer Transcript, 13. Commenting on the phrase, "the evolving standards of decency that mark the progress of a maturing society," Scalia declared: "I detest that phrase, because I'm afraid that societies don't always mature. Sometimes they rot. What makes you think that human progress is one upwardly inclined plane [and that] every day and every way we get better and better? It seems to me that the purpose of the Bill of Rights was to prevent change, not to encourage it, and to have it written into the Constitution."

14. See Antonin Scalia, *A Matter of Interpretation: Federal Courts and the Law* (Princeton, N.J.: Princeton University Press, 1997), 22: "The text is the law, and it is the text that must be observed."

15. 530 U.S. 57 (2000).

16. 530 U.S. 91.

17. 530 U.S. 92–93.

18. *American Trucking Association v. Smith*, 496 U.S. 167, 202 (1990). The negative Commerce Clause is more typically known as the "dormant Commerce Clause."

19. *Dennis v. Higgins*, 498 U.S. 439, 448 (1991).

20. *Westinghouse Electric Corp. v. Tully*, 466 U.S. 388, 402–3 (1984) (emphasis added).

21. *Pharmaceutical Research and Manufacturers Association of America v. Walsh*, 538 U.S. 644, 674 (2003). See also *Tyler Pipe Industries v. Washington State Department of Revenue*, 483 U.S. 232, 254 (1987); *American Trucking Association v. Smith*, 496 U.S. 202; *State of Wyoming v. State of Oklahoma*, 502 U.S. 437, 469 (1992); and *Oklahoma Tax Commission v. Jefferson Lines*, 514 U.S. 175, 200 (1995). See also Scalia, "The Rule of Law as the Rule of Laws," 1185.

22. 496 U.S. 202.

23. As Scalia says in "The Rule of Law as the Rule of Laws," 1185: "The [negative commerce clause] can only be adjudged by a standardless balancing, and so I am not inclined to find an invitation for such judicial enforcement within Article I of the Constitution."

24. 496 U.S. 202, 203.

25. 486 U.S. 888, 906 (1988). See also *Quill Corporation v. North Dakota*, 504 U.S. 298, 320 (1992). Scalia's sustained attack on the negative Commerce Clause has had little or no impact thus far. His criticisms of it have typically occurred in solitary dissents or concurrences in the judgments of the Court.

26. Scalia, *A Matter of Interpretation*, 40–41.

27. 533 U.S. 27 (2001).

28. 533 U.S. 34.

29. 533 U.S. 40 (emphasis in original). See also Scalia's concurring opinion in *Minnesota v. Dickerson*, 508 U.S. 366, 379 (1993): "I take it to be a fundamental principle of constitutional adjudication that the terms in the Constitution must be given the meaning ascribed to them at the time of their ratification. Thus, when the Fourth Amendment provides that 'the right of the people to be secure in their persons, houses, papers, and effects, against unreasonable searches and seizures, shall not be violated,' it 'is to be construed in the light of what was deemed an unreasonable search and seizure when it was adopted.' The purpose of the provision, in other words, is to preserve the degree of respect for the privacy of persons and the inviolability of their property that existed when the provision was adopted—even if a later, less virtuous age should become accustomed to considering all sorts of intrusion 'reasonable.'"

30. 533 U.S. 35–36.

31. 533 U.S. 34. As he declares, "Where, as here, the Government uses a device that is not in general public use, to explore details of the home that would previously have been unknowable without physical intrusion, the surveillance is a "search" and is presumptively unreasonable without a warrant." 533 U.S. at 40.

32. 542 U.S. 296 (2004).

33. 527 U.S. 1, 30 (1999).

34. 527 U.S. 32.

35. 542 U.S. 306.

36. 527 U.S. 30 (emphasis in original). See also his concurrence in the judgment in *Yates v. Evatt*, 500 U.S. 391, 414 (1991); his opinion for the Court in *Sullivan v. Louisiana*, 508 U.S. 275, 280 (1993); and his opinion for the Court in *United States v. Gaudin*, 515 U.S. 506, 511 (1995).

37. 527 U.S. 32.

38. 527 U.S. 32.

39. 530 U.S. 466, 498 (2000).

40. *Blakely v. Washington*, 542 U.S. 313–14.

41. 530 U.S. 499 (emphasis in original).

42. 542 U.S. 304.

43. 524 U.S. 721, 740 (1998).

44. See Ralph A. Rossum, *Antonin Scalia's Jurisprudence: Text and Tradition* (Lawrence: University Press of Kansas, 2006). Consider, for example, Scalia's insistence that the rule of law required full adherence to the original meaning of the text of the Fourth Amendment—*County of Riverside v. McLaughlin*, 500 U.S. 44 (1991) and *National Treasury Employees Union v. Von Raab*, 489 U.S. 656, 681 (1989); the Sixth Amendment's Confrontation Clause—*Coy v. Iowa*, 487 U.S. 1012 (1988), *Craig v. Maryland*, 497 U.S. 836 (1990), and *Crawford v. Washington*, 541 U.S. 36 (2004); and the Fourteenth Amendment's Due Process Clause—*Rogers v. Tennessee*, 532 U.S. 451 (2001).

45. 128 S. Ct. at 2783 (2008).

46. 128 S. Ct. at 2852.

47. 478 F.3d 370, 401 (2007).

48. Joining Justice Scalia's majority opinion were Chief Justice Roberts and Justices Kennedy, Thomas, and Alito. There were two dissents in *Heller*: one by Justice Stevens, who was joined by Justices Souter, Ginsburg, and Breyer; the other by Justice Breyer, who was joined by Justices Stevens, Souter, and Ginsburg.

49. 128 S. Ct. at 2799.

50. 128 S. Ct. at 2788.

51. 128 S. Ct. at 2789.

52. 128 S. Ct. at 2789.

53. 128 S. Ct. at 2789. He parried Justice Stevens's criticism in dissent that since the prefatory clause comes first, it should be discussed first, by noting that "if a prologue can be used only to clarify an ambiguous operative provision, surely the first step must be to determine whether the operative provision is ambiguous." 128 S. Ct. at 2789n4.

54. 128 S. Ct. at 2790.

55. 128 S. Ct. at 2797. Later in his opinion, Scalia cites the following passage from *United States v. Cruikshank*, 92 U.S. 542, 553, 23 L. Ed. 588 (1876): "This is not a right granted by the Constitution. Neither is it in any manner dependent upon that instrument for its existence. The Second Amendment declares that it shall not be infringed." 128 S. Ct. at 2797–98.

56. 128 S. Ct. at 2790.

57. 128 S. Ct. at 2791.

58. See Rossum, *Antonin Scalia's Jurisprudence*, 217.

59. 128 S. Ct. at 2791.

60. 128 S. Ct. at 2792. "'Keep arms' was simply a common way of referring to possessing arms, for militiamen and everyone else." 128 S. Ct. at 2792.

61. 128 S. Ct. at 2793. Scalia continued: "From our review of founding-era sources, we conclude that this natural meaning was also the meaning that 'bear arms' had in the 18th century. In numerous instances, 'bear arms' was unambiguously used to refer to the carrying of weapons outside of an organized militia. The most prominent examples are those most relevant to the Second Amendment: Nine state constitutional provisions written in the 18th century or the first two decades of the 19th, which enshrined a right of citizens to 'bear arms in defense of themselves

and the state' or 'bear arms in defense of himself and the state. It is clear from those formulations that 'bear arms' did not refer only to carrying a weapon in an organized military unit." 128 S. Ct. at 2793.

62. 128 S. Ct. at 2828.

63. 128 S. Ct. at 2794.

64. 128 S. Ct. at 2797.

65. 128 S. Ct. at 2798–99.

66. 128 S. Ct. at 2798–99.

67. 307 U.S. 174, 179 (1939).

68. 128 S. Ct. at 2800 (emphasis in the original).

69. 478 F. 3d, at 405.

70. 128 S. Ct. at 2800–2801.

71. 128 S. Ct. at 2801.

72. 128 S. Ct. at 2802.

73. "This may be considered as the true palladium of liberty. . . . The right to self-defence is the first law of nature: in most governments it has been the study of rulers to confine the right within the narrowest limits possible. Wherever standing armies are kept up, and the right of the people to keep and bear arms is, under any colour or pretext whatsoever, prohibited, liberty, if not already annihilated, is on the brink of destruction." 128 S. Ct. at 2805.

74. William Rawle, *A View of the Constitution of the United States of America* (Philadelphia: H. C. Carey & I. Lea, 1825), 121–22: "No clause in the constitution could by any rule of construction be conceived to give to congress a power to disarm the people. Such a flagitious attempt could only be made under some general pretence by a state legislature. But if in any blind pursuit of inordinate power, either should attempt it, this amendment may be appealed to as a restraint on both." 128 S. Ct. at 2806.

75. Story's *Commentaries* also cite as support Tucker and Rawle, both of whom clearly viewed the right as unconnected to militia service. See 3 Story § 1890, n. 2; § 1891, n. 3. 128 S. Ct. at 2806–7. See 128 S. Ct. at 2807.

76. Scalia cited *Houston v. Moore*, 18 U.S. 1 (1820), *Johnson v. Tompkins*, 13 F. Cas. 840, 850, 852, (CC Pa. 1833), *Aldridge v. Commonwealth*, 4 Va. 447 (Gen. Ct.), *Waters v. State*, 1 Gill 302, 309 (Md. 1843), *Nunn v. State*, 1 Ga. 243, 251 (1846), and *State v. Chandler*, 5 La. Ann. 489, 490 (1850). See 128 S. Ct. at 2808–9.

77. "A Report of the Commission of the Freedmen's Bureau in 1866 stated plainly: "[T]he civil law [of Kentucky] prohibits the colored man from bearing arms. . . . Their arms are taken from them by the civil authorities. . . . Thus, the right of the people to keep and bear arms as provided in the Constitution is infringed." H. R. Exec. Doc. No. 70, 39th Cong., 1st Sess., 233, 236. 128 S. Ct. at 2810. Scalia offered an important insight: "Since those discussions took place 75 years after the ratification of the Second Amendment they do not provide as much insight into its original meaning as earlier sources. Yet those born and educated in the early 19th century faced a widespread effort to limit arms ownership by a large number of citizens; their understanding of the origins and continuing significance of the Amendment is instructive." 128 S. Ct. at 2810.

78. 128 S. Ct. at 2811.

79. 128 S. Ct. at 2811. The passage is from Thomas McIntyre Cooley, *Treatise on Constitutional Limitations* (Boston: Little, Brown and Company, 1868), 350.

80. 128 S. Ct. at 2823.
81. 128 S. Ct. at 2814.
82. 128 S. Ct. at 2816.
83. 128 S. Ct. at 2816. Scalia had introduced this understanding earlier in his opinion: The Second Amendment "right was not unlimited, just as the First Amendment's right of free speech was not. Thus, we do not read the Second Amendment to protect the right of citizens to carry arms for any sort of confrontation, just as we do not read the First Amendment to protect the right of citizens to speak for any purpose." 128 S. Ct. at 2799.
84. 128 S. Ct. at 2817, n. 26.
85. 128 S. Ct. at 2816–17.
86. 128 S. Ct. at 2817. Scalia provided an important insight into his textualist, original-meaning approach to constitutional interpretation when he observed that "[i]t may be objected that if weapons that are most useful in military service—M-16 rifles and the like—may be banned, then the Second Amendment right is completely detached from the prefatory clause. But as we have said, the conception of the militia at the time of the Second Amendment's ratification was the body of all citizens capable of military service, who would bring the sorts of lawful weapons that they possessed at home to militia duty. It may well be true today that a militia, to be as effective as militias in the 18th century, would require sophisticated arms that are highly unusual in society at large. Indeed, it may be true that no amount of small arms could be useful against modern-day bombers and tanks. But the fact that modern developments have limited the degree of fit between the prefatory clause and the protected right cannot change our interpretation of the right."
87. 128 S. Ct. at 2817–18.
88. 128 S. Ct. at 2818.
89. 128 S. Ct. at 2818.
90. 128 S. Ct. at 2822.
91. 128 S. Ct. at 2822. See also his statement that "the Amendment is most naturally read to secure to the people a right to use and possess arms in conjunction with service in a well-regulated militia. So far as appears, no more than that was contemplated by its drafters or is encompassed within its terms." 128 S. Ct. at 2831.
92. Official Transcript of Oral Argument in *District of Columbia v. Heller*, U.S. Supreme Court, March 18, 2008, 4.
93. Speech in the House of Representatives, August 13, 1789, in *Debates of the Congress of the United States*, vol. 1, 736.
94. Speech in the House of Representatives, August 13, 1789, in *Debates of the Congress of the United States*, vol. 1, 734.
95. Respondent's Brief, *District of Columbia v. Heller*, 32.
96. Official Transcript of Oral Argument in *District of Columbia v. Heller*, 31–32.
97. See Rossum, *Antonin Scalia's Jurisprudence*, 37–44.
98. 128 S. Ct. at 2847.
99. 128 S. Ct. at 2852.
100. Stephen Breyer, *Active Liberty: Interpreting Our Democratic Constitution* (New York: Alfred A. Knopf, 2005).
101. Breyer, *Active Liberty*, 3–4.
102. Breyer, *Active Liberty*, 5
103. Breyer, *Active Liberty*, 33.

104. Breyer, *Active Liberty*, 47.
105. Breyer, *Active Liberty*, 121.
106. Breyer, *Active Liberty*, 131.
107. 128 S. Ct. at 2847.
108. 128 S. Ct. at 2866. Contrast Breyer's embrace of the intermediate-level review of constitutional rights with Scalia's assertion that the D.C. handgun ban and gun-lock provisions fail both intermediate review and strict scrutiny. 128 S. Ct. at 2817–18.
109. 128 S. Ct. at 2821. Interestingly, Breyer never mentions—neither in *Active Liberty* nor in his dissent in *Heller*—Article V, the Amendment Article, an obvious way "for all citizens [to] share the governmental authority, participating in the creation of public policy."
110. A. V. Dicey, *Introduction to the Study of the Law of the Constitution*, 8th ed. (London: Macmillan, 1915), 110–16.
111. *Monge v. California*, 524 U.S. at 740.

6

Original-Meaning Jurisprudence, Judicial Restraint, and Democratic Freedom

Edward Whelan

In this chapter, I advocate and defend a judicial methodology that employs the original-meaning approach to the interpretation of legal texts and that supplements that approach with principles of judicial restraint. In part I, I explain what the original-meaning species of originalism is, and I highlight two significant recent developments: Justice Scalia's landmark majority opinion on the meaning of the Second Amendment in *District of Columbia v. Heller*,[1] which expressly endorses original-meaning originalism, and law professor Lawrence B. Solum's monumental work *Semantic Originalism*,[2] which draws on the philosophy of language to demonstrate that the "semantic content" of the Constitution is provided by the original public meaning of the Constitution's provisions. I also address some surprisingly common fallacies about original-meaning jurisprudence and respond to attacks on it. In part II, I explain what judicial restraint and its opposite—judicial activism—are, and what they are not. In part III, I briefly summarize how an original-meaning approach, supplemented by judicial restraint, promotes democratic freedom.

I

A

The term "originalism" sounds obscure and dangerously exotic to the modern ear. As Justice Scalia has put it, people ask him, "When did you first become an originalist?" in much the same tone and manner they might use in asking when he first began eating human flesh.[3] In fact, there is good reason that the term "originalism" is arcane: the term itself appears to be of recent vintage, from the 1980s. Not that there is anything novel about the substance of originalism—precisely the opposite. Until recent decades, originalism had been so unchallenged as constitutional orthodoxy that there was no reason to develop a term that would distinguish it from any rival. As Justice Scalia has put it, "[I]n the past, nonoriginalist opinions have almost always had the decency to lie, or at least to dissemble, about what they were doing."[4] But the abandonment of originalism in recent decades made necessary a label for what everyone had previously recognized as elementary.

An analogous semantic development may illustrate the phenomenon. According to the *Oxford English Dictionary*, the term "heterosexual" came into usage barely a century ago. That is obviously not because heterosexuals did not previously exist, but rather precisely because what we now call heterosexuality had been widely understood to be normative.

What is originalism? Succinctly stated, the term "originalism" identifies the principle that the meaning of various provisions of the Constitution—and of other laws—is to be determined in accordance with the sense they bore at the time they were promulgated.

The commonsense, intuitive appeal of originalism may be shown through an example. Consider a legal provision that, until the recent controversy over John McCain's birth in the Panama Canal Zone, seemed well removed from the distorting effects of political bias: the clause of the Constitution (Article II, Section 1, Clause 5) that sets forth the criteria to be eligible to become president. The first criterion is that one must be "a natural born Citizen." That's an obscure phrase. As Jack Keefe, the protagonist in Ring Lardner's "You Tell Me Al" baseball stories, says when he runs across it on a draft-registration form, "I wonder what they think I am. Maybe they think I fell out of a tree or something."[5] How should we go about figuring out what the phrase "natural born Citizen" means?

One approach, which might fairly be called "current meaning" textualism, would attempt to determine the current meaning of the phrase "natural born Citizen." An adherent of this approach might, for example, note the linguistic connection between "natural born" and "natural childbirth" and conclude that if your mother used epidurals or other painkillers during your birth, you were not "natural born."

A second approach might look to the insights of literature for inspiration. Shakespeare's *Macbeth* would seem to provide particular help. Macbeth finds great comfort in the promise that "none of woman born / Shall harm" him. But his comfort proves unwarranted when Macduff, who "was from his mother's womb / Untimely ripp'd," kills Macbeth. Under the inspiration of this literary approach, it might follow that anyone whose birth was by Cesarean section is not a "natural born Citizen."

Under a third, internationalist approach, a judge might determine that the "natural born Citizen" requirement, whatever it means, is obviously a relic of a benighted and xenophobic past, a past that "evolving standards of decency," as reflected in modern transnational European electoral practices, must be abandoned. It simply isn't fair, this judge would conclude, that any candidates should be excluded by such an arbitrary requirement from running for president. The judge might instead invoke "the right to define one's own concept of existence, of meaning, of the universe, and of the mystery of human life" (*Planned Parenthood v. Casey*, *Lawrence v. Texas*) as he instead substitutes his own arbitrary criteria for eligibility.

A fourth approach, that of originalism, would aim to determine the meaning (or intent, or understanding) of the "natural born Citizen" requirement at the time that phrase was incorporated into the Constitution.

If, as I hope and suspect, it's obvious to you that the fourth approach is the sound one, then I submit that you are an originalist. It's striking that in all the public discussion whether John McCain's birth in the Panama Canal Zone means that he isn't a "natural born Citizen," virtually all commentators purport to undertake an originalist inquiry. (Whether or not they do it well is a separate question.) The same intuition, the same common sense, that you and others apply to this somewhat opaque but relatively noncontroversial provision of the Constitution should apply to all the other provisions.

It is, to be sure, theoretically conceivable that some constitutional provisions were intended to be open-ended and to delegate to judges over time considerable discretion to supply or change their meaning. Imagine, for example, that the Constitution contained a provision expressly stating: "The Supreme Court shall have plenary discretion to invent new constitutional rights whenever it sees fit." Some theorists, trying to fight on the field of originalism, contend that phrases like "due process of law" or provisions like the Ninth Amendment should be understood to confer similar discretion. Now is not the occasion to examine the validity of those contentions or their compatibility with American principles of representative government. It suffices to observe that such theorists either expressly acknowledge or implicitly concede the legitimacy of originalism and merely contest with other originalists what originalism yields.

I strongly suspect that many heterosexual English speakers two or three generations ago disliked the odd term "heterosexual" and were not particularly eager to have the label applied to themselves. I hope that your reaction on discovering that you are an originalist is instead like the delight that Molière's Monsieur Jourdain experienced in learning that he had been "speaking in prose" all his life without knowing it.

B

To state, as I have, that "originalism" means that the provisions of the Constitution are to be construed according to the sense they bore at the time they were promulgated is to begin, not end, the exploration of originalist methodology. Which sense should govern? The subjective intention of the Framers, as "original intent" theory would propose? The ratifiers' understanding (in the approach often labeled "original understanding")? Or, as the "original meaning" school advocates, the objective public meaning of the legal text at the time it was adopted?[6]

The "original meaning" school is now dominant within originalism, and I would like to highlight two recent developments that signal its continued ascendancy within the broader legal culture.

1

The first development is the Supreme Court's June 2008 decision in *District of Columbia v. Heller*, in which the Court ruled, by a five-to-four vote, that the District of Columbia's law banning handgun possession violates the Second Amendment. In Randy Barnett's words, Justice Scalia's majority opinion "is the finest example of what is now called 'original public meaning' jurisprudence ever adopted by the Supreme Court."[7]

Scalia begins his exploration of the meaning of the Second Amendment by setting forth this general tenet of the original-meaning approach:

> In interpreting this text, we are guided by the principle that "[t]he Constitution was written to be understood by the voters; its words and phrases were used in their normal and ordinary as distinguished from technical meaning." *United States* v. *Sprague*, 282 U. S. 716, 731 (1931); see also *Gibbons* v. *Ogden*, 9 Wheat. 1, 188 (1824). Normal meaning may of course include an idiomatic meaning, but it excludes secret or technical meanings that would not have been known to ordinary citizens in the founding generation.

This general tenet is deeply rooted in the American understanding. For example, Thomas Jefferson, as president, wrote: "The Constitution on which our Union rests, shall be administered by me according to the safe and honest meaning contemplated by the plain understanding of the people of the United States at the time of its adoption." Joseph Story, the great justice and constitutional scholar from the early nineteenth century, likewise observed:

> Constitutions are not designed for metaphysical or logical subtleties. . . . They are instruments of a practical nature, founded on the common business of human life, adapted to common wants, designed for common use, and fitted for common understandings. The people make them; the people adopt them; the people must be supposed to read them, with the help of common sense.

Applying this central tenet, Scalia's opinion in *Heller* proceeds to an exhaustive examination of the original public meaning of virtually every word of the Second Amendment, read individually and together. That examination includes contemporaneously adopted provisions of the Constitution; eighteenth-century dictionaries, both general usage and legal; and other Founding-era sources, including state constitutional provisions, legal treatises, the *Federalist Papers*, and the ratification debates. "Putting all of these textual elements together," Scalia determines that the Second Amendment guarantees "the individual right to possess and carry weapons in case of confrontation."

That meaning, Scalia finds in turn, is "strongly confirmed by the historical background of the Second Amendment"—in particular, the Stuart kings' use of disarmament as a means of suppressing political dissidents, and George III's efforts to do the same to the American colonists. Scalia also discusses at length "how the Second Amendment was interpreted from immediately after its ratification through the end of the 19th century"—all in order, he makes clear, to discern their bearing on the public understanding of the Second Amendment at the time of ratification. Thus, he examines the commentary of three important Founding-era legal scholars—the 1803 edition of Blackstone's Commentaries by "law professor and former Antifederalist" St. George Tucker, an 1825 treatise by William Rawle ("who had been a member of the Pennsylvania Assembly that ratified the Bill of Rights"), and Joseph Story's 1833 Commentaries on the Constitution. Scalia also looks to pre–Civil War case law, post–Civil War legislation (which arose amid "an outpouring of discussion of the Second Amendment" but which concededly does "not provide as much insight into its original meaning as earlier sources"), and to post–Civil War commentators like Thomas Cooley.

One particular aspect of Scalia's analysis deserves special mention because it bears on the broader debate over what original-meaning methodology is. Scalia not only rejects, but labels as "bordering on the frivolous," the argument that "only those arms in existence in the 18th century are protected by the Second Amendment." As he puts it:

> We do not interpret constitutional rights that way. Just as the First Amendment protects modern forms of communications, *e.g.*, *Reno* v. *American Civil Liberties Union*, 521 U. S. 844, 849 (1997), and the Fourth Amendment applies to modern forms of search, *e.g.*, *Kyllo* v. *United States*, 533 U. S. 27, 35–36 (2001), the Second Amendment extends, prima facie, to all instruments that constitute bearable arms, even those that were not in existence at the time of the founding.

As I'll discuss below, critics of Scalia have falsely alleged that Scalia's original-meaning jurisprudence is really a jurisprudence of "original expected application" in which the meaning of a provision is limited to those applications specifically contemplated at the time the provision was adopted. That allegation, which was baseless even before *Heller*, is emphatically refuted by Scalia's opinion in *Heller*.

2

In *Semantic Originalism,* Lawrence Solum "offers a theory of constitutional meaning that provides a theoretical foundation for original public meaning originalism."[8] Over the course of 174 single-spaced pages, Solum carefully elaborates four major propositions: (1) the semantic content of a constitutional provision is fixed at the time that provision is adopted (the "fixation thesis"); (2) the semantic content of a constitutional provision is its original public meaning (the "clause meaning thesis"); (3) the semantic content of the Constitution contributes to (but does not fully determine) the content of constitutional law (the "contribution thesis"); and (4) we have a defeasible obligation to respect the semantic content of the Constitution (the "fidelity thesis").

Solum's article is richer and deeper and broader than I can do justice to here. For present purposes, I will pass over his fixation thesis, which does the same work as my "natural born Citizen" test and which Solum correctly points out is held by all species of originalists. Nor will I reach Solum's discussion of the contribution thesis and the fidelity thesis. Instead, I want to highlight Solum's clause-meaning thesis, which powerfully provides the intellectual substructure for the commonsense appeal of original-meaning originalism.

Solum's major contribution is to apply ideas drawn from the philosophy of language and linguistics to the debate over constitutional interpretation. As he puts it:

> The fundamental premise of the move beyond law is that constitutional semantics can only be sensibly understood as applied philosophy of language (or applied linguistic theory). Constitutional texts cannot mean in ways that are fundamentally different than the ways in which other utterances mean. This is not to say that that there is nothing special or different about constitutional interpretation or construction. It is to say that *a theory of constitutional meaning must be reconciled with our understanding of how humans communicate with language in general and written texts in particular*—in a variety of legal and extralegal contexts.[9]

Solum's "central claim" for his clause-meaning thesis is that "understanding the content of the Constitution as focused on its conventional semantic meaning [i.e., its original public meaning] provides the only satisfactory account of the possibility of constitutional communication."[10] The linguistic distinction between "speakers meaning" (i.e., the speaker's intended meaning) and "sentence meaning" (the conventional semantic meaning of the words) parallels the distinction between original-intent originalism and original-meaning originalism, as the former makes controlling the Framers' intended meaning and the latter centers on the conventional original public meaning of the Constitution's clauses. Mirroring the attacks of non-originalists on original-intent theory, Solum draws on linguistics to argue that the Constitution can bear "framers meaning" only if it were "possible for the framers to intend that citizens and officials, contemporaneously and over an indefinite future span, grasp the illocutionary force of the Constitution on the basis of their recognition of the framers' intentions."[11] But the "success conditions" for the Framers' meaning can't be satisfied, as the original intentions of the Framers were "multitudinous and inaccessible" (the "collective intentions" problem).[12] That fact, however, does not render constitutional communication impossible:

> The possibility of constitutional communication was created by the fact that the framers and ratifiers could rely on the accessibility of the public meaning (or conventional semantic meaning) of the words, phrases, and clauses that constitute the Constitution. Not only can such public meanings enable constitutional communication at a time a given constitutional provision is drafted, approved, and first implemented, such meanings can also become stable over time or be recovered if they are lost. In other words, under normal conditions successful constitutional communication requires reliance by the drafters, ratifiers, and interpreters on the original public meaning of the words and phrases.[13]

In short, original-meaning originalism is "grounded both in common sense and widely accepted theoretical ideas about meaning and the nature of law."[14]

One particular aspect of Solum's elaboration of his clause-meaning thesis merits attention, as it resolves an apparent methodological inconsistency in Justice Scalia's majority opinion in *Heller*. Specifically, notwithstanding his general guiding principle that the words of the Constitution "were used in their normal and ordinary as distinguished from technical meaning," Scalia explains one phrase in the Second Amendment—"security of a free State"—as a "term [ ] of art in 18th-century political discourse."[15] How can this departure from "normal and ordinary" meaning be justified? As Solum explains (without reference to *Heller*), the clause-meaning thesis can accommodate the possibility of "terms of art" that are "accessible only to a specialist audience." Using the example of the Constitution's conferral on Congress of the power to "grant Letters of Marque and Reprisal," Solum invokes the theory of the division of linguistic labor to account for constitutional communication of terms of art. Simply put, when ordinary citizens encounter an obscure or technical phrase in the Constitution, they can be expected to recognize the possibility that it may be a term of art and to "defer to the understanding of the term of art that would be the publicly available meaning to those who were members of the relevant group" (i.e., to those who understand the term).[16] In other words, "normal and ordinary" meaning governs terms that have normal and ordinary meaning, but resort to specialized meanings is proper for phrases that don't have normal and ordinary meaning.

3

Let me now expand on what original-meaning jurisprudence is by clarifying what it is not. In particular, I would like to rebut some surprisingly common fallacies.

Let me begin with two common misrepresentations of the methodology of original-meaning originalism. First, originalism is often mistakenly reduced to, or the original-meaning approach is conflated with, the now largely abandoned original-intent species of originalism. This confusion invites dismissive treatment of original-meaning originalism on the basis of the collective-intentions problem.

Second, Justice Scalia and other advocates of original-meaning originalism have been accused of adopting instead a jurisprudence of "original expected application." As Yale law professor Jack Balkin puts the charge, Scalia "insists that the concepts and principles underlying [constitutional text] must be *applied* in the same way that they would have been applied when they were adopted."[17] But Scalia's jurisprudence has not been, and is not, limited to "original expected application," as his *Heller* opinion makes clear. Balkin himself recognizes that, with respect to "new phenomena and new technologies," Scalia agrees that originalist interpretation is (to use Balkin's phrase) "not limited to those applications specifically intended or expected by the framers and adopters of the constitutional text."[18] But Balkin identifies nothing that suggests that Scalia looks only to specific intentions or expectations as to phenomena and technologies that existed at the time of the adoption of the relevant constitutional text. It is true that Scalia rejects (in a passage quoted by Balkin) the notion that "the *very acts* that were perfectly constitutional in 1791 (political patronage in government employment and contracting, for example) may be *un*constitutional today."[19] But that rejection (which, of course, is premised on no intervening amendments of relevance) is not tantamount to looking only to specific intentions or expectations.

It is striking that Balkin cites with evident approval Gary Lawson's argument that originalism "is a hypothetical inquiry that asks how a fully informed public audience, knowing all there is to know about the Constitution and the surrounding world, would understand a particular provision."[20] Scalia may well differ from Lawson on the weight that actual historical understandings should have in this hypothetical inquiry, but it seems clear that Scalia's focus on the objective public meaning of constitutional text reflects this same hypothetical inquiry.[21]

A second set of fallacies misstates the consequences of the original-meaning methodology. One variant, reflected in Margaret Talbot's otherwise largely favorable *New Yorker* profile of Justice Scalia,[22] contends that "in Scalia's hands [originalism] leads to conservative results—at least on social issues like abortion, capital punishment, and gay rights." What Talbot (and others) miss is that on each of these "social issues" Justice Scalia's understanding of the Constitution binds him as a jurist to defer broadly to whatever laws the people might adopt—including, for example, fully funded abortion through all nine months of pregnancy, the abolition of capital punishment, and the redefinition of marriage to encompass same-sex couples. Stated somewhat differently, if Justice Scalia were in fact to read into the Constitution his own (presumed) substantive views on abortion, he would conclude that permissive abortion laws were themselves unconstitutional. Likewise, he would conclude that legislators could not abolish capital punishment and could not create same-sex marriage. His clear rejection of these positions demonstrates that on these issues Justice Scalia's originalism is in fact politically neutral. Originalism will lead to "conservative results" on these issues only if, and to the extent that, elected legislators enact conservative positions into law. Conversely, originalism will lead to liberal results when elected legislators enact liberal laws. And, of course, the free play that originalism gives to the political process on these issues will allow the electorate the flexibility to change its collective positions over time.

A second variant of the bad-consequences objection is that original-meaning jurisprudence lacks the flexibility needed to adapt to changing circumstances. This claim, typically made by proponents of the so-called living Constitution (i.e., make-it-up-as-you-go-along) approach to constitutional interpretation, is doubly defective. First, it ignores the broad play that the Constitution, under original-meaning interpretive principles, gives to the democratic processes to adapt policies to new conditions. Second, insofar as living constitutionalism is used for its primary modern mission—the creation of new rights (rather than, say, the conferral on Congress of greater powers)—it entrenches the current elite's policy preferences in Supreme Court decision making in a manner that deprives future generations of the very adaptability that living constitutionalists say they favor. In short, original-meaning jurisprudence provides the flexibility that the "living Constitution" falsely promises.

The bad-consequences objection leads to a third attack on original-meaning jurisprudence (and on originalism generally). As Cass Sunstein has put it, "Why should we be governed by people long dead?"[23] Sunstein's answer: "It is up to us to decide whether to accept" originalism.[24] Larry Solum's fidelity thesis provides a systematic response to claims like Sunstein's. I'll just observe here that Sunstein's position, beyond resting on a grossly distorted account of the consequences that originalism would entail, has radical anarchistic implications that Sunstein hastens to disguise. He claims that he is not arguing that the Constitution itself should not be taken as binding, but he can argue only that we ought to take it as binding "because it is good to take it as binding."[25] But why, under Sunstein's thinking, couldn't we instead pick and choose the parts of the Constitution that we think would be good and disregard the others? Why, indeed, couldn't each of us reject the legitimacy of any law that we don't like and to which we personally did not consent? Sunstein is so desperate to combat originalism that he would destroy the law itself in the process.

A fourth attack on original-meaning jurisprudence is that it doesn't generate answers to all the legal questions that judges (and other interpreters) must decide. Judge Richard A. Posner, for example, makes this charge in support of his case for pragmatism.[26] Insofar as the charge is that original-meaning principles do not always yield a determinate meaning of a constitutional provision that is sufficiently clear to resolve a controversy, the charge is undoubtedly correct. That's precisely why, as I argue in part II, the original-meaning methodology needs to be supplemented by principles of judicial restraint. But the charge, properly understood, is also of little significance, as original meaning can be the core of a judicial methodology that does generate answers to all the legal questions. Indeed, the charge seeks to recast a fatal vice of nonoriginalist methodologies like living constitutionalism and pragmatism—their amazing ability to generate the desired answer—as a virtue.

Posner goes even further to argue that the Supreme Court is inescapably a "political" court when it deals with constitutional issues. In so doing, Posner intertwines two arguments. His first argument is that a constitution "deal[s] with fundamental issues" that "are *political* issues: issues about political governance, political values, political rights, and political power" (emphasis in original). "Political issues by definition," he asserts, "cannot be referred to a neutral expert for resolution."[27] This argument is simply incoherent. By the same illogic, Posner could argue, say, that legal questions dealing with Department of Agriculture manure regulations are manure issues—issues about manure governance, manure values, manure rights, and manure power—and that manure issues by definition cannot be referred to a nonmanure expert for resolution.

Posner's second argument is coherent, but doesn't come anywhere close to establishing (either by itself or together with his first argument) his proposition that the court is, in ordinary parlance, *necessarily* a "political" court when it deals with constitutional issues. Posner argues that constitutional provisions "tend . . . to be both old and vague" and that the "political preferences [of justices] are [therefore] *likely* to determine how they vote."[28] There is, of course, always a danger that justices will indulge their political preferences. That danger is compounded when justices subscribe to a theory of constitutional decision making (e.g., living constitutionalism or Posner's own pragmatism) that invites them to indulge those political preferences. But Posner offers no evidence for his assertion that each justice's political preferences are "likely" to determine how that justice votes, nor does he recognize that even his threshold of likelihood falls short of establishing that political decision making is inevitable.

4

A final threat to original-meaning originalism comes not from an overt attack but from a supposed embrace: specifically, Jack Balkin's recent effort to effect a grand reconciliation between original meaning and living constitutionalism—and in particular to root a supposed constitutional right to abortion in the original meaning of the Fourteenth Amendment.

As law professors John O. McGinnis and Michael B. Rappaport nicely put it in their brief critique of Balkin's argument, Balkin "undertakes what many previously would have thought a conjuror's trick: he attempts to locate the constitutional right to abortion, the poster child for imposition of the judiciary's own idiosyncratic values, in the original meaning of the Constitution. . . . [His] article has great strategic value [for opponents of conservative originalists]: it attempts to appropriate for the living constitution philosophy the intellectual capital and public respectability that originalism has earned recently in the academy as well as the wider world."[29] Like McGinnis and Rappaport, I believe that Balkin's "conjuror's trick" fails.

Balkin's basic argument can be summarized succinctly: (1) The text of a constitutional provision is properly "judged by contemporary application of [the] concepts (and underlying principles) [that it embodies], not by how people living [at the time of ratification] would have applied those concepts and principles."[30] (2) The original meaning of the Fourteenth Amendment's Equal Protection Clause is to prohibit class legislation, caste legislation, subordinating legislation, arbitrary and unreasonable distinctions, and special or partial laws.[31] (3) Laws criminalizing abortion violate the original meaning of the Equal Protection Clause because they constitute class legislation and subordinating legislation. They "impose special burdens on women not suffered by men."[32] They "help maintain the unequal and subordinate status of women in society because they help commit women, against their will, to lives of domestic labor and economic dependency."[33]

As proposition (1) makes clear, the real divide between Balkin's approach and Scalia's is not, as Balkin would have it, between original meaning and "original expected application," but rather is over which hypothetical public audience should be looked to to determine the original meaning. For Balkin, "each generation"[34]—or at least each generation's professors of constitutional law—interprets constitutional text anew. Balkin's approach would thus seem more deserving of the label "transformable meaning" than "original meaning." For Scalia, the hypothetical public audience consists of those people living when the text was adopted.

As for Balkin's argument that the original meaning of the Fourteenth Amendment's Equal Protection Clause is to prohibit class legislation, caste legislation, subordinating legislation, arbitrary and unreasonable distinctions, and special or partial laws: I will pass over here the question of whether

Balkin has properly determined this original meaning, and I will instead assume *arguendo* that he has done so. (Nor will I bother here to contest his highly contestable characterization of laws criminalizing abortion.) The questions I would like to pose here are: What sort of meaning is that? How can principles so vague and indeterminate convey any generalized meaning?

Balkin, I suspect, might wonder whether I am conflating what he calls the two different questions of fidelity ("what the Constitution means and how to be faithful to it") and of institutional responsibility ("how a person in a particular institutional setting—like an unelected judge with life tenure—should interpret the Constitution and implement it through doctrinal constructions and applications").[35] I accept his distinction—and his related distinction between originalism and judicial restraint. But it seems to me that what Balkin calls the principle of democracy—the principle that the Constitution creates a system of representative government in which issues are presumptively left to the people to decide through their elected representatives[36]—argues powerfully against *anyone's* interpreting the Constitution to embody principles so amorphous and malleable as those Balkin discerns in the Equal Protection Clause.

To state my point somewhat differently: Balkin sees in the Equal Protection Clause "abstract principles and vague standards that would delegate most issues to the future."[37] But issues may be left to future generations in two very different ways. One way—the way Balkin posits—is that it is up to each new generation to determine the *constitutionally compelled application* of these abstract principles and vague standards. A second way would be to read the Equal Protection Clause, insofar as it is vague and indeterminate, as not overriding the Constitution's general reservation to the political processes of the *policy* decision to select among the various otherwise *constitutionally permissible applications*—and to revise those selections over time.

I must also note that Balkin's distinction between the questions of fidelity and of institutional responsibility appears, in his hands, to become an empty one. In particular, there is no indication that principles of judicial restraint meaningfully supplement what Balkin calls his "text and principle" originalism. His "Abortion and Original Meaning" article ends with a lengthy section on "how courts should enforce the [supposed constitutional] right to abortion,"[38] and there is nothing modest about the "discourse shaping" approach[39] that he would have courts play. Further, in "Original Meaning and Constitutional Redemption," Balkin states that his approach makes *Brown v. Board of Education* "a supremely easy case" that "takes about two paragraphs to explain."[40] No doubt. Ditto, evidently, for *Romer v. Evans* and *Lawrence v. Texas*, as this is the entirety of Balkin's explanation why the laws at issue in those cases are unconstitutional: "In my view both laws would violate the principle against class and caste legislation."[41] To be sure, if all a judge need do is attach one of various malleable labels—class legislation, or caste legislation, or subordinating legislation, or arbitrary and unreasonable, or special or partial—to legislation the judge disfavors, the judicial task is quite easy. And representative government operates only at the sufferance of judges.

5

There are, to be sure, significant ongoing methodological challenges that advocates of original meaning face. I will identify three.

First, originalists (with the possible exception of Justice Thomas) have not elaborated a coherent theory of *stare decisis* that would explain the decision to acquiesce in some nonoriginalist precedents and to overturn others. As a result, originalism is vulnerable to Balkin's charge that it has a "play in the joints" that "allows [it] to track particular political agendas and allows judges to impose their political ideology on the law—the very thing that the methodology purports to avoid."[42] This charge is not a complete indictment of originalism. As Justice Scalia writes in *A Matter of Interpretation*, every "theory of interpretation put into practice in an ongoing system of law" faces the same challenge. Further, "[w]here originalism will make a difference is not in the rolling back of accepted old principles of constitutional law but in the rejection of usurpatious new ones." But it would be good, at the very least, to develop clear principles for distinguishing between "accepted old principles" and "usurpatious new ones."

Second, originalists need to explore whether it is possible to develop more fully the role to be played by original expected applications in determining original meaning. It is widely accepted that original meaning is not limited to original expected applications. But do original expected applications form the core of original meaning? And is the process of moving beyond that core one merely of reasoning by analogy? Or is the bearing of original expected applications on original meaning more attenuated? What insights can the philosophy of language shed on these questions? Under what circumstances, if any, may an original expected application of a constitutional provision be outside, and contrary to, the original meaning of that provision?

Third, in determining the original meaning of a provision, what standard of clarity must judges attain—what burden of proof must they meet—in order to apply it, and especially in order to invalidate democratic enactments contrary to the discerned meaning?

II

A

Academics and other nongovernmental actors are free to inquire into constitutional meaning without being constrained by institutional considerations. Their best guesses—and their many wrong guesses—as to original meaning have no direct real-world consequence. Not so for governmental actors whose conduct must be shaped by their assessment of what is and what is not constitutionally permissible. And especially not so for Supreme Court justices and other judges who decide constitutional meaning in the context of specific cases and who must have a legitimate basis for declining to apply (or for declaring invalid) enacted laws.

An original-meaning approach is a necessary component of sound judging. And, for the vast bulk of issues that have been hotly contested in recent decades, it is sufficient. But there are also judicial cases in which original meaning, even together with any appropriate canons of construction, does not yield clear answers. In a democratic republic, principles of judicial restraint properly supplement originalism.

Here I will highlight two principles in particular: First, judges, in crafting rules to implement constitutional meaning, do not have authority to "overenforce" the Constitution. It may well be inevitable that judicial doctrine—which law professor Kermit Roosevelt identifies as the set of rules that judges create to implement the meaning of the Constitution's provisions in particular cases[43]—cannot perfectly comport with constitutional meaning. But (contrary to Roosevelt) judges need to understand that doctrine cannot legitimately overenforce the Constitution and lead them to decline to apply (or to invalidate) legislative enactments that are not, in fact, unconstitutional.

Second, when originalist methodology does not yield a sufficiently clear answer to a constitutional question, judges have no authority to override democratic enactments. Reasonable people can dispute how to define the requisite level of clarity, and it may even be that the level will vary depending on context or the constitutional provision at issue. But a law professor's mere best guess as to constitutional meaning cannot be a judge's basis for trumping the majoritarian process. Thus, when originalism is allied with judicial restraint, the fact that originalism will not always yield sufficiently clear answers is not, as some critics mistakenly think, a fatal or even a significant defect and does not somehow render originalism unworkable. Rather, that situation calls for judges to apply statutory law.

B

Judicial restraint and its antagonist, judicial activism, are widely misrepresented. Here I will identify and respond to the most common misrepresentations.

First, considerations of *stare decisis*, or adherence to precedent, are often confused (frequently deliberately, it would seem) with judicial restraint. But advocacy of judicial restraint and criticism of judicial activism focus first and foremost on the proper role of the courts in a representative government and in a system of separated powers. Judicial restraint is a necessary virtue for the courts because it works to keep courts within their proper bounds. Stare decisis, by contrast, is largely an intrajudicial doctrine. When the Supreme Court addresses a question that it has addressed before, it accords a degree of respect, or deference, to its previous treatment of the question, partly from the presumption that the Court carefully addressed the question the first time, partly from the impracticability of addressing every question anew in every case.

Stare decisis may well have some interbranch implications in some cases, especially, say, where governmental institutions have been designed and maintained in reliance on previous Court rulings. But stare decisis considerations are at their weakest when a previous constitutional ruling by the Court has wrongly overridden the democratic processes. In such instances, a sound understanding of judicial restraint may well call for the Court to revisit its prior ruling. When judges override a legislative enactment, citizens have the right to demand that the judicial decision be right—and that a decision that usurps the political processes be overturned.

A second set of objections attacks the term "judicial activism." One objection is that the term is a meaningless all-purpose epithet. To be sure, the term "judicial activism" is often misused merely to signal one's disagreement with a ruling. It also may well be that the term can be responsibly accorded somewhat different meanings. In my judgment, the term is best used, in the constitutional context, to identify one category of judicial error in interpreting the Constitution: the wrongful overriding of democratic enactments (often through the invention of supposed constitutional rights). That category of judicial error is distinct from a second category, which I call "judicial passivism"—the wrongful failure to enforce constitutional rights. So used, the term "judicial activism" has meaningful core content.

A variant objection is that the term "judicial activism" doesn't perform any analytical work and that whether or not a ruling is activist depends entirely on the underlying theory of sound constitutional judging. That objection is correct, I believe, but largely irrelevant. The term "judicial activism" has descriptive value in succinctly capturing the Court's wrongful invasion of the realm of representative government and the injury that invasion inflicts on the powers of American citizens. More particularly, the expanded term "liberal judicial activism" draws its potency from the Court's repeated entrenchment since the 1960s of the policy preferences of the Left in the guise of constitutional rights. To paraphrase the old Smith Barney commercial, the term "liberal judicial activism" has acquired its stigma the old-fashioned way: it's earned it. Given the ongoing threat that liberal judicial activists pose (both in clinging to ill-gotten gains on matters like abortion and in new or foreseeable incursions like the invention of a constitutional right to same-sex marriage, the conferral of constitutional rights on foreign terrorists, and the invention of a constitutional right to clone), it's no time to retire proper use of the term "liberal judicial activism."

A third variant of the attack on the term "judicial activism" is the effort to neuter the term by redefining it to mean any exercise of judicial review, *whether right or wrong*, that results in the invalidation of a statute or regulation. I'm reminded of the late and great William F. Buckley's response to the leftist charge during the Cold War that the CIA and the KGB were engaged in morally equivalent acts of spycraft. As Buckley put it, that's like "saying that the man who pushes an old lady into the path of a hurtling bus is not to be distinguished from the man who pushes an old lady out of the path of a hurtling bus: on the grounds that, after all, in both cases someone is pushing old ladies around" (*Miles Gone By*).

Another attack on the term "judicial activism" is provided by law professor Kermit Roosevelt in his book *The Myth of Judicial Activism*. Roosevelt mistakenly contends that the concept of judicial activism can make sense only if "determining the plain meaning of the Constitution [is] relatively easy" (a proposition that Roosevelt himself says is "indeed true") and if that "plain meaning" is sufficiently specific to "tell judges how to decide individual cases." Roosevelt asserts that critics of judicial activism believe both these things, but that's simply wrong. Original meaning, for example, will frequently diverge from the generalized "plain meaning" that Roosevelt posits, and there is certainly no consensus among originalists that determining the original meaning of constitutional provisions is "relatively easy." To be sure, most originalists will readily recognize as constitutionally outlandish many of the "rights" recently invented by the Supreme Court. But the fact that easy cases exist does not mean that there aren't plenty of questions with no clear right answer. More fundamentally, Roosevelt's purported demonstration that many controversial cases have no right answer offers no response to critics of judicial activism who ask, On what basis, then, may courts in such cases trump the result that representative democracy has produced? Remarkably, Roosevelt is blind to this fundamental question.

III

An original-meaning approach, supplemented by judicial restraint, promotes democratic freedom in three basic respects.

First, our core democratic freedom of lawmaking is exercised through representative government, and an original-meaning approach provides the only coherent and determinate methodology for interpreting the meaning of the laws—constitutional provisions as well as statutes—that we adopt. As Scalia has written, "[I]t is simply incompatible with democratic government, or indeed, even with fair government, to have the meaning of a law determined by what the lawgiver meant, rather than by [the objective meaning of] what the lawgiver promulgated."[44] As Solum argues, only public-meaning originalism makes possible "constitutional communication"—or any other communication of legal meaning over time.

Second, within broad bounds, the Constitution creates a democratic republic in which the vast bulk of issues, large and small, are left to American citizens to work out through their legislators at the state and national levels. A judicial methodology that supplements the original-meaning approach with principles of judicial restraint preserves the broad realm in which representative government operates. It respects the fundamental democratic freedom of citizens to shape and revise policies over time.

Third, recognizing the threat that democratic freedom could be abused to destroy itself, the Framers (and amenders) of the Constitution have entrenched in the Constitution the protections that experience taught them were necessary to protect against that threat. The original-meaning approach ensures that these fundamental protections of democratic freedom are enforced.

NOTES

1. 128 S. Ct. 2783 (2008).
2. Lawrence B. Solum, *Semantic Originalism* (draft of July 11, 2008), available at http://papers.ssrn.com/sol3/papers.cfm?abstract_id=1120244.
3. Edward Fitzpatrick, "The Law according to Justice Scalia," *The Providence Journal*, April 8, 2008, available at http://www.projo.com/news/content/justice_scalia_04-08-08_LT9M5NV_v38.39db8a5.html (accessed October 4, 2009).
4. Antonin Scalia, "Originalism: The Lesser Evil," *University of Cincinnati. Law Review* 57 (1989): 849, 852.
5. Ring Lardner, *Ring around the Bases: The Complete Baseball Stories of Ring Lardner*, ed. Matthew J. Bruccoli (New York: Charles Scribner's Sons, 1992), 135.
6. There is obviously considerable overlap among these approaches. For example, as law professor Randy Barnett points out, "evidence of the intentions of the Framers and ratifiers is often highly relevant to determining the public meaning of the words they decided to enact." The difference among these approaches, Barnett helpfully explains, "is defined, not by the evidence each includes or excludes from its analysis, but by what each method is trying to prove or disprove by use of evidence." Randy Barnett, "Underlying Principles," *Constitutional Commentary* 24, no. 2 (Summer 2007): 6 (available from http://papers.ssrn.com/sol3/papers.cfm?abstract_id=954601).
7. Randy E. Barnett, "News Flash: The Constitution Means What It Says," *Wall Street Journal*, June 27, 2008.
8. Solum, *Semantic Originalism*, at 3.
9. Solum, *Semantic Originalism*, at 39–40.
10. Solum, *Semantic Originalism*, at 6.
11. Solum, *Semantic Originalism*, at 42.
12. Solum, *Semantic Originalism*, at 6.
13. Solum, *Semantic Originalism*, at 6.

14. Solum, *Semantic Originalism*, at 23.
15. *Heller*, slip op. at 24.
16. Solum, *Semantic Originalism*, at 56.
17. Jack M. Balkin, "Abortion and Original Meaning," *Constitutional Commentary* 24 (2007): 291, 296 (emphasis in original).
18. Balkin, "Abortion and Original Meaning," 295, 297.
19. Antonin Scalia, *A Matter of Interpretation* (Princeton, N.J.: Princeton University Press, 1997), 141 (emphasis in original).
20. See Jack M. Balkin, "Original Meaning and Constitutional Redemption," *Constitutional Commentary* 24 (2007): 427, 447n53.
21. Like Balkin, Ronald Dworkin contends that Scalia embraces what Dworkin calls "'expectation' originalism, which holds that [constitutional] clauses should be understood to have the consequences that those who made them expected them to have," rather than "'semantic' originalism, which insists that the . . . clauses be read to say what those who made them intended to say." See Dworkin's Comment in Scalia, *A Matter of Interpretation*, 119. But Scalia, while accepting Dworkin's distinction, makes clear that he is a "semantic" originalist and, disputing Dworkin's focus on intention, emphasizes that semantic originalists should focus "upon what the text would reasonably be understood to mean, rather than upon what it was intended to mean." Scalia, *A Matter of Interpretation*, 144.
22. Margaret Talbot, "Supreme Confidence," *New Yorker*, March 28, 2005.
23. Cass R. Sunstein, *Radicals in Robes: Why Extreme Right-Wing Courts Are Wrong for America* (New York: Basic Books, 2005), 74.
24. Sunstein, *Radicals in Robes*, 71.
25. Sunstein, *Radicals in Robes*, 74.
26. Richard A. Posner, *How Judges Think* (Cambridge, Mass.: Harvard University Press, 2008).
27. Posner, *How Judges Think*, 272.
28. Posner, *How Judges Think*, 272.
29. John O. McGinnis and Michael B. Rappaport, "Original Interpretative Principles as the Core of Originalism," 1, available at http://papers.ssrn.com/sol3/papers.cfm?abstract_id=962142.
30. Balkin, "Abortion and Original Meaning," 295.
31. Balkin, "Abortion and Original Meaning," 315–16.
32. Balkin, "Abortion and Original Meaning," 323.
33. Balkin, "Abortion and Original Meaning," 324.
34. Balkin, "Abortion and Original Meaning," 293.
35. Balkin, "Abortion and Original Meaning," 308.
36. Balkin, "Abortion and Original Meaning," 306.
37. Balkin, "Original Meaning and Constitutional Redemption," 456.
38. Balkin, "Abortion and Original Meaning," 342.
39. Balkin, "Abortion and Original Meaning," 346.
40. Balkin, "Original Meaning and Constitutional Redemption," 450–51.
41. Balkin, "Original Meaning and Constitutional Redemption," 449n64.
42. Balkin, "Abortion and Original Meaning," 299.
43. Kermit Roosevelt III, *The Myth of Judicial Activism* (New Haven, Conn.: Yale University Press, 2006).
44. Scalia, *A Matter of Interpretation*, 17.

7

Is It Unnatural to Shun Foreign Precedents?

Jeremy Rabkin

In 2002, the U.S. Supreme Court ruled on the application of the death penalty to a man convicted of first-degree murder who was found to be mentally retarded. The five-to-four majority in *Atkins v. Virginia*[1] held that imposing the death penalty in these circumstances would violate the Eighth Amendment prohibition on "cruel and unusual punishment."

By itself, *Atkins* might not have drawn much attention. Thirty years earlier, five justices had ruled that capital punishment, as then practiced in almost all states, was in violation of evolving constitutional norms, with some justices already insisting that resort to capital punishment would be unconstitutional under any circumstances.[2] Shifting majorities had sanctioned death penalties in later cases, but insisted on various restrictions, both procedural and substantive, in its application.[3] *Atkins* was a small skirmish in what was already a long-standing area of constitutional dispute.

What made *Atkins* unusual was a new argument. In addition to pointing out that most states had repudiated capital punishment for defendants of subnormal intelligence, Justice Stevens noted that most foreign governments rejected the death penalty in these circumstances.[4] This appeal to the "opinion of the world community" does not seem to have been decisive for the Court's ruling. It was, in fact, only mentioned in a footnote. Even so, it provoked a sharp rejoinder in a dissenting opinion by Justice Scalia, joined by Justice Thomas and Chief Justice Rehnquist. The "notions of justice" of "the 'world community,'" the conservatives protested, "are (thankfully) not always those of our people."[5]

In 2004, a mere two years after this exchange, the same dispute appeared in a different context. In *Lawrence v. Texas*,[6] the Court held that laws imposing criminal penalties for homosexual sodomy would violate a general right to liberty guaranteed by the Fourteenth Amendment. This time the appeal to foreign practice—ostensibly illustrating the emerging international consensus on the recognition of personal sexual freedom—was in the text. The same three conservatives answered with the same sort of protest against dragging foreign practice into a dispute about how to interpret the U.S. Constitution.

Apparently, neither side was persuaded by these arguments about the propriety of considering foreign law in American constitutional disputes. In 2005, when the Court held, in *Roper v. Simmons*,[7] that capital punishment should not be available to defendants under the age of eighteen, the majority cited the practice of foreign governments and the three conservatives again protested against resort to such arguments in constitutional cases.

Various justices meanwhile began carrying the dispute into nonjudicial forums. In separate public speeches, Justices Breyer and Ginsburg, along with Justice Kennedy and Justice O'Connor, defended the appeal to foreign law while Justice Scalia continued to protest it.[8] In their confirmation proceedings, both John Roberts in 2005 and Samuel Alito in 2006 were questioned about their views of such citations and both came down on Scalia's side. Resolutions condemning appeals to foreign law in constitutional cases were proposed in the House of Representatives in 2005 and then in the Senate in 2006.[9]

Legal scholars have offered what is now a very large body of commentary on the subject. Many scholars have taken sides in the Court's debate, with scholars on the left embracing the practices of judicial liberals and more conservative scholars elaborating the objections of the Court's conservatives. The debate has provoked some scholars to undertake quite extensive reviews of past practice, and their research has shown that appeals to foreign law are not entirely new.[10] Appeals to foreign sources have appeared in Supreme Court opinions almost from the beginning of the Court's history. Such appeals have appeared in a wide range of contexts over the Court's whole history. And they have, almost from the first, regularly provoked protests from other justices, questioning their relevance to decisions the Supreme Court was called on to make.

It may be that the whole debate is disproportionate to the real claims at stake. Even the justices most sympathetic to invoking foreign practice acknowledge that foreign law is not, as such, binding in American constitutional disputes. Even critics of the practice may surmise that cases would have come out much the same way had foreign practice not been mentioned in the opinions.[11]

Yet there are some new features—and some new grounds for concern—in the way the Court has invoked foreign law in recent years. In the past, most references to foreign law arose in cases dealing with explicitly international questions, either because they turned on questions of treaty interpretation or customary international law, such as an early case struggling to define "piracy" on the high seas.[12] In such cases, there were clear grounds to seek to coordinate American law with the practices prevailing among other nations. Even in cases about domestic constitutional issues, appeals to foreign law were, in the past, always defensive in nature or, as one might say, invoked to reinforce arguments for judicial restraint. In no case prior to *Atkins* did the Court invoke foreign citations to hold an American statute invalid. Beginning with *Atkins*, the Court did this three times within three years.

Finally, previous appeals to foreign law often took a very broad view of potentially relevant authorities, citing ancient and medieval legal commentaries as often as contemporary legal decisions to illuminate the broad traditions of Western legal thought. Appeals at that level of abstraction could plausibly claim to be investigating the standards embraced by the Framers of the American Constitution, invoking authorities the Framers might well have studied or been influenced by through the medium of subsequent works. Recent opinions of the Supreme Court have focused on very recent legal trends in other countries, trends often politically coordinated through international institutions such as organs of the United Nations or the Council of Europe.

So there are reasons why contemporary critics of this practice should not necessarily be reassured by claims that past Courts also looked to foreign authorities. At the least, the contemporary debate over this practice tells something about contemporary concerns—and contemporary ambitions.

Some commentators have been quick to make just that point. The debate, as Vicki Jackson of Georgetown Law School has argued, has sometimes triggered "xenophobic hostility" in which "references to foreign law may be cast as a form of judicial disloyalty" but which has also become entangled in ongoing disagreement, at the level of jurisprudential doctrines, between "proponents of originalism and proponents of the 'living constitution.'"[13] Professor Jeremy Waldron of Columbia Law School, in an influential article in the *Harvard Law Review*, sought to frame the debate as a dispute between those who hold to a positivist view of legal interpretation, as simply discerning the will of the lawmaker—implying a narrowly "originalist" view of constitutional interpretation—and those who embrace broader moral perspectives. Those sympathetic to a natural law understanding, Waldron argues, should welcome appeal to foreign citations, since they allow judges to consider the consensus of mankind, much as classic works on natural law appealed to *ius gentium*—the customary law of nations as a guide to fundamental questions of justice.[14]

These arguments are not frivolous. But for many of us, they are more disturbing than reassuring. To think through such arguments certainly helps to clarify what we should and shouldn't mean by the rule of law. Before we get to the most philosophical questions about "law," however, it may be helpful to review some of the easier issues in this debate. Whatever the justices may think, the appeal to natural law by scholarly defenders of the practice is not just decorous rhetoric. The appeal to *ius gentium* functions as a sort of inspirational beacon. Advocates of citing foreign court rulings must regard such arguments as inspiring, because—as Waldron himself concedes—the actual practice of the justices in recent cases is subject to many practical objections: "[W]e should not reject the idea of a theory of the citation of foreign law simply because we see foreign law being cited opportunistically," Waldron cautions, but rather "start thinking directly about legal problems in a way that makes [such a theoretical] account of the citation of foreign law appealing."[15]

It is worth taking some time at the outset, however, to examine these problems in the foreground that the "appealing" theory is supposed to overcome.

FALSE ASSURANCE

One version of the argument in favor of foreign citations is that such citations are not different, in principle, from what common law courts in America have always done when citing rulings from different jurisdictions.[16] It is common practice for a court in one American state to cite an opinion from a state court in another U.S. state. If it is acceptable for Ohio to cite a Massachusetts ruling, why should there be any objection when federal courts cite foreign rulings?

The first and easiest response is that these are, in practice, quite different undertakings. American courts share so much procedure and so many assumptions that it was, down to the 1930s, assumed that federal courts could discern and apply a federal common law, synthesizing the standards of all or almost all states.

The Supreme Court repudiated that practice in 1938[17]—perhaps because, in an age when statutes were displacing so many common law standards, it was no longer so clear that courts in different states should be expected to converge on common standards. Still, American law schools presume that cases from different U.S. jurisdictions will guide students to a proper understanding of common principles. One doesn't need to study cases exclusively originating in Virginia courts to learn the "law of contracts" as it is understood and applied in Virginia.[18] Even when state courts interpret their own state constitutions, if they look at what courts in other American states have said about similar guarantees in other state constitutions, they are looking at judicial reasoning that is, in most respects, readily intelligible, because it shares so many background understandings.

As soon as arguments move from variants within American states to broad patterns across "the international community," the effort to discern common trends becomes vastly more difficult. In most countries, court decisions are not published in English, not grounded in common law procedure and terminology, and not readily accessible in the sort of reporting services that enable American lawyers to track American cases. In practice, when American courts invoke foreign judgments they usually rely on summaries or surveys supplied by anonymous intermediaries.

Atkins already illustrated the dangers. The Court's opinion claimed that opposition to the execution of mentally retarded defendants is "overwhelmingly" rejected by the "world community," so the United States "stands virtually alone" in tolerating this practice. To support the claim, the Court cited an amicus brief submitted by a group of American diplomats, which does assert that even China has repudiated this practice. But the brief offers no citation to any Chinese legal materials to support this assertion, citing only an American journal article which, if one looks it up, turns out not to say anything about the treatment of mentally retarded defendants. The Court also cited a brief submitted by the European Union, which invoked evidence from a UN study on the death penalty. But that study was conducted by a questionnaire distributed to UN member states. It was a survey to which over two-thirds of the states queried did not respond at all and of those that did, the overwhelming majority did not permit capital punishment in any form.

Professor Michael Ramsey, who examined the briefs, concluded that they offered no concrete evidence for the claims they offered: they did "not cite a single person in Atkins' position as having been categorically exempted from an otherwise applicable death sentence because of mental handicap." So the Court's claim was, to say the least, not very well grounded in actual evidence of actual practice by actual governments facing comparable challenges to the one before the American courts; as Ramsay points out, "the Court could not be bothered to cite (nor, presumably, to read) any actual source that even purportedly endorsed its conclusion."[19]

Such carelessness invites the conclusion that foreign citations are not invoked in a serious inquiry but are simply artificial props in a conclusion driven by quite unrelated reasoning. It is not easy for observers to take such appeals seriously when the Court is so haphazard about them.

Professor Roger Alford found a similar pattern in the Court's reliance on foreign trends in *Lawrence v. Texas*. There the Court spoke of an "emerging awareness" in favor of individuals "deciding [freely] how to conduct their private lives in matters pertaining to sex" and cited for this proposition decisions of the UN Human Rights Committee and the European Court of Human Rights, describing the latter as "authoritative in all countries that are members of the Council of Europe." But as Alford points out, human rights advocacy groups portrayed a quite different picture in reports not cited in briefs to the Court in *Lawrence*. In one such report, Human Rights Watch found governmental as well as private discrimination on the basis of sexual orientation to be common in Europe as "in virtually every country in the world." A survey by a gay rights advocacy group found "hardly any support for gay and lesbian rights" among ordinary citizens in 144 countries surveyed.[20] The Court in *Lawrence* simply seized on a few items highlighted in amicus briefs and extrapolated them into a world trend.

One could argue, of course, that the answer to such objections is to make more conscientious efforts in future cases. But American courts are not in a very good position to acquire reliable information about actual legal practices throughout the world. Individual scholars may offer claims in amicus briefs but the broader the claim—as, for example, the claim that a particular American practice is "overwhelmingly rejected" by other nations—the harder it is to examine within the confines (and deadlines) of American litigation. How many lawyers are in a position to challenge claims about what legal systems across Asia or Africa actually do in relation to some disputed practice?

Even if reporting and translation services could overcome the initial information challenges, the ultimate difficulty remains: how to interpret results from such very different countries, whose legal systems operate in such different contexts? What if China—which does sanction capital punishment—turns out to be ready to implement this punishment even against those with mental infirmities? Is China, a one-party dictatorship, a good model for the United States?

Yet China is not a small or insignificant country. China is one of our largest trading partners, so there are few countries with which Americans undertake more legal transactions. If examples from China can be discounted because China is not a democracy, we can't be sure which other countries can be disregarded without a fairly clear definition of "democracy." Is Russia a democracy because it has regular elections and, at least in form, competing parties? In that case, what about Venezuela, Egypt, or Iran, or many other authoritarian regimes that do hold elections but impose many restrictions on the capacity of opposition parties to compete in them?

These are not frivolous questions to judge by the actual practices of justices who favor foreign citations. In a 1999 opinion, dissenting from the Court's denial of certiorari in a capital punishment case, Justice Stephen Breyer cited precedents from the European Court of Human Rights, the Supreme Court of India—and the Supreme Court of Zimbabwe. Breyer himself subsequently conceded that Zimbabwe is "not the human rights capital of the world."[21] But it served his argument at the time to cite Zimbabwe and he had no restraining doctrine to reject such precedent out of hand.

If the crucial criterion is democracy, what about states that have legitimate multiparty democracies, but are obligated by external constraints to conform to policies preferred elsewhere? European countries, for example, have been under great pressure to abandon capital punishment as part of a common European human rights stance. Smaller countries may go along even though they might otherwise prefer to maintain capital punishment. Should all twenty-seven countries in the EU—or all forty-seven in the Council of Europe—count as individual national "votes" against the practice, when they have been pressured to abandon it by outsiders, often against strong local opinion to the contrary?

What if, on the other hand, even the dominant states, like Germany and France, have an agenda that is unrelated to the merits of capital punishment as a criminal justice measure? In 2001, the Council of Europe announced that its number one human rights priority in the world would be its campaign against capital punishment.[22] Part of the purpose, surely, was to draw a contrast with the United States. That probably explains why European authorities took the trouble to submit amicus briefs in cases like *Atkins*, which did not involve any European nationals.

None of these objections are hypertechnical. In *Atkins* and other cases, the Court devoted much attention to the claim that U.S. states were moving in a certain direction. The claim is easy to verify and easy to assess—at least in the sense that American lawyers have a reasonably good notion of what it means for state legislatures or state supreme courts to change local law on some controversial policy issue. The international counterpart to the claim is much harder to interpret. So claims about international trends are much more open to abuse.

That is especially so, as Ramsey points out, when courts have no clear theory about the proper relation between foreign and American practices. The United States is certainly at odds with European practice in relation to capital punishment, where it still clings to views on criminal justice that Europeans rejected decades ago. But the United States is also at odds with Europe on a range of social issues where the American practice reflects more recent innovations by the U.S. Supreme Court. The United States has the most permissive standards on access to abortion and the most permissive standards toward toleration of hate speech. At the same time, it has the most restrictive standards regarding government aid to (or sponsorship of) organized religion. Should European practice count against these U.S. standards? None of the justices who have invoked European practice on other issues has hinted at any willingness to consider European practice in these areas.

Why not? A quite plausible theory—certainly, a quite reasonable suspicion—is that American judges do not wish to be tied down to any particular doctrine or method when it comes to invoking foreign precedent because they want to be able to use foreign or international materials opportunistically: to invoke them when they bolster the outcome they prefer and ignore them when they cut the other way.

One might argue that precisely to the extent that references to foreign law are invoked opportunistically, these references are not in themselves decisive to the results and therefore no serious threat to traditional patterns of American reasoning or judicial decision making. But that is not an entirely reassuring view. If justices persist in invoking these references—despite all the controversy they have provoked—they must feel that they add some degree of authority or persuasiveness for at least some readers of the Court's opinions. And that would seem to imply that the Court reaches for such support when it feels its opinions are otherwise lacking in persuasive power.

In two of the three cases where these appeals featured in majority opinions—that is, in *Lawrence* and *Roper*—the Court was actually reversing its own rulings of less than two decades earlier. If a majority of justices saw the issue one way in relatively recent time, the switch might seem hard to explain or defend as reflecting anything more than differing preferences among the individual justices. To cite foreign precedent might be simply a way to dignify otherwise naked preferences. So justices who can bolster their preferences with foreign citations may feel emboldened to depart from solid reasoning—to depart even from their own precedents—and still feel somewhat "covered" in their conclusions.

If this assessment is correct, it suggests a quite straightforward worry about the current trend. One need not be a strict originalist, a doctrinaire positivist, a pious antiquarian or traditionalist—and one need not be committed to any particular perspective on natural law—to distrust appeals to foreign law in current circumstances. Whatever one thinks are the proper grounds for legal decisions, a good judge should be able to state the proper grounds openly and somewhat persuasively. The simplest objection to foreign citations is that they are too easily deployed as a cover for poorly grounded decisions. And almost any view of law should distrust decisions that are poorly grounded or poorly argued.

JUDICIAL FOREIGN POLICY?

But that is the simplest view and probably the least charitable. One might think these appeals are not decisive to the outcome without viewing them as mere cloaks for decisions that could not stand on other grounds. After all, the justices did offer other reasons in the three cases and elaborated the other grounds at much greater length. Moreover, the justices themselves do offer alternate arguments for the practice. But the most clearly articulated rationale is in itself unsettling—and quite threatening to any reasonable view of the rule of law.

Justice Sandra Day O'Connor gave one of the most explicit versions of this alternate view in a public address delivered a few months after the Court's decisions in *Lawrence*: citing opinions of foreign courts, she said, "will create that all important good impression."[23] Justice Ruth Bader Ginsburg made a similar point in a 2005 speech, where she argued that citations to foreign rulings would fulfill the admonition of the Declaration of Independence to "show a decent respect to the opinions of mankind."[24]

Looked at in this way, the appeal to foreign or international materials might seem more well meaning or high minded. It might seem, if anything, too trustful rather than too cynical. But it is still at odds with the way we have understood the rule of law.

Where the United States has ratified a formal treaty with foreign nations, the treaty may for certain purposes be a legal standard for U.S. courts. That seems to follow from the provision in Article VI of the Constitution that treaties are included, with federal statutes and the federal Constitution, as "supreme law of the land." When courts are called on to interpret a treaty, it makes sense for judges to consider what foreign courts have interpreted the treaty to mean, since the treaty is presumed to aim at a common understanding. Even conservative justices, like Justice Scalia, who normally object to foreign appeals, have embraced the practice in this special context.[25]

But justices who are more open to foreign materials go far beyond this special context. In *Roper*, for example, the Court cited an article in the Covenant on Civil and Political Rights that prohibits the execution of offenders less than eighteen years old—despite the fact that the U.S. Senate, when it ratified this treaty, specifically included a reservation indicating the United States would not be bound by such restrictions. The Court also cited the UN Convention on the Rights of the Child—a treaty the United States has not ratified at all.

The most obvious objection to this practice is that, in the name of interpreting the Constitution, it disregards what the Constitution actually says about treaties. The Constitution prescribes that treaties become law of the land when ratified by two-thirds of the Senate, not when approved by a bare majority of the Supreme Court. When the Senate says it approves a treaty with certain reservations, nothing authorizes the Supreme Court to restore those exceptions. When the Senate says it approves a treaty as an international commitment but not as domestic law, there is no constitutional basis for the Court to disregard this reservation and give treaties direct force in domestic law.

Behind this initial objection about treaties is a deeper point that carries over to other sorts of international understandings. There are a number of sound reasons why treaties are not always regarded as binding in domestic law. *The Federalist* defines treaties as "contracts with foreign nations" and admonishes that "a treaty is only another name for a bargain."[26] The main incentive for a nation to observe a treaty is to retain the compliance of the other parties. When a nation defaults on its treaty obligations, the most ready sanction for other parties is to claim they are no longer bound. The practice is so standard it is acknowledged as proper in the UN Convention on the Law of Treaties.[27]

But it is quite rare for nations to renounce treaty commitments in a formal and public way.[28] What happens more often is that nations fail to comply with their obligations to some extent. Sometimes diplomatic protest is enough to secure correction. Sometimes threats of retaliation must be made explicit but need not be acted on to have the desired effect. Sometimes temporary suspension of treaty commitments is required. For courts to decide when and to what extent treaty commitments should be suspended would require them to undertake quite delicate diplomatic assessments. That challenge is the responsibility of the U.S. president, who is, after all, supplied by an entire Department of State to advise—and help implement—diplomatic undertakings.

The point goes beyond implementation of formal treaty commitments. Treaties are necessarily embedded in a broader range of less-formal foreign policy commitments and signals to other nations about what the United States will do in what circumstances. Even treaties like the NATO pact, promising military assistance in the event of an attack on any of the signatories, depend for their effect on signals we send to allies and potential adversaries before the formal terms of the treaty come into play. The treaty can reassure allies and deter enemies only if, before the obligations of the treaty are actuated by its terms, the United States signals that it is serious about its commitments but not reckless or impulsive in its reactions to changing circumstances. How to do that is not simply a matter of legal parsing of treaty texts—and is far removed from the capacities of courts, deciding individual cases that happen to come before them. Courts are very poorly equipped to conduct American diplomacy. U.S. courts cannot simply give orders to officials of other nations. Even if they limit their orders to American officials, they are not well situated to gauge the effects of such rulings on other issues of concern to our larger foreign policy.

If you think of references to international materials as a show of respect to foreign governments—as Justices O'Connor and Ginsburg have suggested—you must think courts are engaged in a sort of ancillary foreign policy. The same objections can apply even if courts avoid invoking formal treaties. To invoke precedents from foreign courts (even when unrelated to treaties) may imply that our courts are relying on an informal understanding between courts of different nations, something that could be the subject of a treaty but isn't yet, something that the Senate may not even have had the chance to reject.

Take the decision of the UN's Human Rights Committee (HRC), a monitoring body established under the Covenant on Civil and Political Rights. The Supreme Court in *Lawrence* cited an opinion of the HRC as evidence of international support for the right to engage in same-sex sexual relations. The HRC claims that it has authority, under the covenant, not merely to call attention to abuses but to make authoritative interpretations of what the provisions of the covenant must mean on disputed points. The U.S. State Department has rejected this claim.[29] We have agreed to make presentations to the Human Rights Committee when it reviews national policies, but we have not agreed to treat the committee's reactions or conclusions as authoritative for our own understanding of our obligations under the treaty.

It would be a remarkable change in the meaning of the treaty if it were understood to give such authority to a group of international experts elected by the UN General Assembly. The Supreme Court did not endorse that claim in *Lawrence* but did not repudiate it, either. The Court seemed to treat it as at least an open question whether the United States may have some sort of duty to coordinate its policies with decisions of UN bodies like the Human Rights Committee.

In fact, there would be considerable controversy—and considerable constitutional dispute—about whether the United States could actually delegate such authority to an international body. It would allow the meaning of our treaty commitments to evolve over time according to the shifting views of an international body, whose membership was neither answerable to the president nor confirmed by the Senate. The D.C. Court of Appeals ruled in 2005 that delegation of U.S. regulatory authority to an international body would likely violate the Constitution.[30] The Supreme Court ruled in *Medellin v. Texas*[31] in 2008 that the president did not have the authority to override a state court ruling on the death penalty (in a case involving a foreign national who seems to have been deprived of rights guaranteed by an international treaty) even to conform with a direct ruling by the International Court of Justice. If the president does not have this authority, even when trying to conform with the UN's "world court," why would judges, acting on their own, have authority to force states to conform with a random collection of foreign court rulings?

What if an international body, like the UN Human Rights Committee, held that the United States was in violation of international norms by adhering to American constitutional standards? The Supreme Court has held in the past that treaties cannot authorize the U.S. government to violate its obligations under our own Constitution.[32] But the courts have sometimes interpreted constitutional restrictions more leniently in order to accommodate pressing foreign policy concerns, as when the Court approved a presidential agreement suspending private contract claims pending in U.S. courts to secure release of U.S. hostages in Iran in 1981.[33] If courts are conducting a parallel foreign policy, it might seem as reasonable for judges to reinterpret the Constitution to conform with what the judges see as an emerging international rights consensus. That might even seem to be a plausible description of what happened in *Lawrence* and *Roper*.

Is that too far-fetched? One reason to take it seriously is that distinguished scholars advocate such a thing. Ann-Marie Slaughter, dean of the Woodrow Wilson School of Public and International Affairs at Princeton and past president of the American Society of International Law, published a book in 2004 which described such informal coordination among judges on fundamental human rights questions as the most promising path to global governance.[34] The book received quite respectful notice from American scholars.

Meanwhile, the European Union has a Court of Justice, established (like all institutions of the EU) by treaty. The European Court of Justice has held that national courts must uphold its interpretation of European treaty law, even when they run counter to provisions in national constitutions, as interpreted by national constitutional courts.[35] To make this more palatable, the Court of Justice has promised to give consideration to the constitutional norms of the member states—not as binding authority but as a background source for coordinating norms.[36]

Almost all nations of Europe also subscribe to the European Convention on Human Rights, which, by treaty, receives authoritative interpretation by a European Court of Human Rights. Many participating states have given the European Convention direct effect in domestic law so that it functions as a sort of quasi constitution, taking precedence even over subsequently enacted statutes. The Court of Human Rights has not only made a point of citing constitutional rulings of member states to harmonize the convention with national constitutional guarantees; it has also cited opinions of courts outside Europe to reduce the risk that European human rights interpretations turn out to conflict with understandings of international human rights guarantees in UN conventions.[37] And the Human Rights Court views the European Convention as taking priority over subsequent national statutes and treaties, as if it were a constitutional obligation.[38]

If one takes the idea of international human rights law with full seriousness, it may indeed seem logical, even inescapable, to view it as superseding ordinary national laws (since human rights treaties could otherwise be readily nullified by ordinary parliamentary action). But the same logic might then suggest that international human rights law should take priority even over national constitutions, as the European Court of Justice has insisted that EU treaties must take priority over national constitutions.

In the past, the U.S. Supreme Court has emphasized that treaties must conform to the Constitution, so a treaty in violation of the Constitution would not be legally binding. Courts might try to avoid such conflicts, however, by reinterpreting the Constitution to accommodate treaty obligations, as the Constitution has been interpreted to accommodate national security measures by the president in situations of special exigency. Yet why would that be reasonable? What is the special exigency of accommodating international statements about human rights?

The ultimate objection to such recourse is that it blurs the distinction between constitutional authority and foreign policy, between fixed standards at home and necessarily contingent and adaptive responses to challenges from abroad. If courts are adapting the Constitution to their view of foreign policy, then we risk having a foreign policy that is more legalistic than it need be—and a domestic constitutional order that bends and sways with the contingencies of international relations.

The risks were already on display in the Court's ruling in *Boumediene v. Bush*[39] in 2008, holding that the Constitution's guarantee of habeas corpus applies to detainees held in Guantánamo Bay, Cuba. Both critics and defenders of the ruling have seen it as driven, at least in part, by the Court's concern to accommodate criticism of Guantánamo detention procedures by international human rights forums and foreign jurists.[40] The decision does not say that the American military must answer to domestic courts when enemy combatants are detained on foreign battlefields, as in Afghanistan or Iraq. But the decision does not explain why Guantánamo is a unique case. It disclaims reliance on "formal categories" to explain where supervision from American courts will follow the military into overseas actions and where courts will leave the military to make its own decisions.

Meanwhile, the *Boumediene* ruling reaffirmed that continued detention of terror suspects at Guantánamo does not require that they be charged and tried according to normal standards of due process for civilian criminal trials. So the Court's insistence that detentions in Guantánamo are subject to the same judicial supervision as detentions in the United States actually implies that military detentions of terror suspects may be proper within the United States, as long as they meet some standard of due process broadly acceptable to courts—even though not those laid down in the Bill of Rights for criminal trials.[41] Extending constitutional safeguards to military operations overseas means importing some military measures from overseas back into the United States. It is certainly not obvious that the end result will enhance constitutional protections for Americans.

There are good reasons, after all, why courts have not, in the past, tried to extend constitutional supervision to military actions overseas. As the dissenters in *Boumediene* pointed out, the majority opinion could not cite a single case supporting its extension of habeas corpus protection to military actions outside the United States, while the most pertinent precedent (disclaiming jurisdiction over war prisoners in postwar Germany) had firmly repudiated such overseas reach for American courts.[42]

Perhaps the strongest argument for the Court's ruling in *Boumediene* was that it reassured international human rights advocates and many foreign governments. It is even a plausible claim that American foreign policy will be more effective, over all, if American actions are seen to respect the concerns of international human rights advocates. But it is not obvious that this will prove true in every situation, since the security of the United States is not necessarily the highest priority of international human rights advocates. And it is, again, not obvious that courts are equipped to make the necessary policy judgments in balancing security concerns with international prestige among human rights advocates.

That leaves a different argument, which is perhaps most central to the whole dispute. If we are uncertain about how to balance competing concerns—say, between the requirements of national security as against the due process rights of terror suspects—why not consult the opinions of others? Why assume that the particular policy balance preferred by American officials is always better than what others advocate—particularly if many others, speaking for democratic governments facing similar concerns, seem to be converging on a different balance? Why not, finally, be open to the idea that what is endorsed by most nations is likely to be reasonable, even natural? That is the argument advanced by Waldron, which seems to echo natural law theorists back to Hugo Grotius in the seventeenth century and speculations of other thinkers going back even farther. That is, in some way, the deepest level of the contemporary dispute about foreign citations.

THE LAW OF NATURE AND THE RIGHTS OF NATIONS

There is an obvious appeal to the notion that international consensus will point us toward the natural standard. What is generally accepted seems to be more solidly grounded than what happens to be accepted only here or there. But it is not at all clear why, if local majorities are distrusted, we should attribute great authority to global majorities—even if we accept the notion that international conventions or a wide range of national court rulings do reflect the actual views of a global majority. Even the global majority might change its mind. Why give special authority to the views that happen to be held by a majority right at this moment? Why assume these views are more reasonable or more sound than those that may attain currency in some future period?

In the tradition of inquiry into natural justice, nature was associated with something fixed and unchanging. Laws based on local custom may vary, but, as Aristotle said, fire burns the same in Greece as in Persia. So when the seventeenth-century Dutch jurist Hugo Grotius set out to ground the law of nations in a more empirical understanding of natural law, he did not limit his inquiry to the practice of nations in his own day. His immensely influential treatise, *De Jure Bellum ac Pacis* (On The Law of War and Peace), drew most of its examples from the poets and philosophers of ancient Greece, the jurists of ancient Rome, and the patriarchs and prophets of the Hebrew Bible, trying to identify the fundamental principles that had been accepted by civilized nations through the ages.

When the Supreme Court invoked foreign practice in recent cases, however, it did not even pretend to search for consensus extending through many centuries of experience. Quite to the contrary, the Court embraced opinions well known to be quite recent. Only in recent decades have European nations repudiated traditional laws on sexual morality and laws imposing capital punishment for the worst crimes. Why take inspiration from these more recent laws rather than the older laws that they superseded?

The thought in the background seems to be that later laws are better because change implies improvement, because history is a story of progress toward higher and better standards. But modern history—particularly the history of Europe—does not inspire confidence in this idea. Very few people now think the monstrous policies pursued by Communist and Fascist regimes in the mid-twentieth century were improvements on the liberal policies that had prevailed in most of Europe in the nineteenth century.

It may be that European nations have learned lessons from their earlier embrace of monstrous innovations. It is often said that Europeans have embraced stronger guarantees of human rights as a way of ensuring against any revival of abuses perpetrated under Fascist and Communist regimes. But that does not offer any more reason to think Americans must follow the same path. Those who are traumatized by terrible experience are not necessarily the best mentors for people who have led more normal lives; nations that allowed themselves to sink into murderous frenzies may not be the best models for nations that managed to hold themselves within reasonable limits.

Meanwhile, it remains very hard to associate recent European fashions with serious claims about natural law. One can look at all the celebrated natural law thinkers of the past—from Aristotle and Cicero to Aquinas and Suarez, from Grotius to Locke and Kant: not one of them expressed qualms about capital punishment, not one of them embraced a natural right to sexual liberty of the sort articulated in *Lawrence*. And we can still see why such claims did not seem natural to earlier thinkers.

We still distinguish children born in this country from people who come here from foreign countries: the latter can become citizens if they follow prescribed procedures for "naturalization" (as the Constitution calls such laws) but people who were born here are automatically citizens—"naturally" so, as we might say. The natural way a nation perpetuates itself is through the children of current citizens, so nations might seem to have a natural interest in encouraging citizens to form marriage partnerships that can produce children.

If attacked, a nation must be able to defend itself. That means it must have armies and police capable of defending its people. Even today, hardly anyone disputes that lethal force may be used to resist attacks, at least in the extreme case. So it might seem most natural to think that, at least in the extreme case, capital punishment should be available as retribution for attacks that were not prevented or as a deterrent to future attacks.

There are, of course, many plausible objections to such natural conclusions particularly when it comes to applying the general premise to the particular case. But if we are reluctant to give too much weight to what previous generations regarded as "natural," the conclusion that would seem to follow is that a wider range of different policies can now be regarded as acceptable. And if that follows, then we would seem to have not more but *less* reason than previous generations to go searching for indications of some consensus of the nations.

The advocates for citing foreign precedents take the opposite view, however. They seek not less authority for disputable constitutional rulings, but more. Professor Waldron offers this analogy with policy on threats to public health:

> Consider how we would expect our public health authorities to deal with a new disease or epidemic appearing within our borders. It would be ridiculous to say that because this problem had arisen in the United States, we should look only to American science to solve it. On the contrary, we would want to look abroad to see what scientific conclusions and strategies had emerged, had been tested, and had been mutually validated in the public health practices of other countries.[43]

But the fact is that we rarely force citizens to accept medical treatments against their will. If we take as our baseline the practice of medical borrowings based on foreign clinical evidence, the better analogy wouldn't be with binding decisions of constitutional courts—imposed on citizens whether they consent to them or not—but with proposals made to legislative or administrative bodies, where legislators or administrators (and afterward, voters) could decide for themselves how much weight to give to such evidence. Even then, however, the analogy is faulty for a more fundamental reason: the health of individual human bodies—which is the aim of medicine—is much easier to determine and much more readily recognized than the civic health of political bodies.

To offer up such an obviously strained analogy tells something about the background ambition of the project. It looks to provide highly disputable constitutional standards with a moral authority akin to that once associated with natural law—for an era that is otherwise highly skeptical about natural law. In Waldron's telling, the alternative to seeking the consensus of nations is to fall back on a narrowly positivist version of constitutional interpretation, grounded solely in the original understanding of the Framers' intentions: to spurn all inquiries into the consensus of nations is, in this view, to abandon anything akin to natural law or higher law concerns.

It seems a serious challenge because it is known that the American Founders themselves were quite comfortable—sometimes quite insistent—on appeals to natural law. Originalism (in a strictly positivist version) was not the original doctrine of American constitutional law.

Yet contemporary appeals to the consensus of nations are not simply continuations of earlier inquiries into natural law standards. The difference is not just that contemporary appeals are so indifferent to continuity, so disdainful of agreement across time. The contemporary approach also assumes that new understandings can reach down to quite detailed questions. The ostensible issue in *Roper*, for example, was whether capital punishment, if available for crimes committed by eighteen-year-olds, could also be imposed for crimes by seventeen-year-olds. That is far from a bright line distinction when one considers the range of adult responsibilities (from military service to driving automobiles to entering into marriage) that are still authorized for seventeen-year-olds, without arousing much protest or controversy.

It might seem quite implausible: to suppose that the world can make major changes from past views, that it can do so relatively quickly—and then come to agreement not just on general principles but on fine points of distinction. But it looks most implausible if one assumes the process is or could be spontaneous, in the way that (as Grotius tells it, for example), the biblical patriarchs recognized so many of the same principles as the orators of the Greek city-states and the consuls of the Roman republic. The scheme looks less implausible if we assume the agreement will come from coordination, from a background agreement to agree. It is not remarkable that Hawaii and Rhode Island agree on so many fine points of law, such as raising the permissible drinking age to twenty-one. There is a common national legislature (and a common national court system) to impose or cajole such changes.

The assumption that the "world community" is converging on human rights standards is less strange or surprising if you think the world has organized authorities to steer it. It's more plausible that diplomats and judges might reach some sort of consensus than actual electorates across the globe. It is even more plausible that judges and diplomats could often reach consensus—even on new and detailed claims—if they think they have a special duty to do so. But it is not obvious that they do have such a duty, since international human rights conventions do not say that all signatories must interpret them in the same way. Such conventions would have had many fewer signatories if they had announced this requirement. To think that judges can find common ground because they will feel some obligation to do so is to take for granted what is actually disputed—whether agreement is, in itself, a good thing.

Classic works on natural law took a different view. The American Founders, for a notable example, started with an appeal to natural law—to "the Laws of Nature and of Nature's God" in the first sentence of the first American public act, the Declaration of Independence. But the Declaration invokes this seemingly fixed standard on behalf of national independence, the right to "a separate and equal station . . . among the powers of the earth." That right seems to follow from the claim, asserted in the next sentence, that governments derive their "just powers from the consent of the governed": what a "just" government may do seems to depend quite a bit on what its own people find acceptable.[44]

That is not an argument for reducing everything to consent. The Declaration itself goes on to argue that citizens have not only a right but a "duty" to change a government that seems intent on ruling despotically. But it does suggest that when timeless and universal standards are invoked, they must be applied with some regard to what any particular people may find acceptable—what, in the words of the Declaration, "to them ['the people'] shall seem most likely to effect their Safety and Happiness." Grotius, who tried to articulate relatively detailed natural standards for dealings between states, also acknowledged that governments must not interfere in the domestic affairs of other states except in extreme cases, since there are few transnational standards for domestic government: "[T]he mother of municipal law is the obligation that arises from mutual consent [of the governed] and since this obligation derives its force from the law of nature, nature may be considered, so to say, the great-grandmother of municipal law."[45]

The idea that judges and diplomats can establish detailed standards for safeguarding human rights among all peoples might seem most objectionable for risking the establishment of a global tyranny, where all are compelled to follow the same prescriptions whether they do or do not find them suitable to their own circumstances. Why suppose that judges and diplomats, even if drawn from many nations, really know what is best for each nation—and really will focus on what is best for each nation rather than most convenient for those with the most clout in the councils of the consensus builders?

But the more likely danger is not that appeals for international consensus will invest too much power in global opinion leaders. Agreements among judges and diplomats are agreements about words. No one has proposed to place police or military forces on call to enforce the human rights nostrums of international opinion leaders when these standards are disregarded by recalcitrant governments in nations like China or Saudi Arabia. The real question is, what happens to constitutional standards in countries that do have meaningful constitutional safeguards at home? Decisions of constitutional courts in these countries can be quite important because those who do control police and armies feel bound to obey them. In constitutional countries, officials generally obey court rulings even when they may be unpopular, because citizens expect to obey court rulings even when they don't endorse them.

But what is the argument for bowing to controversial court rulings? There is obvious force to the claim that courts are acting properly when they continue to uphold the standards bequeathed by past generations. Without stability, there is no reliable law; without law, no reliable constitution; without a reliable constitution, no government worthy of trust; without a trustworthy government, no assurance that a nation will not crumble to pieces. If citizens feel they are not protected by their own government, they will look elsewhere for such protection and their loyalties will migrate with their search for security. There are reasons, as the Declaration of Independence says, why "governments long established should not be changed for light and transient causes."

It is less obvious why a law that is hostage to shifting international opinion is a law that critics must accept. It is still less obvious why the law must be respected when it is not even law made by representatives of the people it purports to govern but is simply the current consensus of judges and diplomats. Why defer to these custodians of international opinion when they do not even commit to follow their own prescriptions in the future? Why defer to them when they do not even claim their prescriptions are adjusted to the best interests of any particular people but are merely generic admonitions for all peoples—just for this moment.

It may be true that confidence in law—and the sense of obligation to obey the law—requires some belief that the law is reasonable. But many things might be regarded as reasonable without engaging any strong sense of commitment or obligation. The question for any constitution is not whether it can operate in times of comfort but whether it can sustain itself in times of stress and crisis. If judges and government officials are swayed by moral pressure from international human rights advocates and foreign governments, will they have the stamina to withstand more violent or angry threats from other directions?

The questions are hardly hypothetical. Over the past decade, the Organization of the Islamic Conference has demanded that nations enforce laws against "Islamophobia," by which it means public speech critical of Islam. European nations have expressed concerns about threats to free speech in this program—but abstained at crucial votes in UN human rights forums. Meanwhile, European human rights institutions have urged that some balance be struck, since citizens should be protected against incitements to intolerance. Which is more likely to bend its current notions of proper free speech protection to accommodate the demands of Islamist advocates—Europe or the United States? In a number of countries, advocates have urged that Muslim communities should be allowed to enforce *sharia* law on fellow Muslims, even in Western countries with very different notions about the freedom of individuals. Which is more likely to abandon their own national standards to accommodate demands for local *sharia*—Europe or the United States?

Americans, at least, have long experience holding to their own views. The United States is one of the only countries to enshrine a right to bear arms in its national bill of rights. In 2008, the Supreme Court ruled that this guarantee means what it says.[46] Presidential candidates of both major parties agreed that the Court was right to say so. The United States adheres not only to a whole range of eighteenth-century governing principles, but even to such old traditions as the English system of weights and measures, in a world where even England and all other English-speaking countries have converted to the metric system.

Meanwhile, European countries have abandoned their own constitutions to avoid confrontations with judges and bureaucrats at the European level. National electorates have repeatedly rejected the European constitution when allowed to express their own views in direct referenda. National electorates have then subsided into passivity when governments found ways to circumvent referenda results and embrace the rejected European "constitution." If national leaders and national electorates will not fight for their own constitutions, why would anyone expect them to remain staunch supporters of international human rights standards? If there is no strong political support for these standards and opponents threaten violence and social turmoil if they are not removed, should we really expect judges in Europe to remain staunch defenders of the current standards?

Standards that purport to be universal or broadly international may have much less capacity to maintain themselves than national standards. If this is so, it presents a powerful challenge: a standard that cannot maintain itself forfeits its claim to be called a law.

CONCLUSION: NOT THE CITATIONS BUT THE THOUGHT BEHIND THEM

Almost all commentators—and seemingly all justices—agree that foreign citations are appropriate in some circumstances. No one disputes that it is appropriate for American judges to look at how foreign courts or foreign governments have interpreted treaties to which the United States is a party, since treaties are, by definition, efforts to coordinate policies of different nations. Even in constitutional cases, there is no serious dispute about the potential relevance of foreign legal sources from before the American Revolution, which may have informed the intentions of the Constitution's Framers. In some situations, it may even be pertinent to notice more recent foreign *experience* insofar as it offers cautionary lessons. Justice Rehnquist, for example, cited Dutch experience with medical abuses when deciding a case on the right to medically assisted suicide.[47]

At the heart of the contemporary dispute about citation of foreign law is dispute about whether American courts should be interpreting the American Constitution to coordinate American standards with foreign *opinion* on disputed social issues. The project looks plausible to many advocates in an era when many countries and many international institutions profess support for common standards of protection for human rights.[48] But it is certainly something new for American courts to judge the requirements of the U.S. Constitution by trends in international human rights discourse. The dispute is not about the proper style of Court opinions but about whether constitutional interpretation should be shared in this way—even if done with qualifications or hesitations. The underlying dispute is likely to be with us for decades to come, even if justices sympathetic to this approach are more cautious about what they actually cite in their opinions.

Whatever else one might say about this underlying dispute, it is not persuasive to frame it as simply the latest version of ongoing disputes between advocates of natural law and advocates of a confined or positivistic reading of the Constitution. Some justices who have shown sympathy for natural law arguments, notably Justice Thomas, have still voiced sharp protest against appeals to foreign precedents in U.S. constitutional decisions.[49] Those who do embrace appeals to foreign or international precedents, on the other hand, seem to have strayed very far from any traditional understanding of natural law.

Over many centuries, there have been many different understandings of what the law of nature teaches. But if there is one underlying idea in the tradition of natural law inquiry it is that nature has implanted certain immediate perceptions of justice in human beings and no government can simply ignore these perceptions on the ground that its law is law and can't be questioned. To go beyond our own Constitution to some supposed consensus of global experts on human rights—or worse, experts on the latest emerging trends in human rights policy adjustment—seems to be seeking an authority so global that it can't be readily questioned. It is unlikely that international human rights organs or networks of national judges nodding to each other's human rights pronouncements will ever attain such unshakeable authority. But that may say not that the project is safe, but that it is unnatural. The animating dream seems to be of a world where nations are not separately constituted. The end result may be that there is less and less left in the world that we could recognize as constitutional *law*.

NOTES

1. *Atkins v. Virginia*, 536 U.S. 304 (2002).

2. *Furman v. Georgia*, 408 U.S. 238 (1972).

3. Starting with *Gregg v. Georgia*, 428 U.S. 153 (1976) (death penalty acceptable after separate jury deliberation on its application); *Woodson v. North Carolina*, 428 U.S. 280 (1976) (rejecting mandatory capital sentences); *Coker v. Georgia*, 433 U.S. 584 (1977) (rejecting death penalty for rape); *Ford v. Wainwright*, 477 U.S. 399 (1986) (rejecting death penalty for insane offenders); *Thompson v. Oklahoma*, 487 U.S. 815 (1988) (rejecting death penalty for offenders under sixteen).

4. "[W]ithin the world community, the imposition of the death penalty for crimes committed by mentally retarded offenders is overwhelmingly disapproved." 356 U.S. 304 at 316n21.

5. 356 U.S. at 347–48.

6. *Lawrence v. Texas*, 549 U.S. 577 (2003).

7. *Roper v. Simmons*, 543 U.S. 551 (2005).

8. Sandra Day O'Connor, "Remarks at the Southern Center for International Studies," October 28, 2003; Ruth Bader Ginsburg, "A Decent Respect to the Opin-

ions of Humankind: The Value of a Comparative Perspective in Constitutional Adjudication," address to the American Society of International Law Annual Meeting, April 1, 2005.

9. H. R. Res. 568, 108th Cong., 2004; S. Res. 92, 109th Cong., 2005.

10. The most thorough is Steven G. Calabresi and Stephanie Dotson Zimdahl, "The Supreme Court and Foreign Sources of Law," *William and Mary Law Review* 47 (December 2005): 743.

11. For example, John Yoo, "Peaking Abroad? The Supreme Court's Use of Foreign Precedents in Constitutional Cases," *Hawaii Law Review* 26 (Summer 2004): 385, while offering strong criticism of the practice, begins by acknowledging it "is difficult to know how seriously to take this development. One possibility is that Justices may be using foreign constitutional decisions simply as an ornament, merely to illuminate or decorate their opinions" (385).

12. *United States v. Smith*, 18 U.S. (5 Wheat.) 153 (1820).

13. Vicki Jackson, "The International Migration of Constitutional Norms in the New World Order," *Fordham Law Review* 75 (November 2006): 921, 922, 925.

14. Jeremy Waldron, "Foreign Law and the Modern Ius Gentium," *Harvard Law Review* 119 (November 2005): 129.

15. Waldron, "Modern Ius Gentium," 131–32.

16. For one version of this argument, see Daniel Farber, "The Supreme Court, the Law of Nations and Citations to Foreign Law," *California Law Review* 95 (2007): 1355–61 (on borrowings between states within the United States).

17. *Erie R. R. Co. v. Tompkins*, 304 U.S. 64 (1938).

18. My own law school, funded by taxpayers of Virginia as part of the state university system, is a case in point. Even the first-year courses on "contract," "property," "torts," and so on, rely on national textbooks, which give only glancing attention to cases that happen to arise in Virginia. Only one course in all the school's offerings (Virginia Practice) focuses on Virginia-specific cases. Can we really imagine a law school curriculum in which almost all courses rely predominantly on foreign cases?

19. Michael Ramsey, "International Materials and Domestic Rights," *American Journal of International Law* 98 (January 2004): 77–78.

20. Roger P. Alford, "The United States Constitution and International Law: Misusing International Sources to Interpret the Constitution," *American Journal of International Law* 98 (January 2004): 65–66.

21. Zimbabwe citation in *Knight v. Florida*, 528 U.S. 990 at 997–98; subsequent concession in Justices Antonin Scalia and Stephen Breyer, "Discussion at the American University Washington College of Law: Constitutional Relevance of Foreign Court Decisions," January 13, 2005.

22. Agence France-Press, "Council of Europe Urges U.S., Japan to End Death Penalty," June 5, 2001.

23. See note 8 above.

24. It may be telling that Justice Ginsburg's appeal to the Declaration starts by translating its language into the politically correct terminology favored by some feminists today: "A Decent Respect to the Opinions of [Human]kind': The Value of a Comparative Perspective in Constitutional Ajudication," speech to the ASIL, April 1, 2005. In addition to speaking of "mankind" without embarrassment, the authors of the Declaration did not, as it happens, bother to cite a single foreign precedent in making the American case for independence. In the same case (on the

constitutional validity of racial preferences) Justice Thomas cited the "principles" of the Declaration, while Justice Ginsburg cited (to bolster a different conclusion), the International Convention on the Elimination of Racial Discrimination. *Grutter v. Bollinger*, 539 U.S. 306 (2003) at 304.

25. The Court "can and should look to decisions of other signatories when we interpret treaty provisions." *Olympic Airways v. Husain*, 540 U.S. 644 (2004) at 660 (Scalia dissenting).

26. *Federalist* 75, ed. C. Rossiter and C. Kesler (New York: Signet, 2003), 449; *Federalist* 64, ed. C. Rossiter and C. Kesler (New York: Signet, 2003), 392.

27. Vienna Convention on the Law of Treaties (1969), Art. 60.

28. A survey of some 32,000 multilateral treaties, registered with the UN between 1945 and 2004, found fewer than 5 percent of ratifications were ever withdrawn and fewer than 4 percent of these treaties were subject to even one act of withdrawal. Larry Helfer, "Exiting Treaties," *Virginia Law Review* 91 (November 2005): 1579.

29. The State Department (during the Clinton administration) protested that the International Covenant on Civil and Political Rights did not "impose . . . an obligation to give effect to the Committee's interpretation or confer on the Committee the power to render definite interpretations of the Covenant." The statement was reprinted in *Human Rights Law Journal* 16 (1995): 422.

30. *Natural Resources Defense Council v. Environmental Protection Agency*, 464 F.3d 1 (D.C. Circ., 2006).

31. *Medellin v. Texas*, 128 S.Ct. 1346 (2008).

32. *Reid v. Covert*, 354 U.S. 1 (1957).

33. *Dames & Moore v. Regan*, 453 U.S. 654 (1981).

34. Anne-Marie Slaughter, *A New World Order* (Princeton, N.J.: Princeton University Press, 2004), esp. chap. 2, "Judges: Constructing a Global Legal System."

35. *Internatiionale Handelsgesellschaft MBH v. Einfuhr-Und-Vorratsstelle*, Case 11/70, [1970] ECR 1125.

36. *Liselotte Hauer v. Land Rheinland-Pfalz*, Case 44/79, [1979]ECR 3727.

37. In *Tyrer v. United Kingdom* (judgment of April 25, 1978), the Court of Human Rights held "birching" to be improper punishment, because by then quite unusual and evaluation of proper punishment could not "but be influenced by developments and common standards . . . in the member states of the Council of Europe, rather than anywhere else." But by 2005, after many such appeals to a supposed emerging consensus among parties to the European Convention on Human Rights, the Court (in a case objecting to the United Kingdom's denial of voting rights to convicted felons), looked as well to the Supreme Court of Canada and the Constitutional Court of South Africa. (*Hirst v. UK*, No. 74025/01, ECHR 2005-IX). In 2007, in a case dealing with education rights of the gypsy minority in the Czech Republic, the Human Rights Court considered parallel or possibly relevant guarantees in the International Covenant on Civil and Political Rights, the International Convention on Elimination of Race Discrimination, the Convention on the Rights of the Child, and pronouncements of various UN organs. (*D.H. and Others v. Czech Republic*, No. 57325/0012 Nov. 2007). A recent publication by the court includes a contribution from the Chief Justice of Ireland questioning this jurisprudence: "Can recent consensus, emerging consensus or trends [among various jurisdictions in or out of Europe] be properly described as a true consensus? Is it not simply a majority view? And a current one at that." He cites, with evident sympathy, from the dissent-

ing opinion of Justice Scalia in *Roper*. A judge of the Belgian Constitutional Court worries, on the other hand, that allowing the Human Rights Court (rather than national judges) to have the last word in discerning emerging trends may threaten "the rule-making power [of national courts] that has enabled a European judicial [*sic*] democracy to form." ECHR, *Dialogue between Judges* (2008), 65, 48, 94.

38. The Court insists that states that subscribe to the convention are obligated to change their national law to make it "coherent and consistent" with the Court's interpretation of the convention—but it is "for the respondent state [in a case] alone to take the measures it considers appropriate to assure" this result. *Marckx v. Belgium* (judgment of June 13, 1979).

39. *Boumediene v. Bush*, 128 S. Ct. 2229 (2008).

40. Eric A. Posner, "*Boumediene* and the Uncertain March of Judicial Cosmopolitanism," and David D. Cole, "Rights Over Borders: Transnational Constitutionalism and Guantanamo Bay," both in *Cato Supreme Court Review 2007–2008*.

41. *Hamdi v. Rumsfeld*, 542 U.S. 507 (2004).

42. *Johnson v. Eisentrager*, 339 U.S. 763 (1950).

43. *Johnson v. Eisentrager*, 339 U.S. at 143.

44. Professor Waldron interprets Locke's failure to provide for judicial enforcement of constitutional limits—or natural law limits—in this way in an earlier work: "I think what Locke wants to say is that whenever there are controversies about natural law, it is important that a *representative* [original emphasis] assembly resolve them. . . . The institution which comprises our representatives and the institution which resolves our ultimate differences in moral principle ought to be one and the same. It is by combining these functions that it embodies our civic unity and our sense of mutual sympathy. . . . I think this is a powerful and appealing position. It embodies a conviction that these issues are 'ours' to deal with, so that even if they must be dealt with by some institution which comprises fewer than all of us, it should nonetheless be an institution that is diverse and plural and which, through something like electoral accountability, embodies the spirit of self-government." Jeremy Waldron, *The Dignity of Legislation* (Cambridge: Cambridge University Press, 1999), 86–87.

45. Hugo Grotius, *The Law of War and Peace*, trans. Francis W. Kelsey (Oxford: Oxford University Press, 1925), Prolegomena, par. 16, p. 15.

46. *District of Columbia v. Heller*, 128 S.Ct. 2783 (2008).

47. *Washington v. Glucksberg*, 485 U.S. 702 (1997) at 724.

48. For example, Daniel Bodansky, "Use of International Sources in Constitutional Opinion," *Georgia Journal of International and Comparative Law* 32 (2004): 421; Sarah H. Cleveland, "Our International Constitution," *Yale Journal of International Law* 31 (2006): 1.

49. Compare Justice Thomas's protest in *Foster v. Florida*, 557 U.S. 990 (2002) ("this Court's Eight Amendment jurisprudence should not impose foreign moods, fads or fashions on Americans") with his appeal the following year to principles preceding the Constitution in *Grutter v. Bollinger*, 539 U.S. 306 (2003) ("the principle of equality embodied in the Declaration of Independence.") or earlier in *Troxel v. Granville*, 530 U.S. 57 (200) (suggesting the Due Process Clause may protect basic rights derived from natural law principles).

8

Progressivism and the Decline of the Rule of Law

Bradley C. S. Watson

In this chapter I discuss the philosophical origins of the "living Constitution" approach to judicial review, a Progressive-historicist approach to constitutional interpretation that today dominates American jurisprudential thought and presents the most significant threat to the Founders' Constitution and the rule of law. I begin with a brief account of the meaning of the rule of law and American constitutionalism and then proceed to review recent examples of threats to that constitutionalism in cases from the United States Supreme Court. In the next two sections of the chapter I examine how social Darwinism and pragmatism transformed American political thought at the end of the nineteenth and early parts of the twentieth century, forming the basis for intellectual progressivism. This last ideology—progressivism—would infiltrate institutional attitudes and American politics more generally through the twentieth century and have significant implications for the new science of jurisprudence. I review these implications in the concluding section of the chapter.

THE RULE OF LAW, PROGRESSIVISM, AND TODAY'S SUPREME COURT

The rule of law in liberal democracies involves the invocation and enforcement by the state of authoritative norms that have been consensually and publicly adopted and that bind equally state and nonstate actors, having as their end the protection of the fundamental and timeless natural rights of human beings. The rule of law thus cannot be the rule of men, cannot stem from the posting of norms in a manner such that they cannot be known, and cannot involve the alteration of norms in a contingent or nonconsensual manner.

The now common notion that the Constitution is a living document, creating an organic constitutional order that is subject to ceaseless change or "growth" at the behest of the least republican branch of government, is incompatible with the idea and implementation of the rule of law as defined above. The judicial branch, more than any other, has adopted a historicist view of the Constitution and constitutionalism. Under this view, the exact nature and degree of change or growth in the constitutional order is to be dictated by judicial elites in accordance with their perceptions of the new realities that the progress of History imposes on constitutional interpretation. This jurisprudential progressivism relies on a theory of History, with a capital *H*—a History that unfolds inexorably in a democratic, egalitarian direction, requiring occasional help from jurists who are in a position to see, and remove, obstacles in the way of historical progress. The view is not simply that we have, of necessity, an interpretable Constitution, but that we have one that must be interpreted in light of a particular understanding of the historically situated, contingent nature of the state, the individual, society, and constitutionalism itself.

This understanding is in a considerable amount of tension with the rule of law and the earlier American constitutionalism that attempted to enshrine the rule of law through the creation of a constitutional order of limited and dispersed powers serving the "laws of nature and nature's God." As Herman Belz has noted,

> The conception of the constitution as a formal legal instrument or code giving existence to government and prescribing and limiting the exercise of its powers, rather than as the basic structure of the polity, not consciously constructed but growing organically through history, was one of the distinctive achievements of the American Revolution, and oriented constitutional description and analysis in the early republic toward a legalistic approach.[1]

In 1863 Abraham Lincoln declared that America "was conceived in liberty, and dedicated to the proposition that all men are created equal." It is in Lincoln we can see the culmination of the older understanding of the American constitutional order and the political principles it enshrined. Both were, in Lincoln's view, handed down by the Founding Fathers, who bequeathed them to later generations to preserve. From relatively early in his adult life, through the coming and prosecution of the Civil War, Lincoln exemplified the belief in legalistic constitutionalism, overlaid with the complementary belief in the necessity of active statesmanship for preserving it.

The political rhetoric and actions of Lincoln remain among the greatest statements that there are such things as natural rights that do not change with time, that the American Constitution is dedicated to preserving them, and that the role of great political actors, while responding to urgent necessities, is to look backward rather than forward. For Lincoln, the state is more formal than organic, history is not destined to unfold in a democratic direction, and democracy itself, because of its indissoluble link with the passions rather than reason, is always combustible. Certainly the judicial branch—as evidenced by the *Dred Scott* case—is hardly to be relied on as the engine of progress. Moral and political regress are as likely as, and perhaps more likely than, progress.

Furthermore, there are certain fixed principles beyond which progress is impossible. Sharing with Plato and Aristotle the belief that negative regime change is an ever-present possibility, Lincoln was profoundly wary of the very notion of progress; evolution, growth and an organic constitutionalism were not part of his political vocabulary. American political thought subsequent to Lincoln has, for the most part, amounted effectively to an attack on the Founders' and Lincoln's conception of the American Constitution and the philosophical proposition on which it rests. This transformation has been reflected in, and driven by, twentieth- and twenty-first-century constitutional jurisprudence.

One need not seek long or hard for recent examples of the Progressive-historicist, as opposed to legalistic, approach to jurisprudence. For example, in the early 1990s, the plurality opinion of the U.S. Supreme Court in *Planned Parenthood v. Casey* (1992)[2] famously asserted or reasserted an individual right to be "free from unwarranted governmental intrusion into matters so fundamentally affecting a person as the decision whether to bear or beget a child." It went on to add that such "intimate and personal choices" are "central to personal dignity and autonomy" and to the liberty protected by the Fourteenth Amendment, which has at its heart "the right to define one's own concept of existence, of meaning, of the universe, and of the mystery of human life," which beliefs "define the attributes of personhood." Affirming this language a decade later, Justice Anthony Kennedy, writing for the majority in *Lawrence v. Texas* (2003),[3] also asserted the importance of an "emerging recognition" of new rights worthy of judicial protection, in this case concerning homosexual conduct. "In all events," he claimed, "we think that our laws and traditions in the past half century are of most relevance here. These references show an emerging awareness that liberty gives substantial protection to adult persons in deciding how to conduct their private lives in matters pertaining to sex." Only through recognition of such liberty, argued Justice Kennedy, can we avoid stigmatizing and demeaning the autonomous choices of individuals, whose dignity is revealed in time. In fact,

> [h]ad those who drew and ratified the Due Process Clauses of the Fifth Amendment or the Fourteenth Amendment known the components of liberty in its manifold possibilities, they might have been more specific. They did not presume to have this insight. They knew times can blind us to certain truths and later generations can see that laws once thought necessary and proper in fact serve only to oppress. As the Constitution endures, persons in every generation can invoke its principles in their own search for greater freedom.

In striking down the state statutes at issue, these decisions relied on purported substantive due process protections of the Fourteenth Amendment—in Justice Kennedy's phrasing, the "due process right to demand respect for conduct protected by the substantive guarantee of liberty." But in so doing, they also put forth particular, interlocking understandings of constitutionalism, individuality, and a dynamic of historical unfolding—or History, as more than a mere record of events. Along with these understandings is a theory, adopted *sub silentio*, of the judiciary's role in History.

This is a theory adopted more explicitly by the late Justice William J. Brennan, when he claimed judges must recognize that "the genius of the Constitution rests not in any static meaning it might have had in a world that is dead and gone, but in the adaptability of its great principles to cope with current problems and current needs."[4] According to Brennan, the "vision of our time" is destined to be different from the vision of other times, and a central part of the judicial role is to act as visionary. Although the Constitution is in some degree a "structuring text" marking out the bounds of government, it is, more fundamentally, a visionary document demanding ever more democracy and respect for individual dignity.[5] To inject meaning into these terms, the judge will eschew "a technical understanding of the organs of government" in favor of "a personal confrontation with the wellsprings of our society."[6] Asserting that individual dignity is the most important of all political values, Brennan sees the judge's job as articulating its meaning as that meaning reveals itself in time.

This revelation is aided by the full play of ideas. The reason for the protection of "broad and deep rights of expression"[7] is that they are related to the intellectual and spiritual growth over time that lends dignity to the human creature. Citing approvingly Justice Brandeis's dictum in *Whitney v. California* (1927)[8] that the state has no end beyond ensuring full development of human faculties, Brennan avers that the "demands of human dignity will never cease to evolve."[9] Dignity is not fixed—it has no principles or laws beyond those governing its internal evolutionary dynamic. In fact, the very act of looking for fixed principles or laws is regressive, for in so acting we cast a glance toward a past wherein dignity was, always and everywhere, less developed and more stultified.

A corollary of this view is that the scope and power of government—whether state or national—are in principle unlimited, because of the need to support human dignity and the constant development of human faculties. Courts merely adjudicate at the "collision points" between state and society, and are on guard against anything that stifles salutary development.[10] The task of judging is therefore itself protean, accurately reading and responding to the constant flux of human aspiration.[11] The Supreme Court has the last word on constitutional interpretation, but the last word for any one time is not the last word for all time, or the Constitution "falls captive" to the "anachronistic views of long-gone generations."[12] The Constitution is timeless only because its interpretations are time bound; its genius lies in its recognition of the inevitability of the "evolutionary process."[13] Adaptation to the "ever-changing conditions of national and international life"[14] is the sine qua non of constitutionalism, and the motor of this process is the judicial branch.

Brennan's colleague on the Court, the late Justice Thurgood Marshall, also pointedly claimed that the meaning of the Constitution was not fixed in Philadelphia, nor anywhere else.[15] The Constitution that emerged from Philadelphia was merely "a product of its times,"[16] as is the Constitution we now have. The changes we have witnessed in our constitutional fabric were not, and could not have been, foreseen or accepted by those who gathered in 1787 to draft the document.[17] The constitutional text itself lies dead in a vault in the National Archives.[18] The views of our own time are all that live. Constitutional interpretation involves perceiving and clearly articulating the direction of evolutionary change for an organic document that serves the needs of an organic state. Those who possess an insight into History must redefine outdated notions of liberty, justice, and equality. Their aim is to aid a process that is outside the full control of any one individual or institution. The historical process is an immense struggle for survival of the good over the bad, and good fortune is indispensable to a proper unfolding of History.[19]

On some questions, History moves rapidly. It is the job of the wise majority of the Court to recognize its direction and clear the obstacles, often in the form of state laws, which stand in its way. The rapidity of Historical change is illustrated by the difficulty even the Court has in keeping up with it. Certain minority opinions gain majority status in remarkably short periods of time. It took only seventeen years for *Lawrence* to overturn *Bowers v. Hardwick* (1986), [20] in which a five-to-four majority of the Supreme Court upheld a Georgia antisodomy statute. According to Justice Kennedy in *Lawrence,* even as *Bowers* was being decided, there was an "emerging recognition" of the substantial liberty of adult persons to choose freely in "matters pertaining to sex." The Court's majority in *Bowers* failed by failing to recognize the stamp of approval that History had already placed on homosexual conduct—but this Historical fact was not lost on the *Bowers* dissenters. For example, Justice Harry Blackmun quoted approvingly Oliver Wendell Holmes—the Court's first social Darwinist—in condemning a rule of law whose grounds "have vanished long since." Such "blind imitation of the past"[21] is senseless because the ethical grounds on which such statutes were based have shifted radically over time. For our time, at least, "much of the richness of a relationship will come from the freedom an individual has to *choose* the form and nature" of that relationship. Human personality must be allowed to develop by keeping the state out of the business of restricting "intimate associations." The asserted primacy of freedom of choice thus allows us to define our natures as we see fit, subject only to the principle of mutual consent. The process of redefinition is in principle virtually unlimited, and will continue to unfold as new understandings of human personality manifest themselves in History.

A mere eight years before *Lawrence*, in *Hurley v. Irish-American Gay, Lesbian, and Bisexual Group of Boston* (1995), [22] the Court had held unanimously that a privately organized parade could exclude groups that wished to convey a message contrary to that favored by the parade organization, thus protecting the organization's First Amendment rights. However, just five years later in *Boy Scouts of America v. Dale* (2000), [23] the Court could only muster a slim five-to-four majority for the proposition that an open homosexual did not have the right to join the Boy Scouts as an adult leader because his presence in the organization would convey a message contrary to the one the Boy Scouts wished to convey. What had happened in the intervening five years?[24]

The dissent in *Boy Scouts*, penned by Justice Stevens, gives us some clues. For him, unfavorable views of homosexuals are rooted in ancient prejudices, best likened to the "equally atavistic opinions about certain racial groups," which opinions have "been nourished by sectarian doctrine." Only "habit, rather than analysis" grounds the man-woman distinction. Thus does Justice Stevens, in a single paragraph, take on and dismiss both revelation and classical moral reasoning. And he goes on, in the same paragraph, to substitute for them History and historical progress, including the findings of social science as revealed in History:

> Over the years . . . interaction with real people, rather than mere adherence to traditional ways of thinking about members of unfamiliar classes, have modified these opinions. A few examples: The American Psychiatric Association's and the American Psychological Association's removal of "homosexuality" from their lists of mental disorders; a move toward greater understanding within some religious communities; Justice Blackmun's classic opinion in *Bowers*; Georgia's invalidation of the statute upheld in *Bowers*; and New Jersey's enactment of the provision at issue in this case. Indeed, the past month alone has witnessed some remarkable changes in attitudes about homosexuals.

Justice Stevens's reasoning, not coincidentally, bears a close resemblance to the reasoning of the unanimous Court in *Brown v. Board of Education* (1954)[25] wherein sociological jurisprudence, in the form of reliance on psychological studies, takes the place of constitutional or common-law reasoning. As Chief Justice Earl Warren then wrote, what is true, or at least fashionable, "in these days," is sufficient warrant for the Court to lay down an enduring constitutional principle. This is a sensible course of action if and only if History is reliably progressive, steadily revealing new and legally relevant "truths" in time.

A series of "right to die" cases further illustrate the centrality of historical reasoning to some members of the Court. In *Cruzan v. Missouri Department of*

Health (1990),[26] the five-to-four majority of the Court held that a competent person has a constitutionally protected Fourteenth Amendment liberty interest in refusing unwanted medical treatment, but that the state of Missouri could require clear and compelling evidence of an incompetent person's wishes concerning the withdrawal of lifesaving medical treatment. Justice Scalia, in a concurring opinion, would have had the Court stand back from "right to die" questions entirely, for the Constitution is silent on the matter, and indeed it has never been the case that states have been prohibited from interfering with such a purported right, the contours of which "are neither set forth in the Constitution nor known to the nine Justices of this Court any better than they are known to nine people picked at random from the Kansas City telephone directory." But in considering right to die cases nonjusticiable on constitutional grounds, Scalia was a minority of one.

In *Washington v. Glucksberg* (1997),[27] the Court upheld a Washington state statute that outlawed assisted suicide. In writing for the majority, Chief Justice Rehnquist noted the cases in which the Court held that the Fourteenth Amendment's Due Process Clause offers substantive protections of liberty going beyond fair procedure. These have included, among other things, the right to marry, the right to marital privacy, and, in *Casey*, the right to abortion. But Rehnquist also asserted the reluctance of the Court to expand substantive due process to other areas because of the fundamentally political nature of the enterprise, and the superiority of legislative debate, experimentation, and compromise to judicially imposed substantive standards. However, in a concurring judgment, Justice Souter agreed that the experimentation of the legislative process is to be preferred, but only for the present time. "The Court should accordingly stay its hand to allow reasonable legislative consideration. While I do not decide for all time that respondents' claim should not be recognized, I acknowledge the legislative institutional competence as the better one to deal with that claim at this time." For Souter, judicial intervention is not called for until it is called for. Facts revealed as History unfolds, rather than common law or constitutional principles, determine the justiciability of fundamental moral-political questions.

Souter offered a similar concurrence in *Vacco v. Quill* (1997),[28] which was heard in conjunction with *Glucksberg*. In *Vacco*, an equal protection claim was raised against a New York law that allowed competent patients to refuse medical treatment but made it a crime to assist a competent person to commit suicide, including by prescription of lethal medication. The argument in favor of striking down the law alleged that this resulted in different treatment for similarly situated patients, one subset of whom chose suicide by refusal of treatment, the other by ingestion of medication. Justice Rehnquist for the Court maintained as rational the distinction between refusal of treatment and assisting with suicide—the former resulting in death from "an underlying fatal disease or pathology," the latter involving the intention on the part of a doctor that "the patient be made dead." In his concurrence, Justice Souter would say only that he did "not conclude that assisted suicide is a fundamental right entitled to recognition at this time." According to Justice Souter's reasoning, for the time being—but only for the time being—the state statutes in *Glucksberg* and *Vacco* are not unconstitutional under either the due process standard or the equal protection standard. But History will be the ultimate judge.

SOCIAL DARWINISM AND THE TRANSFORMATION OF AMERICAN POLITICAL THOUGHT

As we can see from even this brief sampling, the modern historical, nonlegalistic approach to jurisprudence has been embraced by judicial appointees of different presidents, from different decades, Democrat and Republican, "liberal" and "conservative." A major transformation in American political thought was necessary to bring such a diverse cast of characters to their organic view of the Constitution. This transformation is little understood. Legal historians have preferred to concentrate on legal education or legal theory narrowly construed, rather than the philosophical categories that animate thought and action.[29] Political theorists have for the most part not filled the gap. We can only begin to assess the new constitutionalism—as well as the new science of jurisprudence that is its handmaid—by tracing its philosophical origins.[30]

This transformation in political thought, commencing after Reconstruction and running through the Progressive era of the early twentieth century, undergirds many forms of political action in America. The transformation involves the coalescing of social Darwinism and pragmatism into a powerful intellectual progressivism that decisively informs institutional attitudes and behaviors, particularly, starting in the early twentieth century, those of the judicial branch.

In the America of the late nineteenth century, the old understanding of the nature and permanent limits of politics was dead or dying. The death of this understanding was necessarily linked to a reevaluation and reconfiguration of the American Founders' political categories. The death was hastened, and arguably caused, by the arrival on the intellectual scene of the various doctrines and philosophical assumptions commonly, though subsequently, associated with the phrase "social Darwinism." As Richard Hofstadter has observed, "In some respects the United States during the last three decades of the nineteenth and at the beginning of the twentieth century was *the* social Darwinian country."[31]

On the foundation laid by the social Darwinists and those in allied philosophical movements, many of the most influential American political thinkers and actors—particularly judicial actors—came, in the twentieth century, to share six core, overlapping understandings of the nature of politics and constitutional government.

First, that there are no fixed or eternal principles that govern, or ought to govern, the politics of a decent regime. Old political categories are just that, and Lincoln's understanding of the Founders' Constitution, to the extent it is worthy of any consideration at all, is a quaint anachronism.

Second, that the state and its component parts are organic, each involved in a struggle for never-ending growth. Contrary to the Platonic ideal of *stasis*, and contrary too to the Aristotelian notion of natural movement toward particular ends, the new organic view of politics suggests movement itself is the key to survival and what can perhaps loosely be termed the political "good."

Third, that democratic openness and experimentalism, especially in the expressive realm, are necessary to ensure vigorous growth—they are the fertilizer of the organic state. Such experimentalism implies a particular sort of consequentialism or utilitarianism when judging institutions and laws.

Fourth, that the state and its component parts exist only in History, understood as an inexorable process, rather than a mere record of events.

Fifth, that some individuals stand outside this process and must, like captains of a great ship, periodically adjust the position of this ship in the river of History—to ensure that it continues to move forward, rather than run aground and stagnate. Politics demands an elite class, possessed of intelligence as a method, or reason directed to instrumental matters rather than fixed truth. This elite class springs into action to clear blockages in the path of historical progress, whether in the form of anachronistic institutions, laws, or ideas. These blockages will form in the path of the ship of state when openness or experimentalism proves inadequate.

Sixth, and a direct corollary to the strong historicism just mentioned, is that moral-political truth or rightness of action is always relative to one's moment in History, or the exact place of the ship in the river of time.

According to the social Darwinists and those who would follow in their footsteps, a new social science was indebted to Darwin, whose organic, genetic and experimental logic could be brought to bear on an array of human problems heretofore considered insoluble, or at least perennial. Darwin came to be understood as a political philosopher and political scientist rejecting old modes and orders. No one more clearly explicates the nature of this new science than John Dewey in a great essay entitled "The Influence of Darwinism on Philosophy."[32] By the time he wrote it in 1909, he was effectively summarizing the intellectual tenor of his times. He was giving an account of the origins of an already regnant pattern of American social and political thought.[33]

As Dewey avers, the publication of the *Origin of Species* marked a revolution not only in the natural sciences, but the human sciences as well, which can continue in their old form only under the pressures of habit and prejudice. To speak of an "origin" of species is itself a revolution in thought, implying that the organic sciences as well as the inorganic can concentrate on change rather than stasis. In Dewey's words, "The influence of Darwin upon philosophy resides in his having conquered the phenomena of life for the principle of transition, and thereby freed the new logic for application to mind and morals and life." Darwin, more than anyone else, allows us to move from old questions that have lost their vital appeal to our perceived interests and needs. We do not solve old questions, according to Dewey—"we get over them. Old questions are solved by disappearing, evaporating, while new questions corresponding to the changed attitude of endeavor and preference take their place. Doubtless the greatest dissolvent in contemporary thought of old questions, the greatest precipitant of new methods, new intentions, new problems, is the one effected by the scientific revolution that found its climax in the 'Origin of Species.'"

Dewey's Darwin lays hands "upon the sacred ark of permanency" that had governed our understanding of human beings. Darwin challenges the most sacred cow in the Western tradition, one that had been handed down from the Greeks: the belief in the "superiority of the fixed and final," including "the forms that had been regarded as types of fixity and perfection." The Greeks dilated on the characteristic traits of creatures, attaching the word "species" to them. As they manifested themselves in a completed form or final cause, these species were seen to exhibit uniform structure and function, and to do so repeatedly, to the point where they were viewed as unchanging in their essential being. All changes were therefore held "within the metes and bounds of fixed truth."[34] Nature as a whole came to be viewed as "a progressive realization of purpose." The Greeks then propounded ethical systems based on purposiveness.

Henceforth, "genetic" and "experimental" processes and methods can guide our inquiries into the human things. In fact, on Darwinian terms, change is of the essence of the good, which is identified with organic adaptation, survival, and growth. With maximally experimental social arrangements, change in useless directions can quickly be converted into change in useful directions. The goal of philosophy is no longer to search for absolute origins or ends, but for the processes that generate them.[35] What *materially* is becomes more important than what ought to be because only the former can be an object of the new empirical science. In the absence of fixity, morals, politics, and religion are subject to radical renegotiation and transformation. Essences are no longer the highest object of inquiry, nor indeed any object of inquiry. Rather, science concentrates on particular changes and their relationship to particular salutary purposes, which depend on "intelligent administration of existent conditions."[36] Philosophy is reduced from the "wholesale" to the retail level.[37] Through the emphasis on administration of concrete conditions, Dewey claims responsibility is introduced to philosophy. Instead of concentrating on metaphysics, or even politics in the full Aristotelian sense, we are in effect freed to concentrate on policy—or, in Dewey's language, "the things that specifically concern us."

Darwin broke down the last barriers between scientific method and reconstruction in philosophy and the human sciences generally because of his overcoming of the view that human nature is different from the physical sciences and therefore requires a different approach. This is contrary to Aristotle's understanding that different methods of inquiry are required for different kinds of beings—there is no one scientific or philosophic mode of inquiry that applies across the board, though philosophy and science are seen as synonymous. Philosophy or science—the human striving after wisdom or knowledge—seeks an understanding of the *highest* things through an examination of *all* things, according to methods appropriate to each. One way of understanding Dewey's enterprise is to view it as an attempt to reintegrate science and philosophy, which had been torn asunder by modernity. While Dewey seeks their reintegration, he does so on uniquely modern terms—philosophy is *reduced* to empirical, naturalistic science—the process, without the ends, or essences, or highest things.[38] We can therefore reduce human sciences, including politics, to relatively simple principles, contrary to the Aristotelian or ancient view, which held that politics is much *harder* than physics precisely because one must take into account unpredictable behavior, and choice-worthy, purposive behavior toward *complex* ends—rather than more predictable motions and processes toward simple ends. The human sciences, which at the highest level involve statesmanship, are, for Aristotle, more complex than the physical, and rely on great practical, experiential wisdom as well as theoretical wisdom.[39] By contrast, for Dewey and his generation, Darwinism seemed to break down the barriers between the human and the nonhuman.

Dewey's elucidation of the utility of Darwinism to social science and the new philosophy of man abstracts from the thought of a number of the major social Darwinist thinkers, including William Graham Sumner, Lester Frank Ward, and W. E. B. Du Bois. Together with Dewey, these men provided many of the intellectual categories of their age. And these categories continue to exert a powerful control over political and jurisprudential discourse to the present day. Collectively, they point to a view of society as an organism that, constantly in the throes of change, must grow or die. For the social Darwinists, to look backward—whether to Founding principles or any other fixed standard of political right—inevitably reflects a death wish. While to some degree borrowing Hegelian historical categories, American social Darwinism shares no single rational end point with Hegelianism. Change in itself becomes the end in many instances, and is always preferable to its opposite.

PRAGMATISM AND PROGRAMMATIC LIBERALISM

Despite its defining many of the terms of intellectual discourse in late nineteenth-century America, social Darwinism would not become known as the quintessential American philosophy. This honor belongs to pragmatism. In fact, it has recently been suggested that, by the 1890s, social Darwinism was a "fading ideology."[40] However, the links between pragmatism and social Darwinism are wide and deep, and it is impossible to understand the "American philosophy" of pragmatism without understanding its relationship to social Darwinism. It is also impossible to dismiss social Darwinism's enduring influence on American political thought. The pragmatic tradition worked "with the basic Darwinian concepts—organism, environment, adaptation," and spoke "the language of naturalism."[41]

William James's reflections on "What Pragmatism Means"[42] elucidate the links between these two schools of thought. James recognizes himself as the popularizer of Charles Peirce's argument that the only meaning of a thought or idea is what conduct or consequences it is fitted to produce.[43] Even though James rejected the Hegelian/Darwinian historical categories that were never far from the thinking of his fellow pragmatist and younger contemporary John Dewey, the two shared a thoroughgoing skepticism of the tradition of absolutes, a faith in progress, and an emphasis on the process, rather than essence, of human life and activity. With Darwinism, pragmatism rejects the "rationalist temper" that is ossifying rather than instrumental, and accepts the displacement of design from scientific consciousness.[44] According to James, all ideas must be interpreted in light of practical consequences, rather than purposes or metaphysical underpinnings. If no practical difference in the realm of consequences can be found, the debate over any competing notions is idle.[45] There are no important differences in abstract truth that do not express themselves in concrete fact—no principles, absolutes, or a prioris can govern the pragmatic method, which is an attitude of casting one's glance away from first things toward last things, meaning the "fruits, consequences, facts" of life.[46]

While pragmatism has much in common with earlier empiricism, it is purer in its rejection of finality and its concentration on action and power. However, it does so without the materialist or anti-ideological bias that characterizes empiricism.[47] Ideas "become true just in so far as they help us to get into satisfactory relation with other parts of our experience."[48] James's pragmatism therefore contains a theory of truth, not just meaning. New ideas are true if they gratify "the individual's desire to assimilate the novel in his experience."[49] The test of the truth of a proposition is its ability to marry what we know to new facts. Pragmatism thus becomes a method and means to bind old belief to a new set of facts when new beliefs are inchoate, providing a kind of psychic tranquility that prevents cognitive dissonance. "The reason why we call things true is the reason why they *are* true."[50] In short, what works for us is true, and the pragmatist understanding of what works is linked to the inevitability of change and growth. At the very end of his essay "The Will to Believe," James quotes approvingly Fitzjames Stephen: "We stand on a mountain pass in the midst of whirling snow and blinding mist. . . . If we stand still we shall be frozen to death. If we take the wrong road we shall be dashed to pieces. We do not certainly know whether there is any right one."[51]

It is hardly clear that these two understandings of pragmatism—as a theory of method to arrive at objective reality, and as a theory of subjective satisfaction that might affect the questions we choose to ask—are entirely compatible. Nonetheless, James runs with them, going so far as to argue that even mystical experiences are true if they have practical consequences. If "God" works for us—if religious belief is effective in guiding our actions or giving us comfort—then pragmatism can't deny it.[52] Religion—the will to believe—can have its place. For James personally, belief in the Absolute might clash with other truths whose benefits he hates to give up,[53] but for others it might not. If belief in the absolute could be restricted "to its bare holiday-giving value" it would not clash with James's other truths,[54] for such a belief would understand religious symbols in purely secular terms. Alas, James cannot allow it, for underlying the belief is a logic and metaphysics of which he is the enemy.[55]

Of course, this opens James, and pragmatism, to the same lines of criticism that can be directed toward utilitarianism or laissez-faire economics: there can be different truths or goods for different people, depending on what is expedient for them. James's pragmatism here comes perilously close to reducing all human beings to atomized individuals seeking the greatest good not even for the greatest number, but for themselves. It has no fixed ends beyond growth and practicality, but the direction of this growth is not rationally intelligible in a way that transcends a consequentialist analysis. As James argues,

> Rationalism sticks to logic and the empyrean. Empiricism sticks to the external senses. Pragmatism is willing to take anything, to follow either logic or the senses and to count the humblest and most personal experiences. She will count mystical experiences if they have practical consequences. She will take a God who lives in the very dirt of private fact—if that should seem a likely place to find him.
>
> Her only test of probable truth is what works best in the way of leading us, what fits every part of life best and combines with the collectivity of experience's demands, nothing being omitted. . . .
>
> But you see already how democratic she is. Here manners are as various and flexible, her resources as rich and endless, and her conclusions as friendly as those of mother nature.[56]

It is indeed the very protean nature of pragmatism—its willingness to take *anything*—combined with its democratic ethos and faith in scientific intelligence, that has made it an enduringly popular doctrine for Americans—politicians and jurists no less than private-sector entrepreneurs. Indeed, in the pragmatic understanding, it seems any idea or pursuit can be justified, if it serves this ethos and this faith. The fact that versions of pragmatism are today espoused in all branches of American government—though they were not at the time of the Founding—is telling with respect to the development of our constitutional understandings. Many have noted the movement in twentieth-century political rhetoric away from discussions of the Constitution or constitutionalism, and toward discussion of policy.[57] This move is at least partly a reflection of the hold of pragmatism on the American political imagination.

Dewey brought pragmatism and social Darwinism together as a compact set of political ideas, while showing their mutually reinforcing character. Dewey's pragmatism in some respects follows James, but it remains reliant on the intellectual categories of "left" social Darwinism. James's purer pragmatism all but did away with the categories of nature and natural law that were still central, albeit only in a materialist sense, to the Darwinists. Dewey's pragmatism, by contrast, reinjects natural forces and a strong sense of historical unfolding with which any method must comport itself. It is in Dewey that we can see how social Darwinism and pragmatism together become an intellectual and political force to be reckoned with: a modern liberalism whose goal is to help history along its democratic path, relying on the intellectual inputs of an elite vanguard that need not directly consult the people or ask for their consent.

While still a graduate student at Johns Hopkins, Dewey had fortuitously heard the social Darwinist Lester Frank Ward give his "Mind as a Social Factor" paper.[58] But more fundamentally, Dewey was deeply antagonistic—as was an increasing proportion of the intellectual class of his day—toward classical economics and philosophical individualism. Like Ward, Dewey conceived of human beings as having the capacity and responsibility for choices aimed at directing organic social and individual growth that is stifled by outmoded notions of competition and individual rights. Such choices and the policies that flow from them are always provisional responses to the flux of life, but their ultimate end is a more democratic society. Ideas grow and survive not because they are true or transcend human experience, but because they respond to it most effectively. "Social action" is called for once we understand that scientific intelligence can in fact superintend the unfolding of History.[59]

In his short book *Liberalism and Social Action*, based on a series of lectures, Dewey offers a history of liberalism, an analysis of the crisis it faces, and its prospects for a renaissance that will cement it as the guiding force of social life. As reason became purely instrumental, no longer concerned with ultimate truths but only "concrete situations,"[60] liberalism comes into its own. According to Dewey, the Western understanding of liberalism has moved from Locke's natural rights, to Smith's dynamic economism, to Bentham's psychology of pleasure and pain that seeks the greatest happiness for the greatest number. Bentham's theory argued for judging law by its consequences, and the supremacy of the national over the local. Furthermore, Bentham picked up on Hume's denial of natural rights—which exist only in "the kingdom of mythological social zoology"[61]—and thereby set the stage for the final move from individualist to collectivist liberalism.[62] Interestingly, Dewey notes that the source of factory laws and other reforms in England was not Benthamite liberalism alone. Rather, liberalism was informed by evangelical piety, humanitarianism, literary romanticism, and Tory hostility to industry. Also, German idealism played a role, emphasizing the organic connection of individuals to the collective and the creation of the conditions for positive freedom. Together, all these strains form a collectivism concerned with the organic whole of state and individual.[63]

Still, there was nothing fundamental to Bentham's doctrine "that stood in the way of using the power of government to create, constructively and positively, new institutions if and when it should appear that the latter would contribute more effectively to the well-being of individuals."[64] Liberalism accommodated and assimilated a wide range of doctrines, but never lost its historicism, consequentialism, or scientism. The result is "the majority who call themselves liberals today are committed to the principle that organized society must use its powers to establish the conditions under which the mass of individuals can possess actual as distinct from merely legal liberty."[65] The challenge for this modern liberalism is to make itself a "compact, aggressive force."[66]

This new liberalism is far from its outmoded earlier version because it makes itself relevant to the problems of social organization and integration of various historically situated forces. In fact, the lack of a historical sense on the part of earlier liberals blinded them to the fact that their own interpretations of liberty were historically conditioned, rather than immutable truths. Historical relativity finally frees liberalism to recognize that economic relations are the "dominantly controlling" forces of modernity and that they require social control for the benefit of the many.[67] Free competition and removal of artificial barriers are no longer enough. Instead, the individual's powers must be "fed, sustained, and directed"[68] through cooperative control of the forces of production.[69] Individuality itself does not simply exist, but is attained through continuous growth.[70]

> The demand for a form of social organization that should include economic activities but yet should convert them into servants of the development of the higher capacities of individuals, is one that earlier liberalism did not meet. If we strip its creed from adventitious elements, there are, however, enduring values for which liberalism stood. These values are liberty, the development of the inherent capacities of individuals made possible through liberty, and the central role of free intelligence in inquiry, discussion, and expression.[71]

In Dewey we see a dominant theme of American progressivism and twentieth-century liberalism: the belief that there is an intelligence, or "method of intelligence," that can be applied to solve social problems, which are themselves primarily economic in nature. It is this intelligence, which makes no pretense to knowledge except as a result of a pragmatic experimentation,[72] that captures the spirit of democracy more so than any philosophical or institutional analysis. While all social relations are historically situated and in flux, there is one constant: the application of intelligence as a Progressive ideal and method. "For the only adjustment that does not have to be made over again . . . is that effected through intelligence as a method."[73] It is the only simulacrum of God in an otherwise desiccated world of process, evolution, and growth.

Dewey rounds out his discussion by giving us insight into the nature of a "renascent liberalism." Growth must be physical, intellectual, and moral, and all classes and individuals must benefit. This of course means that there must be constructed a vast state mechanism that is confidently dedicated to ensuring growth, by means of progressive education, the welfare state, and redistribution of capital. The older political science of the Founding era, including that of *The Federalist,* is easily swept aside by Dewey. While the exact contours of public power and policy are not necessarily the same for him as they are for Progressive political actors such as Theodore Roosevelt and Woodrow Wilson, all agree that there are no inherent limits on state power. Like Roosevelt and Wilson's, Dewey's political theory is impatient with constitutional restraints and institutional forms. Separation of powers is a doctrine rooted in stasis and therefore political death. Meanwhile, concerning oneself with constitutional forms and formalities is to give to institutions an abiding character they do not deserve. Certainly Dewey did not concern himself with the possibility that many publics are formed by complex industrial societies and that a theory of representation is needed to integrate them. Such considerations are subsumed to the newly political categories of change and growth. Long before "the courage to change" became an effective presidential campaign slogan, Dewey helped ensure "change" would have a central position in American political rhetoric.

As constitutional restraints are seen as counterproductive and even dangerous, the restraints of character take their place in a decent political order. Education becomes a check on the power of the state, as it creates citizens capable of fully participating in the republic of experimentation.[74] But the old virtues—whether they be of Aristotle's *Ethics,* or Plato's *Republic,* or the Judeo-Christian Bible—are out. In their stead are the new virtues inculcated by a democratic education, including noncompetitive striving, cooperation, and self-actualization. All-around growth, peculiarly, seems to exclude certain *individual* strivings, such as those after honor, money, or power. Dewey seems concerned about the exercise of arbitrary power, but has little concern for the aggregate power of the state.

The cure for a powerful democratic state seems to be constant evolution in the direction of more democracy. The key to the perpetuation of our political institutions is far removed from either the constitutionalism of the Founders or the statesmanship of Lincoln.

In a beautiful encapsulation of social Darwinism, progressivism, and contemporary liberalism, Dewey claims: "[Flux] has to be controlled that it will move to some end in accordance with the principles of life, since life itself is development. Liberalism is committed to an end that is at once enduring and flexible: the liberation of individuals so that realization of their capacities may be the law of their life."[75] Human life therefore *is* nothing in particular, beyond a continual unfolding and advancement, and liberalism is dedicated to its liberation through social policy. When the economic necessities are provided, individuals may pursue the higher life according to their spiritual needs, whatever they might be, and however they might change. And change they will. Dewey's vision of liberalism is ultimately of an individual free of the various constraints that were previously thought by so many to be necessitated by a dangerous, and eternal, nature. This vision of liberalism is a version of Marx's notion that truly free men may fish in the afternoon and criticize after dinner. Although today's constraints happen to be, for Dewey, largely economic in nature, it is not materialism but growth toward freedom that is at the heart of modern liberalism.

THE PROGRESSIVE SYNTHESIS AND THE NEW SCIENCE OF JURISPRUDENCE

Progressivism as an intellectual and political (as opposed to populist) movement amounts to the *politicizing* of the twin doctrines of social Darwinism and pragmatism. By harnessing these doctrines for political ends—as Dewey hoped—the Progressives were able to usher in a new order of the ages that would overtake American politics. Commencing in the early years of the twentieth century, political and judicial actors borrowed freely from pragmatic and Darwinist accounts of politics, constitutionalism, and human life. The age-old question of "what works," politically, was increasingly divorced from a sense of constitutional restraint, as it was informed by an organic conception of a state unlimited in principle, whose only end was growth and development to buttress certain contemporary understandings of democracy and the choosing self. By the late twentieth century, as we have seen, the Progressive synthesis was bearing full fruit.

Like its overtly political counterpart, progressivism in jurisprudential guise is marked by a disposition to step outside the bounds of Madisonian constitutionalism for the sake of faith in the future rather than the past. The Progressive task is to read the public mind and loosen the chains of society enough to allow individual and social growth.

There is a residual incoherence to Progressive jurisprudence. It alternates between two poles. On the one hand, it expresses the desire to make decisions that are legitimate in the eyes of the community—ones that respond to something like, in Oliver Wendell Holmes's words, the "felt necessities" of the age, and, on the other, decisions that counter what it claims is illegitimate majority will. But neither pole is rooted in constitutional text, tradition, logic, or structure, but rather in the judge's view of just what necessities are most deeply felt, and most likely to encourage social and personal growth. The practical result, in contemporary jurisprudence, is that art trumps economics, expression trumps the common good, subjectivity trumps morality, freedom trumps natural law, and will trumps deliberation. Such is the face of Progressive jurisprudence, a face that now seems barnacle encrusted from its triumphal march of a hundred years' duration. Having rooted itself so firmly in the historicist thought that guides America and—under different names—the Western world as a whole, and having gained so much strength and momentum on its virtually uninterrupted path, the triumph of this jurisprudence will not be reversed anytime soon. Its success is marked by the fact that it no longer seeks victory, only legitimation in a constitutional order formally dedicated to the rule of law.

NOTES

This chapter is adapted from chapters 1 and 3 of my book, *Living Constitution, Dying Faith: Progressivism and the New Science of Jurisprudence* (Wilmington, Del.: ISI Books, 2009). Used by permission of the publisher.

1. Herman Belz, "The Constitution in the Gilded Age: The Beginnings of Constitutional Realism in American Scholarship," *The American Journal of Legal History* 13, no. 2 (April 1969): 111.
2. *Planned Parenthood of Southeastern Pennsylvania v. Casey*, 505 U.S. 833 (1992).
3. *John Geddes Lawrence and Tyron Garner v. Texas*, 539 U.S. 558 (2003).
4. William J. Brennan, "The Constitution of the United States: Contemporary Ratification," *South Texas Law Review* 27 (1986): 438.
5. Brennan, "Constitution of the United States," 438–39.
6. Brennan, "Constitution of the United States," 440.
7. Brennan, "Constitution of the United States," 442.
8. *Whitney v. California*, 274 U.S. 357.
9. Brennan, "Constitution of the United States," 443.
10. Brennan, "Constitution of the United States," 439–40.
11. Excepting those areas where the judge's position apparently should be "fixed and immutable"—for example, in opposition to capital punishment as a violation, in all circumstances, of the Eighth Amendment ban on cruel and unusual punishment. See Brennan, "Constitution of the United States," 443.
12. Brennan, "Constitution of the United States," 444.
13. Brennan, "Constitution of the United States," 445.
14. Brennan, "Constitution of the United States," 445.

15. Thurgood Marshall, "The Constitution: A Living Document," *Howard Law Journal* 30 (1987).

16. Marshall, "The Constitution," 918.

17. Marshall, "The Constitution," 919.

18. Marshall, "The Constitution," 919.

19. Marshall, "The Constitution," 919.

20. *Bowers v. Hardwick*, 478 U.S. 186 (1986).

21. This is a quotation from Holmes's essay, "The Path of the Law."

22. *Hurley v. Irish-American Gay, Lesbian, and Bisexual Group of Boston*, 515 U.S. 557 (1995).

23. *Boy Scouts of America v. Dale*, 530 U.S. 640 (2000).

24. For an extended discussion of the relationship of this and similar cases to the doctrine of stare decisis, see John C. Eastman, "Stare Decisis: Conservatism's One-Way Ratchet Problem," in *Courts and the Culture Wars*, ed. Bradley C. S. Watson (Lanham, Md.: Lexington Books, 2002), 127–37.

25. *Brown v. Board of Education*, 347 U.S. 483 (1954).

26. *Cruzan v. Missouri Department of Health*, 497 U.S. 261 (1990).

27. *Washington v. Glucksberg*, 521 U.S. 702 (1997).

28. *Vacco v. Quill*, 521 U.S. 793 (1997).

29. The reluctance of historians to deal with philosophical categories, including those of the old constitutionalism that was replaced by the new, has been noted by Mark Warren Bailey, in *Guardians of the Moral Order* (DeKalb: Northern Illinois University Press, 2004), 2–6.

30. As Belz notes, a strain of constitutional realism became evident in historical studies written in the years after Reconstruction, by such pre-Progressive scholars as John W. Burgess, Herman Edward von Holst, J. Franklin Jameson, Alexander Johnston, Brooks Adams, George Bancroft, Christopher Tiedeman, and Sidney George Fisher. These men emphasized the importance of extraconstitutional influences on the practice of American politics and the development of constitutional understandings, from the growth of political parties to the particular actions of the branches of government. While they went "beyond the façade of the formal written document" and examined particular historical circumstances, they did not, for the most part, rely on a strong theory of History, or concentrate their attention on the role of the Supreme Court in promoting organic growth. See Belz, "The Constitution in the Gilded Age," *passim*. Woodrow Wilson would become the most prominent exponent of a theory of History that suggested evolution in a particular direction—though he saw the executive rather than judicial branch as primary expositor and superintendent of this evolution.

31. Richard Hofstadter, *Social Darwinism in American Political Thought*, rev. ed. (Boston: Beacon Press, 1955). The phrase "social Darwinism" gained widespread intellectual currency as an appropriate descriptor of an amalgam of ideas only with the publication of the first edition of this book in 1944.

32. John Dewey, "The Influence of Darwinism on Philosophy," in *The Influence of Darwinism on Philosophy and Other Essays in Contemporary Thought* (New York: Henry Holt and Co., 1951).

33. The only other contender for the throne was the vigorous, pragmatic individualist frontier strain of thought associated with such figures as Frederick Jackson Turner and Mark Twain. But this strain was never as theoretically unified as social

Darwinism, and never found the same acceptance among the intellectual classes. Not coincidentally, perhaps, it could not be said to have undermined, in any direct or consistent manner, the principled understanding of the American Founding articulated by Lincoln.

34. There are problems with this Deweyan tendency to identify nature as final cause or form with changelessness. Such an account comes close to capturing the essence of Plato's forms, but for Aristotle there are no fixed, immutable ideas separate from matter. Rather, things develop to their natural perfection, which for human beings is happiness, relying on a combination of intellectual and moral virtue. There is a tension in Aristotle between philosophy (man as knower) and politics (man as political animal, i.e., a virtuous actor, rather than, or in addition to, a knower). It is far from clear, in either Aristotle or Plato, how these virtues interact at all levels. But what is clear is that there is no simple teleology in Aristotle when it comes to human beings. Simple teleologies are for the lower forms, whereas for humans there are choices involving politics, ethics, and philosophy, and nature many times misses its mark. Furthermore, for Aristotle, essence is not form simply, but activity or what a thing does. In his science, repose does not represent the highest state of being. Although there is a good amount of truth to Dewey's characterization of Western science, or philosophy, as the search for the transcendent, he seems wrong insofar as he puts a Platonic gloss on Aristotle.

35. Dewey, "Influence of Darwinism on Philosophy," 13.

36. Dewey, "Influence of Darwinism on Philosophy," 15.

37. Dewey, "Influence of Darwinism on Philosophy," 16.

38. See, for example, John Dewey, *Reconstruction in Philosophy* (Boston: Beacon Press, 1957), *passim.*

39. This is the reason why we do not expect great statesmen—exercising practical and theoretical wisdom—to be young, whereas mathematicians might be.

40. Louis Menand, *The Metaphysical Club* (New York: Farrar, Straus and Giroux, 2001), 302.

41. Hofstadter, *Social Darwinism*, 125.

42. William James, "What Pragmatism Means," in William James, *Essays in Pragmatism*, ed. Alburey Castell (New York: Hafner Press, 1948); originally delivered by James as a lecture in 1906.

43. James, "What Pragmatism Means," 142–43.

44. James, "What Pragmatism Means," 153–54.

45. James, "What Pragmatism Means," 141–42.

46. James, "What Pragmatism Means," 146.

47. James, "What Pragmatism Means," 144–45, 154.

48. James, "What Pragmatism Means," 147.

49. James, "What Pragmatism Means," 150.

50. James, "What Pragmatism Means," 150 (emphasis in original).

51. William James, "The Will to Believe" (1896), in *Pragmatism: A Reader*, ed. Louis Menand (New York: Vintage Books, 1997), 92.

52. James, "What Pragmatism Means," 154–55.

53. James, "What Pragmatism Means," 156–57.

54. James, "What Pragmatism Means," 157.

55. Interestingly, U.S. courts, in establishment clause jurisprudence, have come to deal with the Absolute in similarly pragmatic terms. If government celebration of

or teaching about religious holidays, institutions, or symbols can be understood in purely secular terms, it passes constitutional muster. Unlike James, many judges do not appear to suffer cognitive dissonance as a result.

56. James, "What Pragmatism Means," 157–58.

57. One need only compare the constitutional rhetoric of Lincoln to virtually any recent president to see this difference in stark relief. See Jeffrey K. Tulis, *The Rhetorical Presidency* (Princeton, N.J.: Princeton University Press, 1987).

58. Menand, *Metaphysical Club*, 302.

59. Indeed, Louis Menand notes that the growth of American social science disciplines was a consequence of the rejection of the notion that evolutionary laws govern in a way that cannot be improved on by public policy. See Menand, *Metaphysical Club*, 302.

60. Dewey, *Liberalism and Social Action* (Amherst, N.Y.: Prometheus Books, 2000; orig. pub. 1935), 29.

61. Dewey, *Liberalism and Social Action*, 27.

62. This move was delayed in the United States due to the more agrarian nature of its economy and the lack of a Benthamite influence. See Dewey, *Liberalism and Social Action*, 27–28.

63. Dewey, *Liberalism and Social Action*, 30–35.

64. Dewey, *Liberalism and Social Action*, 24.

65. Dewey, *Liberalism and Social Action*, 35.

66. Dewey, *Liberalism and Social Action*, 36.

67. Dewey, *Liberalism and Social Action*, 42.

68. Dewey, *Liberalism and Social Action*, 40.

69. Dewey, *Liberalism and Social Action*, 59.

70. Dewey, *Liberalism and Social Action*, 46.

71. Dewey, *Liberalism and Social Action*, 40.

72. Dewey, *Liberalism and Social Action*, 80.

73. Dewey, *Liberalism and Social Action*, 55–56.

74. See, especially, John Dewey, *Democracy and Education: An Introduction to the Philosophy of Education* (New York: The Free Press, 1966; orig. pub. 1916).

75. Dewey, *Liberalism and Social Action*, 61.

III

WAR, NATIONAL SECURITY, AND THE RULE OF LAW

9

National Security Law

The Judicial Role

Louis Fisher

Contemporary federal judges sometimes claim they lack both jurisdiction and competence over matters of war and national security. This attitude has no basis in law or practice. Federal courts handled those cases on a regular basis until the Vietnam War years, when judges used a variety of threshold arguments (standing, ripeness, political questions, etc.) to duck a lawsuit. Over the previous century and a half, federal courts accepted war power cases and decided the legal and constitutional issue presented. Federal judges today seem to be largely unaware of the role played by the judiciary in the past. Without a judiciary comfortable and knowledgeable about its duties and authority, broad assertions by executive officials of emergency power will undermine constitutional rights and individual liberties.

I. FUNDAMENTAL PRINCIPLES

The Framers recognized that the president possessed an implied authority to use military force for certain defensive actions, but that grant of authority was narrowly defined. As Roger Sherman remarked at the Philadelphia Convention, the president "shd. be able to repel and not to commence war." Elbridge Gerry agreed, saying he "never expected to hear in a republic a motion to empower the Executive alone to declare war." George Mason spoke "agst giving the power of war to the Executive, because not safely to be trusted with it; . . . He was for clogging rather than facilitating war."[1] The first two presidents, George Washington and John Adams, fully understood that they could exercise defensive powers but that the decision to mount offensive operations was reserved solely to Congress.[2] In 1801, President Thomas Jefferson sent a small squadron of frigates to the Mediterranean to protect against possible attacks by the Barbary pirates. He told Congress that he was "unauthorized by the Constitution, without the sanction of Congress, to go beyond the line of defense." It was up to Congress to authorize "measures of offense also."[3]

Federal courts understood this jurisdictional line between Congress and the president and decided cases consistent with that principle. The Quasi-War against France (1798–1800) reached the Supreme Court in two cases in 1800 and 1801, both of which acknowledged that Congress can resort to authorization of war rather than formal declaration. There was no hesitation on the part of the Court to accept and decide these cases because they concerned questions of war and national security. In the first case, the Court had to determine whether France was statutorily an "enemy" in the absence of a declaration of war. Treating the matter as a legal issue to be decided by the judiciary, the Court ruled that the conflict amounted to war and Congress under the Constitution could either declare or authorize war.[4] Justice Chase noted that Congress authorized hostilities only on the high seas and not on land.[5]

A year later, Chief Justice John Marshall wrote the second case on the Quasi-War. He said without reservation that the "whole powers of war being, by the constitution of the United States, vested in congress, the acts of that body can alone be resorted to as our guides in this inquiry." Congress may authorize "general hostilities, in which case the general laws of war apply to our situation; or partial hostilities, in which case the laws of war, so far as they actually apply to our situation, must be noticed."[6] For Marshall, legislative statutes provided the sole guides for judicial inquiry. Unlike some contemporary observers, federal courts never looked to the Commander in Chief Clause as a source of independent presidential authority to initiate war.

A speech that Marshall gave in 1800, as a member of the U.S. House of Representatives, has been mischaracterized by the Supreme Court and the Justice Department to support a position he never held. It is the so-called sole organ doctrine, regularly unfurled to justify unilateral, inherent, plenary, and independent presidential authority over external affairs, including war. This is what Marshall said on March 7, 1800: "The President is the sole organ of the nation in its external relations, and its sole representative with foreign nations."[7] When one reads the entire speech and understands it in the context of the House's effort either to impeach or censure President John Adams, nothing said by Marshall supported exclusive or extraconstitutional power for the president. His only objective was to defend Adams's authority to carry out an extradition treaty by handing over to England a British subject charged with murder. The president was not the sole organ in formulating the treaty. He was the sole organ in *implementing* it.

Marshall was stating what should have been obvious. Under the express language of Article II it is the president's duty to "take Care that the Laws be faithfully executed." Under Article VI, all treaties made "shall be the supreme Law of the Land." President Adams was not attempting to make foreign policy single-handedly. He was carrying out a policy made jointly by the president and the Senate (for treaties). On other occasions the president might be charged with carrying out a policy made by statute.

Even in carrying out a treaty, Marshall said, the president could be restrained by a subsequent statute. Congress "may prescribe the mode" of carrying out a treaty.[8] Later, Congress provided that in all cases of treaties of extradition between the United States and another country, federal and state judges were authorized to determine whether the evidence was sufficient to sustain the charge against the individual to be extradited.[9] In his capacity as chief justice, Marshall held firm to his position that the making of foreign policy is a joint exercise by the executive and legislative branches, through treaties and statutes, and not a unilateral or exclusive authority of the president. When a presidential proclamation issued in time of war conflicted with a statute enacted by Congress, Chief Justice Marshall ruled in 1804 that the statute prevails.[10]

II. RETHINKING *CURTISS-WRIGHT*

Despite the clear meaning of Marshall's speech in 1800, the Supreme Court and legal analyses by the Justice Department repeatedly cite the "sole organ" doctrine as a source of inherent presidential power. The misconception first appeared in a decision by Justice Sutherland in *United States v. Curtiss-Wright Corp* (1936).[11] On January 19, 2006, the Justice Department invoked the sole organ doctrine in defending the National Security Agency (NSA) surveillance program. The department associated the doctrine with inherent power, pointing to "the President's well-recognized inherent constitutional authority as Commander in Chief and sole organ for the Nation in foreign affairs."[12] Later in this memo the department stated: "the President's role as sole organ for the Nation in foreign affairs has long been recognized as carrying with it preeminent authority in the field of national security and foreign intelligence."[13] Only by relying on the erroneous dicta by Justice Sutherland in *Curtiss-Wright* could language like that be used. Nothing in Marshall's speech offers any support for inherent or preeminent authority for the president.

Of all the misconceived and poorly reasoned judicial decisions that have inflated presidential power in the field of national security, confused the judiciary, weakened the rule of law, and endangered individual rights, *Curtiss-Wright* stands in a class by itself. The case had absolutely nothing to do with presidential power. It concerned only the power of Congress. The constitutional dispute was whether Congress by joint resolution could delegate to the president *its* power, authorizing President Franklin D. Roosevelt to declare an arms embargo in a region in South America.[14] In imposing the embargo, President Roosevelt relied solely on this statutory—not inherent—authority. He acted "under and by virtue of the authority conferred in me by the said joint resolution of Congress."[15] President Roosevelt made no assertion of inherent, independent, exclusive, plenary, or extraconstitutional authority.

Litigation on his proclamation focused on legislative power because, in 1935, the Supreme Court twice struck down the delegation by Congress of *domestic* power to the president.[16] The issue in *Curtiss-Wright* was whether Congress could delegate legislative power more broadly in international affairs than it could in domestic affairs. A district court held that the joint resolution impermissibly delegated legislative authority but said nothing about any reservoir of inherent or independent presidential power.[17] None of the briefs discussed the availability of inherent or independent presidential power. For the Justice Department, the question before the Court went to "the very power of Congress to delegate to the Executive authority to investigate and make findings in order to implement a legislative purpose."[18] The joint resolution passed by Congress, said the Department of Justice (DOJ), contained adequate standards to guide the president and did not fall prey to the "unfettered discretion" found by the Court in the two 1935 decisions.[19]

The brief for the private company, Curtiss-Wright, focused solely on the issue of delegated power and did not explore the availability of independent or inherent powers for the president.[20] A separate brief, prepared for other private parties, concentrated on the delegation of legislative power and did not attempt to locate any freestanding or freewheeling presidential authority.[21] Given President Roosevelt's stated dependence on statutory authority and the lack of anything in the briefs about inherent presidential power, there was no need for the Supreme Court to discuss independent sources for executive authority.

Anything along those lines would be dicta. The extraneous matter added by Justice Sutherland in *Curtiss-Wright* has been subjected to highly critical studies by scholars. One article regarded Sutherland's position on the existence of inherent presidential power to be "(1) contrary to American history, (2) violative of our political theory, (3) unconstitutional, and (4) unnecessary, undemocratic, and dangerous."[22] Other scholarly works found similar deficiencies with Sutherland's dicta.[23]

Federal courts repeatedly cite *Curtiss-Wright* to sustain delegations of legislative power to the president in the field of international affairs and at times to support the existence of inherent and independent presidential power for the president in foreign policy. Although some justices of the Supreme Court have described the president's foreign relations power as "exclusive," the Court itself has not denied to Congress its constitutional authority to enter the field and reverse or modify presidential decisions in the area of national security and foreign affairs.[24]

The Supreme Court continues to cite *Curtiss-Wright* haphazardly. In the recent *Boumediene* case, Justice Anthony Kennedy spent seventy pages explaining why President Bush lacked the authority he claimed over the detainees at Guantánamo Bay and why they are entitled to habeas relief. In the last few pages, as though he sensed he might have gone too far and was on tenuous ground, Kennedy remarked: "In considering both the procedural and substantive standards used to impose detention to prevent acts of terrorism, proper deference must be accorded to the political branches. See *United States v. Curtiss-Wright Export Corp.*, 299 U.S. 304, 320 (1936)."[25] And what might be on page 320? Why, of course Sutherland's dicta about the president as "sole organ." Remarkably, the language on that page speaks of independent and inherent presidential powers, precisely the kind of power the majority denied in *Boumediene*. The president, Sutherland claimed on page 320, operated not only on the basis of statutory authority but also on "the very delicate, plenary and exclusive power of the President as the sole organ of the federal government in the field of international relations—a power which does not require as a basis for its exercise an act of Congress, but which, of course, like every other governmental power, must be exercised in subordination to the applicable provisions of the Constitution." If the president does indeed have plenary and exclusive power, how could the Court locate restrictions in 2008?

III. FROM 1789 TO THE CIVIL WAR

Beginning with the Quasi-War cases in 1800 and 1801 and *Little v. Barreme* in 1804, federal courts decided cases of war and national security throughout the next century and a half. An early example of this pattern is a decision by a circuit court in 1806, reviewing the indictment of Colonel William S. Smith for engaging in military actions against Spain. He claimed that his operation "was begun, prepared, and set on foot with the knowledge and approbation of the executive department of our government."[26] He was accused of violating the Neutrality Act of 1794, which prohibited American citizens from providing any assistance to military expeditions against "a foreign prince or state, with whom the United States are at peace."[27]

Far from shying away from the dispute, the court reviewed Smith's assertion and forcefully rejected his argument: "The president of the United States cannot control the statute, nor dispense with its execution, and still less can he authorize a person to do what the law forbids."[28] The court considered whether it should subpoena the secretary of state to determine whether Smith had acted pursuant to any type of presidential instruction. It concluded that even if it were to confirm Smith's account, the testimony of the secretary of state or anyone in the Jefferson administration would be immaterial. Congress had already established U.S. policy. The president had no independent constitutional authority to direct military expeditions on the part of private citizens.[29] Executive officials, including the president, could not waive statutory provisions. Drawing on the distinction between the "defensive" power of the president to resist invasion and the "offensive" authority to undertake military actions against foreign countries, the court had no difficulty in assigning the latter exclusively to Congress:

> If, indeed, a foreign nation should invade the territories of the United States, it would I apprehend, be not only lawful for the president to resist such invasion, but also carry hostilities into the enemy's own country; and for this plain reason, that a state of complete and absolute war actually exists between the two nations. In the case of invasive hostilities, there cannot be war on the one side and peace on the other. . . . There is a manifest distinction between our going to war with a nation at peace, and a war being made against us by an actual invasion, or a formal declaration. In the formal case, it is the exclusive province of congress to change a state of peace into a state of war.[30]

The president, said the court, had no constitutional power to initiate war. Does the president, the court asked, "possess the power of making war? That power is exclusively vested in congress."[31]

Federal courts continued accepting and deciding cases involving military operations. If the U.S. government discovered British property in the country at the commencement of hostilities in the War of 1812, could it be seized as enemy property as a necessary consequence of a declaration of war? Did any congressional statute authorize the seizure? The Supreme Court in 1814 concluded that the declaration of war did not authorize the seizure and no explicit statutory authorization existed.[32] The seizure of enemy property needed action by "the legislature, not of the executive or judiciary."[33]

In 1827, the Court examined the president's authority to call forth state militia to repel invasion from abroad or to suppress internal insurrections. Beginning in 1792, Congress had passed legislation defining the president's power.[34] Guided by statutory authority, the Court held that the power to respond to emergencies rested with the president.[35] When presented with the legal issue, the Court did not step aside. The Court acknowledged a broad discretionary power for the president by analyzing the statutory policy of Congress: "Whenever a statute gives a discretionary power to any person, to be exercised by him, upon his own opinion of certain facts, it is a sound rule of construction, that the statute constitutes him the sole and exclusive judge of the existence of those facts. And in the present case, we are all of opinion that such is the true construction of the act of 1795."[36]

In 1849, the president's power to call out the militia and declare martial law was again before the Supreme Court. As before, it accepted the case and decided it by analyzing statutory language.[37] The Court conceded that the president could abuse the discretionary power placed in his hands.[38] If the president acted improperly or invaded the rights of the people, "it would be in the power of Congress to apply the proper remedy."[39]

The Mexican War brought many cases to the Supreme Court. In 1850, it offered a restrictive interpretation of the Commander in Chief Clause, explaining that it was to be employed to carry out the statutory policy of Congress. The president was authorized to direct the movements of naval and military forces "placed *by law* at his command."[40] The Court did not invite some kind of inherent, unchecked emanations from Article II. In case of threats from abroad, the president "may invade the hostile country, and subject it to the sovereignty and authority of the United States. But his conquests do not enlarge the boundaries of the Union, *nor extend the operation of our institutions and laws beyond the limits before assigned to them by the legislative power*."[41] The question before the Court turned in part on the construction of an 1846 statute setting duties on goods imported from a foreign country.[42] Enlarging the boundaries of the United States could not be done by the president: "[T]his can be done only by the treaty-making power or the legislative authority, and is not a part of the power conferred upon the President by the declaration of war."[43] Far from dodging or ducking the issue, the Court decided that Tampico was "a foreign port when this shipment was made."[44]

In another Mexican War case, the Court fully acknowledged its authority to take jurisdiction, and decide, the legal issue regarding a dispute over the seizure of property. The Court granted a U.S. citizen damages for the seizure of his property by an officer of the U.S. Army. It ruled that orders of a superior officer will not justify unlawful seizure, even when the orders invoke the traditional argument of military necessity. It was the duty of the Court "to determine under what circumstances private property may be taken from the owner by a military officer in a time of war."[45] Under the facts of the seizure, the Court concluded "that the law does not permit it."[46]

Other Mexican War cases deserve mention. An American vessel had been seized by a U.S. officer upon suspicion of trading with the enemy and condemned as lawful prize by an officer authorized by the president to exercise admiralty jurisdiction. The Supreme Court held that "[e]very court of the United States . . . must derive its jurisdiction and judicial authority from the Constitution or the laws of the United States."[47] The Court ruled that "neither the President nor any military officer can establish a court in a conquered country, and authorize it to decide upon the rights of the United States, or of individuals in prize cases, nor to administer the laws of nations."[48] The constitutional authorities to create tribunals inferior to the Supreme Court, define and punish offenses against the law of nations, and make rules concerning captures on land and water were assigned to Congress under Article I. In 1854, the Court decided that military commanders could impose duties on imports during the conquest, but after the treaty those duties were illegal. The power of Congress to make rules and regulations respecting territory belonging to the United States prevailed over military decisions.[49]

The judicial reasoning in Colonel Smith's 1806 case reappeared in *The Prize Cases* of 1863. The Supreme Court upheld President Abraham Lincoln's blockade on the rebellious states, but Justice Grier observed that the president as commander in chief "has no power to initiate or declare a war either against a foreign nation or a domestic State."[50] During oral argument, the executive branch took exactly the same position. Richard Henry Dana Jr., who was representing the president, acknowledged that Lincoln's actions had nothing to do with "the right *to initiate a war, as a voluntary act of sovereignty*. That is vested only in Congress."[51]

At times federal courts were unsuccessful in limiting military actions by a president. Lincoln's suspension of the writ of habeas corpus was opposed by Chief Justice Taney, sitting as circuit judge. Taney lost that face-off, but not because he refused to take jurisdiction or decided he lacked competence. He ruled that Lincoln lacked authority to suspend the writ and the prisoner, John Merryman, should be set free. Prison officials, acting under Lincoln's policy, refused to let Taney's marshal serve a document at the prison to release Merryman. Taney noted: "I have exercised all the power which the constitution and laws confer upon me, but *that power has been resisted by a force too strong for me to overcome.*"[52]

Federal judges continued to challenge President Lincoln's authority to suspend the writ without the sanction of Congress.[53] After Congress on March 3, 1863, passed legislation authorizing the president to suspend the writ, federal judges found suspension "valid and efficient in law."[54] Also during this period, the federal judiciary decided a number of cases concerning military courts and military commissions.[55] In 1876 the Supreme Court struck down a military order that attempted to annul a decree issued by a civil court concerning an issue that arose during the Civil War. The Court regarded the order as "an arbitrary stretch of authority" and considered it "an unbending rule of law, that the exercise of military power, where the rights of the citizen are concerned, shall never be pushed beyond what the exigency requires."[56]

IV. THE RECONSTRUCTION PERIOD

In two cases following the Civil War, the Supreme Court found it prudent not to accept and decide a case involving military power and the Commander in Chief Clause. The first involved an injunction brought by Mississippi to prevent President Andrew Johnson from using the military to implement two Reconstruction acts. Chief Justice Chase, writing for the Court, rejected the argument that the duties placed on the president were purely ministerial and could be directed by the courts. The Court decided it lacked jurisdiction to issue the injunction because presidential duties in this area were "purely executive and political," lying outside the scope of "judicial interference with the exercise of Executive discretion."[57] Looking down the road, the Court saw formidable hazards. First, if President Johnson refused to comply with a judicial order, how would the Court enforce its process?[58] More worrisome, suppose Johnson complied with the court order and invited impeachment by being in contempt of congressional statutes? Would the Court then step in to support him against Congress? If the House impeached Johnson he would be tried in the Senate, with the chief justice serving as presiding officer. Facing those scenarios, the Court decided to step aside.

Shortly after this case came *State of Georgia v. Stanton*. Georgia brought the case under the Court's original jurisdiction against Secretary of War Edwin M. Stanton, General of the Army Ulysses S. Grant, and Major General John Pope, who was assigned to command the Third Military District consisting of Georgia, Florida, and Alabama. The district was organized under the Reconstruction Acts. The lawsuit claimed that Stanton, Grant, and Pope, acting under orders from President Johnson, were using the army "to take military possession of the States, and threatened to subvert her government, and to subject her people of military rule."[59]

Writing for the Court, Justice Nelson called attention to the "distinction between judicial and political power."[60] He said Georgia's lawsuit called "for the judgment of the court upon political questions, and upon rights, not of persons or property, but of a political character, will hardly be denied."[61] Actually, the military's presence in Georgia did bear on persons and property, but in the Court's judgment the risk of judicial activity was too great. Consequently, Justice Nelson concluded that the Court "possesses no jurisdiction over the subject-matter presented in the bill for relief."[62] Chief Justice Chase dissented on some grounds but agreed that the Court had no jurisdiction.[63]

Cases immediately after the Civil War involved the judiciary in passing judgment about decisions to conduct the war. In 1870, the Court was asked to decide whether Congress, in enacting the Legal Tender Acts of 1862, possessed "the power to make United States notes a legal tender in payment of all debts [as] a means appropriate and plainly adapted to the execution of the power to carry on war."[64] Could the Court, looking back to a period when Congress decided that paper money was the only available means of financing the war, second-guess and overturn the legislative judgment? It decided it could, and did, by a four-to-three vote. A year later, after President Ulysses S. Grant had added two justices, the Court swung around and reversed itself.[65]

From 1870 to 1872, the Court issued three decisions to define when the Civil War commenced and when it ceased. Those rulings were necessary to resolve a number of claims to be reimbursed for land and other possessions.

To what extent could private property be taken to further the interests of a military operation? The war did not begin or end at the same time in all the states, requiring the Court to interpret proclamations by the president.[66]

V. SPANISH-AMERICAN WAR TO VIETNAM

The war against Spain in 1898 placed several issues before the Supreme Court. In 1901, it held that the president's authority as commander in chief over a conquered area is governed by the "laws of war."[67] The question involved the decision of the U.S. military commander to impose duties on goods coming from the United States into Puerto Rico. The Court ruled that the duties imposed under presidential authority were valid prior to the ratification of the peace treaty, but those collected after ratification had been unlawfully imposed.[68]

In 1904, the Court reviewed the seizure by U.S. military and naval forces of a vessel owned by a Spanish corporation. The question was whether the vessel had been properly seized as enemy property used for war purposes. To decide that issue, the Court needed to determine when the war had ended and the effect of the peace treaty. It ruled that the war had not ceased until the exchange of ratifications of the Treaty of Paris in April 1899.[69] Litigants argued that the war had ended with the protocol and presidential proclamation of August 12, 1898, suspending hostilities. To the Court, "[a] truce or suspension of armies . . . does not terminate the war, but . . . [only] suspends its operations."[70]

During this period, a circuit court decided a dispute arising from the Boxer Rebellion in China. Although there had been no declaration of war by Congress and President William McKinley declared that his sending of five thousand U.S. troops to China "involved no war against the Chinese nation," the Court interpreted Article of War 58 to create a "condition of war" that provided legal justification for a general court-martial.[71] A district court in 1912 decided whether military authorities had acted properly in making arrests without a warrant. Congress had empowered the president to employ the army to prevent a nongovernmental military expedition from the United States against the territory of any foreign state "with whom the United States are at peace."[72]

Notwithstanding this statutory support, the court held that the president lacked authority, in time of peace, to use the military to arrest without a warrant and imprison without trial an alien merely suspected of violating the neutrality laws. Military authorities were attempting to secure evidence from him. The arrest, said the court, contravened the Fourth Amendment and his continued detention was "repugnant not only to the fifth amendment, but also the sixth."[73] The detention was "unlawful" and represented "the exercise of arbitrary power by the military authorities."[74]

In several cases from 1919 to 1924, the Supreme Court regarded the exercise of the war power by the political departments as subject to judicial review: "The war power of the United States, like its other powers and like the police power of the States, is subject to applicable constitutional limitations."[75] Several of these cases involved the constitutionality of the War-Time Prohibition Act, challenged partly on the ground that Congress was continuing to prohibit the liquor traffic as a means of increasing war efficiency *after* the armistice with Germany had been signed. The Court had to decide how long the war power could be exercised after hostilities have ended.[76]

The *Curtiss-Wright* case of 1936 has already been discussed. A year after writing that decision, Justice Sutherland claimed that "the conduct of foreign relations was committed by the Constitution to the political departments of the government, and the propriety of what may be done in the exercise of this political power was not subject to judicial inquiry or decision."[77] Sutherland vastly overgeneralized. This particular case involved an executive agreement between the United States and Russia. What if an executive agreement affected private claims or violated statutory and constitutional provisions? As the State Department concedes, an executive agreement cannot be "inconsistent with legislation enacted by the Congress in the exercise of its constitutional authority."[78] A number of court decisions have limited the reach of executive agreements.[79]

World War II ushered in a range of cases testing the limits of the war power. On repeated occasions federal courts decided those cases rather than sidestep them.[80] In 1943 and 1944, the Court upheld first the curfew order and later the internment of 120,000 Japanese Americans living on the West Coast.[81] While not expressly refusing the cases on political-question grounds, the Court came close to it, explaining that "we cannot say" that the elected branches lacked reason for its actions.[82] In one of three dissents in the internment case, Justice Jackson suggested that the Court might have been wiser not to take and decide the case:

> Much is said of the danger to liberty from the Army program for deporting and detaining these citizens of Japanese extraction. But a judicial construction of the due process clause that will sustain this order is a far more subtle blow to liberty than the promulgation of the order itself. A military order, however unconstitutional, is not apt to last longer than the military emergency. Even during that period a succeeding commander may revoke it all. But once a judicial opinion rationalizes such an order to show that it conforms to the Constitution, or rather rationalizes the Constitution to show that the Constitution sanctions such an order, the Court for all time has validated the principle of racial discrimination in criminal procedure and of transplanting American citizens.[83]

During martial law in Hawaii, federal courts at the district level repeatedly challenged actions by military authorities. Eventually the Supreme Court, after the war was over, rejected the continuation of military rule.[84]

This represents a record of judicial deference on the whole, but the cases were taken and decided and in some cases federal district judges were willing to confront military leaders.

The Steel Seizure Case of 1952 is a vivid example of judicial independence and competence in reviewing military actions. President Harry Truman ordered the secretary of commerce to take possession of and operate most of the nation's steel mills. Believing that a threatened strike would jeopardize national defense and limit the raw materials needed to prosecute the war in Korea, his executive order was based not on specific statutory authority but on the general "emergency" powers of the president to act "within the aggregate of his constitutional powers as the Nation's Chief Executive and the Commander in Chief of the Armed Forces of the United States."[85]

In district court, the Justice Department told Judge David Pine that the presidential power to seize the mills was inherent and plenary and not subject to judicial scrutiny or control. Only two checks limited the president and both were political: the ballot box and impeachment.[86] Judge Pine repudiated this claim of "unlimited and unrestrained Executive power," as did the Supreme Court.[87] Strengthening judicial resolve in this case was a war that had become increasingly unpopular, an executive argument badly presented in court, a Congress that decided to let President Truman dangle on a limb without statutory support, and claims of private property by major steel corporations.[88] Following this decision, federal courts were asked whether the hostilities in Korea amounted to a "war" in terms of life insurance policies. Although the Truman administration artificially argued that the country was engaged in a "police action," not war, federal judges had no difficulty in concluding that the country was at war.[89]

VI. THE VIETNAM CASES

The war in Vietnam and Southeast Asia provoked dozens of lawsuits challenging the constitutionality of U.S. military involvement. From 1966 to 1970, cases were initially dismissed on different grounds: they presented a political question or an unconsented suit against the United States, or the plaintiffs lacked standing. The Supreme Court regularly denied petitions seeking review. For the first time in the nation's history, the courts were using the political-question doctrine, or variants of it, consistently to avoid constitutional challenges about the war power.

The avoidance pattern began with a Vietnam case in 1966. A district judge claimed that courts "may not substitute themselves for the Commander in Chief of the Army and Navy and determine the disposition of the Armed Forces."[90] In affirming that ruling, the D.C. Circuit found the subject matter so obviously unfit for the judiciary "that no discussion or citation of authority is needed."[91] Subsequent cases denying jurisdiction relied heavily on that holding. Each time the Supreme Court denied certiorari.[92] In one case Justice Douglas objected: "To call issues of that kind 'political' would be to abdicate the judicial function which the Court honored in the midst of the Civil War in the *Prize Cases*."[93]

After four years of ducking these cases, federal courts began to edge toward the merits. Instead of mechanically citing the political question doctrine, the Second Circuit understood that it could have a legitimate role on certain constitutional questions. One possible opening: "Since orders to fight must be issued in accordance with proper authorization from both branches under some circumstances, executive officers are under a threshold constitutional 'duty [which] can be judicially identified and its breach judicially determined.'"[94] Another: "If the executive branch engaged the nation in prolonged foreign military activities without any significant congressional authorization, a court might be able to determine that this extreme step violated a discoverable standard for *some* mutual participation by Congress in accordance with Article I, section 8."[95]

In this case, the Second Circuit concluded that Congress in the Gulf of Tonkin Resolution of 1964 had provided sufficient authority. Moreover, Congress had participated "impliedly through appropriations and other acts in support of the project over a period of years."[96] Inadvertently perhaps, but the court opened up additional issues. Suppose Congress repealed the Gulf of Tonkin Resolution? Does an appropriations bill constitute authorization? When the case was remanded to district court, the plaintiff provided expert witnesses to testify that appropriations bills "do not encompass major declarations of policy." Both the House and the Senate have rules against including legislation in appropriations bills, and many lawmakers voted funds to support the armed forces in Indochina without endorsing the administration's policy.[97] District Judge Judd rejected that line of reasoning, stating there "is no doubt" that Congress had authorized the president to send U.S. troops to South Vietnam to engage in hostilities.[98] That "some members of Congress talked like doves before voting with the hawks is an inadequate basis for a charge that the President was violating the Constitution in doing what Congress by its words had told him he might do."[99]

Plaintiffs lost that case but not because of standing, jurisdiction, the political question doctrine, or other threshold tests. Judge Judd proceeded to the merits, pointing out that the dispute was not like the steel seizure case, where President Truman "relied on his own power without any supporting action from Congress."[100] Also in 1970, a district court held that an order directing a serviceman to report for Vietnam war duty was justiciable and was not barred by the political question doctrine: "No unusual subject matter is presented. Decisions in the entire area of the taking and arresting of combat action are exclusively political in kind, but determining whether or not a political decision has been taken by the appropriate set of governmental acts inescapably presents a purely judicial question" about the existence or nonexistence of a valid authorization.[101]

The district court reached the merits on other issues. The language of the Constitution and the debates at the time left no doubt "that the power to declare war and wage war was pointedly denied to the presidency . . . the power to make war and peace are legislative."[102] This decision was affirmed by the Second Circuit, which agreed that judicial scrutiny of the congressional duty to participate in war making was not foreclosed by the political-question doctrine.[103] It ruled that the president had no constitutional authority to take unilateral action in initiating offensive military action, and that Congress had to share in the decision to wage war. The task of the judiciary was therefore to determine whether Congress had sufficiently authorized or ratified the military operation.[104] The Second Circuit concluded that congressional action had satisfied those requirements.

In 1970, a district court held that men enlisted in the armed forces reserves had standing to challenge the constitutionality of the Vietnam War. Nor was the suit was barred by the doctrine of sovereign immunity or the political-question doctrine. The only issue, the court said, was the "narrow, legal question" of whether the war was "being waged by and under the authority of the branch of our government in which such power is constitutionally vested."[105] That position was reversed by the Ninth Circuit, which decided that the plaintiffs lacked standing.[106]

In 1971, the Second Circuit went to the merits in deciding whether congressional action in extending the Selective Service Act and appropriating funds was sufficient to ratify and approve military operations in Vietnam. At the time of the court's decision, Congress had repealed the Gulf of Tonkin Resolution.[107] The court agreed that the two political branches had to be mutually engaged in prosecuting military activities in Vietnam, but regarded the particular means used to wind down the conflict and disengage the nation as "a political question and outside of the power and competency of the judiciary."[108] And yet not quite. If the president decided to escalate the struggle instead of decreasing it, "additional supporting action by the Legislative Branch over what is presently afforded, might well be required."[109] The Supreme Court continued to deny certification.[110]

Although the Second Circuit implied that the judiciary might have a role in case of escalation without specific congressional backing, it backed away when that opportunity presented itself. Judges, it argued, lacked "vital information upon which to assess the nature of battlefield decisions" and could not possibly determine whether a specific military operation constituted escalation or "merely a new tactical approach within a continuing strategic plan."[111] Unwilling to close the door to judicial review entirely, the Second Circuit conceded that some war power issues might be appropriately adjudicated, such as a "radical change in the character of war operations—as by an intentional policy of indiscriminate bombing of civilians without any military objective."[112] Why this turn of events would be more suitable for judicial resolution than military escalation the court did not explain. Finally, the court suggested that judicial review might be required if Congress cut off funding.[113]

During this period of judicial soul-searching, other courts continued to rely on standing and the political-question doctrine to dismiss cases.[114] Even when courts sidestepped these cases, many insisted on at least some level of joint action by the president and Congress. Mutual cooperation between the two branches in the war effort became a dominant and recurrent principle. By clear implication, presidential military initiatives in the absence of legislative support could be invalidated by the courts.[115]

In 1973, the D.C. Circuit felt compelled to reject the position in *Luftig* that it was beyond judicial competence to determine the allocation of the war powers. It stated: "[W]e are now persuaded that there may be, in some cases, such competence."[116] In this case, Judge Charles Wyzanski revisited the argument that Congress, by appropriating funds and extending the draft serve, had consented to the war. He said that lawmakers in voting for an appropriation or draft law did not necessarily approve of the war: "We should not construe votes cast in pity and piety as though they were votes freely given to express consent."[117]

Also in 1973, in one of the first cases brought after the withdrawal of American combat troops from Vietnam and the release of American prisoners of war, a district court held that the president could be enjoined from engaging in combat activities in Cambodia.[118] During this litigation, Congress took steps to prohibit the use of funds for the bombing of Cambodia. But President Nixon vetoed the bill and Congress could not muster a two-thirds majority in each chamber for the override. The political branches settled on language to allow the bombing to continue until August 15, 1973, after which point the use of funds for military activities in Southeast Asia would be prohibited. The compromise, said the court, could not amount to congressional ratification of the bombing. It "cannot be the rule that the President needs a vote of only one-third plus one of either House in order to conduct a war, but this would be the consequence of holding that Congress must override a Presidential veto in order to terminate hostilities which it has not authorized."[119]

This decision was reversed by the Second Circuit, which held that the challenge presented a nonjusticiable question outside the scope of its cognizance.[120] This apparent lack of judicial competence did not prevent the court from noting that the "August 15 Compromise" constituted evidence that Congress had consented, by this language, to the Cambodian bombing.[121] The Second Circuit's decision was sustained by the Supreme Court.[122] What had firmed up as a war powers case capable of being decided by the courts was mooted by a political compromise by the elected branches.

VII. CONTEMPORARY ATTITUDES

Many war power cases have gone to the courts in the post-1973 period and in a large number of instances they have been treated as unsuitable for judicial resolution unless Congress and the president reached a constitutional impasse or deadlock. Congress needed to assert its institutional powers to make the clash ripe for adjudication. As the then judge Ruth Bader Ginsburg said in 1985, "[A] gauntlet has to be thrown down . . . by a majority of the members of Congress" before the judiciary will act.[123] Lawsuits brought by members of Congress were typically dismissed by the courts because Congress had not fully used its institutional powers. In some cases, lawmakers who defended the president's military actions intervened and submitted their own briefs.[124]

This line of analysis differed fundamentally from the Steel Seizure Case. The Supreme Court did not insist that Congress confront President Truman with legislative action before the case could be successfully litigated. It was a matter of examining whether Truman possessed constitutional or statutory authority to do what he did, and the Court found he did not. Is a gauntlet necessary every time? If the president withdrew funds from the Treasury without an appropriation, would Congress have to act legislatively to make the dispute ripe for the courts?

Judges who dismissed these cases often took time to examine and reject executive branch positions. An example is Judge Harold Greene in 1990, who faced a lawsuit against President George H. W. Bush because he was preparing for war against Iraq. In the end, Judge Greene dismissed the case on grounds of ripeness but not before disagreeing with the Justice Department that only the political branches are able to determine whether or not the country is at war: "This claim on behalf of the Executive is far too sweeping to be accepted by the courts. If the Executive has the sole power to determine that any particular offensive military operation, no matter how vast, does not constitute war-making but only an offensive military attack, the congressional power to declare war will be at the mercy of a semantic decision by the Executive. Such an 'interpretation' would evade the plain language of the Constitution, and it cannot stand."[125]

To Judge Greene, "courts do not lack the power and the ability to make the factual and legal determination of whether this nation's military actions constitute war for purposes of the constitutional War Clause."[126] He had "no hesitation in concluding that an offensive entry into Iraq by several hundred thousand United States servicemen under the conditions described above could be described as a 'war' within the meaning of Article I, Section 8, Clause 11, of the Constitution."[127] Although the Constitution "grants to the political branches, and in particular to the Executive, responsibility for conducting the nation's foreign affairs, it does not follow that the judicial power is excluded from the resolution of cases merely because they may touch upon such affairs. The court must instead look at 'the particular question posed' in the case. . . . In fact, courts are routinely deciding cases that touch upon or even have a substantial impact on foreign and defense policy."[128]

For those reasons, Judge Greene did not dismiss the case on the political-question doctrine.[129] Moreover, the plaintiffs had "adequately alleged a threat of injury in fact necessary to support standing."[130] He decided that the doctrine of remedial discretion did not require dismissal of the suit. The lawmakers did not have a remedy available from their fellow legislators and "cannot gain 'substantial relief' by persuasion of their colleagues alone."[131] Having crisply decided the merits in many areas, Judge Greene nevertheless decided that the doctrine of ripeness constituted an obstacle to rendering a decision. He expressed concern that Congress might yet vote its approval for the war.[132] Why was that an obstacle to judicial relief? He could have decided on the merits that if the president proceeded to mount an offensive war, it could begin only after Congress either declared or authorized the war. He could have issued an injunction, as requested by the plaintiffs, subject to the condition that the injunction would be lifted if Congress passed a declaration or authorization.

Litigation on the war in Kosovo offers competing views about judicial competence. Several members of Congress sought a declaration that President Clinton violated the War Powers Clause of the Constitution and the War Powers Resolution by conducting air strikes in the Federal Republic of Yugoslavia without congressional authorization.[133] The court held that the plaintiffs lacked standing because their complaint (the alleged "nullification" of congressional votes) was not sufficiently "concrete and particularized."[134] As for the political question doctrine, the court noted: "To the extent that the President is arguing that *every* case brought by a legislator alleging a violation of the War Powers Clause raises a non-justiciable political question, he is wrong."[135]

The D.C. Circuit affirmed on the ground of standing.[136] Two judges offered markedly different positions on the political-question doctrine. In a concurrence, Judge Laurence Silberman stated that "no one" is able to bring a challenge of "a President's arguably unlawful use of force."[137] He deemed the case nonjusticiable because of a lack of "judicially discoverable and manageable standards" to address the issue.[138] There were "no standards to determine either the statutory or constitutional questions raised in this case, and the question of whether the President has intruded on the war-declaring authority of Congress fits squarely within the political question doctrine."[139]

In this Kosovo litigation, Judge Silberman was reluctant to decide a national security case even in the presence of express constitutional powers.

Two years later, as part of the FISA Court of Review, he showed no hesitancy in deciding a case on the basis of "inherent" powers of the president to conduct national security surveillance. Without providing any reasoning or citing any evidence, he wrote: "We take for granted that the President does have that [inherent] authority and, assuming that is so, FISA could not encroach on the President's constitutional power."[140]

Judge David Tatel agreed with Silberman that the plaintiffs lacked standing to bring the case but denied that the lawsuit posed a nonjusticiable political question. Manageable standards were available to guide the courts. Whether the military operation in Yugoslavia "amounted to 'war' within the meaning of the Declare War Clause . . . is no more standardless than any other question regarding the constitutionality of government action." Courts have "proven no less capable" of developing standards to resolve war power issues than with Fourth Amendment or First Amendment actions.[141] Citing *Bas v. Tingy*, *Talbot v. Seeman*, and *The Prize Cases*, Tatel wrote: "Since the earliest years of the nation, courts have not hesitated to determine when military action constitutes 'war.'"[142]

From 2004 to 2008, the Supreme Court decided four major cases involving national security: *Hamdi*, *Rasul*, *Hamdan*, and *Boumediene*.[143] The first involved the right of a U.S. citizen not to be held indefinitely without being charged, given counsel, and tried. Only one justice, Clarence Thomas, argued that the Court lacked competence to decide the case. In *Rasul*, the Court rejected the administration's position that the naval base at Guantánamo Bay created a jurisdiction beyond the reach of federal courts. All justices agreed that the Court could hear and decide the case. They split only on how to apply an earlier holding, *Johnson v. Eisentrager* (1950). Justices disagreed with the administration's argument during oral argument that the "question of sovereignty is a political question."[144]

The third case, *Hamdan*, rejected the administration's claim that the president possessed inherent constitutional authority to create military commissions. Justice Antonin Scalia (joined by Clarence Thomas and Samuel Alito) dissented, not primarily on whether the Court had jurisdiction to hear and decide the case but on the interpretation the majority gave to the Detainee Treatment Act of 2005. The dissent by Justice Thomas (joined in part by Scalia and Alito) concluded that the Court lacked jurisdiction to hear the case and should have deferred to the president's judgment.

Finally, the Court split five to four in *Boumediene* in upholding the jurisdiction of federal district courts to hear habeas actions from detainees at the Guantánamo naval base. The four dissenters did not fundamentally question whether the Court had jurisdiction to take the case and reach the merits. Instead, they offered different views on how to read the Detainee Treatment Act, *Eisentrager*, the Insular Cases, English common law, the Habeas Corpus Act of 1679, and other historical precedents.

CONCLUSION

Contrary to the general impression that war power disputes present political questions beyond the scope of judiciary authority and competence, federal courts have often regarded the exercise of war power by the political departments as subject to independent judicial scrutiny. Throughout the past two centuries, judges have reviewed a broad range of issues involving foreign and domestic conflicts: the executive's right to seize property in wartime, annex territory, establish duty rates, suspend the writ of habeas corpus, and define when war begins and ends. Recent cases on detainees and military tribunals fit well within the jurisdiction and duties of federal courts. How well those decisions are written and decided is open for debate, but that is true of every judicial ruling, congressional statute, and presidential action. Competence by a branch to decide a matter of public policy does not guarantee a result pleasing to all parties.

NOTES

1. Max Farrand, ed., *Records of the Federal Convention of 1787*, vol. 2 (New Haven, Conn.: Yale University Press, 1937), 318–19.
2. Louis Fisher, *Presidential War Power*, 2nd ed. (Lawrence: University Press of Kansas, 2004), 17–19, 23–25.
3. James D. Richardson, ed., *A Compilation of the Messages and Papers of the Presidents, 1789–1902*, vol. 1 (Washington, D.C.: Bureau of National Literature and Art, 1904), 314.
4. *Bas v. Tingy*, 4 Dall. (4 U.S.) 37, 40 (1800) (emphasis in original).
5. *Bas v. Tingy*, 4 Dall. (4 U.S.) at 43.
6. *Talbot v. Seeman*, 5 U.S. (1 Cr.) 1, 28 (1801).
7. *Annals of Congress*, 10th Congress, 613.
8. *Annals of Congress*, 10th Congress, 614.
9. 9 Stat. 320 (1846), upheld in *In re Kaine*, 55 U.S. 103, 111–14 (1852).
10. *Little v. Barreme*, 2 Cr. (6 U.S.) 170, 179 (1804).
11. 299 U.S. 304, 320 (1936).
12. Office of Legal Counsel, U.S. Department of Justice, "Legal Authorities Supporting the Activities of the National Security Agency Described by the President," January 19, 2006, 1.
13. Office of Legal Counsel, "Legal Authorities," 30.
14. 48 Stat. 811, chap. 365 (1934).
15. 48 Stat. 811, at 1745.
16. *Panama Refining Co. v. Ryan*, 293 U.S. 388 (1935); *Schechter Corp. v. United States*, 295 U.S. 495 (1935).
17. *United States v. Curtiss-Wright Export Corp.*, 14 F.Supp. 230 (S.D. N.Y. 1936).
18. U.S. Justice Department, Statement as to Jurisdiction, *United States v. Curtiss-Wright*, No. 98, Supreme Court, October Term, 1936, 7.

19. U.S. Justice Department, Statement as to Jurisdiction, *United States v. Curtiss-Wright,* No. 98, Supreme Court, October Term, 1936, 15.

20. Brief for Appellees, *United States v. Curtiss-Wright,* No. 98, Supreme Court, October Term 1936, 3.

21. Brief for Appellees Allard, *United States v. Curtiss-Wright,* No. 98, Supreme Court, October Term, 1936.

22. C. Perry Patterson, "*In re the United States v. the Curtiss-Wright Corporation,*" *Texas Law Review* 22 (1944): 286, 297.

23. Those works are summarized in Louis Fisher, "Presidential Inherent Power: The 'Sole Organ' Doctrine," *Presidential Studies Quarterly* 37 (2007): 139, 149–50. For more detailed treatment of the sole organ doctrine, see my August 2006 study for the Law Library. The article and the study are available at http://www.loc.gov/law/help/usconlaw/constitutional_law.html#agency.

24. See pp. 23–28 of the August 2006 study cited in N. 23.

25. *Boumediene v. Bush,* 128 S. Ct. 2229 (2008), memo op., 68.

26. *United States v. Smith,* 27 Fed. Cas. 1192, 1229 (C.C.N.Y. 1806) (No. 16,342).

27. 1 Stat. 384, 7 (1794).

28. *United States v. Smith,* 27 Fed. Cas., 1229.

29. *United States v. Smith,* 27 Fed. Cas., 1228–31.

30. *United States v. Smith,* 27 Fed. Cas., 1230.

31. *United States v. Smith,* 27 Fed. Cas., 1230.

32. *United States v. Brown,* 12 U.S. (8 Cr.) 110, 123, 126–27 (1814).

33. *United States v. Brown,* 12 U.S. (8 Cr.) 128–29.

34. Louis Fisher, "Domestic Commander in Chief: Early Checks by Other Branches," *Cardozo Law Review* 29 (2008): 961, 975–76.

35. *Martin v. Mott,* 25 U.S. (12 Wheat.) 19, 28 (1827).

36. *Martin v. Mott,* 25 U.S. (12 Wheat.) 30.

37. *Luther v. Borden,* 48 U.S. (7 How.) 1, 43 (1849).

38. *Luther v. Borden,* 48 U.S. (7 How.) 44.

39. *Luther v. Borden,* 48 U.S. (7 How.) 45.

40. *Fleming v. Page,* 50 U.S. (9 How.) 603, 615 (1850) (emphasis added).

41. *Fleming v. Page,* 50 U.S. (9 How.) 603, 615 (1850) (emphasis added).

42. 9 Stat. 42 (1846).

43. 50 U.S. 614–15.

44. 50 U.S. 616.

45. *Mitchell v. Harmony,* 54 U.S. (13 How.) 115, 135 (1851).

46. *Mitchell v. Harmony,* 54 U.S. (13 How.) 115, 135 (1851).

47. *Jecker v. Montgomery,* 54 U.S. (13 How.) 498, 515 (1852).

48. *Jecker v. Montgomery,* 54 U.S. (13 How.) 498, 515 (1852).

49. *Cross v. Harrison,* 57 U.S. (16 How.) 164 (1854).

50. *The Prize Cases,* 67 U.S. 635, 668 (1863).

51. *The Prize Cases,* 67 U.S. 660 (emphasis in original).

52. *Ex parte Merryman,* 17 Fed. Cas. 144, 153 (C.C. Md. 1861) (No. 9,487) (emphasis in original).

53. *Ex parte Benedict,* 3 Fed. Cas. 159 (D.N.Y. 1862) (No. 1,292); *Ex parte Field,* 9 Fed. Cas. 1 (C.C.Vt. 1862) (No. 4,761). See Louis Fisher, *Military Tribunals and Presidential Power: American Revolution to the War on Terrorism* (Lawrence: University Press of Kansas, 2005), 60–62.

54. *In re Dunn*, 8 Fed. Cas. 93 (S.D.N.Y. 1863) (No. 4,171); *In re Fagan*, 8 Fed. Cas. 947 (D. Mass. 1863) (No. 4,604).

55. *Dynes v. Hoover*, 61 U.S. (20 How.) 65 (1858); *Ex parte Milligan*, 71 U.S. (4 Wall.) 2 (1866).

56. *Raymond v. Thomas*, 91 U.S. 712, 716 (1876).

57. *Mississippi v. Johnson*, 71 U.S. (4 Wall.) 475, 499 (1867).

58. *Mississippi v. Johnson*, 71 U.S. (4 Wall.) 500–501.

59. *State of Georgia v. Stanton*, 73 U.S. (6 Wall.) 50, 51 (1867).

60. *State of Georgia v. Stanton*, 73 U.S. (6 Wall.) 71.

61. *State of Georgia v. Stanton*, 73 U.S. (6 Wall.) 77.

62. *State of Georgia v. Stanton*, 73 U.S. (6 Wall.) 77.

63. *State of Georgia v. Stanton*, 73 U.S. (6 Wall.) 77–78.

64. *Hepburn v. Griswold*, 75 U.S. (8 Wall.) 603, 616-17 (1870).

65. *Legal Tender Cases*, 12 Wall. 457 (1871).

66. *United States v. Anderson*, 76 U.S. (9 Wall.) 56, 70–71 (1870); *United States v. Russel*, 13 Wall. 623 (1871); The Protector, 12 Wall. 700 (1872).

67. *Dooley v. United States*, 182 U.S. 222, 231 (1901).

68. *Dooley v. United States*, 182 U.S. 234.

69. *Hijo v. United States*, 194 U.S. 315, 323 (1904).

70. *Hijo v. United States*, 194 U.S. 315, 323 (1904) (citing Kent's Commentaries).

71. *Hamilton v. McClaughrey*, 136 Fed. 445, 449-51 (C.C. Kan. 1905); 13 Messages and Papers of the Presidents 6423 (December 3, 1900).

72. 35 Stat. 1090, sec. 14 (1909).

73. *Ex parte Orozco*, 201 F. 106, 112 (W.D. Tex. 1912), dismissed, 229 U.S. 633 (1913).

74. *Ex parte Orozco*, 201 F. 107.

75. *Hamilton v. Kentucky Distilleries Co.*, 251 U.S. 145, 156 (1919).

76. See *Ruppert v. Caffey*, 251 U.S. 264 (1920); *United States v. Standard Brewery*, 251 U.S. 210 (1920); *United States v. Cohen Grocery Co.*, 255 U.S. 81 (1921); *Commercial Trust Co. v. Miller*, 262 U.S. 51 (1923); *U.S. Trust Co. v. Miller*, 262 U.S. 58 (1923); *Ahrenfeldt v. Miller*, 262 U.S. 60 (1923); *Chastleton Corp. v. Sinclair*, 264 U.S. 543 (1924).

77. *United States v. Belmont*, 301 U.S. 324, 328 (1937).

78. 11 Foreign Affairs Manual 723.2-2(C).

79. *United States v. Guy W. Capps, Inc.*, 204 F.2d 655, 660 (4th Cir. 1953), aff'd on other grounds, 348 U.S. 296 (1955); *Seery v. United States*, 127 F.Supp. 601, 606 (Ct. Cl. 1955); *Reid v. Covert*, 354 U.S. 1, 16 (1957).

80. *United States v. Bethlehem Steel Corp.*, 315 U.S. 289 (1942); *Yakus v. United States*, 321 U.S. 414 (1944); *Bowles v. Willingham*, 321 U.S. 503 (1944); *Woods v. Miller Co.*, 333 U.S. 138 (1948). *Lichter v. United States*, 334 U.S. 742 (1948).

81. *Hirabayashi v. United States*, 320 U.S. 81 (1943); *Yasui v. United States*, 320 U.S. 115 (1943); *Korematsu v. United States*, 323 U.S. 214 (1944).

82. *Korematsu v. United States*, 323 U.S. 218.

83. *Korematsu v. United States*, 323 U.S. 246.

84. *Duncan v. Kahanamoku*, 327 U.S. 304 (1946). See also Fisher, Military Tribunals and Presidential Power, 135–38.

85. *Youngstown Co. v. Sawyer*, 343 U.S. 579, 582 (1952).

86. Oral argument in district court, reprinted at H.R. Doc. No. 534, 82d Cong., 2d Sess. 255–58, 362–63, 371–72 (1952).

87. *Youngstown Sheet & Tube Co. v. Sawyer*, 103 F.Supp. 569, 577 (D.D.C. 1952); *Youngstown Co. v. Sawyer*, 343 U.S. 579 (1952).

88. Fisher, *Presidential War Power*, 115–16.

89. *Weissman v. Metropolitan Life Ins. Co.*, 112 F.Supp. 420, 425 (D. Cal. 1953); *Gagliormella v. Metropolitan Life Ins. Co.*, 122 F.Supp. 246, 249–50 (D. Mass. 1954); *Carius v. New York Life Insurance Co.*, 124 F.Supp. 388, 390–91 (D. Ill. 1954). Prior to the Korean War, courts had also decided whether war existed within the meaning of life insurance claims; *New York Life Ins. Co. v. Durham*, 166 F.2d 874 (10th Cir. 1948).

90. *Luftig v. McNamara*, 252 F.Supp. 819, 821 (D.D.C. 1966).

91. *Luftig v. McNamara*, 373 F.2d 664, 665-66 (D.C. Cir. 1967), cert. denied, 387 U.S. 945 (1967).

92. *United States v. Mitchell*, 354 F.2d 767 (2d Cir. 1966), aff'd, 369 F.2d 323 (2d Cir. 1966), cert. denied, 386 U.S. 972 (1967); *United States v. Hart*, 382 F.2d 1020 (3d Cir. 1967), cert. denied, 391 U.S. 956 (1968); *United States v. Holmes*, 387 F.2d 781 (7th Cir. 1967), cert. denied, 391 U.S. 936 (1968); *Morse v. Boswell*, 289 F.Supp. 812 (D. Md. 1968), aff'd, 401 F.2d 544 (4th Cir. 1968), cert. denied, 393 U.S. 1052 (1969); *Mora v. McNamara*, 387 F.2d 862 (D.C. Cir. 1967), cert. denied, 389 U.S. 934 (1967); *United States v. Sisson*, 294 F.Supp. 511 (D. Mass. 1968); *McArthur v. Clifford*, 402 F.2d 58 (4th Cir. 1968), cert. denied, 393 U.S. 1002 (1968); *Velvel v. Johnson*, 287 F.Supp. 846 (D.D.C. 1968); aff'd, *Velvel v. Nixon*, 415 F.2d 236 (10th Cir. 1969), cert. denied, 396 U.S. 1042 (1970); *Pietsch v. President of the United States*, 434 F.2d 861 (2d Cir. 1970); *Davi v. Laird*, 318 F.Supp. 478 (W.D. Va. 1970); *Massachusetts v. Laird*, 400 U.S. 886 (1970).

93. *McArthur v. Clifford*, 393 U.S. 1002 (1968).

94. *Berk v. Laird*, 429 F.2d 302, 305 (2d Cir. 1970) (quoting *Baker v. Carr*, 369 U.S. 186, 198 [1962]).

95. *Berk v. Laird*, 429 F.2d 302, 305 (2d Cir. 1970) (emphasis in original).

96. *Berk v. Laird*, 429 F.2d 302, 305 (2d Cir. 1970).

97. *Berk v. Laird*, 317 F. Supp. 715, 718–21 (E.D. N.Y. 1970).

98. *Berk v. Laird*, 317 F. Supp. 716.

99. *Berk v. Laird*, 317 F. Supp. 724.

100. *Berk v. Laird*, 317 F. Supp. 729.

101. *Orlando v. Laird*, 317 F.Supp. 1013, 1016 (E.D. N.Y. 1970).

102. *Orlando v. Laird*, 317 F.Supp. 1013, 1016 (E.D. N.Y. 1970).

103. *Orlando v. Laird*, 443 F.2d 1039, 1042 (2d Cir. 1971), cert. denied, 404 U.S. 869 (1971).

104. *Orlando v. Laird*, 443 F.2d 1039, 1042 (2d Cir. 1971), cert. denied, 404 U.S. 869 (1971).

105. *Mottola v. Nixon*, 318 F.Supp. 538, 540 (N.D. Cal. 1970).

106. *Mottola v. Nixon*, 464 F.2d 178 (9th Cir. 1972).

107. *DaCosta v. Laird*, 448 F.2d 138, 1369 (2d Cir. 1971); 84 Stat. 2055, sec. 12 (1971).

108. *DaCosta v. Laird*, 448 F.2d 138, 1370.

109. *DaCosta v. Laird*, 448 F.2d 138, 1370.

110. 405 U.S. 979 (1972).

111. *DaCosta v. Laird*, 471 F.2d 1146, 1155 (2d Cir. 1973).

112. *DaCosta v. Laird*, 471 F.2d 1156.

113. *DaCosta v. Laird*, 471 F.2d 1157.

114. *Campen v. Nixon*, 56 F.R.D. 404 (N.D. Cal. 1972); *Atlee v. Laird*, 347 F. Supp. 689 (E.D. Pa. 1972) (three-judge court), aff'd, 411 U.S. 911 (1973); *Gravel v. Laird*, 347 F. Supp. 7 (D.D.C. 1972); *Sarnoff v. Connally*, 457 F.2d 809 (9th Cir. 1972); *Head v. Nixon*, 342 F.S upp. 521 (E.D. La. 1972), aff'd, 468 F.2d 951 (5th Cir. 1972).

115. *Commonwealth of Massachusetts v. Laird*, 327 F. upp. 378, 381 (D. Mass. 1971); *Commonwealth of Massachusetts v. Laird*, 451 F.2d 26, 34 (1st Cir. 1971); *Atlee v. Laird*, 347 F. Supp. 689, 694 (E.D. Pa. 1972), aff'd summarily, 411 U.S. 911 (1973); *Drinan v. Nixon*, 364 F. Supp. 854, 856, 860–61 (D. Mass. 1973).

116. *Mitchell v. Laird*, 488 F.2d 611, 614 (D.C. Cir. 1973).

117. *Mitchell v. Laird*, 488 F.2d 615.

118. *Holtzman v. Schlesinger*, 361 F. Supp. 553 (E.D. N.Y. 1973).

119. *Holtzman v. Schlesinger*, 361 F. Supp. 565.

120. *Holtzman v. Schlesinger*, 484 F.2d 1307 (2d Cir. 1973).

121. *Holtzman v. Schlesinger*, 484 F.2d 1313.

122. 414 U.S. 1304, 1316, 1321 (1973).

123. *Sanchez-Espinoza v. Reagan*, 770 F.2d 202, 211 (D.C. Cir. 1985).

124. For a representative list of these cases, see *Crockett v. Reagan*, 558 F. Supp. 893 (D.D.C. 1982), aff'd, *Crockett v. Reagan*, 720 F.2d 1355 (D.C. Cir. 1983); *Conyers v. Reagan*, 578 F. Supp. 324 (D.D.C. 1984), dismissed as moot, *Conyers v. Reagan*, 765 F.2d 1124 (D.C. Cir. 1985); *Sanchez-Espinoza v. Reagan*, 568 F. Supp. 596 (D.D.C. 1983), aff'd, *Sanchez-Espinoza v. Reagan*, 770 F.2d 202 (D.C. cir. 1985); *Lowry v. Reagan*, 676 F.Supp. 33 (D.D.C. 1987), aff'd, No. 87-5426 (D.C. Cir. 1988); *Dellums v. Bush*, 752 F. Supp. 1141 (D.D.C. 1990). Legal challenges by private plaintiffs fared no better. *Rappenecker v. United States*, 509 F. Supp. 1024 (N.D. Cal. 1980); *Ange v. Bush*, 752 F. Supp. 509 (D.D.C. 1990); *Pietsche v. Bush*, 755 F. Supp. 62 (E.D. N.Y. 1991).

125. *Dellums v. Bush*, 752 F. Supp. 1141, 1145 (D.D.C. 1990).

126. *Dellums v. Bush*, 752 F. Supp. 1146.

127. *Dellums v. Bush*, 752 F. Supp. 1146.

128. *Dellums v. Bush*, 752 F. Supp. 1146.

129. *Dellums v. Bush*, 752 F. Supp. 1144n5.

130. *Dellums v. Bush*, 752 F. Supp. 1148.

131. *Dellums v. Bush*, 752 F. Supp. 1149. Judge Greene later contradicted himself on this point: "In short, unless the Congress as a whole, or by a majority, is heard from, the controversy here cannot be deemed ripe; it is only if the majority of the Congress seeks relief from an infringement on its constitutional war-declaration clause that is may be entitled to receive it." *Dellums v. Bush*, 752 F. Supp. 1151.

132. *Dellums v. Bush*, 752 F. Supp. 1149–50.

133. *Campbell v. Clinton*, 52 F. Supp.2d 34 (D.D.C. 1999).

134. *Campbell v. Clinton*, 52 F. Supp.2d 43.

135. *Campbell v. Clinton*, 52 F. Supp.2d 40n5 (emphasis in original).

136. *Campbell v. Clinton*, 203 F.3d 19 (D.C. Cir. 2000).

137. *Campbell v. Clinton*, 203 F.3d 24.

138. *Campbell v. Clinton*, 203 F.3d 24–25.

139. *Campbell v. Clinton*, 203 F.3d 28.

140. *In Re: Sealed Case*, 310 F.3d 717, 742 (Foreign Int.Surv.Ct.Rev. 2002).

141. *Campbell v. Clinton*, 203 F.3d 37.

142. *Campbell v. Clinton*, 203 F.3d 37.

143. *Hamdi v. Rumseld,* 542 U.S. 507 (2004); *Rasul v. Bush,* 542 U.S. 466 (2004); *Hamdan v. Rumsfeld,* 548 U.S. 557 (2006); *Boumediene v. Bush,* **128 S. Ct. 2229** (2008). See Louis Fisher, *The Constitution and 9/11 Recurring Threats to America's Freedoms* (Lawrence: University Press of Kansas, 2008), 190–97, 231–39, 245–47.

144. U.S. Supreme Court, *Rasul v. Bush,* oral argument, April 20, 2004, 51 (Solicitor General Theodore Olson).

10

When the Rule of Law Can Undermine the Rule of Law

Hamdi and *The Federalist* on War and Necessity

Anthony A. Peacock

The United States Supreme Court's decision in *Hamdi v. Rumsfeld* (2004)[1] was one of the most significant war powers decisions in the Court's history, addressing what judicial process, if any, was owed to an American citizen detained as an enemy combatant in the United States. The citizen in question, Yaser Hamdi, was captured in Afghanistan in 2001 shortly after America went to war in that country against al Qaeda and the Taliban regime that supported it. Hamdi had been caught by the Northern Alliance, a U.S. ally, and was accused by the United States of being an enemy combatant, having taken up arms against American forces and their allies. The government contended that Hamdi's designation as an enemy combatant justified his indefinite detention without formal charges or proceedings. Among other things, the government maintained that Hamdi constituted an ongoing threat to U.S. troops.

Hamdi's father disagreed. Filing pleadings on behalf of himself and his son, Hamdi senior claimed that his son had been wrongly accused of being an enemy of the United States, that Hamdi's due process rights under the Fifth Amendment had been violated, and that Hamdi was entitled to a habeas corpus hearing. A plurality on the Supreme Court agreed with these last contentions, holding that citizens who sought to challenge their classifications as enemy combatants were entitled to notification of the factual basis for their classification as well as a fair opportunity to challenge the government's assertions before a neutral decision maker.[2]

Hamdi centered on what is a perennial problem that confronts any liberal democratic regime involved in a military conflict: what to do about the dilemma of war and necessity, specifically, how should government address those exigencies arising in war that do not lend themselves to legal resolution? The principal problem in *Hamdi* was not merely, as its critics have argued, that the Supreme Court was arrogating to itself what only the political branches of government could decide (although that was certainly a significant problem) but that the majority of its members were trying to "legalize" an area of political decision making that could not be reduced to rules. Not only would the decision in *Hamdi* result in the judiciary displacing the political branches of government, the president and Congress, as the final arbiter of national security policy, but because of legalizing these types of war policy questions, judges and lawyers would be making terrorism policy rather than politically responsible representatives exercising fact-contingent discretion.

The impossibility of regulating war by fixed rules of law is a problem as old as Western civilization. In *The Peloponnesian War*, for instance, Thucydides detailed how necessity curtailed political choice during war, perpetually confronting the Athenian and Spartan coalitions with decisions that required breaking laws, violating treaties, denying long-standing political customs, and alienating allies.

The problem of war and necessity was also familiar to America's Founders, whose Constitution was specifically designed to address it. Indeed, the first paragraph of *The Federalist* distinguished between those "political constitutions" established through "reflection and choice" and those established by "accident and force," highlighting that a critical issue for any government is preserving the freedom to choose and to choose wisely.[3] As we will see below, the most important *Federalist* numbers on national security similarly addressed the necessity of the Constitution accommodating both the positive law, or those rules freely chosen by the people's representatives, and extralegal discretion, the exercise of political judgment confronted by necessity that can never be reduced to rules.

In this chapter I examine the *Hamdi* decision with a view to defending Justice Thomas's dissenting opinion in the case as the position most consistent with the defense of strong executive powers advanced in *The Federalist*. Justice Thomas's position in *Hamdi* was that the judiciary could decide only whether the executive's detention of Yaser Hamdi was lawful, *not* whether his designation as an enemy combatant was correct. Thomas's position, which defended the concept of a unitary executive, was the most categorical of any assumed in *Hamdi* since it contemplated *no* role for the courts in addressing this principal issue in the case, the only opinion to do so. Yet Thomas's opinion was the only one that reflected an adequate understanding of the role of necessity in politics and in particular the necessities of war. This issue was front and center in *The Federalist* and was arguably the most difficult issue the authors of that work had to address.

It was also no accident that *The Federalist* itself was at the center of debate in *Hamdi*. Its authority on the issues in dispute remains unquestioned. But what exactly was that authority or, rather, what did *The Federalist* have to say about the issues raised in *Hamdi*? Although the plurality made no reference to the work, the remaining three opinions—by Justices Souter, Scalia, and Thomas—made eleven references to eleven *Federalist* numbers, just about as many as one will find in any Supreme Court decision. The three justices who cited *The Federalist* did so to buttress their own particular interpretation of presidential war powers but obviously enough those opinions conflicted, as did the justices' constructions of *The Federalist*. Which of the opinions more closely approximated the sense of the Constitution as it was understood by Publius (the pseudonym under which *The Federalist* was authored) is not merely of academic interest but of practical concern since it may not only help explain the legal and political theory underlying the Constitution's war powers but the complaints lodged against the Court by legal scholars and others following *Hamdi*.

The theme of this chapter is that insistence on government, particularly the executive, strictly adhering to the rule of law or fixed legal rules during times of war can not only be dangerous to the nation's security but can undermine the rule of law. *The Federalist* teaches us to understand how the natural rights preserved by the Constitution must be moderated by prudence, how the positive law must be moderated by the natural law, and how the rule of law may be inadequate to all political exigencies. The right to self-preservation is the most fundamental natural right that trumps all other rights in the constitutional order. Providing the executive absolute power to protect this right—to protect national security—was a paramount priority of the Constitution's Founders. It was the threat posed by *Hamdi* and subsequent decisions by the Court, all seeking to ensnare the government in a labyrinth of further legal rules and regulations, that drew the ire of the dissenting justices in those cases. However, it was not just the dissenters who were concerned about this development in law. Legal scholars, many of whom have participated in the government's war on terror, have also complained of the overregulation of those constitutional war powers necessary to fight radical Islam. The penultimate section of this chapter will review some of this literature and its relation to *Hamdi* and the other detainee cases the Court has decided this decade.

Before that, I begin below by outlining the positions taken in *Hamdi* with particular emphasis on those opinions that used *The Federalist* for support of their holdings in the case. I then proceed to examine *The Federalist* itself on the question of war and necessity, and apply this examination to the earlier issues raised in *Hamdi*. The review outlined above follows as well as some concluding remarks.

HAMDI ON *THE FEDERALIST*

What then were the positions staked out in *Hamdi*, especially on the constitutional issues relevant to *The Federalist*?

The plurality took the position that Hamdi was entitled to at least some due process allowing him to challenge the president's determination that he was an enemy combatant. Applying the balancing test from *Mathews v. Eldridge* (1976),[4] a case involving a denial of disability benefits, the Court held "that the process due in any given instance is determined by weighing 'the private interest that will be affected by the official action' against the Government's asserted interest, 'including the function involved' and the burdens the Government would face in providing greater process."[5] Lower courts and the Supreme Court would have to assess claims like Hamdi's in future weighing these competing considerations. Although Justice Thomas was skeptical the judiciary could achieve this balancing act, his more fundamental criticism was that by using the *Mathews* scheme the Court had "fail[ed] adequately to consider basic principles of the constitutional structure as it relates to national security and foreign affairs."[6]

But what precisely were those basic principles of constitutional structure? There was little agreement on the Court. Justice Souter, who had made a single reference to *The Federalist*, had cited Madison's remark in *Federalist* 51 about the constitutional separation of powers: "[T]hat 'the constant aim is to divide and arrange the several offices in such a manner as that each may be a check on the other—that the private interest of every individual may be a sentinel over the public rights.'"[7] Souter used Madison's authority to support his assertion that the principal tension in American constitutional government was the perennial one "between security and liberty. . . . In a government of separated powers, deciding finally on what is a reasonable degree of guaranteed liberty whether in peace or in war (or some condition in between) is not well entrusted to the Executive Branch of Government, whose particular responsibility is to maintain security."[8] Justice Souter then would allow the judiciary to scrutinize executive branch decisions over the designation of individuals, such as Yaser Hamdi, as enemy combatants since to fail to do so would place dangerous, unchecked power in the hands of an executive who might not adequately respect those private rights that constituted one of the fundamental objects Founders such as James Madison had designated as the highest ends of American constitutionalism.

Justice Scalia had similarly described the conflict at issue in *Hamdi* as one between the competing demands of national security and a citizen's right to personal liberty. Scalia was careful to qualify that the Supreme Court was in no position to second-guess what was necessary to meet the government's security needs and that his ruling applied only to citizens, like Hamdi, who had been "detained within the territorial jurisdiction of a federal court."[9] Those outside such jurisdiction did not enjoy the same constitutional benefits that those under the auspices of federal courts enjoyed. However, when citizens were detained in places where federal courts were open, the government had two options: it could charge the citizen with a crime or it could suspend the writ of habeas corpus pursuant to Article I, Section 9 of the Constitution.[10] No other options existed.

To buttress this contention Scalia cited Alexander Hamilton's proclamation in *Federalist* 84 that habeas corpus was a bulwark against arbitrary imprisonments and tyranny. "Indeed, availability of the writ under the new Constitution (along with the requirement of trial by jury in criminal cases, see Art. III, §2, cl. 3) was [Hamilton's] basis for arguing that additional, explicit procedural protections were unnecessary. See The Federalist No. 83."[11] For Scalia, citizens detained during wartime had a right to full constitutional due process made available through the writ of habeas corpus. Although during war aliens might be detained until the cessation of hostilities, citizens could not be. Procedurally, citizens were to be treated no differently during wartime than they were during peacetime. There was no such thing as detaining citizens indefinitely because they posed a threat to America or its troops. "It is unthinkable that the Executive could render otherwise criminal grounds for detention noncriminal merely by disclaiming an intent to prosecute, or by asserting that it was incapacitating dangerous offenders rather than punishing wrongdoing."[12] The tradition in the United States has been to treat citizens who have aided the enemy as traitors subject to criminal process. The Constitution certainly recognized that necessity of depriving citizens of their due process rights during times of need but this required an explicit congressional act suspending the writ of habeas corpus, "the Constitution's only 'express provision for exercise of extraordinary authority because of a crisis.'"[13]

Scalia further cited *The Federalist* in support of his contention that the executive's lack of indefinite wartime detention powers over citizens was consistent with the Founders' suspicion toward military wherewithal permanently at the executive's disposal.

> In the Founders' view, the "blessings of liberty" were threatened by "those military establishments which must gradually poison its very fountain." The Federalist No. 45. . . . No fewer than 10 issues of the Federalist were devoted in whole or in part to allaying fears of oppression from the proposed Constitution's authorization of standing armies in peacetime. Many safeguards in the Constitution reflect these concerns.[14]

Scalia also cited Hamilton's discussion of executive power in *Federalist* 69 to demonstrate that the president's military authority would be much more diminished than it was for the British king. The president was only to assume command of military forces while the British king enjoyed the power of declaring war as well as of raising and regulating fleets and armies, powers that only Congress could exercise under the Constitution. Scalia concluded: "A view of the Constitution that gives the Executive authority to use military force rather than the force of law against citizens on American soil flies in the face of the mistrust that engendered these provisions."[15]

But did Scalia have the Founders right here? Or did he impute to them Whig prejudices about the potential abuse of executive power that had led to such disastrous consequences under the Articles of Confederation that the Constitution was designed to overcome?

In contrast to both Justice Souter and Justice Scalia, Justice Thomas did not believe federal courts had any authority either to second-guess the executive's detention determinations, like that at issue in *Hamdi*, or to require the imposition of habeas corpus where the government had not suspended the writ, as Justice Scalia suggested was required. Thomas advanced three principal arguments, all derivative of arguments initially advanced by Alexander Hamilton in *The Federalist*.

The first was that the principal purpose of the federal government was to provide for security, both against "internal convulsions" and "external attacks," to use Hamilton's language from *Federalist* 23.[16] Second, the federal government had to have power sufficient to provide for national security. Thomas again paraphrased from *Federalist* 23:

> The power to protect the Nation "ought to exist without limitation . . . *[b]ecause it is impossible to foresee or define the extent and variety of national exigencies, or the correspondent extent & variety of the means which may be necessary to satisfy them*. The circumstances that endanger the safety of nations are infinite; and for this reason no constitutional shackles can wisely be imposed on the power to which the care of it is committed."[17]

The emphasis here is Hamilton's and his point is clear: since the variety of potential threats to the United States was unlimited, so too had to be the power of the national government to deal with those threats. In a Constitution of limited government, the implications of this were significant. We will examine them in more detail in the next section.

Finally, Justice Thomas emphasized that the structural advantages of a unitary executive led the Framers to place primary responsibility for national security and the nation's foreign relations in the hands of the president. As *Federalist* 70 implored, energy in the executive was critical both to the promotion of good government and to protection against foreign attacks. In addition, unity was the key ingredient to energy in the executive because it promoted "'[d]ecision, activity, secrecy, and dispatch," all of which were best achieved in the hands of one rather than many.[18] Citing *Federalist* 70, Thomas concluded: "'Of all the cares or concerns of government, the direction of war most peculiarly demands those qualities which distinguish the exercise of power by a single hand.'"[19] As I noted earlier, Thomas was content to allow the judiciary to decide whether Hamdi's detention was lawful but he disagreed that the Court had either the legal authority or institutional capacity to determine whether Hamdi was an "enemy combatant." That was a factual question to be determined by the political branches.[20] The judiciary was unauthorized and incompetent to assess such issues.

In the context of *The Federalist*, then, we might reduce the critical questions raised in the opinions of Justices Souter, Scalia, and Thomas to two. First, would the authors of *The Federalist* agree with Justices Souter and Scalia—as well as the plurality in *Hamdi*—that the judiciary had the constitutional authority to intercede in the dispute involving Yaser Hamdi and question his designation as an enemy combatant? If so, what procedures might they allow the judiciary to provide Hamdi and on what constitutional basis would those procedures be provided? On the other hand, if the authors of *The Federalist* were more inclined to adopt Justice Thomas's position in *Hamdi*, why would they be so inclined? What arguments in addition to those raised by Thomas's remarks above might we find in *The Federalist* that might further flesh out the details of executive war powers and the problem of war and necessity in American politics as Publius conceived them?

THE FEDERALIST ON WAR AND NATIONAL SECURITY

My answer to the first question above is that Publius likely would not agree with allowing the judiciary to intercede to challenge an executive determination of Hamdi as an enemy combatant because of the fundamentally political and discretionary nature of war-related questions. Accordingly, no consideration need be given to what procedures might be allowed detainees such as Hamdi.

Justice Scalia's argument that the Constitution permits citizens detained within the jurisdiction of federal courts to assert habeas rights absent a suspension of habeas corpus is compelling but ultimately fails to explain how the political branches of government can act constitutionally in all cases of necessity that might confront the country in war. Justice Souter's opinion similarly suffers from trying to regulate exercises of executive discretion by law and granting the power to do so to the most unaccountable and incompetent branch of the federal government: the judiciary.

The Constitution emerged above all from a concern over national security.[21] The single greatest failure of the Articles of Confederation was their ineptitude in the face of national security threats, both foreign and domestic. Following *Federalists* 1 and 2, which introduced the work, the next eight numbers of *The Federalist* (2–10) were dedicated to safety—from foreign threats (3–5), strife between the states (6–8), and domestic faction (9–10).[22] Jay emphasized in *Federalist* 3 that "[a]mong the many objects to which a wise and free people find it necessary to direct their attention, that of providing for their *safety* seems to be the first."[23] The key to this primal urge in politics, as Jay highlighted in *Federalists* 3–5, was union. Union was critical to American safety. Madison went so far in *Federalist* 41 as to proclaim that a united America, "without a single soldier, exhibit[ed] a more forbidding posture to foreign ambition than America disunited, with a hundred thousand veterans ready for combat."[24] Madison's review of ancient and modern confederacies provided in *Federalists* 18–20 demonstrated that the real threat to federal bodies was not so much "tyranny in the head" as "anarchy among the members."[25] Moreover, weak constitutions necessarily dissolved either because they did not have the powers necessary for public safety or because they had to usurp those powers requisite for that end. "Tyranny has perhaps oftener grown out of the assumptions of power, called for, on pressing exigencies, by a defective constitution, than out of the full exercise of the largest constitutional authorities."[26] The great danger to the United States was not that the new federal union might acquire too much power but that, like the Amphictyonic council or Achaean league, it would disintegrate from too few.

If the union was to survive then the Constitution would have to provide national security powers sufficient to keep an extensive territory the size of the United States together. What Americans needed was a more energetic constitution, and it was in the executive above all that energy was to be found. As *Federalist* 70 implored:

> Energy in the Executive is a leading character in the definition of good government. It is essential to the protection of the community against foreign attacks; it is not less essential to the steady administration of the laws; to the protection of property against those irregular and high-handed combinations which sometimes interrupt the ordinary course of justice; to the security of liberty against the enterprises and assaults of ambition, of faction, and of anarchy.[27]

Presidential power had to be commensurate with presidential responsibility. Because *Federalist* 23 made clear that responsibility was virtually infinite—given the impossibility of foreseeing or defining "the extent and variety of national exigencies"—presidential power would have to be correspondingly infinite. Article II of the Constitution recognized this necessity by vesting *all* executive power "in a President of the United States" and further charging him—and him only—with being the "commander in chief" of the armed forces.[28] As John Yoo has recently demonstrated, the text, structure, and ratification of the Constitution all make clear that similar to the British legal tradition, the executive under the American Constitution was fully authorized to commence war and any other military hostilities necessary to protect the general welfare. As *Federalist* 74 recognized, the Constitution, following many state constitutions of the Founding era, "concentrated the military authority in [the executive] *alone*."[29] And for good reason. The discretion necessary to conduct war and to respond to its exigencies could not be fixed by law, constitutional or otherwise. The Declare War Clause of Article I, Section 8, Subsection 11 of the Constitution, like the other legalistic provisions of that subsection, was simply a legal provision that notifies the enemy and American citizens that a formal state of war has been declared. Although of obvious significance for international and domestic law, the orthodoxy in American academic circles and among some of the federal judiciary that the Declare War Clause requires the president to obtain the consent of Congress before engaging the country in war is refuted not only by constitutional practice and the history of the Constitution but by the Constitution's language itself. Article I, Section 10, for instance, explicitly states that "no State shall, without the Consent of Congress . . . engage in War, unless actually invaded, or in such imminent Danger as will not admit of delay." No such explicit requirement of consent from Congress is required by Article I, Section 8, Subsection 11. As Yoo writes, "Article I, Section 10 . . . shows the faults of [the orthodox] approach, because it requires us to believe that the Framers did not know how to express themselves in one part of the Constitution but did in another part of the Constitution on exactly the same subject."[30] Although the president has more or less complete control over foreign relations and war under the Constitution, Congress does retain control over the domestic effects of the president's decisions by controlling federal legislation and funding.[31]

It is worth noting that it was not just Hamilton but Madison too in *The Federalist* who made the argument for the necessity of unlimited discretion in the case of national defense, that too much of the rule of law could undermine the rule of law. Justice Thomas cited *Federalist* 41 immediately following his citation of *Federalist* 23 as authority for the proposition that discretionary power for purposes of war had to be unlimited. In *Federalist* 41 Madison remarked:

> The means of security can only be regulated by the means and the danger of attack. They will, in fact, be ever determined by *these rules*, and by *no others*. It is in vain to oppose constitutional barriers to the impulse of self-preservation. It is worse than in vain; because it plants in the Constitution itself necessary usurpations of power, every precedent of which is a germ of unnecessary and multiplied repetitions.[32]

Justice Thomas recognized the implications of these intriguing statements from Hamilton and Madison about unlimited national security powers in *Federalists* 23 and 41. The Court's oversight in *Hamdi* with respect to the issue of who gets to decide military questions (the political branches or the judiciary), like Justice Scalia's and Justice Souter's, undermined two critical elements of American constitutionalism: its republicanizing of energetic executive power and its constitutionalizing of prerogative power.

Harvey Mansfield has observed that until the Constitution strong executive power had never been republicanized.[33] The history of republics, as Hamilton and Madison both made clear in *The Federalist*, was a history of imbecility. "[T]he history of the petty republics of Greece and Italy," for instance, was one of a "rapid succession of revolutions by which they were kept perpetually vibrating between the extremes of tyranny and anarchy. If they exhibited occasional calms, these only serve as short-lived contrasts to the furious storms that are to succeed."[34] In *Federalist* 1, Publius warned his readers that those like him who advocated more energetic government such as that proposed under the Constitution would be denounced as "fond of power and hostile to the principles of liberty." But he reminded his readers that it is "equally forgotten that the vigor of government is essential to the security of liberty."[35] Arguably the most difficult task *The Federalist* faced was addressing the "idea . . . that a vigorous Executive is inconsistent with the genius of republican government."[36] It had been an article of faith held by advocates of republican government since time immemorial that strong executives were a threat to liberty. This idea had been almost fatal to America under the Articles of Confederation and it had to be abandoned.

A critical element to improving American government was acceding to the necessity of constitutionalizing prerogative and granting this power to an executive who could exercise it uniformly. The British political philosopher John Locke had famously defined prerogative as the "Power to act according to discretion, for the publick good, without the prescription of the Law, and sometimes even against it." Prerogative was necessary because

> in some Governments the Law-making Power is not always in being, and is usually too numerous, and so too slow, for the dispatch requisite to Execution: and because also it is impossible to foresee, and so by laws to provide for, all Accidents and Necessities, that may concern the publick; or to make such Laws, as will do no harm, if they are Executed with an inflexible rigour, on all occasions, and upon all Persons, that may come in their way, therefore there is a latitude left to the Executive power, to do many things of choice, which the Laws do not prescribe.[37]

The two supreme powers in Locke's constitutional regime were the positive law and extralegal discretion. This latter power, prerogative power, could not be reduced to rules. "For *Prerogative is nothing but the Power of doing publick good without a Rule.*"[38] Yet prerogative, as Locke made clear, was a power as essential to good government as the positive law, a power necessary to security and that recognized the limits to political choice and to the rule of law that necessity imposed on that choice and that law.[39]

Publius largely accepted Locke's assessment and prescriptions regarding prerogative. He observed, for instance, in *Federalist* 28:

> That there may happen cases in which the national government may be under the necessity of resorting to force, cannot be denied. Our own experience has corroborated the lessons taught by the examples of other nations; that emergencies of this sort will sometimes exist in all societies, however constituted . . . that the idea of governing at all times by the simple force of law (which we have been told is the only admissible principle of republican government), has no place but in the reverie of those political doctors, whose sagacity disdains the admonitions of experimental instruction.[40]

You could not have a more explicit rejection by Publius of the idea that republican government requires all actions by public officials, particularly those charged with national security, to be regulated by law. Indeed, Publius denounces those who hold to such a position as dreamers, "political doctors" devoid of prudential wisdom. Publius not only suggests that the discretionary powers of prerogative are necessary to good government but as his remarks in *Federalist* 41 above (and *Federalist* 25 quoted below) make clear, both the positive law and the discretionary powers of prerogative will be part of the law of the Constitution. Publius is certainly cognizant of the potential for abuse that prerogative poses, unlimited as it is by law, but like Locke he indicates that the president cannot act any way he likes, but only in a manner consistent with the public good.[41] Moreover, unlike the unelected British monarch, the American president is elected by the people (or the electors of the Electoral College) who can dispatch the president any time he abuses his powers. As *The Federalist* illustrates then, the Constitution remedies Locke's problem of requiring government to rise above the law or to even act against it when exercising prerogative by constitutionalizing prerogative. No such contravention of the law will occur under the Constitution since exercising executive prerogative powers will be constitutional.[42]

During the Revolutionary War, Hamilton had learned that the nature of modern warfare made the necessity of unity and discretion in the executive even more imperative than it otherwise might have been. The war against the British had educated Hamilton on the ineptitude of republican governments and their almost fatal reliance on legislative rule and the rule of law. As I indicate in the introduction to this book, republican governments are inherently lawmaking and law-abiding governments, governments that create legal rules through legislative process that it is expected that everyone abide by, including those who make the law. To be sure, this is one of the great virtues of republicanism: that it facilitates precisely that respect for the rule of law, with its concomitant of the equal treatment of individuals who are not subject to the arbitrary rule of others. This virtue, however, can turn into vice when republican governments, as *The Federalist* warned time and again, rely excessively on legislative rule. "The legislative department is everywhere extending the sphere of its activity, and drawing all power into its impetuous vortex," *Federalist* 48 warned.[43] Separation of powers, with an independently acting energetic executive, was critical to the success of the new Constitution, as America's experience during the Revolution revealed.[44]

Single direction in the conduct of war was critical to national security, particularly in the modern era of total and global war. In an age of large, professionally trained standing armies and imperial navies, danger could bring itself to the shores of the United States in very short order.[45] Publius implored that what America needed was not only its own standing army and navy but an energetic executive. The first ingredient of such an executive—as Justice Thomas observed in *Hamdi*—was unity. In *Federalist*

70 Hamilton had challenged the traditional Whig assumption that lay at the heart of the republican prejudice in favor of legislative over executive power. That assumption, "derived from that maxim of republican jealousy," considered "power as safer in the hands of a number of men than of a single man." Hamilton emphasized, however, that "all multiplication of the Executive is rather dangerous than friendly to liberty."[46] The Whig assumption of safeguarding against the abuse of power by multiplying its agency was not universally applicable and could be positively fatal in the case of emergencies that confronted nations. Those emergencies required immediate, decisive, and energetic action, action that could generally only be effectively taken by a single hand.

Energetic government also might require secretive executive action, which again did not lend itself to regulation by law. One of the most controversial themes of *The Federalist,* which at times was explicit and at other times less explicit, was that necessity confronts republican regimes with the imperative of acting in unrepublican ways. Americans needed "a Constitution, at least equally energetic with the one proposed," which is to say, however excessive the congressional and executive powers provided for under the Constitution may have seemed to its critics in 1787, they were *the least* that were required for the preservation of the Union. Yet that minimum provided for under the Constitution nevertheless allowed for *unlimited means* for dealing with national security crises. The "*means* ought to be proportioned to the *end,*"[47] *Federalist* 23 proclaimed, and as we have seen, the ends for purposes of national security outlined in that same number required unlimited discretionary action. The means to attain such ends also therefore had to be unlimited.

But if this is so, where does this leave the individual rights referred to in *Hamdi*? If the political branches of government and specifically the executive have unlimited discretionary powers during times of national emergency or war, does this not leave all individual rights so sacred to the American constitutional order exposed to abuse by government? What relevance, for instance, is the writ of habeas corpus, whose existence is explicitly contemplated by Article I, Section 9 of the Constitution, if the government can simply act as it pleases during emergencies, incarcerate citizens, and then defend this as an act of emergency powers or prerogative? The interpretation of war powers provided above seems to make *any* constitutional limitations, including those provided for in the Suspension Clause, irrelevant. Or does it?

WAR POWERS, INDIVIDUAL RIGHTS, AND THE PROBLEM OF JUDICIAL RATIONALISM

In *Hamdi,* Justice Scalia had emphasized that there were numerous *Federalist* numbers that warned against the dangers of standing armies and that sought to address the "general mistrust of military power permanently at the Executive's disposal." Scalia paraphrased Madison's warning in *Federalist* 45 that "the 'blessings of liberty' were threatened by 'those military establishments which must gradually poison its very fountain.'"[48] Hamilton himself had admonished against unrestricted executive power in the *Federalist* numbers dealing with the executive, allaying for instance readers' concerns by demonstrating in *Federalist* 69 that the president's powers would be far less extensive than what the British king enjoyed. Hamilton further indicated in *Federalist* 71 that the president would be "subordinate to the laws" even if he was not "to be dependent on the legislative body."[49] This certainly suggested that the president would enjoy no rights of prerogative, at least not in the normal course of things.

Yet despite these concessions about the dangers of military establishments and broad, unchecked executive power, as the last section suggests, *The Federalist* was equally, if not more, emphatic about the necessity for more energetic government, the very standing armies the Constitution's critics were so skeptical of, and as broad executive and political powers as were necessary to deal with any national exigencies that might arise. In *Federalist* 26, where Hamilton made the case for the necessity of standing armies in times of peace, he proclaimed that "[i]t was a thing hardly to have been expected that in a popular revolution the minds of men should stop at that happy mean which marks the salutary boundary between POWER and PRIVILEGE, and combines the *energy of government* with the *security of private rights*. A failure in this delicate and important point is the great source of the inconveniences we experience."[50] This passage, made in that part of *The Federalist* stressing the need for more energetic government and in a *Federalist* number specifically advocating more energetic government through the vehicle of a standing army, followed Hamilton's concluding paragraph to *Federalist* 25, where similar to Madison's proclamation in *Federalist* 41 against placing any "constitutional barriers to the impulse of self-preservation," Hamilton again implored

> that nations pay little regard to rules and maxims calculated in their very nature to run counter to the necessities of society. Wise politicians will be cautious about fettering the government with restrictions that cannot be observed, because they know that every breach of the fundamental laws, though dictated by necessity, impairs that sacred reverence which ought to be maintained in the breast of rulers toward the constitution of a country, and forms a precedent for other breaches where the same plea of necessity does not exist at all, or is less urgent and palpable.[51]

Federalist 26 makes clear that Hamilton considered the balance struck between energy in government and the protection of individual rights to be a crucial consideration in any reasonable constitutional thinking but it also makes clear that he did not believe that balance had been correctly struck following the Revolution. In particular, he seemed to believe that too little attention had been paid to energy in government because there had been an overzealous vigilance on behalf of individual rights, which translated under the Articles of Confederation into virtual legislative omnipotence. Hamilton's caution in *Federalist* 25 that nations will disregard "rules or maxims calculated in their very nature to run counter to the necessities of society" and that "wise politicians" will not fetter "government with restrictions that cannot be observed" further suggests yet again that legalistic burdens or legislative maxims that impede national security will be—and *should* be—overlooked by those charged with maintaining it. The Constitution had to accommodate prerogative.

How then do these remarks from *The Federalist* bear on the issues raised in *Hamdi*? Where is the balance to be struck between disputes over energy in government and security of private rights, and can such disputes be resolved in a judicial, rather than a political, forum as the Court suggested in *Hamdi*?

Justice Thomas's position was that the courts had no business second-guessing President Bush's designation of Yaser Hamdi as an enemy combatant. Thomas was not saying that individual rights needed to be ignored, only that the proper balance to be struck between individual rights and national security is a political question for the political branches—the executive and Congress—to decide. The plurality, Justice Souter, and Justice Scalia all disagreed, countering that the courts had a role in questioning the president's actions. Justice Scalia conceded that national security decisions were for the president to make, but absent suspension of the writ of habeas corpus, full criminal due process rights had to be accorded citizens such as Hamdi where federal courts had jurisdiction. Thomas's response to Scalia on this score spoke to the broader problem of attempting to judicialize war powers questions of the sort at issue in *Hamdi*—the problem that such questions did not lend themselves readily, if at all, to legal resolution.

Article I, Section 9 provides that "[t]he privilege of the Writ of Habeas Corpus shall not be suspended, unless when in Cases of Rebellion or Invasion the public Safety may require it." As Justice Thomas highlighted, the Suspension Clause applies only to cases of rebellion and invasion and not to all potential emergencies that could arise when it might be necessary to detain enemy combatants. Accordingly, should these situations that fall outside the ambit of the Suspension Clause occur,

> Congress would then have to choose between acting unconstitutionally and depriving the President of the tools he needs to protect the Nation. Second, [Thomas did] not see how suspension would make constitutional otherwise unconstitutional detentions ordered by the President. It simply removes a remedy. JUSTICE SCALIA'S position might therefore require one or both of the political branches to act unconstitutionally in order to protect the Nation. But the power to protect the Nation must be the power to do so lawfully.[52]

It is this fact perhaps above all that undermines Justice Scalia's assertion that his position in *Hamdi* most closely comports with the teachings of *The Federalist.* The declarations of Hamilton and Madison in *Federalists* 28 and 41 seemed to make clear that the power to defend the nation must be the power to do so constitutionally. Justice Scalia's opinion does not seem to allow the federal government to act legally or constitutionally in all situations of national exigency, as *The Federalist* seemed to propose. But this is not all *The Federalist* said with respect to the issue of individual rights and national security.

If Justice Thomas's interpretation is correct, what does this imply about the rights guarantees in the Constitution during times of war, particularly during a war that may go on indefinitely? Do citizens not have *any* recourse to dispute executive findings of fact, for instance, in the face of an administration that might detain them for years, perhaps the better part of their lives? And might Justice Thomas's position not lead to a political regime of potentially unlimited powers during wartime? Was this itself consistent with the Constitution's principles and the teaching of *The Federalist*?

The difficulty here concerns the priority of the Constitution's objects and the structural issues Thomas referred to regarding the separation of powers, both of which implicate a distinction between political and judicial decision making. In *Hamdi* none of the justices, other than Thomas, provided an account of the political consequences once *any* judicial review of the executive's decision making regarding the status of enemy combatants is allowed. Even if only *minimal* judicial process is permitted, as Justice Thomas emphasized, it will undermine unity and responsibility in the executive since it gives the ultimate power of deciding war powers questions to the judiciary, not the executive or Congress. Justice Souter's citation of *Federalist* 51 as an example of Madison's argument that the separation of powers requires vigilant scrutiny of one branch by another, failing which individual rights might be jeopardized, gets Madison's account of the separation of powers only half right. The distinction between the ends of Madison's constitutionalism, the protection of private rights and the promotion of the public good, receives its constitutional expression in the distinction between the judicial and the political branches of government. As much as it may be based on a political anthropology that seeks to counteract ambition with ambition—as Souter suggested—Madison's separation of powers is also based on a *functional* distinction between the capacities and competencies of the three branches of government.[53] As Donald Horowitz has written, "If the separation of powers reflects a division of labor according to expertise, then relative institutional capacity becomes relevant to defining spheres of power and particular exercises of power."[54] And in the case of war, the judiciary possesses virtually no capacity—and even less responsibility—to address the questions *Hamdi* would have it address. What is constitutionally novel in *Hamdi* is that the Court not only counsels the executive about what must be accounted for when it acts but is *exercising the executive power itself* to the extent that it seeks to balance individual interests against what it understands to be the government's national security interests.

Justice Thomas was on firm constitutional ground for his propositions that national security was the most fundamental governmental interest,[55] that that governmental interest could at times trump an individual's liberty interest,[56] and that the president had broad powers of war that could not be judicially questioned because they constituted political, rather than judicial, questions.[57] This last holding was of course challenged by other members of the *Hamdi* Court—hence *Hamdi*'s importance as a precedent. The nub of Thomas's opinion was perhaps captured most succinctly by the passage he cited from *Chicago & Southern Airlines, Inc. v. Waterman S.S. Corp.* (1948). There FDR's former attorney general, Justice Robert Jackson, had this to say on behalf of the Court:

> The President, both as Commander-in-Chief and as the Nation's organ for foreign affairs, has available intelligence services whose reports are not and ought not to be published to the world. It would be intolerable that courts, without the relevant information, should review and perhaps nullify actions of the Executive taken on information properly held secret. Nor can courts sit *in camera* in order to be taken into executive confidences. But even if courts could require full disclosure, the very nature of executive decisions as to foreign policy is political, not judicial. Such decisions are wholly confided by our Constitution to the political departments of government, Executive and Legislative. They are delicate, complex, and involve large elements of prophecy. They are and should be undertaken only by those directly responsible to the people whose welfare they advance or imperil. They are decisions of a kind for which the Judiciary has neither aptitude, facilities nor responsibility and which has long been held to belong in the domain of political power not subject to judicial intrusion or inquiry.[58]

Justice Jackson here was emphatic: the judiciary had *no* role in foreign policy disputes. Courts not only lacked the "aptitude, facilities [and] responsibility" to make foreign policy decisions. Such decisions were inherently *political*. That is why the Constitution "wholly confided" such powers "to the political departments of government."

This point was crucial to *Federalist* 78, where Publius emphasized that "the general liberty of the people can never be endangered from [the courts of justice] . . . so long as the judiciary remains truly distinct from both the legislature and the Executive." Publius agreed that "there is no liberty, if the power of judging be not separated from the legislative and executive powers."[59] Where the judiciary exercises legislative or executive powers, then, liberty will be in jeopardy.

Here then was the irony of *Hamdi*: Contrary to the plurality's assertion, its intervention on behalf of Yaser Hamdi may have threatened the liberty of individuals—particularly individual Americans other than Hamdi whose own fundamental rights to security might be seriously threatened by his release—more than served it. As Justice Jackson's opinion suggested, it is impossible for the Court to address disputes of the nature of those in *Hamdi* in anything but a politically partisan way. The plurality in *Hamdi* proposed to weigh "'the private interest that will be affected by the official action' against the Government's asserted interest, 'including the function involved' and the burdens the Government would face in providing greater process."[60] But how could the Court make such an assessment, Justice Jackson might ask, without taking sides in a heated, partisan dispute with enormous political implications? How could it, for instance, possibly know the real "burdens the Government would face" without taking in "executive confidences" on foreign policy—classified information, surveillance portfolios, witness statements, information obtained from detention and interrogation, as well as covert military actions, and the like—precisely what Justice Jackson admonished the judiciary could not do since these were "delicate, complex" decisions that had to be made "by those directly responsible to the people"? The Court's balancing test in *Hamdi* would require that the Court be party to whatever intelligence information, assessments of military risks, liabilities, and so on that were necessary to know what the government's true "asserted interests" were. But this was something the Court had neither the constitutional authority nor the institutional capacity to assess.

The *Hamdi* plurality's response to such a proposed hands-off approach was to counter that the Court had "long since made clear that a state of war is not a blank check for the President when it comes to the rights of the Nation's citizens."[61] In the absence of the suspension of the writ of habeas corpus, some process had to be given to citizens like Hamdi even if it was not the full criminal due process Justice Scalia was proposing. What fate lay in wait for detainees such as Hamdi who might sit in a detention facility for years in an interminable war should the Court not intervene in some fashion in his case?

One of the strongest arguments Justice Scalia raised in *Hamdi* was to point out that Alexander Hamilton in *Federalist* 84 had highlighted the importance of habeas corpus as a fundamental protection—perhaps *the* fundamental protection—citizens enjoyed against governmental tyranny. "[T]he *habeas-corpus* act," Hamilton proclaimed in *Federalist* 84, was referred to by William Blackstone as "'the BULWARK of the British Constitution.'"[62] Central to Blackstone's understanding, Scalia emphasized, was that the *right* of due process would be secured through the *instrument* of habeas corpus, two concepts that found constitutional embodiment in the Due Process and Suspension clauses.[63] This was powerful stuff that clearly indicated the extent to which Hamilton considered habeas rights fundamental to any constitutional order, including the American constitutional order, as Justice Scalia and the plurality had emphasized.

But *Federalist* 84 was as much a warning *against* bills of rights and the formalistic or legalistic reasoning the plurality and Scalia were proposing as it was an encomium for habeas rights. Rights-based reasoning of the sort bills of rights invited tended to look at constitutionally guaranteed rights in isolation or in absolute terms. Bills of rights provided little, if any, guidance on how to assess those rights within the broader context of competing political considerations or when other constitutionally guaranteed rights conflicted with those rights. To enumerate a list of rights, as a bill of rights does, tells us nothing about how to assess or prioritize competing rights claims.[64] As Hamilton observed in *Federalist* 84:

> What signifies a declaration, that "the liberty of the press shall be inviolably preserved"? What is the liberty of the press? Who can give it any definition which would not leave the utmost latitude for evasion? I hold it to be impracticable; and from this I infer, that its security, whatever fine declarations may be inserted in any constitution respecting it, must altogether depend on public opinion, and on the general spirit of the people and of the government. And here, after all, as is intimated upon another occasion, must we seek for the only solid basis of all our rights.
>
> . . . The truth is, after all the declamations we have heard, that the Constitution is itself, in every rational sense, and to every useful purpose, A BILL OF RIGHTS.[65]

According to Hamilton, the structure of the Constitution was intended to compel the sort of comprehensive political deliberation contemplated in *Federalist* 84 and that a bill of rights necessarily discourages. This among other reasons is why Hamilton maintained that bills of rights are "not only unnecessary" but "dangerous." They "are, in their origin, stipulations between kings and their subjects" and have "no application to constitutions, professedly founded upon the power of the people, and executed by their immediate representatives and servants."[66] Those representatives are charged with engaging in the political reasoning necessary to assess rights claims that challenge political decision making. They are in a better position to engage in the sort of balancing between competing political claims that all politics engenders both because they are involved in the political process, and are thus cognizant of the broader repercussions of particular decisions in a way the judiciary is not, and because they are electorally accountable. These observations are not applicable necessarily to all rights-based determinations—particularly those involving rights of property, contract, claims of negligence, and other *private* matters[67]—but Hamilton suggests that they are applicable to the most important constitutional decisions that might involve the most fundamental of rights in *political* contests, including those at issue in national security decisions. Those fundamental rights, which might be provided for in a bill of rights "between kings and their subjects," are, in republics, to be addressed as Hamilton makes clear by the people's "representatives."

In *Hamdi*, the Court acknowledged that President Bush had the authority to detain enemy combatants, including citizens like Hamdi, and that the Authorization for Use of Military Force (AUMF), passed by Congress in 2001, provided Bush with whatever congressional authorization he needed to do so. Justice Scalia's position in the case avoided second-guessing Bush's war powers decisions but it did so at the expense of flexibility, requiring full criminal due process rights for citizens such as Hamdi any time the writ of habeas corpus had not been suspended. The plurality's position, by contrast, did have flexibility and was prepared to recognize the complexity of emergency situations that might arise in cases of war by allowing for a balancing of the competing individual and governmental interests at stake but its decision made clear that it was the courts, not the executive or Congress, that got the final say about balancing those interests. The specific question raised by Justice Thomas (and by Justice Scalia, who also criticized the plurality on this score) was why the Court was in a better position to be the arbiter of the balancing of the interests of individuals and the government on questions of war than the president or Congress. Like Hamilton in *Federalist* 84, Justice Thomas had stressed the importance of constitutional structure in resolving these kinds of disputes, that by granting Hamdi's petition the plurality had failed "adequately to consider basic principles of the constitutional structure as it relates to national security and foreign affairs."[68]

Critics of today's Supreme Court have suggested that the recent history of judicial activism and America's experience with independent counsels should caution us against the idea that judges or lawyers can be nonpartisan overseers of politics. If anything, this recent experience has proven such an assumption to be a myth.[69] Over the last two generations, the Supreme Court has arrogated to itself the power to decide questions of reapportionment and redistricting, a labyrinthine array of regulations affecting political speech, questions of abortion and homosexual rights, the extent to which race preferences can or cannot be used in university admissions, employment relationships, and elections, and a host of other matters that affect American politics at its most fundamental level. I have referred to this expansion of judicial power in both the United States and in Canada as the emergence of a new "judicial rationalism" where the courts have presumed to possess the moral, social, and political knowledge necessary to regulate those aspects of national life that they have decided might be reshaped in their own vision.[70] *Hamdi*, I propose, is just one more recent example of such a development. Although *Hamdi* itself did not necessarily reveal the partisan qualities of so many of the Court's recent decisions that have split along decisive liberal and conservative lines, the Court's other key military detainee decisions, *Rasul v. Bush* (2004),[71] *Hamdan v. Rumsfeld* (2006),[72] and *Boumediene v. Bush* (2008),[73] did. As one might expect from the nature of these political disputes, the more liberal members of the Court sided with the petitioners, while the more conservative members sided with the Bush administration.

THE CONSEQUENCES OF JUDICIALIZING WAR POWERS FOR THE RULE OF LAW

The *Hamdi* decision illustrates the difficulty of attempting to subject political decision making to judicial or legal reasoning. This was the substance of Justice Jackson's remarks in *Chicago & Southern Airlines* as well as of Justice Thomas's remarks in *Hamdi*. These conflicts between legal and political reasoning, particularly on matters of war and other affairs of necessity, were anticipated by *The Federalist*. The argument there recognized that the necessity of energetic government and the need for uniformity of executive action might indeed at times jeopardize individual liberties in the name of the more fundamental object of national security, but it also recognized that these imperatives would almost certainly be undermined by an excessively legalistic approach to war questions.

Justice Thomas's opinion in *Hamdi* provided little solace to those who see the president's exercise of war powers as a threat to civil liberties. In addition, as much as he criticized Justice Scalia's position for failing to account for those emergencies requiring the detention of enemy combatants that could fall outside the ambit of the Suspension Clause, he did not answer what purpose that clause or the Fifth Amendment's Due Process Clause might serve in the overall constitutional order during wartime. As Justice Scalia emphasized,

> If the Suspension Clause does not guarantee the citizen that he either be tried or released, unless the conditions for suspending the writ exist and the grave action of suspending the writ has been taken; if it merely guarantees the citizen that he will not be detained unless Congress by ordinary legislation says he can be detained; it guarantees him very little indeed.[74]

Scalia touches on what is arguably the most difficult question that presents itself to the American constitutional order: how to reconcile citizens' individual rights with national security interests during a time of war.

But the message of *The Federalist* is that this is an issue that cannot be resolved in some fixed, legalistic manner, as though the Constitution can establish defined legal processes in cases involving questions of war and necessity that lend themselves to ready judicial enforcement.[75] The point of Publius's discussion of war and necessity in *Federalists* 23, 28, 41, and elsewhere is that to try to legalize questions of war is impossible, even suicidal, an imperative that will eventually denigrate the rule of law—particularly the law of the Constitution—by requiring that law to be broken to preserve national security. As *Federalist* 41 further indicates, every time government has to violate the Constitution to meet the exigencies of war, it will not only undermine "sacred reverence" for the Constitution but form "a precedent for other breaches where the same plea of necessity does not exist at all, or is less urgent and palpable." In other words, it will invite further violations of the Constitution.

National security cases like Hamdi's implicate not only a detainee's rights but the rights of all other Americans whose lives may be jeopardized by the release of potential terrorist threats like Hamdi. Casting *Hamdi* as a conflict between individual rights and national security thus obscures two important points: first, that what is at issue is in fact a conflict between the rights of Yaser Hamdi, on the one hand, and the rights of all other Americans, on the other; and second, that war is a unique constitutional question, one that cannot be reduced to legalistic reasoning and that implicates the age-old distinction between politics and law or political and judicial decision making.

This last distinction has been at the center of attention in commentary over war powers issues post-9/11. Recent books, for instance, by Jack Goldsmith, who served in the Office of Legal Counsel under President George W. Bush, and Andrew McCarthy, who led the federal prosecution against the 1993 World Trade Center bombers, have counseled against unnecessary legalization of questions of war.

Despite working for President Bush, in his book *The Terror Presidency: Law and Judgment inside the Bush Administration*, Goldsmith is critical of President Bush, particularly for what Goldsmith believes were Bush's many failures to exercise the sort of political judgments that presidents like Abraham Lincoln and Franklin D. Roosevelt exercised during the war crises they faced. Lincoln himself was not perfect. Goldsmith takes him to task for going beyond John Locke's and Thomas Jefferson's concept of prerogative to embrace "the very different and more dangerous idea that it was legal for the President to do whatever is necessary to protect the nation." Goldsmith cites Lincoln's famous Civil War letter to Albert Hodges of April 4, 1864, in which Lincoln declares "that 'measures, otherwise unconstitutional, might become lawful, by becoming indispensable to the preservation of the constitution, through the preservation of the nation.'" We might disagree with Goldsmith's assessment of Lincoln's concept of prerogative, which he describes—following Arthur M. Schlesinger Jr.—as a "striking innovation," but Goldsmith concedes that Lincoln's "was an innovation that Franklin Roosevelt, who also studied Lincoln, closely, would employ."[76]

As our discussion of *The Federalist* makes clear and as other scholarship on Lincoln makes equally evident, Lincoln's understanding of prerogative was hardly an innovation and was consistent with the natural right thinking of many Founders as well as earlier political philosophers who knew that natural right always had to be moderated by prudence, the positive law by the natural law.[77] Lincoln recognized, as FDR acknowledged, the distinction between political or prudential judgments and legal judgments, both of which are accommodated in the Constitution. FDR followed Lincoln's lead in this regard. As Goldsmith writes, "While Roosevelt was not hostile to law itself, he derided what he called 'legalisms,' and he was, according to Robert Jackson, 'a strong skeptic of legal reasoning.'"[78] On Roosevelt's reading, "'rights should yield to the necessities of war.' He thought that '[r]ights came after victory, not before,' because he thought the Constitution did not prevent what military necessity demanded."[79] Goldsmith adds that FDR could adopt the position he did "because the law governing presidential authority during his era was largely a *political* rather than a *judicial* constraint on presidential power."[80]

Since that time things have changed dramatically. The press, Congress, and intellectuals have become skeptical of, if not openly hostile to, executive power and the military; the civil rights and international human rights revolutions of the 1960s and beyond have given a new impetus to universal rights enforcement; and the "post-Watergate hyper-legalization of warfare"[81] has imposed enormous additional constraints on the executive, even precipitating what has been called "lawfare," what Air Force Brigadier General Charles Dunlap has defined as "'the strategy of using or misusing law as a substitute for traditional military means to achieve an operational objective.'"[82] As Goldsmith emphasizes, following 9/11

> President Bush faced national security imperatives akin to those that Roosevelt faced. But for the first time ever, the president's ultimate obligation to do what it takes to protect the nation from devastating attack was checked by a hornet's nest of complex criminal restrictions on his traditional wartime discretionary powers.[83]
>
> [N]ever in the history of the United States had lawyers had such extraordinary influence over war policy as they did after 9/11. The lawyers weren't necessarily expert on al Qaeda, or Islamic fundamentalism, or intelligence, or international diplomacy, or even the requirements of national security. But the lawyers—especially White House and Justice Department lawyers—seemed to "own" the issues that had profound national security and diplomatic consequences. . . .
>
> The main reason why lawyers were so involved is that the war itself was encumbered with legal restrictions as never before. Everywhere decisionmakers turned they collided with confining laws that required a lawyer's interpretation and—in order to avoid legal liability—a lawyer's sign-off.[84]

Goldsmith points out that what happens when "lawyers make terrorism policy" is that everyone from the president on down to lower-level officials in the Department of Defense, the CIA, the National Security Agency, and other governmental bodies feels a sense of paralysis due to exposure to legal liability. Thus they become apprehensive about taking those risks necessary to preserve national security.[85] The safety of Americans at all levels of government accordingly suffers from the legalization of terrorism policy.

Andrew McCarthy similarly cautions against the danger of an excessive legalization of war. McCarthy particularly admonishes against employing a counterterrorism strategy of law enforcement that treats war as though it can be reduced to crime and prosecuted accordingly. This is what was done in the case of the World Trade Center bombers. The attitude of the FBI and government more generally in that case as well as against international terrorism subsequently was to regard "alien security threats as if they were legal issues to be spotted and adjudicated rather than enemies to be smoked out and defeated before they can kill."[86] Again, the failure according to McCarthy consisted of refusing to account for the limitations of the law.

> The Law is our noble, all-purpose abstraction. Reason, free from passion, said Aristotle. Who could argue with that? To doubt the fitness of law to resolve all our problems, including the most intractable, is to invite ostracism from polite society. Yet, doubt it we must. The law's majesty lies in the consent of the governed to abide by it, and the capacity of the governed to compel adherence to it. Outside their body politic, in the international arena, it is a fantasy. In the hands of barbarians, it is an offensive weapon. . . .
>
> . . . If we are too obsessed with law, and liability, we are shrinking from our highest duty: to protect lives.[87]

Yet in *Hamdi* this legalization of war, particularly the war against radical Islam, seems to be precisely what the Supreme Court has imposed. The burdens on national security that *Hamdi, Rasul, Hamdan,* and *Boumediene* have placed on Congress and the executive have not been minor but enormous, creating a host of new legal constraints that have strangled the administration in its prosecution of the war and encouraged a swarm of lawyers to act on and expand the new laws and rules the Court has created.

At the time *Hamdi* and *Rasul* were decided there were over six hundred enemy combatants resident at the U.S. naval base at Guantánamo Bay and potentially thousands more in Afghanistan, Iraq, and elsewhere. *Rasul* overruled a half-century-old precedent, *Johnson v. Eisentrager* (1950),[88] and for the first time in history extended a federal habeas statute to aliens held by the military both within and without U.S. territorial jurisdiction. In *Hamdan* the Court again rejected the Bush administration's assessment of military necessity and held that the administration could not try the appellant (Hamdan) by military commission. In *Boumediene* the Court conferred, again for the first time in history, a constitutional right to habeas corpus on alien enemies detained abroad by U.S. military forces in the course of an ongoing war. Striking down a host of procedural measures designed by the political branches specifically to deal with such detainees, the Court failed to specify what due process rights these individuals had and left it to future courts to define these, thus leaving in abeyance all parties who would now have to divine what procedures might or might not pass constitutional muster before the Court in future.[89]

Both Chief Justice Roberts and Justice Scalia in separate dissenting opinions in *Boumediene* referred to the majority's decision as a game of bait and switch. In response to *Rasul* the Defense Department had established Combatant Status Review Tribunals (CSRTs) at Guantánamo. In response to *Hamdan*, where the Court granted statutory habeas rights for alien detainees despite explicit language in the Detainee Treatment Act (DTA) of 2005 stripping the Court of this power, Congress immediately enacted the Military Commissions Act of 2006 (MCA). This again, in Justice Scalia's words, "emphatically reassert[ed] that [Congress] did not want these prisoners [at Guantánamo] filing habeas petitions."[90] Civil courts were to stay out of this process.

Yet in *Boumediene*, the Court ignored the better judgment of Congress and the president, finding that the MCA did not suspend the writ of habeas corpus and that the DTA of 2006 was unconstitutional because it did not provide an effective substitute for the alien detainees' habeas rights. Astonishingly, in *Boumediene* the Court granted alien enemy combatants greater habeas rights than citizens themselves were determined to enjoy in *Hamdi*.[91] The Court in its earlier 2004 and 2006 decisions had baited Congress and the president to provide statutory procedural remedies to enemy combatants and then when Congress responded with CSRTs and the DTA and MCA of 2006, the Court said, in Justice Scalia's characterization, it was "just kidding."[92] That will not do.

In *Boumediene*, Chief Justice Roberts and Justice Scalia contended that the Court's decision put national security in serious danger. Justice Scalia went so far as to assert that the Court's "game of bait-and-switch" on "the Nation's Commander in Chief" would "almost certainly cause more Americans to be killed."[93] *Boumediene* would impose procedural and evidentiary requirements on military officials beyond what Congress had deemed appropriate, requiring these officials' appearance before civilian courts to defend their actions. The Court's decision would further afford "the detainees increased access to witnesses (perhaps troops serving in Afghanistan?) and to classified information."[94] In his dissent, Chief Justice Roberts queried:

> So who has won? Not the detainees. The Court's analysis leaves them with only the prospect of further litigation to determine the content of their new habeas right, followed by further litigation to resolve their particular cases, followed by further litigation before the D.C. Circuit—where they could have started had they invoked the DTA procedure. Not Congress, whose attempt to "determine—through democratic means—how best" to balance the security of the American people with the detainees' liberty interests . . . has been unceremoniously brushed aside. . . . Not the rule of law, unless by that is meant the rule of lawyers, who will now arguably have a greater role than military and intelligence officials in shaping policy for alien enemy combatants. And certainly not the American people, who today lose a bit more control over the conduct of this Nation's foreign policy to unelected, politically unaccountable judges.[95]

Like *Hamdi, Boumediene* further judicialized war powers disputes, adding yet another layer of legal regulations to war powers decisions and ultimately displacing the responsibility for deciding "sensitive foreign policy and national security decisions from the elected branches to the Federal Judiciary."[96]

CONCLUSION

In *Hamdi* the Court acknowledged the government's position regarding the "practical difficulties that would accompany a system of trial-like process. In its view, military officers who are engaged in the serious work of waging battle would be unnecessarily and dangerously distracted by litigation half a world away, and discovery into military operations would both intrude on sensitive secrets of national defense and result in a futile search for evidence buried under the rubble of war." In response to this, the Court reassured the government—and the American people—that these burdens could be "properly taken into account in our due process analysis."[97] Court skeptics might not be too certain.

Justice Scalia concluded his opinion in *Hamdi* with the declaration that "[w]hatever the general merits of the view that war silences law or modulates its voice, that view has no place in the interpretation and application of a Constitution designed precisely to confront war and, in a manner that accords with democratic principles, to accommodate it."[98] But the Founders' Constitution, as interpreted by *The Federalist*, accommodated the necessities of war by according the president precisely those discretionary powers necessary to fight wars of unforeseen variety. *Hamdi* illustrates as well as any recent Court decision the potential impossibility of reconciling the Constitution's twin objectives of respecting individual rights—at least in as comprehensive a manner as we might like—with the protection of national interests, here security—at least in a manner that we might need. Addressing the Constitution's critics who thought that the federal government's powers, particularly its war powers, would result in a diminishment of state powers, Madison rejoined in *Federalist* 45: "The more adequate, indeed, the federal powers may be rendered to the national defence, the less frequent will be those scenes of danger which might favor their ascendancy over the governments of the particular states."[99] Ironically, the *Hamdi* Court's solicitation of a more zealous protection of citizen liberties during times of war may have worsened the political conditions necessary to conduct, and ultimately end, a war that might better secure those liberties for all Americans.

NOTES

1. 542 U.S. 507.

2. 542 U.S. at 533, O'Connor, J., opinion of the Court; see also 542 U.S. 509.

3. Alexander Hamilton, John Jay, and James Madison, *The Federalist: A Commentary on the Constitution of the United States*, ed. Robert Scigliano (New York: Modern Library, 2001); *Federalist* 1, 3. All subsequent references to *The Federalist* are to this edition.

4. 424 U.S. 319.

5. *Hamdi v. Rumsfeld*, 542 U.S. at 529.

6. 542 U.S. 579, Thomas, J., dissenting.

7. 542 U.S. 545, Souter, J., dissenting, citing *The Federalist*, ed. Jacob E. Cooke (Middletown, Conn.: Wesleyan University Press, 1961), 349.

8. *Hamdi v. Rumsfeld*, 542 U.S. at 545.

9. 542 U.S. 577, Scalia, J., dissenting.

10. 542 U.S. 564.

11. 542 U.S. 558.

12. 542 U.S. 556.

13. 542 U.S. 562, citing *Youngstown Sheet & Tube v. Sawyer*, 343 U.S. 579, 650 (1952) (Jackson, J., concurring).

14. *Hamdi v. Rumsfeld*, 542 U.S. at 568.

15. 542 U.S. 569.

16. 542 U.S. 580, Thomas, J., dissenting.

17. 542 U.S. citing *The Federalist*, ed. Cooke, 147, emphasis in original. Thomas also cited *Federalist* 34 and 41 in support of this proposition.

18. 542 U.S. 581, citing *Federalist* 70.

19. 542 U.S. 581, citing *Federalist* 74.

20. *Hamdi v. Rumsfeld*, 542 U.S., 585–86 and 589.

21. As *Federalist* 40 highlights, the delegates to the convention in Philadelphia "were to frame a *national government*, adequate to the *exigencies of government*, and *of the Union*; and to reduce the articles of Confederation into such form as to accomplish these purposes" (emphasis in original).

22. See *The Federalist*, liii.

23. *The Federalist*, 13.

24. *The Federalist*, 259.

25. *Federalist* 18, 111.

26. *Federalist* 20, 121. See also *Federalist* 45, 294–95: "We have seen, in all the examples of ancient and modern confederacies, the strongest tendency continually betraying itself in the members, to despoil the general government of its authorities, with a very ineffectual capacity in the latter to defend itself against the encroachments."

27. *Federalist* 70, 447.

28. See Thomas L. Krannawitter, *Vindicating Lincoln: Defending the Politics of Our Greatest President* (Lanham, Md.: Rowman & Littlefield, 2008), 326.

29. *Federalist* 74, 475 (emphasis added).

30. See John Yoo, *The Powers of War and Peace: The Constitution and Foreign Affairs After 9/11* (Chicago: University of Chicago Press, 2005), 146. See also Yoo, *The Powers of War and Peace*, 5–6, 9–16, 22–27, 32–34, 51–52, and 147.

31. Yoo, *The Powers of War and Peace*, 8. See also Krannawitter, *Vindicating Lincoln*, 325–26.

32. *Federalist* 41, 258 (emphasis added).

33. Harvey C. Mansfield Jr., *Taming the Prince: The Ambivalence of Modern Executive Power* (Baltimore: Johns Hopkins University Press, 1993), 247.

34. *Federalist* 9, 47.
35. *Federalist* 1, 5.
36. *Federalist* 70, 447. See also Mansfield, *Taming the Prince*, 249.
37. John Locke, *Second Treatise of Government*, in *Two Treatises of Government*, ed. Peter Laslett (New York: Cambridge University Press, 1988), sec. 160, 375.
38. Locke, *Second Treatise of Government*, sec. 166, 378, (emphasis in original).
39. See Mansfield, *Taming the Prince*, 255–264.
40. *Federalist* 28, 168.
41. See Krannawitter, *Vindicating Lincoln*, 324.
42. Mansfield, *Taming the Prince*, 251–52 and 258–59. In 1923 Charles Thach outlined how Gouverneur Morris, while working on the Constitutional Convention's committee of style, had modified the language of Articles I and III of the Constitution in such a way as to broaden the scope of Article II. As Thach pointed out, following Morris's work, Article I referred to "[a]ll legislative Powers *herein granted* shall be vested in a Congress," while Article III similarly limited the judicial powers to those enumerated in the Article by the circumscribing language "the judicial Power shall *extend to*." Article II, by contrast, remained unchanged by Morris and did not circumscribe executive powers. "The Executive Power shall be vested in a President," read the Vesting Clause. Thach referred to the latter wording as Morris's "joker," contending that "whether intentional or not, it admitted an interpretation of executive power which would give to the President a field of action much wider than that outlined by the enumerated powers." Charles C. Thach Jr., *The Creation of the American Presidency, 1775–1789* (New York: Da Capo Press, 1969), 138–39. (Thach's book was originally published by Johns Hopkins University Press in 1923.)

Twenty years after Thach wrote, constitutional scholar Edward Corwin attributed Locke's concept of prerogative to the American presidency, apparently being the first scholar to do so. See Edward S. Corwin, *The President: Office and Powers, 1787–1948*, 3rd rev. ed. (New York: New York University Press, 1948). What was more, as Robert Scigliano has pointed out, Corwin defined Locke's prerogative in broad terms. Corwin had quoted from Locke's chapter, "Of Prerogative," in the *Second Treatise of Government*, where Locke had defined prerogative as the "Power to act according to discretion, for the publick good, without the prescription of the Law and sometimes even against it." Cited in Robert Scigliano, "The President's 'Prerogative Power,'" in *Inventing the American Presidency*, ed. Thomas E. Cronin (Lawrence: University Press of Kansas, 1989), 236, 237. Locke further provided that "'[t]is fit that the Laws themselves should in some Cases give way to the Executive Power. . . . For since many accidents may happen, wherein a strict and rigid observation of the Laws may do harm . . . 'tis fit, the Ruler should have a Power, in many Cases, to mitigate the severity of the Law, and pardon some Offenders." Cited in Scigliano, "President's 'Prerogative Power,'" 240. As Scigliano pointed out, despite Corwin's attribution of Lockean prerogative to the executive, Corwin elsewhere suggested that in Article II's provision that the president "take Care that the Laws be faithfully executed," many Founders believed that they had inoculated against any possibility of future presidents' ever acting contrary to the law. Corwin's equivocation about executive powers, torn as he was between two competing visions, "one mak[ing] the president subordinate to Congress . . . the other allow[ing] him to be autonomous and self-directing within broad limits," would set the stage for subsequent scholarly disputes over the extent of executive powers. Scigliano, "President's 'Prerogative Power,'" 238.

43. *The Federalist*, 316.

44. In his letter to James Duane of September 3, 1780, Hamilton had complained of the "want of method and energy in the administration" of the Continental Congress, what had resulted "in a great degree from prejudice and the want of a proper executive. Congress have kept power too much into their own hands and have meddled too much with details of every sort." Letter to James Duane, September 3, 1780, in *The Papers of Alexander Hamilton*, ed. Harold C. Syrett and Jacob E. Cooke (New York: Columbia University Press, 1961), hereinafter *Papers*, 2:400, 404.

In *The Continentalist No. 1* (1781) Hamilton had similarly admonished that republican governments, particularly those framed on the heels of a popular revolution against an unpopular monarch, can suffer from "[a]n extreme jealousy of power." "In a government framed for durable liberty, not less regard must be paid to giving the magistrate a proper degree of authority, to make and execute the laws with rigour, than to guarding against encroachments upon the rights of the community. As too much power leads to despotism, too little leads to anarchy, and both eventually to the ruin of the people." *Papers*, 2:649, 650–51.

The Continentalist No. III (1781), again stressed how Americans had failed to realize how difficult it would be to exhaust the resources of an energetic nation like Great Britain and had additionally failed to account "for the immense advantage to the enemy, of having their forces, though inferior, under a single direction." *Papers*, 2:660, 663.

45. See *Federalist* 24, 149.

46. *Federalist* 24, 455.

47. *Federalist* 23, 140–41 (emphases in original).

48. *Hamdi v. Rumsfeld*, 542 U.S. at 568, Scalia, J., dissenting.

49. *The Federalist*, 459.

50. *The Federalist*, 157 (emphasis added).

51. *The Federalist*, 156.

52. *Hamdi v. Rumsfeld*, 542 U.S. at 594, Thomas, J., dissenting.

53. *Federalist* 51, 330–35. See also Anthony A. Peacock, *Deconstructing the Republic: Voting Rights, the Supreme Court, and the Founders' Republicanism Reconsidered* (Washington, D.C.: AEI Press, 2008), 10.

54. Donald L. Horowitz, *The Courts and Social Policy* (Washington, D.C.: Brookings Institution, 1977), 18–19.

55. *Aptheker v. Secretary of State*, 378 U.S. 500, 509, *Haig v. Agee*, 453 U.S. 280, 307 (1981), and *Youngstown Sheet & Tube Co. v. Sawyer*, 343 U.S. 579, 662 (Clark, J., concurring).

56. *United States v. Salerno*, 481 U.S. 739, 748 (1987).

57. *Fleming v. Page*, 9 How. 603, 615 (1850), *Prize Cases*, 2 Black 635, 668, 670 (1863), *United States v. Curtiss-Wright Export Corp.*, 299 U.S. 304, 320 (1936), and *Chicago & Southern Airlines, Inc. v. Waterman S.S. Corp.*, 333 U.S. 103, 111 (1948).

58. *Chicago & Southern Airlines*, 333 U.S., at 111, cited at *Hamdi v. Rumsfeld*, 542 U.S. at 582, Thomas, J., dissenting.

59. *Federalist* 78, 497. On the question of why the Court itself must remain politically neutral if it is to arbitrate neutrally on matters of rights, see Gordon S. Wood, *The Radicalism of the American Revolution* (New York: Alfred A. Knopf, 1992), 324–25; and Jeremy Rabkin, *Judicial Compulsions: How Public Law Distorts Public Policy* (New York: Basic Books, 1989), 45.

60. *Hamdi v. Rumsfeld,* 542 U.S. at 529.
61. 542 U.S. 536.
62. *Federalist* 84, 548. See, also, *Hamdi v. Rumsfeld,* 542 U.S., at 555.
63. *Hamdi v. Rumsfeld,* 542 U.S., at 555–56, Scalia, J., dissenting.
64. For a good discussion of this issue, see Hadley Arkes, *Beyond the Constitution* (Princeton, N.J.: Princeton University Press, 1990), esp. chap. 4, "On the Dangers of a Bill of Rights: Restating the Federalist Argument," 58–80.
65. *The Federalist,* 550–51.
66. *Federalist* 84, 549–50.
67. See Rabkin, *Judicial Compulsions,* 44–48.
68. *Hamdi v. Rumsfeld,* 542 U.S. at 579, Thomas, J., dissenting.
69. See Nathaniel Persily, "Reply: In Defense of Foxes Guarding Henhouses: The Case for Judicial Acquiescence to Incumbent-Protecting Gerrymanders," *Harvard Law Review* 116 (December 2002): 649, 650–52, 677.
70. See Peacock, *Deconstructing the Republic,* 2–3; and Anthony A. Peacock, "Judicial Rationalism and the Therapeutic Constitution: The Supreme Court's Reconstruction of Equality and Democratic Process under the Charter of Rights and Freedoms," in *The Myth of the Sacred: The Charter, the Courts, and the Politics of the Constitution of Canada,* ed. Patrick James, Donald E. Abelson, and Michael Lusztig (Montreal and Kingston: McGill-Queen's University Press, 2002), 17.
71. 542 U.S. 466.
72. 126 S. Ct. 2749.
73. 128 S. Ct. 2229.
74. *Hamdi v. Rumsfeld,* 542 U.S. at 575, Scalia, J., dissenting.
75. See Yoo, *The Powers of War and Peace,* 6, 8.
76. Jack Goldsmith, *The Terror Presidency: Law and Judgment inside the Bush Administration* (New York: W. W. Norton, 2007), 83.
77. For a good account of Lincoln's understanding of prerogative, see Krannawitter, *Vindicating Lincoln,* 322–28.
78. Goldsmith, *Terror Presidency,* 48.
79. Goldsmith, *Terror Presidency,* 44.
80. Goldsmith, *Terror Presidency,* 48.
81. Goldsmith, *Terror Presidency,* 81.
82. Goldsmith, *Terror Presidency,* 58.
83. Goldsmith, *Terror Presidency,* 68–69.
84. Goldsmith, *Terror Presidency,* 129–30.
85. Goldsmith, *Terror Presidency,* 90–91, 94–95, 99.
86. Andrew C. McCarthy, *Willful Blindness: A Memoir of the Jihad* (New York: Encounter Books, 2008), 12.
87. McCarthy, *Willful Blindness,* 13.
88. 339 U.S. 763.
89. See *Boumediene v. Bush,* 128 S. Ct., at 2279, Roberts, C. J., dissenting.
90. 128 S. Ct. 2296, Scalia, J., dissenting.
91. See 128 S. Ct. 2280–81, Roberts, C. J., dissenting.
92. 128 S. Ct. 2296, Scalia, J., dissenting.
93. 128 S. Ct. 2294.
94. 128 S. Ct. 2295.
95. 128 S. Ct. 2293, Roberts, C. J., dissenting.

96. 128 S. Ct. 2280.
97. *Hamdi v. Rumsfeld*, 542 U.S. at 531–32.
98. 542 U.S. 579, Scalia, J., dissenting.
99. *Federalist* 45, 298.

IV

VOTING RIGHTS, REPRESENTATION, AND THE RULE OF LAW

11

A Decline in Adherence to Traditional Districting Standards Undermines Fair Representation in the United States

Katharine Inglis Butler

I contend that geographically based representation—the form of representative democracy in place since the founding of our nation—is at a critical crossroad. In many states, election districts have been unleashed from their historic mooring in independently significant and identifiable geographic areas. In the not-too-distant past, most states relied heavily on counties, or their equivalents, as the basis for state legislative districts and as the primary building blocks for their congressional districts. The change in South Carolina's congressional districts from1982 (figure 11.1) to 1992 (figure 11.2) is typical.

The highlighted 6th Congressional District is by no means an extreme example of kinds of post-1990 districts that cannot be described in meaningful geographic terms. A number of factors have contributed to a decline in districts closely connected to political subdivisions, and also in districts created in accordance with other generally recognized districting principles. However, the catalyst for the near abandonment of districting standards in some states was a movement to enhance the opportunities for the election of racial and ethnic minorities through the creation of "majority-minority" districts. Laudable though their purpose was, these districts and their partisan and politically motivated siblings are inconsistent with geographically based representation. These districts are in fact an attempt to impose "interest representation" for a few groups (minorities, extreme partisans, and incumbents) on a system not designed to directly accommodate group representation at all.

Most of the world's democracies elect their legislators in proportional representation systems, which by design provide for direct representation of parties in accordance with the share they receive of the vote. In these systems, parties are organized to accommodate political interests ranging

Figure 11.1. South Carolina Congressional Districts, 1982

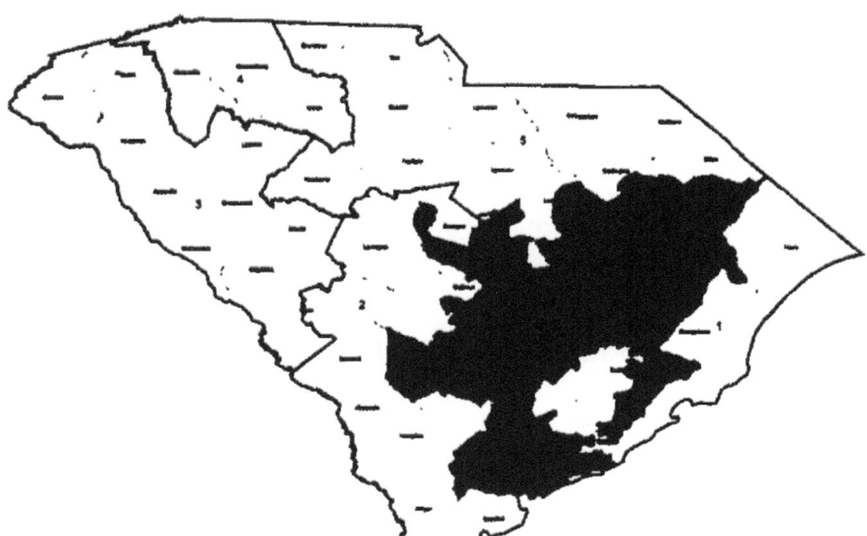

Figure 11.2. South Carolina Congressional Districts, 1992

from broad political-philosophical perspectives to ethnicity. By contrast, our legislators represent the populations of their geographic districts, including the portions that voted for someone else. Thus, a Republican legislator represents his district, not his party. There is much room to debate the relative merits of geographically based "winner take all" representation versus interest-group representation. Proponents of our system argue that it produces more stable and more effective governments, while proponents of proportional representation systems note that they are, indeed by design, more reflective of the diversity of interests in the electorate.

Its relative merits aside, our geographically based system has been in place since the founding of the nation, and currently is the system by which virtually all legislative bodies from Congress to town councils are elected. The most basic component of this system is the geographically defined unit (usually a district) from which representatives are elected. If we expect our geographic system to function effectively, we must continue to follow, or in many cases return to, the standards that produce districts for that purpose. If on the other hand, interest-group representation is now thought to be essential for minorities, it should be provided directly and not by manipulation of district boundaries. If geographic representation is deemed inadequate for modern times, perhaps because too few political interests are tied to one's residence, an alternative should be provided for all. If such a drastic change is in order for the nation or some part thereof, it can fairly be accomplished only if the affected electorate, with full understanding of the merits, openly and forthrightly abandons geographic representation. In short, we should either fix the system we have, or, as a people, decide to adopt a different one.

In the pages that follow, I explain how congressional and state legislative districts, once based predominantly on political subdivisions, have come to include a substantial number of districts that defy geographic description—a phenomenon more common in areas with significant concentrations of minority citizens. I outline how, in an odd turn of events, a series of Supreme Court decisions invalidating bizarre districts drawn specifically to aid the election of minorities ended up opening the door to unrestrained political gerrymandering, which the Court has demonstrated little interest in containing. I point out how, in 1991, gerrymandering opportunities, both racial and political, were unwittingly greatly enhanced by the Census Bureau and, of course, by the availability of increasingly sophisticated computer technology. Finally, I suggest that in places where gerrymandering for racial and political reasons has produced the most geographically distorted districts, those of us who are not strongly supportive of incumbents, highly partisan, or minorities, are effectively limited in our ability to impact electoral outcomes and have no political means to address the problem. We have become "filler" for districts specifically designed to further interests not our own.

I. THE EVOLUTION OF ELECTION DISTRICTS[1]

From the founding of the nation until 1962, the Supreme Court left the manner of electing state and local representatives to the states. In *Baker v. Carr*[2] the Court announced the end of its forbearance, when a majority of the justices decided that huge disparities in intrastate political influence because of malapportionment could no longer be tolerated. *Baker* was followed by a series of cases, starting with *Reynolds v. Sims*,[3] that would require adjustments in the representational schemes of most states and the redesign of election districts at every level of government.

A. Election Districts before *Reynolds v. Sims*

Generally, the original thirteen states modeled their legislative systems after the federal system. In one house, representatives were assigned to fixed geographic units, and in the other house, representatives were apportioned to these units taking account differences in population. As states were added to the nation, there were many variations in the details of the representational systems adopted. However, it is a fair generalization to say that up to time of the one-person, one-vote decisions, the use of fixed units—typically counties or their equivalents, and sometimes other political subdivisions—remained important components of the states' representational schemes in both houses in various ways. Population changes over time were taken into account by "reapportionment" (changing the number of representatives assigned to fixed geographic units) and not generally by "redistricting" (changing district boundaries).[4]

Some common arrangements using counties as districts, or building blocks, were: (a) individual counties served as districts, with population taken into account in the number of representatives apportioned to each county in at least one house of a bicameral legislature and sometimes in both[5] (in the "little federal" variation of this scheme, each county was assigned one seat in the upper house, and was apportioned seats in the lower house roughly based on its population[6]); (b) counties were aggregated to form districts, sometimes with "rotation requirements" so that the legislative seat was rotated from county to county within the district, with party primaries being held only in the county whose "turn" it was to have the seat;[7] and (c) in states where population was the official basis for apportioning representatives for both houses, counties and other political subdivisions were nevertheless the most common building blocks for districts and the number of representatives per county, groupings of counties, or other political subdivision would be adjusted for population differences.[8]

For virtually all states, including those for which some measure of population equality was mandated, almost never in their histories would their legislative districts have complied with the one-person, one-vote standards the Court would ultimately announce. Of course, the population inequalities by the time of *Baker* were exponentially worse in the numerous states where reapportionment had not taken place in decades.

Counties were also important components of congressional districting, when either by choice or pursuant to congressional dictates, the states elected their congressional seats from single-member districts. Before *Baker*, no state with multiple congressional seats would have approached the degree of population equality the Supreme Court would ultimately conclude was mandated by Article I, Section 2 of the Constitution.[9]

B. The Reapportionment Revolution Necessarily Limited the Role of Counties and Other Fixed Political Subdivisions

The reapportionment cases of 1964, led by *Reynolds v. Sims*,[10] set out population equality standards that would invalidate most of the nation's state legislative election schemes.

Initially, many states for which counties had been essential to the definition of election districts took steps to continue their use, even while adapting to new population equality measures. Whole counties were aggregated to come up with a total population that when divided by the required "population per representative" came relatively close to a whole number.[11]

As the Supreme Court tightened the deviation permitted from absolute population equality, states had greater difficulty retaining a connection between counties and districts. "Reapportionment" of representatives to fixed units (counties, and groupings of counties) became impossible. Thus at a minimum, it was necessary to rearrange the county groupings. To continue to use counties as districts or as building blocks for districts required some number of multimember districts, which presented problems of their own. The most significant was the tendency of such districts, particularly those containing a substantial portion of the state's population, to submerge many interests—partisan, racial, and simply parochial—that would have had a more direct legislative voice in a single-member district system. Pressure from multiple sources eventually led to a decline in the use of large multimember districts and with it the use of whole counties and other political subdivisions as building blocks for state legislative districts.

When counties no longer served as election districts, other principles were devised to encourage sensible districts and to discourage gerrymandering. However, no doubt as a result of most states' long histories of using counties and political subdivisions in the construction of election districts, respect for county and/or other political subdivision boundaries remained an important standard for drawing districts.[12] Other standards were added, such as creating compact districts with recognizable boundaries, and respecting "communities of interests," such as neighborhoods, or regions sharing similar economies.

Today, few would disagree with the view that fair representation must be based significantly on population. Elevation of "population equality across districts" to constitutional status eliminated huge disparities in the political influence of rural and urban populations. Before *Reynolds*, many state legislative bodies were controlled by rural legislators, even though the majority of the state's population lived in urban areas. The legislature's failure to address these disparities was a form of political gerrymandering—by not taking greater account of population in assigning representatives, rural legislators held on to seats that otherwise would have been allocated to the cities.

Nevertheless, *Reynolds* and its progeny were highly controversial at the time—particularly the Court's seemingly inflexible focus on population equality that significantly reduced the ability to retain long-standing "area-specific" representation. Often even the beneficiaries of these decisions found the loss of "area-specific" representation alarming.[13] Instinctively, it seemed, people recognized that, in terms of the purpose behind geographic representation, the Court's reapportionment decisions presented a conceptual conundrum. Adherence to "population equality" inevitably undercut the connection between legislators and "independently significant," geographic areas. Finding a meaningful and objective substitute for "fixed" political subdivisions was not easy. Districting standards not tied to political subdivisions were subject to interpretation and to manipulation by line drawers, who in most states were the legislators themselves, or individuals susceptible to their influence.

Unleashing representation from objectively determined boundaries clearly had the potential to encourage unrestrained gerrymandering. Generally speaking, three factors limited the extent to which the gerrymandering urge was acted. First, the districting standards developed post-*Reynolds*, even though flexible, did limit the degree to which legislators were likely to obviously distort districts. Whether they were mandated by law or followed by tradition, these standards tended to produce districts that retained an association with identifiable, and sometimes independently significant, geographic areas. So long as the districts created were ones in which grassroots political organization was possible, gerrymandering could influence, but not guarantee, their political outcomes. Second, legislators who had been elected in districts created in accordance with traditional districting principles were likely to prefer such districts, and to limit "manipulations" to measures that substituted one "standard" district for another. Moreover, a seriously distorted district was likely to draw the attention of the press, and possibly incur the wrath of the electorate. Third, and this may in time turn out to have been the most significant factor, the absence of census data for small geographic areas, and inadequate technical tools, imposed physical limits on the degree to which greatly distorted districts could be produced. It simply was not possible, absent enormous expense, to create districts that resembled bug splats before the 1990 census.

In summary, despite *Reynolds*, legislators so inclined could, by adhering to generally accepted geographically based districting principles, create sensible districts, often with significant continuity from decade to decade. While these standards could not prevent gerrymandering, they did significantly reduce the line drawers' ability to effectively insulate themselves from successful challenge and to totally thwart the electoral opportunities of the minority party.

II. DISTRICTS CREATED TO ELECT MINORITIES HAD A DEVASTATING IMPACT ON GEOGRAPHICALLY SENSIBLE DISTRICTS

Section 5 of the Voting Rights Act, and to a lesser extent Section 2 of the act, provided the primary impetus to design districts to elect minorities, and when necessary, without regard to traditional districting standards. Section 5, the so-called preclearance provision, was one of several key components of the 1965 act that applied in only a limited number of states and counties, mainly in the South.[14] Section 5's purpose was to prevent these "covered jurisdictions" from adopting new discriminatory devices to block political participation by African Americans, soon to be enfranchised by the act's ban on literacy tests as a prerequisite to registration.

Covered jurisdictions must obtain prior federal approval—either from the U. S. attorney general or the Federal District Court for the District of Columbia—before implementing any changes in their procedures affecting voting. Most changes are submitted to the attorney general, rather than the court, and the preclearance process is administered by the Department of Justice, Voting Section ("Justice"). As discussed below, Justice's power to withhold preclearance has given it the de facto ability to dictate the districting decisions of covered jurisdictions.

Section 2, a provision that applies nationwide, was amended in 1982 to allow challenges to districting plans that result in minorities having less opportunity than others in the electorate to elect representatives of their choice. It has been the chief contributor to geographically distorted districts in jurisdictions not subject to Section 5. It too will be discussed below.

A. Mixed Signals from the Supreme Court on "Interest Group" Representation

Several post-*Reynolds* Supreme Court cases provided modest encouragement for the proposition that "population content" (partisan and racial) rather than "geographic makeup" was the appropriate measure of "fair" districts.

The Court's 1973 decision in *Gaffney v. Cummings*[15] was a harbinger of a change that would come to full fruition in the post-2000 redistrictings. The lower court found the redrawing of Connecticut's house districts to be unconstitutional, in part on political gerrymandering grounds. It was undisputed that the dominant consideration for the new districting plan was that it mirror the statewide partisan vote,[16] something that could be accomplished only by ignoring the state's constitutional prohibition against dividing towns (political subdivision equivalent to counties). The result was numerous geographically distorted districts.

The Supreme Court reversed, holding that benign political gerrymandering did not violate the Constitution. Justice White noted that "judicial interest [in the political process underlying districting] should be at its lowest ebb when a State purports fairly to allocate political power to the parties in accordance with their voting strength and, within quite tolerable limits, succeeds in doing so." He went on to say:

> The very essence of districting is to produce . . . a more "politically fair" result than would be reached with elections at large. . . . [There is no federal basis] to invalidate a state plan . . . because it undertakes, not to minimize or eliminate the political strength of any group or party but to recognize it and, through districting, provide a rough sort of proportional representation in the legislative halls.[17]

Justice White's equation of "politically fair" with "partisan proportionality" was clearly understood by those who had challenged the plan as inconsistent with the underlying rationale for geographic representation. A system "premised upon legislators [representing] the local or regional interests of [their] district[s] . . . is subverted [by a] districting plan [designed] to elect legislators on the basis of a state-wide formulate related to prior state-wide party vote." [18]

Certain of the Supreme Court's voting rights cases implied that "fair" districting for minorities was to be measured by their percentage of the electorate, a concept clearly more consistent with interest-group, rather than geographic, representation. In *Allen v. Board of Elections,*[19] which held that Section 5's preclearance requirement extended to change in election practices beyond those affecting registration, the Court referenced *Reynolds v. Sims*[20] for the proposition that "the right to vote can be affected by a dilution of voting power as well as by an absolute prohibition on casting a ballot."[21] Reliance on *Reynolds* implied that minority "voting power" was equal to the group's portion of the electorate and would be "diluted" when the group's votes did not translate into a comparable number of representatives.

The Court made a similar observation in *Perkins v. Matthews,*[22] when it noted that an annexation was subject to Section 5 preclearance because it had the potential for racial discrimination in that it "dilutes the weight of the votes of the voters to whom the franchise was limited before the annexation."[23] Because all voters within a city have the impact of their votes reduced by the annexation of additional voters, the Court's comment implied that if black and white voters had different political interests, anything that added to the support blacks needed from whites to elect candidates of their choice could be seen as "diluting" the group's influence.

Despite dicta in these cases, when actually confronted in *Whitcomb v. Chavis*[24] with recognizing a cognizable minority group's "right" to proportional representation, the Court rejected it. Subsequently, in *White v. Register*,[25] the Court held that under certain circumstances—a combination of past and present discrimination against a minority group, and an election system that permitted racially polarized voting to exclude the group from full political participation—modifications to the election structure would be required to provide the group with an opportunity to elect candidates of its choice.

The strongest implication that the Court might *mandate* interest-group representation for racial and ethnic minorities in areas with histories of racial discrimination in voting came in *City of Richmond v. United States*,[26] the Court's first interpretation of "discriminatory effects" within the meaning of Section 5. Richmond sought preclearance of an annexation that would result in a drop in the black percentage of the city from 52 percent to 42 percent. Under pressure from Justice, Richmond had changed from at-large elections to single-member districts. The Court held that the change to single-member districts "neutralized" the loss of influence blacks otherwise would have suffered by virtue of the annexation, so long as "a fairly drawn" district plan provided blacks "representation reasonably equivalent to their political strength in the enlarged" city.[27]

The combination of the holdings and pronouncements in *Allen*, *Perkins*, *Whitcomb*, *White*, and *City of Richmond* strongly implied that at least in Section 5 jurisdictions—jurisdictions subject to federal scrutiny of their election law changes precisely because of their past discrimination against minorities—a nondiscriminatory districting system was one that provided minorities with proportional representation *at least to the extent feasible using standard single-member districts*. This was an important limitation that would later be overlooked.

B. "Nonretrogression," Not Proportional Representation Became the Standard for Section 5 Preclearance

The ink had hardly dried on *City of Richmond* when the Court announced a standard for Section 5 that clearly did not mandate proportional representation, even when it could be accomplished without violating traditional districting standards. In *Beer v. United States*,[28] the City of New Orleans challenged Justice's objection to the post-1970 census redistricting of the city's council districts. Since 1954, New Orleans had had a seven-member council comprised of five members elected from single-member districts and two elected at large. Although by 1970 blacks made up 45 percent of the city's total population, none of the existing (post-1960 census) districts was majority black.[29]

The city's proposed plan retained the north-south orientation of the existing districts, which were adjusted for population by following ward and precinct lines. Blacks were a majority of the registered voters in one district and of the population in another. The attorney general rejected the plan, indicating that the vertical orientation of the districts diluted black voting strength. He noted that the predominantly black neighborhoods were "located generally in an east to west progression," and consequently were divided by north-south district lines. Although the districts' shapes were driven by the shape of the city's seventeen wards, "the wards do not of themselves define official boundaries bearing upon the election or on representation by city council members, and adherence to the traditional shape of wards may not serve to justify the resulting prohibited dilution of black voting strength under Section 5."[30] The letter went on to say that drawing a nondilutive plan would be very difficult if vertical districts were used, an orientation that was "not necessary to achieve a successful reapportionment of the city's population."[31]

Note that the attorney general's letter did not say that the plan divided a geographically distinct black neighborhood or failed to follow traditional districting standards, or even that a more natural configuration for the districts would have been an east-west orientation. It did not suggest that modest shifts in populations between districts would have created additional majority black districts. Absent any allusion that improper criteria had been followed, or "unnatural" districts had been produced, Justice's objection became, if it was possible to draw a *different* plan, which could have provided a greater number of majority black districts, Section 5 mandated that the city do so. Seemingly, all districting standards, save equal population, would have to be sacrificed, if necessary to achieve this goal.[32]

Despite earlier hints of a proportional representation-like standard, the Supreme Court took a different tack altogether when it concluded that because minority voters fared better under New Orleans's proposed plan than under its previous one, the new plan was entitled to preclearance.[33] Thereafter, *Beer's* "retrogression" standard was the official measure of a discriminatory effect under Section 5. In light of *Beer*, the Court's earlier pronouncements in *Richmond* concerning "fairly drawn districts" should have been seen as limited to annexations and other changes that decreased the collective impact of the black vote. A retrogressive annexation could nevertheless obtain preclearance if the city adopted single-member districts that provided blacks with roughly proportional representation.

C. Despite *Beer*, Justice Was Able to Use Its Power under Section 5 to Coerce Majority-Minority Districts and in the Process, It Wreaked Havoc on Geographic Representation in Section 5 States

While *Beer*'s retrogression standard clearly was less harmful to geographic representation than a proportional representation mandate would have been, it nevertheless contributed to a decline in districts created in accordance with traditional standards. To retain an existing number of majority black districts, given likely population shifts between censuses, covered jurisdiction could well be required to deviate significantly from traditional districting standards.[34]

To avoid problems with Justice, many covered jurisdictions maintained their existing number of majority-minority districts, ignoring their own districting standards when necessary. Some perhaps could have avoided retrogression, while still following traditional districting standards, but only by sacrificing other interests—often as not, reelection of some number of incumbents. I am aware of situations where "barbell" districts (two noncontiguous population concentrations connected by a narrow, often unpopulated, strip of land) were voluntarily created for one or both of these purposes. If the nonretrogression standard was to mean that all majority black and Hispanic districts had to be retained, even at the expense of sensible districts, it was inevitable that over time, fewer and fewer districts in covered jurisdictions would be constructed in accordance with traditional district standards.

That said, any reasonable interpretation of *Beer* should have limited Justice's ability to demand an actual increase in the number of minority districts as the price of preclearance. Justice, however, found ways around *Beer*, including simply ignoring it. Justice routinely coerced covered jurisdictions to move toward proportional representation for minorities in circumstances where the change at issue was not retrogressive and any claim that the change had been adopted for a discriminatory purpose was tenuous at best and pretextual at worst. This added measurably to the distortion of geographic districts.[35]

Justice often refused to preclear a redistricting plan because it failed to fairly reflect existing minority voting strength—a position clearly at odds with the Court's decision in *Beer*. The New Orleans redistricting plan, which the Court held not to be retrogressive, had only one majority black district out of seven seats. The plan as a whole would not have satisfied any reasonable definition of "fairly reflects."

Justice refused to preclear plans containing multimember districts, even when including such districts was not new, because, it said, "fairly drawn" single-member districts would better recognize black voting strength. This position also seemingly was specifically rejected by the Court's holding in *Beer* that New Orleans's two at-large seats, carried over as a part of the new plan, were not subject to preclearance because their retention did not equal "a change."[36]

Justice objected to "packed" minority districts and to district lines that fractured minority population concentration. The term "packed" implies that district lines have been manipulated to include a greater concentration of minority population than was "natural" in a district. "Fractured" implies that district lines have been manipulated to divide a population when a more natural configuration would be to retain the population "intact." When truly the product of "gerrymandering," packing and fracturing justify a finding of intentional discrimination. However, all too often these claims are nothing more than observations that a different alignment of the districts would have resulted in more of them having black majorities. In some cases these objections could be overcome only by affirmatively ignoring the jurisdiction's race-neutral districting standards in order to produce additional majority-minority districts.

Justice objected when the jurisdiction rejected alternatives more favorable to the minority community without satisfactory reasons—another position not only at odds with *Beer*, but also uncabinable. This claim could be made any time there was a "standard" plan more favorable to the group than the "standard" plan the legislature eventually adopted. Thus, it was just one more variation of "you could have done better."

Of course, when it was consistent with creating additional minority districts, the attorney general did object to noncompact, oddly shaped districts; districts that did not follow natural boundaries; and districts that departed from the state's own districting standards. Given that the positions Justice would eventually take after the 2000 census opened up exponentially greater gerrymandering opportunities, these early objections appear to be the order, "Covered jurisdictions, follow sound districting standards unless we find that your ignoring them will produce more majority-minority districts."

Justice's power to influence the drawing of districts in covered jurisdictions was further enhanced by the 1982 amendment of Section 2 of the Voting Rights Act. Section 2, as amended, gave minorities the ability to sue to set aside any election system that had the effect of depriving them of the opportunity to elect legislators of their choice on account of race. The amendment was motivated by the Supreme Court's decision in *City of Mobile v. Bolden*,[37] which held that to establish a claim of unconstitutional racial vote dilution, plaintiffs had to prove that the allegedly dilutive electoral system had been adopted, or was being maintained, for the purpose of diluting minority voting strength. The amendment restored the "discriminatory result" standard based on the factors set out in *White v. Register* and *Whitcomb v. Chavis*.[38]

Whether or not it was an accurate reading of the Court's position on the standards for amended Section 2, *Thornburg v. Gingles*[39] was widely perceived as mandating the creation of districts for any minority group "sufficiently numerous and sufficiently geographically compact" to constitute a majority of a district. Under threat of Section 2 litigation, many states and political subdivisions gave up multimember districts and at-large elections, and restructured existing single-member districts in order to create more districts favorable to the election of minorities. The post-1980 redistrictings produced a new crop of single-member districts, a substantial number of them with black or Hispanic majorities. All majority-minority districts in Section 5 states would become part of the benchmark plan for the next round of redistricting in 1990. It is very likely that many of these districts were distorted to create a sufficient number to satisfy plaintiffs, or to preserve the reelection possibilities for incumbents displaced by the new minority districts, or both. Retaining the same number of minority districts in the next round almost certainly led to more geographically distorted districts.

After Section 2 was amended in 1982, and before its position was rejected by the District of Columbia Court in *Bossier Parish v. Reno*,[40] Justice objected to a change if it believed the new plan violated Section 2. Given the very subjective assessment of whether a Section 2 violation has occurred, this position gave Justice carte blanche authority to reject plans not to its liking. It was on this basis that Justice refused to allow preclearance of South Carolina's 1982 senate redistricting plan—the state's first all-single-member district plan, which included nine majority black districts compared to none in its previous plan.[41]

Outside of Section 5 jurisdictions, actual suits and threats of suits under Section 2 contributed to the collection of distorted districts. Indeed, some of the candidates for most bizarre districts from the 1990s were produced under the guise of "compliance with Section 2." Despite *Thornburg*'s strong implication that a minority group must be able to benefit from a geographically compact district to obtain relief under Section 2, a federal court in Illinois concluded that a bizarre district drawn to benefit Hispanics satisfied this requirement.[42] The congressional district, which the court itself described as resembling a "Rorschach blot turned on its side," used a narrow C-shaped corridor to join together two Hispanic population concentrations that were separated from each other by an entire additional district.[43]

Eventually the Supreme Court would hold that neither Section 5 nor Section 2 required majority-minority districts that could be created only by violating traditional districting standards. As discussed in the next section, the cases so holding not only came too late to save traditional districting standards, but actually encouraged gerrymandering for nonracial reasons.

III. THE SUPREME COURT'S DECISIONS LIMITING THE USE OF RACE TO CREATE DISTRICTS HAD LITTLE IMPACT ON RESTORING TRADITIONAL DISTRICTING STANDARDS

It was not until the round of redistrictings following the 1990 census that the degree to which Justice was prepared to push Section 5 jurisdiction to adopt minority districts became obvious. Before then, the damage Justice had done to traditional districting standards by stretching *Beer*'s holding was somewhat limited.

Prior to the 1990 census, population information for small geographic areas generally was not available outside certain metropolitan areas; this lack imposed a physical limit on the degree to which line drawers could dissect out racial or political population for pinpoint gerrymandering purposes. Moreover, the ability to aggregate small clumps of population for the creation of districts was limited by the available technology. In 1990, the Census Bureau reported population information for every closed polygon in America, which, when joined with greatly improved technology, exponentially increased the options for aggregating tiny segments of geography to create districts.

Districts like North Carolina's congressional district, which used a corridor no wider than the interstate down which it ran to connect black population concentrations in several cities, drew the attention of the press and the ire of some citizens. Suits in several states challenged some of the distorted districts, eventually resulting in eight Supreme Court decisions, known collectively as the "*Shaw* cases" (after the first case, *Shaw v. Reno*) or "affirmative racial gerrymandering" cases (because all the challenged districts allegedly had been created to elect minorities).[44] In these cases, the Supreme Court held that the use of race to create districts was unconstitutional, unless it was narrowly tailored to satisfy a compelling state interest. The Court further held that neither Section 5 nor Section 2 required the creation of majority-minority districts that violated traditional districting standards and thus these provisions did not provide a "compelling state interest" that justified the use of race to design districting.

Those who challenged these districts generally were not concerned that they contained a majority of minority voters, but rather that the legislatures had deliberately aggregated pockets of minority population to create them, grossly violating traditional districting standards in the process. In the course of its *Shaw* decisions, the Court gave an occasional positive nod to sound districting principles.[45] But in the end, the Court's concern was not the districts' bizarre shapes, but, rather, that the legislature's predominant consideration in their creation had been their racial content, which they manipulated by "sorting" population concentrations into and out of districts on the basis of their racial makeups.

So, while the challengers were concerned primarily with the impact of distorted districts on effective geographic representation and the implications of creating districts specifically "for" groups, the Court's concern was more limited. Geographic distortions and violations of traditional districting standards merely constituted evidence that the lines could have been driven primarily by racial concerns, thus triggering strict scrutiny. These decisions have had little impact on racial gerrymandering, and have in the long run made their own substantial contribution to the decline in sensible election districts.

The only positive news these cases provided was that if legislatures wish to create bizarre districts for other reasons, they can no longer hide behind the "need for minority districts." The Court affirmed that majority-minority districts created in accordance with traditional districting standards raise no constitutional concerns, a proposition that, standing alone, is desirable and unassailable. Unfortunately, even the apparent limitation on racial gerrymandering may turn out to be illusory.

The bad news the decisions provided for geographic representation overwhelms the good. While Justice's misuse of Section 5 can be seen as the catalyst for the decline of traditional districting standards, these decisions may turn out to be their death knell. The reasons for my pessimism are explained below.

A. Challenges to Future Bizarre Districts, Even on Racial Grounds, Will Have Little Chance of Success

The value of the Court's *Shaw* line of cases is limited by the requirement that, to trigger strict scrutiny, a challenger must demonstrate that the legislature subordinated traditional race-neutral districting principles to racial considerations. "Race must . . . [be] . . . the *predominant* factor motivating the legislature's districting decision[.] Plaintiffs must show that a facially neutral law is unexplainable on grounds other than race."[46] The original challengers had no difficulty making this showing because the legislatures had justified the bizarre shapes of districts as "necessary" to make them majority-minority.

Now educated, legislators will not make that assertion again. Indeed, the last of the *Shaw* decisions, *Easley v. Cromartie*,[47] provided a road map for legislators who wished to continue to create bizarre districts for minorities. The case involved a challenge to a very modest redrawing of the North Carolina "interstate" district, invalidated in one of the earlier cases. The legislature used "political" rather than "racial data" to redraw it, basically selecting for inclusion in the "new district" areas that previously had voted overwhelmingly Democratic. To no one's surprise, the district turned out to be not only heavily black, but also not very different from the original district.[48] Despite what seems to have been a subterfuge, a majority of the Court found the use of political data sufficient evidence that politics, not race, was responsible for the district's bizarre shape. In the future, only the ill-informed are likely to produce districts that can be challenged as racial gerrymanders. Do not be surprised if in 2010, many districts are constructed of precincts that voted overwhelmingly for the Democratic presidential candidate in 2008!

B. Gerrymandering for Nonracial Reasons Is (Mostly) OK, Maybe Even a Legitimate Political Goal

The greatest damage to sensible districts no doubt came from *Cromartie*'s direct sanctioning of the use of political data, which clearly had been selected because it correlated highly with the race of the electorate, and a statement in the opinion in effect *endorsing* the legitimacy of partisan and incumbency-based gerrymandering, so long as it did not rise to the level of unconstitutionality, a level to date never established.[49] The Court described North Carolina's representation that its new "interstate district" was drawn as "Democratic gerrymander" to protect the incumbent as "a legitimate political explanation."[50]

But surely "not unconstitutional" does not equate with "legitimate." Given the long tradition in all the states involved in the *Shaw* cases of generally following traditional districting standards, their massive gerrymandering in violation of these standards hardly seems "legitimate." Regardless of what the Court actually meant by its backhanded endorsement of political gerrymandering, it appears to have been enthusiastically taken literally by many a legislator as an invitation to sit at her computer and design, guilt free, a district whose sole purpose is to guarantee her reelection.

If we are now to have a free-for-all, it hardly seems fair that racial gerrymandering is to be the only form banned. A race-based district often would satisfy one basis for a sensible district—that a majority of its inhabitants have sufficient common political interests to be represented by the legislator it elects. As it has turned out, there was no obvious decrease in efforts to create majority-minority districts in 2002. This was perhaps driven by the fact that Section 5 jurisdictions still had to obtain preclearance of their redistricting plans, and all jurisdictions still wanted to avoid Section 2 litigation.

C. The Politics of Distorted Districts

An admittedly unscientific perusal of the districts nationwide after the 2000 census suggests that "distorted districts" beget more distorted districts. States initially coerced into creating bizarre districts have kept them and adopted more. Georgia's congressional districts are examples. Georgia's longstanding practice of religiously using counties as the building blocks for congressional districts was highly disrupted in 1992 when Justice coerced it to ignore county boundaries in order to create additional majority-minority districts—districts later successfully challenged as affirmative racial gerrymanders. Even though free to return to its prior districting practices, Georgia adopted congressional districts in 2002 that were more distorted than ever. Figure 11.3 cannot fully capture the extent to which the plan violated traditional districting standards.[51]

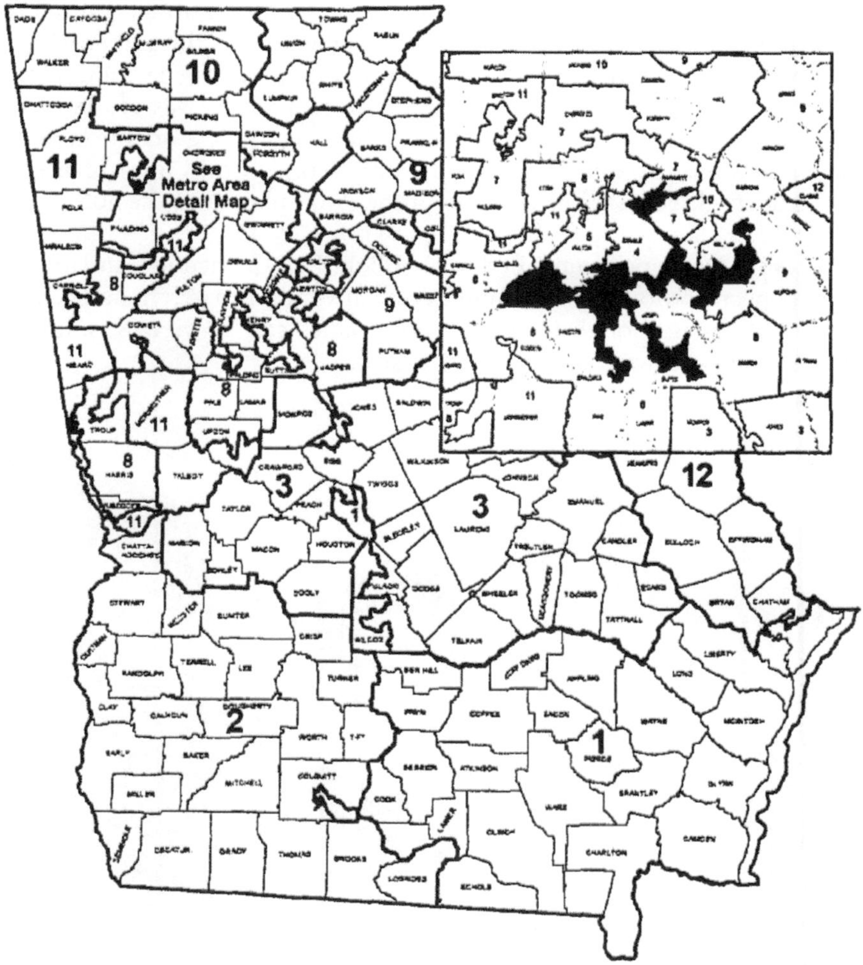

Figure 11.3. Georgia Congressional Districts in 2002, Emphasizing the 13th District

Georgia subsequently redrew its congressional districts in 2005, substantially altering the most distorted of its districts. The reapportionment committee indicated that new districts were needed, in part, to avoid the bizarre shapes of the old ones, and to limit the number of split counties and precincts. The old plan split thirty-four counties and eighty-five precincts, and the new one split eighteen counties and twenty precincts. In terms of respect for traditional districting standards, the new districts were a substantial improvement. The lei-like shape of District 13 was replaced by a district with more regular boundaries, and the squiggly projections into and out of some of the other districts largely were eliminated.[52]

Nevertheless, the new plan was less consistent with traditional districting standards, particularly respect for political subdivisions lines, than Georgia's plans prior to Justice's intervention in 1990.[53] Georgia's 1982 plan, for example, divided only three counties, one of which was too large to be contained within a single district, and the geographic description of its ten districts took up only three pages in the Georgia Code, in comparison to the thirty-three pages in Westlaw of the 2005 plan, and the 105 pages of the 2001 plan.

States that were not compelled to abandon their districting standards in 1992 appear not to have taken the Court's invitation to gerrymander. The post-2000 congressional districts of most states can be viewed online.[54] Ohio's plan is depicted in figure 11.4, below.

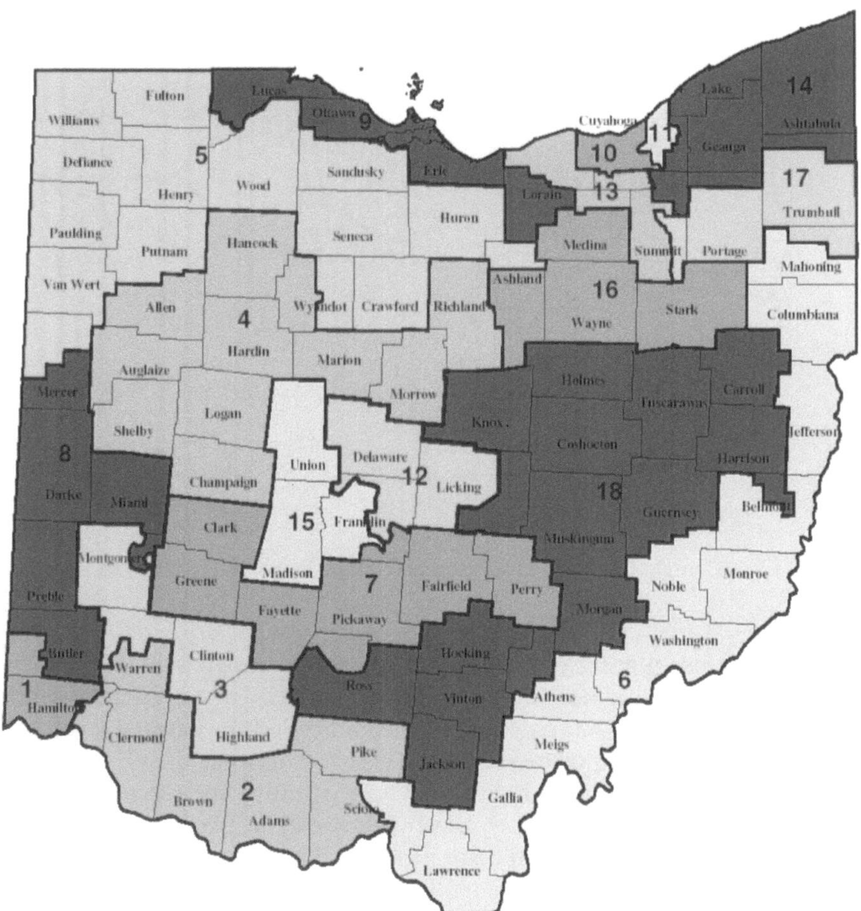

Figure 11.4. Ohio Congressional Districts, 2002

It retrospect, it was perhaps naive to believe that the states that had been coerced to adopt distorted districts would return to normal ones after *Shaw*. The geographic distortions necessary to create minority districts or to help incumbents displaced by them, necessarily rippled though a state's entire districting plan, inevitably producing additional "nonstandard" districts. Most distorted districts were never challenged. For those that were, only the "race-based" districts had to be redrawn, and, as *Cromartie* demonstrates, this did not necessarily involve a return to standard districts, even for the "corrected" districts, and left in place equally bizarre districts created for nonracial purposes.

In most cases, the race-based districts were challenged after jurisdiction-wide elections had been held, as was true in North Carolina. Those elected no doubt believed the boundaries of their districts, even if distorted, were just fine. When time came to adjust the districts invalidated in *Shaw*-type litigation, legislators would be inclined to make as few modifications to those districts as possible to lessen the ripple effect on the remaining districts. Thus, the natural self-preservation instincts of incumbents would result in redrawn districts changing only sufficiently to remedy the racial gerrymandering. By substituting "political data" for "racial data," a "racially gerrymandered district" could simply became an unassailable "Democratic gerrymander" and have virtually no impact on the surrounding districts.

Once elected, minority incumbents enjoyed the consideration legislators often afford their own. Even in an era of seemingly virulent partisanship, particularly in redistricting, minority incumbents, including very junior ones, got "bys" from both parties.[55] No doubt some legislators were motivated by compassion for the new incumbents, and others by a genuine belief in the importance of diversity in the legislative body. These motivations aside, Republican legislators understood that their electoral opportunities improved in districts from which minority voters (sure Democratic votes) had been removed in order to create majority-minority districts. Democrats understood that reality as well, but nevertheless recognized their party's dependence on minority voters, thereby limiting their objections even when increasing the number of minority districts inevitably would reduce the total number of Democratic legislators.[56] Thus, if a minority incumbent believed he needed a majority-minority to be reelected, and this could be accomplished only with a "distorted district," he probably got it.

When it was time to redistrict again following the 2000 census, many legislators were in geographically distorted districts to which they were understandably attached, but which would now have to be redrawn to satisfy population equality standards. Once hooked on the personal and partisan advantages of districts drawn without regard for traditional districting standards, it was easy to draw more districts with even less regard for standards. As three distinguished voting rights scholars recently noted:

> In earlier decades, respect for these [traditional districting] principles imposed tacit constraints on the extent to which self-interested redistricters could manipulate district design to insulate preferred incumbents and candidates from political competition and electoral accountability. As with other tacit constraints, once these informal, generally accepted limitations on unmediated pursuit of political self interest begin to break down, a race to the bottom quickly ensures the virtual elimination of these traditional constraints altogether.[57]

IV. TRADITIONAL DISTRICTING STANDARDS REALLY DO MATTER

It should be self-evident that districts drawn down interstate highways, resembling bug splats and Rorschach blots, are nonfunctional from the perspective of all participants in the political process, save their intended beneficiaries. The man on the street would be surprised to find that many disagree, at least as to distorted districts created to elect minorities.[58] Many commentators argued that there is no relationship between the shape of a district and "fair and effective" representation. But surely that depends in large part on "what" is to "fairly and effectively" represent in a system based on geography. As noted earlier, if it is the collective interest of "groups," racial or otherwise, geographic representation simply cannot deliver.

Perhaps those prepared to undermine the basic units of geographic representation, to accomplish goals more appropriate to a proportional representation system, have allowed their hearts to overtake their heads. These highly distorted districts have indeed produced in the jurisdictions that adopted them something much closer to proportional "interest-group representation" for minorities, but at what cost for the functioning of their systems as a whole? When legislators deprive their citizens of the most basic tool for playing the political game, they are left with geographic representation in name only.

It should be common ground that we expect geographic districts to do more than simply corral the population into groups containing the requisite number of "people per representative." The "more" we expect is sensible districts that will serve as vehicles for fair and competitive elections and for effective representation of all citizens. In this regard, a sensible district for a geographically based representation is one for which voters can easily determine its boundaries, which is conducive to citizens' political participation as voters and candidates, and which is capable of being effectively represented by its elected representative(s).

Judge Edith Jones captured the consequences of ignoring standards that tie representation to significant and identifiable geography when she wrote:

> When natural geographic and political boundaries are arbitrarily cut, the influence of local organizations is seriously diminished. After the civic and veterans groups, labor unions, chambers of commerce, religious congregations, and school boards are subdivided among districts, they can no longer importune their congressman and expect to wield the same degree of influence they would if all their members were voters in his district. Similarly, local groups are disadvantaged from effectively organizing in an election campaign because their numbers, money, and neighborhoods are split. Another casualty . . . is likely to be voter participation. . . . A citizen will be discouraged from undertaking grassroots activity if . . . she [cannot locate her congressman's district's boundaries].
>
> [A]s the influence of truly local organizations wanes, that of special interests waxes. Incumbents are no longer as likely to be held accountable by vigilant, organized local interests after those interests have been dispersed. The bedrock principle of self-government, the interdependency of representatives and their constituents, is thus undermined by ignoring traditional districting principles.[59]

V. CAN GEOGRAPHIC REPRESENTATION BE SAVED?

For districting systems that already deviate significantly from traditional districting standards, the prospects are dim for reassociating election districts with independently significant geographic units, unless legislators themselves are willing to face the personal upheavals that would produce. The failure of legislatures to take advantage of the Court's *Shaw* holding is indicative of how quickly a "bizarre" district becomes "normal" in the mind of its beneficiary. Having discovered the personal and partisan advantages to unrestrained gerrymandering, legislators may be no more likely to give it up than an addict his heroin. As noted earlier, legislators elected in "standard districts" have greater affinity for them, and therefore should be less inclined to outrageously distort them.

There is no reason to believe that Justice will grant Section 5 preclearance to plans that reduce the number of minority-controlled districts, even if that number can be maintained only by total abandonment of all districting standards—if there remain Section 5 jurisdictions where this has not already happened.[60] Ironically, the mess Justice precipitated by its "black maximization" policy of the 1990s (declared unlawful in *Shaw*) has made it easier to insist that districting standards give way if necessary to avoid retrogression.[61] Where legislators have abandoned districting standards for their own purposes, they can hardly argue that they should not be required to do the same to maintain the number of minority-controlled districts.

Moreover, in 2006, Congress not only extended Section 5 for an additional twenty-five years, it also restored to Justice one of its most malleable tools to coerce covered jurisdictions to follow its directives. The amendment specifies that preclearance is to be denied to a change that was adopted for *any* discriminatory purpose. It was intended to overrule the Court's decision in *Reno v. Bossier Parish School Board*, which held that the only discriminatory purpose sufficient to support a denial of preclearance was the intent to cause retrogression.[62] Congress's new subjective and vague standard gives Justice much latitude to be "unconvinced" that a redistricting plan not to its liking was the product of "some" discriminatory purpose, a conclusion it tended to reach before *Bossier Parish* anytime it was possible to create additional minority districts.

Attacking bizarre districts as partisan gerrymanders is de facto impossible. Moreover, it should be clear that the harm caused by these districts is of a different sort and a greater magnitude than that caused by past partisan gerrymandering that was constrained by geography and technology. Old gerrymandered districts skewed partisan outcomes, but in many cases, electoral competition no doubt shifted from the general election to the primary of the dominant party, leaving grassroots political participation largely intact.

Bizarre districts, on the other hand, disrupt basic political participation from voting to running for office, and serve the interests only of the "group" for which they were designed. Those of us who are not strongly supportive of incumbents, highly partisan, or minorities, are effectively limited in our ability to impact electoral outcomes. We have become "filler" for districts specifically designed to further interests not our own. Any new strategy for challenging these districts should not be based on their disparate partisan impact, or even on the improper use of race in their creation, but on their depriving the electorate of the basic tool with which to play the political game—a functional election district.

NOTES

1. Of course, much has been written on this topic and each state has a unique tale. Here I can provide only generalizations, which will not exactly fit the history of any one state, and for which there are no doubt many exceptions, perhaps even including states for which nothing I report will apply.

2. 369 U.S. 186 (1962).

3. 377 U.S. 533 (1964).

4. *Reynolds v. Sims*, 377 U.S. 533, 602–10 (Harlan, J., dissenting) (detailing the provisions of various states from the ratification of the Fourteenth Amendment forward).

5. New York, for example, from 1894 until its system was declared unconstitutional in 1964, apportioned both senators and "assemblymen" to counties in accordance with a complicated formula very loosely based on population. County-level boards in "multimember" counties then created single-member subdistricts, which by state law were not permitted to divide certain political subdivisions. Robert G. Dixon, *Democratic Representation, Reapportionment in Law and Politics* (New York: Oxford University Press 1968), 202.

6. South Carolina's constitution mandates this model. S.C. Constitution, art III. A number of other states adopted variations of this model, among them California, Maryland, and Colorado. Dixon, *Democratic Representation*, app. B.

7. Malcolm E. Jewell, "State Legislatures in Southern Politics," *Journal of Politics* 26 (1964): 181. Before the arrangement was invalidated after *Baker v .Carr*, Georgia's three-county senate districts not only rotated the shared seat among the counties, but the seat was actually elected solely by the voters of the designated county. Jewell, "State Legislatures," 181.

8. *Reynolds v. Sims*, 377 U.S. 533, 602–10 (Harlan, J., dissenting).

9. Dixon, *Democratic Representation*, app. B.

10. 377 U.S. 533 (1964).

11. In South Carolina, for example, following the 1970 census, the General Assembly adopted sixteen senatorial districts, three single-member districts and thirteen multimember, with from two to five senators each. The ideal population necessary for one seat was 56,316 (2,590,516 [total population] divided by 46 [the number of senators specified in the state constitution]). Indiana adopted a similar system for both of its legislative houses. James L. McDowell, "Indiana," in *Reapportionment Politics, the History of Redistricting in the 50 States*, ed. Leroy Hardy, Alan Heslop, and Stuart Anderson (Beverly Hills: Sage, 1981), 110.

12. For example, when Iowa adopted new districting standards in 1980, respect for political subdivision boundaries was second in importance only to population equality. District boundaries were to coincide with political subdivision boundaries to the extent possible. The number of counties and cities divided was to be as small as possible, with more populous subdivisions divided before less populous ones, except in the case of a district boundary that followed a county line through a city lying in more than one county. Compactness was important, but was not to take precedent over political subdivision lines. John M. Liittschwager, "Iowa," in *Reapportionment Politics, the History of Redistricting in the 50 States*, ed. Leroy Hardy, Alan Heslop, and Stuart Anderson (Beverly Hills: Sage, 1981), 116.

13. When the Court held that the one-person, one-vote mandate could not be overcome by a statewide referendum (*Lucas v. Forty-Fourth Gen. Assembly*, 377 U.S. 713, 736 [1964], out of Colorado), several attempts were made in Congress to adopt a constitutional amendment to allow the states to have one house of a bicameral legislature based on "area" representation without regard to population. 111 Cong. Rec. 19,363 (1965) (failure of the Dirksen Amendment).

14. The entire states of Alabama, Georgia, Louisiana, Mississippi, South Carolina, and Virginia, plus forty counties in North Carolina and a smattering of other counties elsewhere, were "covered" in 1965. The state of Alaska was also caught by the coverage formula, but was able to obtain a declaratory judgment letting it "bail out." Additional states and counties were added to the list of covered jurisdictions in 1975 to provide similar protection for Hispanics.

15. 412 U.S. 735 (1973). David I. Wells was one of the few experts to see this well-known case as an early indication that the Supreme Court either did not understand the premise of geographically based representation, or rejected it. Two of his articles appeared in the legislative history of the 1982 Voting Rights Act amendments: "Con Affirmative Gerrymandering," *Policy Studies Journal* 9 (1980–1981): Special #3; and "'Affirmative Gerrymandering' Compounds Districting Problems," *National Civic Review* (January 1978). Hearing before the Subcommittee on the Constitution of the Senate Committee on the Judiciary, 97th Cong., vol. 2 appendix (1982).

16. The state redistricting body "overtly adopted and followed a policy of 'political fairness,' which aimed at a rough scheme of proportional representation of

the two major political parties. Senate and House districts were structured so that the composition of both Houses would reflect 'as closely as possible . . . the actual (statewide) plurality of vote on the House or Senate lines in' [three preceding statewide elections], and, on that basis, created what was thought to be a proportionate number of Republican and Democratic legislative seats." 412 U.S. at 738.

17. 412 U.S. at 753–54.

18. Appellant Brief, *Gaffney v. Cummings*, 1972 WL 135814 (U.S. 1972) (No. 71-1476) (making reference to James M. Edwards, "The Gerrymander and 'One Man, One Vote,'" *New York University Law Review* 46 (1971): 879.

19. 393 U.S. 544 (1969).

20. 377 U.S. 533 (1964).

21. 393 U.S. at 569.

22. 400 U.S. 379 (1969).

23. 400 U.S. at 388.

24. 403 U.S. 124 (1971).

25. 412 U.S. 755 (1975).

26. 422 U.S. 358 (1975).

27. 422 U.S. at 370. "Fairly drawn" was not explained, but the most reasonable definition would have been a plan drawn to produce equally populated single-member districts, following traditional districting standards—one neither gerrymandered to avoid creating majority black districts, nor gerrymandered to accomplish that result.

28. 425 U.S. 130 (1976).

29. From the age-structure differences between blacks and whites reported in *Beer*, it appears that blacks made up about 33 percent of the voting-age population.

30. Letter of objection, on behalf of the attorney general (July 9, 1973) (reproduced in part in the District Court opinion, *Beer v. U.S.*, 374 F. Supp. 363, 371n33 (D.C.D.C. 1974)).

31. 374 F. Supp. at 371n33.

32. After it failed to obtain preclearance from Justice, New Orleans brought a new action in the District Court for the District of Columbia. The court was more explicit about the problem with the plan—it simply failed to provide black voters with 2.42 seats, which in the court's view was "their share." This failure was justified only if the city could demonstrate that no plan could be produced that was "less burdensome" to minority voters. Perhaps concerned about this theory, the court's backup position was that the proposed plan was "dilutive" as the concept had been defined by the Supreme Court in *Whitcomb v. Chavis*, 403 U.S. 124 (1971), and *White v. Register*, 412 U.S. 755 (1975). The district court appeared to be on firmer footing here, particularly in light of the Court's prior indications that the capacity of redistricting plans to dilute black voting strength was the reason Section 5 preclearance was required.

33. 425 U.S. at 141–42.

34. The most logical interpretation of *Beer* was that the number of majority black districts in the existing districting plan had to be maintained. *United Jewish Org. v. Carey*, 97 S. Ct. 996, 1007 (1977) (apportionment in New Orleans approved in *Beer* because it created a majority black district when none existed before; had some number of majority black districts existed in the prior plan, the proposed plan could not decrease that number). The Court eventually would

indicate that its retrogression standard did not mandate that these standards be ignored, but not until many, many distorted districts had been adopted to avoid a literal interpretation of nonretrogression. In *Bush v. Vera*, 517 U.S. 952 (1996), the Court rejected Texas's argument that a "bug splat" majority-minority district was necessary to avoid retrogression, indicating that "[n]onretrogression is not a license for the State to do whatever it deems necessary to insure continued electoral success; it merely mandates that the minority's opportunity to elect representatives of its choice not be diminished, *directly or indirectly* by the State's actions." 517 U.S. at 955, 983 (emphasis added).

35. Specific examples of Justice's objections to post-*Beer* redistrictings on the grounds set out below can be found in Katharine Inglis Butler, "Reapportionment, the Courts, and the Voting Rights Act: A Resegregation of the Political Process?" *University of Colorado Law Review* 56 (1984): 1.

36. 425 U.S. at 138–39.

37. 466 U.S. 55 (1980).

38. *Whitcomb v. Chavis*, 403 U.S. 124 (1971); *White v. Register*, 412 U.S. 755 (1975).

39. 478 U.S. 30 (1986).

40. 907 F. Supp. 434 (D.D.C 1995), aff'd, *Reno v. Bossier Parish*, 520 U.S. 471 (1997).

41. Justice also argued that South Carolina's old "one senator per county system," which was unconstitutional after *Reynolds v. Sims*, was a "single member districts system," and was the benchmark against which the proposed plan should be measured. Both positions were extreme "reaches" to justify Justice's effort to squeeze one additional majority black district out of the state. To equate representation of "counties as counties" to a single-member district system is equivalent to saying that U.S. senators are elected in a double-member districting system.

42. *Hastert v. State Bd. of Elections*, 777 F. Supp. 634 (N.D. Ill. 1991).

43. 777 F. Supp. at 648n24. A federal court in Florida produced two similarly bizarre minority districts for Florida's 1992 congressional districting plan, one resembling a loop of flowers, and the other appropriately labeled the "condom district." The court justified these bizarre districts by noting that the important requirement was that the minority, not the district, be compact, and that, while districting standards such as respecting county boundaries were desirable, "this aesthetic requirement should not undercut the primary goal of creating minority districts." *DeGrandy v. Wetherell*, 794 F. Supp. 1076, 1085 (N.D. Fla. 1992).

44. The cases were: *Shaw v. Reno*, 509 U.S. 630 (1993) (a challenge to two of North Carolina's congressional districts); *Miller v. Johnson*, 515 U.S. 900 (1995) (a challenge to two of Georgia's congressional districts); *Bush v. Vera*, 517 U.S. 952 (1996) (a challenge to three of Texas's congressional districts); *Shaw v. Hunt* (*Shaw II*), 517 U.S. 899 (1996) (North Carolina's districts a second time); *Abrams v. Johnson*, 521 U.S. 74 (1997) (Georgia's districts a second time); *Hunt v. Cromartie*, 526 U.S. 541 (1999) (North Carolina's districts a third time); and *Easley v. Cromartie*, 532 U.S. 234 (2001) (North Carolina's districts a fourth time).

45. For example, in *Miller v. Johnson*, the Court suggested that states could avoid strict federal scrutiny of their districting plans "altogether by respecting their own traditional districting principles," 517 U.S. at 978, and noted in *Abrams v. Johnson* that Section 2 liability, at a minimum, required the existence of a geographically compact

minority group taking into account "traditional districting principles such as maintaining communities of interest and traditional boundaries." 521 U.S. at 92.

46. *Easley v. Cromartie*, 532 U.S. 234, 241–42 (2001) (internal quotation marks and citations omitted) (ellipsis in original) (quoting *Hunt v. Cromartie*, 526 U.S. 541, 546, 547 [1999]); *Bush v. Vera*, 517 U.S. 952, 959 (1966).

47. 532 U.S. 234 (2001).

48. The precincts included in the "new" Democratic district were ones that had voted overwhelmingly for Democrats, including the black Democrat who ran in the original challenged district. Under the circumstances, the use of political data was so patently a pretext for maintaining the district's black percentage as close as possible to that of the original, that *Cromartie* makes it appear that the Court changed its mind about these cases. Perhaps the Court, too, is susceptible to "political correctness" pressures. This case made it "four for four" against the North Carolina District Court. The Supreme Court rejected the lower court's finding of constitutionality three times, and when the district court finally found a plan unconstitutional, the Court rejected that as well. Ironically, the basis for reversing the final time was that the lower court's finding that race was the predominant factor in creating the district was clearly erroneous.

49. Theoretically, and to date, the possibility of partisan gerrymander violating the Constitution still exists. It awaits merely the genius who can provide standards for a "discriminatory effect" on the minority party that will satisfy the Court. *League of United Latin Am. Citizens v. Perry*, 548 U.S. 399 (2006).

50. *Easley*, 532 U.S. at 242. The Court indicated that caution (in concluding the state has drawn district lines on the basis of race) "is especially appropriate in this case where the State has articulated a legitimate political explanation for its districting decisions." 532 U.S. at 234.

51. Some indication of the gerrymandering effort that went into the 13th District comes from knowing that its geographic description (the description of the individual units of census geography it includes), takes up multiple pages, whereas Georgia's entire congressional districting plan for 1982 was described in just a few lines of text in the Georgia Code. Georgia was not alone in its seeming voluntary abandonment of districting standards. Today, in jurisdictions subject to Section 5, election districts at all levels of government are highly irregular. Mississippi's state legislative districts may take the prize for the most distorted—distortion that cannot be appreciated in black and white. The district "in color" can be found online at http:// nationalatlas.gov/printable/congress.html.

52. The old and new districts can be seen side by side at www.legis.state.ga.us/legis/2005_6/ communications/presentations/hb499redistricting.ppt.

53. The degree to which concern for effective geographic districts has been replaced by concern for "district content" is demonstrated by a social science article analyzing the voting patterns in two of the revised districts—districts that were held by white Democratic incumbents at the time the lines were redrawn. M. V. Hood III and Seth C. McKee, "Gerrymandering on Georgia's Mind: The Effects of Redistricting on Vote Choice in the 2006 Midterm Election," *Social Science Quarterly* 89 (2008): 60. These researchers saw the redrawing of the districts as merely a partisan endeavor: "Of course, the primary motive for redrawing the congressional map was [to] greatly increase the likelihood for Republicans to win additional seats." Hood and McKee, "Gerrymandering on Georgia's Mind," 64. "Because the redistricting was

implemented by a Republican-controlled legislature, it is no surprise that the newly drawn portions of these districts reduce the black voting-age populations in addition to infusing them with large shares of redrawn voters." Hood and McKee, "Gerrymandering on Georgia's Mind," 65. Almost certainly, the new districts were more favorable to the election of Republicans, but the authors fail to note that the previous plan was a racial and Democratic gerrymander, which could only be accomplished by using bizarre boundaries. The natural result of fixing the bizarre boundaries of the prior plan, without also reducing the black percentages in any of districts with black incumbents, was to improve the electoral opportunities of Republicans. The authors did not suggest an alternative plan that would simultaneously avoid retrogression in the black incumbent districts, eliminate the most egregious of the bizarre district lines, and yet avoid substantially redrawing the two districts they analyzed. Perhaps they are in the category of scholars who see no value in traditional districting standards, at least not if they produce "unacceptable" political outcomes.

54. Congressional Districts–110th Congress, http:// nationalatlas.gov/printable/congress. html#list (accessed October 11, 2008).

55. When North Carolina redrew the 12th Congressional District, part of its "political explanation" for making virtually no changes in the district was to protect its incumbent, Democrat Mel Watts, an African American, and also to avoid pitting him against a Republican incumbent, which would, the state alleged, have been the unavoidable result of adopting a more "standard" district. *Easley*, 532 U.S. at 248. Similarly, when the new Republican majority in Georgia's legislature redrew the state's congressional districts in 2005, it appears to have preserved the reelection opportunities of the state's four African American congressmen (all Democrats).

56. The vast majority of researchers and commentators recognized the connection between the increase in the number of Republicans elected and creating majority-minority districts. Political scientist Timothy O'Rourke details the various assessments of this connection in "*Shaw v. Reno*: The Shape of Things to Come," *Rutgers Law Journal* 26 (1995): 724–28 (text and notes).

57. Brief of Samuel Issacharoff, Burt Neubrone, and Richard H. Pildes as Amici Curiae in Support of Appellants 26, *League of United Latin Am. Citizens v. Perry*, No. 05-204; *Travis County v. Perry*, No. 05-254; *Eddie Jackson v. Perry*, No. 05-276; *GI Forum of Texas v. Perry*, No. 05-439 (U.S. January 10, 2006).

58. See Mark Monmonier, *Bushmanders and Bullwinkles: How Politicians Manipulate Electronic Maps and Census Data to Win Elections* (Chicago: University of Chicago Press, 2001), 154 (arguing that North Carolina's interstate district and some of the intricate inner-city districts, such as Chicago's 4th Congressional District approved in *Hastert v. State Bd. of Elections*, 777 F. Supp. 634 (N.D. Ill. 1991), are more functional than their critics suggest). See also the comments of Judge Philips in *Shaw v. Hunt*, 861 F. Supp. 408 (E.D.N.C. 1994), rev'd, 517 U.S. 899 (1996), indicating that "compactness, contiguity, and respect for political subdivision lines have little inherent value in the districting process." 861 F. Supp. at 451. He further noted that these standards once were thought necessary to fair and effective representation, because they produced districts of citizens likely to share common political needs and interests, and made it easy for legislators to stay in contact with their constituents, but "are no longer necessary" or even appropriate today. 861 F. Supp. at 451–52.

59. *Vera v. Richards*, 861 F. Supp. 1304, 1335 n. 43. (S.D. Tex. 1994), aff'd sub nom. *Bush v. Vera*, 517 U.S. 952 (1996).

60. Mississippi has totally abandoned districting standards for its house and senate district, this can be seen online.

61. There is little dispute that the jurisdictions involved in the *Shaw* cases abandoned their former districting standards under pressure to satisfy what the Supreme Courted labeled Justice's "black-maximization" policy. See *Miller v. Johnson*, 515 U.S. 900, 921 (1965).

62. 528 U.S. 320 (2000). The Court reasoned that because Section 5's purpose is to prevent backsliding, an intent to perpetuate an existing discriminatory system did not make minorities worse off than they were before the change. 528 U.S. at 335. Aspects of *Bossier Parish* are discussed in Katharine Inglis Butler, "Redistricting in a Post-*Shaw* Era: A Small Treatise Accompanied by Districting Guidelines for Legislators, Litigants, and Courts," *University of Richmond Law Review* 36 (2002): 191–95.

Index

About the Contributors

Katharine Inglis Butler, Distinguished Professor Emerita, University of South Carolina School of Law, is a nationally recognized expert on the Voting Rights Act. She began her career in the Voting Section, Civil Rights Division, of the Department of Justice. She joined the South Carolina Law Faculty in 1978. Professor Butler's writings on voting rights and redistricting have appeared in books, law reviews, and in popular printed and electronic legal publications. Much of her recent work has focused on the impact of the Voting Rights Act on geographically based representation. She has advised governing bodies at every level on compliance with the act and on redistricting issues and has served as an expert to the court in several voting rights/redistricting cases.

Louis Fisher is a specialist in constitutional law for the Law Library of Congress. His views expressed in this book are personal, not institutional. Previously Fisher worked for Congressional Research Service as a specialist in separation of powers and was research director of the House Iran-Contra Committee in 1987, writing major sections of the final report. He has testified before congressional committees on constitutional issues more than fifty times.

Joyce Lee Malcolm, professor of law at George Mason University School of Law, is a historian and constitutional scholar focusing on the development of individual rights in Great Britain and America. She is the author of seven books, including *To Keep and Bear Arms: The Origins of an Anglo-American Right*; *Guns and Violence: The English Experience*; a two-volume collection, *The Struggle for Sovereignty: Seventeenth-Century English Political Tracts*; and most recently *Peter's War: A New England Slave Boy and the American Revo-*

lution (2009). Malcolm's essays have been widely published in legal and historical journals and the popular press.

Anthony A. Peacock is an associate professor in the political science department at Utah State University, where he is also the director of The Project on Liberty and American Constitutionalism. He is the author or editor of five books on American and Canadian law and politics. He has also published numerous articles, book chapters, and book reviews. At Utah State, Peacock teaches courses on constitutional law; constitutional theory; law and policy; and law, politics, and war.

Joseph Postell is assistant director of the B. Kenneth Simon Center for American Studies at The Heritage Foundation. He has published on the political theory of the American Founding, and is currently working on a study of the relationship between political theory, regulation, and contemporary administrative law.

Jeremy Rabkin is professor of law at George Mason University, where he teaches courses on international law and the American Founding. He serves on the Board of Directors of the Center for Individual Rights (a public interest law firm) and the U.S. Institute of Peace (a federal research and advisory agency). He holds a Ph.D. in political science from Harvard University and a B.A. from Cornell. His most recent book is *Law without Nations?*

Ralph A. Rossum is director of the Rose Institute of State and Local Government and Henry Salvatori Professor of American Constitutionalism at Claremont McKenna College; he is also a member of the faculty of Claremont Graduate University. He earned his M.A. and Ph.D. from the University of Chicago and is the author or coauthor of nine books, including *American Constitutional Law,* a two-volume work now in the eighth edition (2010), and *Antonin Scalia's Jurisprudence: "Text and Tradition"* (2006). Rossum has also written over sixty-five book chapters or articles in law reviews and professional journals.

V. James Strickler is an assistant professor of political science at Utah State University, where he teaches in their law and constitutional studies major and works with The Project on Liberty and American Constitutionalism. He earned his J.D. from the J. Reuben Clark Law School at Brigham Young University and his Ph.D. from Stanford University. He has previously published in the *Georgia Law Review* and the *Harvard International Journal of Press/Politics*. Originally from Sweet Home, Oregon, he now lives in Logan, Utah, with his wife, Kathleen, and their seven young children.

Bradley C. S. Watson is the Philip M. McKenna Professor of American and Western Political Thought at Saint Vincent College in Pennsylvania. He has held visiting faculty appointments at Princeton University and Claremont McKenna College and has authored or edited many books, including *Living Constitution, Dying Faith: Progressivism and the New Science of Jurisprudence* (2009).

Edward Whelan is president of the Ethics and Public Policy Center and writes widely on the Supreme Court, constitutional law, and the judicial confirmation process. Mr. Whelan has served in positions of responsibility in all three branches of the federal government—as a law clerk to Supreme Court Justice Antonin Scalia and to Judge J. Clifford Wallace of the U.S. Court of Appeals for the Ninth Circuit, as principal deputy assistant attorney general for the Office of Legal Counsel in the United States Department of Justice, and as general counsel to the U.S. Senate Committee on the Judiciary. He is a graduate of Harvard College and Harvard Law School.

www.ingramcontent.com/pod-product-compliance
Ingram Content Group UK Ltd.
Pitfield, Milton Keynes, MK11 3LW, UK
UKHW041126071026
15587UKWH00009B/256

9 780739 136188